MW00572252

HUMAN
RIGHTS
WATCH

WORLD REPORT

2010

EVENTS OF 2009

Front cover photo: *Sri Lankan Tamils wait behind barbed wire during a May 2009 visit by United Nations Secretary-General Ban Ki-moon to Menik Farm camp, where the government interned several hundred thousand people displaced in the final months of the war between the government and the Tamil Tiger separatists.* © 2009 Joe Klamar/AFP/Getty Images

Back cover photo: *Relatives of prominent reformers and other people detained after Iran's disputed June 2009 election gather outside the prosecutor's office in Tehran calling for the release of their family members.* © 2009 Sipa

Cover and book design by Rafael Jiménez

350 Fifth Avenue, 34th floor
New York, NY 10118-3299 USA
Tel: +1 212 290 4700
Fax: +1 212 736 1300
hrwnyc@hrw.org

1630 Connecticut Avenue, N.W., Suite 500
Washington, DC 20009 USA
Tel: +1 202 612 4321
Fax: +1 202 612 4333
hrwdc@hrw.org

2-12 Pentonville Road, 2nd Floor
London N1 9HF, UK
Tel: +44 20 7713 1995
Fax: +44 20 7713 1800
hrwuk@hrw.org

27 Rue de Lisbonne
75008 Paris, France
Tel: +33 (0) 1 43 59 55 35
Fax: +33 (0) 1 43 59 55 22
paris@hrw.org

Avenue des Gaulois, 7
1040 Brussels, Belgium
Tel: + 32 (2) 732 2009
Fax: + 32 (2) 732 0471
hrwbe@hrw.org

64-66 Rue de Lausanne
1201 Geneva, Switzerland
Tel: +41 22 738 0481
Fax: +41 22 738 1791
hrwgva@hrw.org

Poststraße 4-5
10178 Berlin, Germany
Tel: +49 30 2593 06-10
Fax: +49 30 2593 0629
berlin@hrw.org

1st fl, Wilds View
Isle of Houghton
Boundary Road (at Carse O'Gowrie)
Parktown, 2198 South Africa
Tel: +27-11-484-2640, Fax: +27-11-484-2641

#4A, Meiji University Academy Common bldg. 7F, 1-1,
Kanda-Surugadai, Chiyoda-ku
Tokyo 101-8301 Japan
Tel: +81-3-5282-5160, Fax: +81-3-5282-5161
tokyo@hrw.org

*Chawkatly Building, 7th Floor
Charles Helou Ave, Saifi/Port Area
Beirut, Lebanon
Tel: +961-1-447833, Fax +961-1-446497
* *Registration in process.*

www.hrw.org

Human Rights Watch is dedicated to protecting the human rights of people around the world.

We stand with victims and activists to prevent discrimination, to uphold political freedom, to protect people from inhumane conduct in wartime, and to bring offenders to justice.

We investigate and expose human rights violations and hold abusers accountable.

We challenge governments and those who hold power to end abusive practices and respect international human rights law.

We enlist the public and the international community to support the cause of human rights for all.

HUMAN RIGHTS WATCH

Human Rights Watch is one of the world's leading independent organizations dedicated to defending and protecting human rights. By focusing international attention where human rights are violated, we give voice to the oppressed and hold oppressors accountable for their crimes. Our rigorous, objective investigations and strategic, targeted advocacy build intense pressure for action and raise the cost of human rights abuse. For over 30 years, Human Rights Watch has worked tenaciously to lay the legal and moral groundwork for deep-rooted change and has fought to bring greater justice and security to people around the world.

Human Rights Watch began in 1978 with the founding of its Europe and Central Asia division (then known as Helsinki Watch). Today, it also includes divisions covering Africa, the Americas, Asia, and the Middle East and North Africa; a United States program; thematic divisions or programs on arms, business and human rights, children's rights, health and human rights, international justice, lesbian, gay, bisexual and transgender rights, refugees, terrorism/counterterrorism, and women's rights; and an emergencies program. It maintains offices in Amsterdam, Beirut, Berlin, Brussels, Cairo, Chicago, Geneva, Johannesburg, London, Los Angeles, Moscow, New York, Paris, San Francisco, Tokyo, Toronto, Washington DC, and Zurich, and field presences in around a dozen more locations globally. Human Rights Watch is an independent, nongovernmental organization, supported by contributions from private individuals and foundations worldwide. It accepts no government funds, directly or indirectly.

The staff includes Kenneth Roth, Executive Director; Michele Alexander, Development and Outreach Director; Clive Baldwin, Senior Legal Advisor; Carroll Bogert, Associate Director; Emma Daly, Communications Director; Ian Gorvin, Senior Program Officer; Barbara Guglielmo, Finance and Administration Director; Peggy Hicks, Global Advocacy Director; Iain Levine, Program Director; Andrew Mawson, Deputy Program Director; Dinah PoKempner, General Counsel; Aisling Reidy, Senior Legal Advisor; James Ross, Legal and Policy Director; Joe Saunders, Deputy Program Director; and Minky Worden, Media Director.

The division directors of Human Rights Watch are Brad Adams, Asia; Joseph Amon, Health and Human Rights; John Biaggi, International Film Festival; Peter Bouckaert, Emergencies; Holly Cartner, Europe and Central Asia; Richard Dicker, International Justice; David Fathi, United States; Bill Frelick, Refugees; Georgette Gagnon, Africa; Arvind Ganesan, Business and Human Rights; Liesl Gerntholtz, Women's Rights; Steve Goose, Arms; Scott Long, Lesbian, Gay, Bisexual and Transgender Rights; Joanne Mariner, Terrorism/Counterterrorism; José Miguel Vivanco, Americas; Lois Whitman, Children's Rights; and Sarah Leah Whitson, Middle East and North Africa.

The advocacy directors of Human Rights Watch are Steve Crawshaw, United Nations–New York; Juliette De Rivero, United Nations–Geneva; Jean-Marie Fardeau, Paris; Marianne Heuwagen, Berlin; Lotte Leicht, European Union; Tom Porteous, London; and Tom Malinowski, Washington DC.

The members of the board of directors are Jane Olson, Chair, Bruce J. Klatsky, Vice Chair, Sid Sheinberg, Vice Chair, John J. Studzinski, Vice Chair, Karen Ackman, Jorge Castañeda, Geoffrey Cowan, Tony Elliott, Hassan Elmasry, Michael G. Fisch, Michael E. Gellert, James F. Hoge, Jr., Betsy Karel, Wendy Keys, Robert Kissane, Joanne Leedom-Ackerman, Susan Manilow, Kati Marton, Barry Meyer, Pat Mitchell, Joel Motley, Joan R. Platt, Neil Rimer, Victoria Riskin, Amy L. Robbins, Shelley Rubin, Kevin P. Ryan, Jean-Louis Servan-Schreiber, Darian W. Swig, John R. Taylor, Catherine Zennström.

Emeritus board members are Robert L. Bernstein, Founding Chair, 1979-1997, Jonathan F. Fanton, Chair, 1998-2003, Lisa Anderson, David M. Brown, William D. Carmichael, Vartan Gregorian, Alice H. Henkin, Stephen L. Kass, Marina Pinto Kaufman, Josh Mailman, Samuel K. Murumba, Peter Osnos, Kathleen Peratis, Bruce Rabb, Sigrid Rausing, Orville Schell, Gary Sick, and Malcolm B. Smith.

Acknowledgments

A compilation of this magnitude requires contribution from a large number of people, including most of the Human Rights Watch staff. The contributors were:

Fred Abrahams, Pema Abrahams, Brad Adams, Chris Albin-Lackey, Anna Alekseyeva, Henrik Alffram, Joseph Amon, Evelyn Astor, Luiza Athayde, Leeam Azulay-Yagev, Clive Baldwin, Nadia Barhoum, Jo Becker, Andrea Berg, Sebastian Brett, Christen Broecker, Jane Buchanan, David Buchbinder, Maria Burnett, Elizabeth Calvin, Juliana Cano Nieto, Holly Cartner, Grace Choi, Sara Colm, Tatyana Cooper, Andrea Cottom, Zama Coursen-Neff, Steve Crawshaw, Emma Daly, Philippe Dam, Kiran D'Amico, Sara Darehshori, Juliette De Rivero, Fernando Delgado, Kristina DeMain, Rachel Denber, Richard Dicker, Steven Dudley, Corinne Dufka, Dahlia El Zein, Jon Elliott, Jessica Evans, Elizabeth Evenson, Jean-Marie Fardeau, David Fathi, Jamie Fellner, Eva Fortes, Bill Frelick, Chloë Fussell, Georgette Gagnon, Arvind Ganesan, Meenakshi Ganguly, Liesl Gerntholtz, Neela Ghoshal, Brent Giannotta, Thomas Gilchrist, Allison Gill, Giorgi Gogia, Eric Goldstein, Steve Goose, Ian Gorvin, Jessie Graham, Eric Guttschuss, Andreas Harsono, Ali Dayan Hasan, Leslie Haskell, Marianne Heuwagen, Peggy Hicks, Nadim Houry, Peter Huvos, Claire Ivers, Rafael Jiménez, Tiseke Kasambala, Aruna Kashyap, Elise Keppler, Nadya Khalife, Juliane Kippenberg, Kyle Knight, Kathryn Koonce, Mignon Lamia, Adrianne Lapar, Leslie Lefkow, Lotte Leicht, Iain Levine, Maria Lisitsyna, Diederik Lohman, Tanya Lokshina, Scott Long, Anna Lopriore, Linda Louie, Drake Lucas, Tom Malinowski, Joanne Mariner, Abigail Marshak, David Mathieson, Géraldine Mattioli, Veronica Matushaj, Andrew Mawson, Maria McFarland, Omid Memarian, Lisa Misol, Marianne Mollmann, Heba Morayef, Priyanka Motaparthy, Rasha Moumneh, Siphokazi Mthathi, Jim Murphy, Samer Muscati, Dipika Nath, Agnes Ndige Muriungi Odhiambo, Stephanie Neider, Rachel Nicholson, Jessica Ognian, Diana Parker, Alison Parker, Elaine Pearson, Rona Peligal, Sunai Phasuk, Sarah Pinho, Enrique Piraces, Dinah PoKempner, Tom Porteous, McKenzie Price, Daniela Ramirez, Ben Rawlence, Rachel Reid, Aisling Reidy, Meghan Rhoad, Sophie Richardson, Lisa Rimli, James Ross, Kenneth Roth, Abby Rubinson, Abderrahim Sabir, Joe Saunders, Ida Sawyer, Rebecca Schleifer, Max Schoening, Kathryn Semogas, Kay Seok, JeffreySeverson, Kavita Shah, Bede Sheppard, Cecile Shrestha, Emma Sinclair-Webb, Param-Preet Singh, Mickey Spiegel, Xabay Spinka, Nik Steinberg, Joe Stork, Stacy Sullivan, Judith Sunderland, Veronika Szente Goldston, Tamara Taraciuk, Letta Tayler, Laura Thomas, Sarah Tofte, Simone Troller, Wanda Troszczynska Van Genderen, Bill Van Esveld, Gauri Van Gulik,

Anneke Van Woudenberg, Nisha Varia, José Miguel Vivanco, Janet Walsh, Ben Ward, Katharine Weis, Matthew Wells, Kerri West, Lois Whitman, Sarah Leah Whitson, Christoph Wilcke, Daniel Wilkinson, Minky Worden, Arezo Yazd , Michael Ybarra, Iwona Zielinska.

Ian Gorvin edited the report with assistance from Iain Levine, Andrew Mawson, and Joe Saunders. Dahlia El Zein coordinated the editing process. Layout and production were coordinated by Grace Choi and Rafael Jiménez, with assistance from Anna Lopriore, Veronica Matushaj, Jim Murphy, and Enrique Piraces.

Pema Abrahams, Evelyn Astor, Leeam Azulay-Yagev, Dahlia El Zein, Chloë Fussell, Kyle Knight, Mignon Lamia, Adrianne Lapar, Abigail Marshak, Stephanie Neider, Jessica Ognian, Sarah Pinho, McKenzie Price, Daniela Ramirez, and Jeffrey Severson proofread the report.

For a full list of Human Rights Watch staff, please go to our website: www.hrw.org/about/info/staff.html.

This year's Human Rights Watch World Report is dedicated to two courageous colleagues we tragically lost in 2009:

Alison Des Forges was senior adviser to Human Rights Watch's Africa division for almost two decades. She died in February in a plane crash in the United States. Alison dedicated her life to working on Rwanda and the Great Lakes region of Africa, and was the world's leading expert on the 1994 Rwanda genocide. She appeared as an expert witness in international trials of *genocidaires*, yet remained scrupulously even-handed, typified by her persistent calls for justice for victims of abuses committed by forces that defeated the genocidal regime as well. Alison also trained an entire generation of human rights activists—in Rwanda, Burundi, and the Democratic Republic of Congo— and was a mentor to many at Human Rights Watch. Her rigor, intelligence, principle, energy, compassion, and commitment were without peer.

Natalia Estemirova was the foremost investigator of human rights abuses in Chechnya, the war-torn region in the south of Russia still wracked by insecurity. A Chechnya-based researcher with the Russian human rights group Memorial, in July she had just completed a joint mission with Human Rights Watch into government-sanctioned abuses when she was abducted in Grozny and murdered, a crime that remains unpunished. Natalia had been honored for her work by Human Rights Watch in 2007.

TABLE OF CONTENTS

THE ABUSERS' REACTION: INTENSIFYING ATTACKS ON HUMAN RIGHTS DEFENDERS, ORGANIZATIONS, AND INSTITUTIONS

By Kenneth Roth

Every government is at times tempted to violate human rights. To encourage governments to resist that temptation, the human rights movement seeks to raise the price of abuse—to shift the cost-benefit calculus behind a government's actions.

The human rights movement's ability to raise that price has grown substantially in recent years. Today, activists are capable of exposing abuses most anywhere in the world, shining an intense spotlight of shame on those responsible, rallying concerned governments and institutions to use their influence on behalf of victims, and in severe cases, persuading international prosecutors to bring abusers to justice. These are effective tools, and they have retained their power even as certain traditional allies wavered in their support for human rights. That effectiveness has spawned a reaction, and that reaction grew particularly intense in 2009.

Certain abusive governments, sometimes working together, sometimes pursuing parallel tracks, are engaged in an intense round of attacks on human rights defenders, organizations, and institutions. The aim is to silence the messenger, to deflect the pressure, to lessen the cost of committing human rights violations.

These attacks might be seen as an unwitting tribute to the human rights movement. If governments were not feeling the heat, they would not bother trying to smother the source. But the cynicism of their motives does not mitigate the danger. Under various pretexts, these governments are attacking the very foundations of the human rights movement.

The techniques vary from the subtle to the transparent, from the refined to the ruthless. In some cases, human rights activists—be they advocates, journalists, lawyers, petition-gatherers, or others who document and publicize abuses or defend victims—have been harassed, detained, and sometimes killed.

Organizations have been shut down or crippled. The tools used range from the classic police raid to the more novel use of regulatory constraints.

International institutions have also been targeted. The emergence of an international system of justice—especially the International Criminal Court—has been the focus of particular venom by government leaders who fear prosecution. The aim is apparently to suppress any institution that is capable of penalizing those who violate human rights. The attacks are built on a series of arguments that have resonance but cannot ultimately be reconciled with the imperative of justice for the worst international crimes. In addition, the Human Rights Council, the United Nations' foremost intergovernmental human rights body, has become victim of concerted efforts to undermine its potential by restricting voices that are independent of government control.

The emergence of a strong human rights movement has not, of course, meant the end of human rights abuses. Pressure sometimes works to mitigate or curb abuses, but at other times governments see such advantages to violating human rights that they are willing to brave the cost. The trend, however, is that a growing number of governments hope to have their cake and eat it too—to violate human rights without paying a price. They hope to achieve that abuser's paradise by subverting the individuals and institutions that impose a cost for human rights abuse

Governments, of course, have long been tempted to attack the bearer of bad news. There is a long, sordid history of human rights defenders being censored, imprisoned, "disappeared," or killed. But now, as the human rights movement has grown more powerful and effective, the silence-the-messenger efforts of many governments have grown in subtlety and sophistication. Murders are committed deniably. Politically motivated prosecutions are disguised by common criminal charges. Censorship is accomplished through seemingly neutral regulatory regimes. Funding streams are blocked. As the UN special rapporteur on human rights defenders noted in August 2009, "the ways and means applied in certain countries in order to restrict the activities of human rights organizations are now even more widely used in all regions of the world."

The perpetrators of these attacks are not limited to classic authoritarian governments such as Cuba and China. Democracies such as Sri Lanka have increased the pressure on local and international human rights groups that documented violations, as have governments that hold elections but fall short of democratic rule, such as Russia.

These efforts have yet to succeed in diminishing pressure from the human rights movement. Most human rights defenders accept the unintentional compliment behind the attacks and redouble their efforts. But the campaign to undermine human rights activism is nonetheless dangerous. By highlighting it in this year's World Report, Human Rights Watch seeks to expose and help to reverse the trend. A strong defense of human rights depends on the vitality of the human rights movement that is now under assault. We appeal to governmental supporters of human rights to help defend the defenders by identifying and countering these reactionary efforts..

Attacks on Human Rights Defenders

Murder and Other Violent Attacks

Governments have long used murder to silence human rights criticism. But instead of acting openly, abusers today tend to hide behind the work of "unknown assailants" whose killing is then conveniently ignored by national justice institutions.

RUSSIA

In 2009, Russia was at the forefront of murderous retaliation against human rights defenders. Several of the victims had in common their reporting on arbitrary detention, torture, and summary execution committed in the war-torn republic of Chechnya by forces under the de facto control of Chechen President Ramzan Kadyrov. Russian authorities have fostered a culture of impunity for abuse that cannot but have emboldened the authors of these killings. For example:

- In July, Natalia Estemirova, the leading Chechnya researcher for the Russian human rights group Memorial, was abducted by unidentified men near her home in Grozny, the Chechen capital, and later found murdered.

3

- In August, law enforcement personnel abducted Zarema Sadulayeva and her husband, Alik Dzhabrailov, from their Grozny office; they were found shot dead the next day. They worked for Save the Generation, a charity that provides assistance to children affected by the conflict in Chechnya.

- In January, Umar Israilov, a former security guard for Kadyrov who had filed a complaint for torture against him before the European Court of Human Rights, was murdered by an unknown assailant in Vienna, Austria.

Also in January, human rights lawyer Stanislav Markelov, along with a journalist who was with him, Anastasia Baburova, were killed in Moscow just after he held a press conference. Two suspects have been arrested, and one reportedly confessed to personal motives behind the shooting, allegedly linked to Markelov's work against Russian neo-fascists. At this writing it is unclear whether that was indeed the motive for the murder. Markelov was also representing the family of a young Chechen woman who had been killed by a Russian colonel. He had previously represented Anna Politkovskaya, a journalist who specialized in reporting on abuses under Kadyrov. She was killed in Moscow in 2006, and her murder has never been solved.

Some Russian human rights defenders have faced violence because of their work outside the context of Chechnya.

- Anti-corruption activist Andrei Kulagin, who worked for the group Spravedlivost (Justice) in Petrozavodsk, in northwest Russia, was found dead in July 2009, two months after he went missing. In Khimki, just outside Moscow, Albert Pchelintsev, who works to expose local corruption, was attacked in July by two men who shot him in the mouth "to shut him up," according to the attackers.

- In August, the office of Mothers of Dagestan for Human Rights, a group of mothers whose sons are believed to have been forcibly disappeared, was the subject of an arson attack, after some of its staff members were among those named in a pamphlet calling for the murder of human rights defenders.

- In June, Aleksei Sokolov, a human rights defender from Yekaterinburg in the Ural region, was arrested on clearly spurious charges. A member of a public prison monitoring group, he was beaten by the police as they taunted, "You think *you* have oversight over *us*?"

OTHER COUNTRIES

Russia was not alone in violently attacking human rights defenders. Other countries where rights activists were murdered, "disappeared," or seriously assaulted in 2009 include:

- Kenya, where Oscar Kamau Kingara and John Paul Oulu of the Oscar Foundation, a legal aid organization, were murdered by unidentified assailants in Nairobi in March after they had briefed UN Special Rapporteur Philip Alston on summary executions by the police.

- Burundi, where Ernest Manirumva of the anti-corruption organization OLU-COME was murdered in April. The government initially set up a commission that conducted a sham investigation. Under pressure, it appointed a seemingly more genuine investigative commission in October.

- Sri Lanka, where in May uniformed armed men abducted and "disappeared" Stephen Suntharaj of the Centre for Human Rights and Development. He has not been seen since. He had just been released from two months in police detention upon order of the Supreme Court.

- Afghanistan, where Sitara Achakzai, a prominent human rights advocate from Kandahar, was gunned down in April. She had complained to government officials for weeks about threats that she had been receiving but they had done nothing to protect her—a common complaint among Afghan women in public life, including politicians, journalists, and human rights activists. The authorities have made little or no effort to find Achakzai's killers.

- Malaysia, where Finardo Cabilao, a social welfare attaché at the Philippines embassy, was found bludgeoned to death in August. He appears to have been targeted because of his work combating human trafficking.

- India, where lawyers who represented terrorism suspects were physically attacked by other lawyers often affiliated with militant Hindu parties and threatened by mobs. The government failed to take action against those responsible for such attacks. For example in March, pro bono lawyer Anjali Waghmare volunteered to represent Ajmal Amir Kasab, the sole surviving gunman of the November 2008 Mumbai attacks. A mob of 200 people, led by local leaders of the extremist Shiv Sena party, surrounded her Mumbai home, throwing stones and shouting obscenities. A judge ordered special protection for the lawyer, but none of the attackers has yet been prosecuted.

- Uzbekistan, where three members of the Human Rights Alliance of Uzbekistan—Elena Urlaeva, Salomat Boimatova, and Ilnur Abdulov—were stopped by suspected plainclothes police as they made their way to the UN office in Tashkent in May 2009 to deliver a report on human rights defenders in Uzbekistan. When the alliance members objected to a request to visit the police station, three officers beat Abdulov and forced the three into a waiting police car. At the station, they were questioned about no crime in particular and quickly released. Urlaeva was forced to sign a statement that she would not participate in any human rights activities until June 10, the day of the European Union-Uzbekistan Human Rights Dialogue. Despite that intensifying repression, the EU in October lifted an arms embargo on Uzbekistan, the last remaining sanction imposed after the Andijan massacre of 2005.

Closed Societies and Restricted Conditions for Activism

Some governments are so oppressive that no domestic human rights movement can exist openly. No one dares. These governments typically also preclude visits by international human rights monitors. Noteworthy in this regard are Eritrea, North Korea, and Turkmenistan. Burma and Iran have small, embattled human rights movements but bar international groups from entering. Saudi Arabia does not acknowledge nongovernmental human rights promotion, sometimes ignoring solitary activists, but more often immediately clamping down when those brave individuals find broader resonance, especially in the Western media. Somalia is so dangerous that open human rights monitoring is virtually impossible: the past three years of brutal conflict have seen civil society decimated, with many activists killed or fleeing the country.

Libya has allowed international visits but effectively bars independent domestic monitoring because the concept of an independent civil society contradicts Libyan leader Mu`ammar al-Gaddafi's theory of government by the masses without intermediary. In Syria, all human rights groups remain unlicensed, as officials consistently deny their requests for registration. The National Organization for Human Rights has challenged before an administrative court the decision of the Ministry of Social Affairs and Labor to deny its registration request. The ministry responded by calling for the organization's members to be prosecuted.

Some generally open societies bar international human rights groups from visiting the sites of certain serious abuses. Indonesia has prohibited the International Committee of the Red Cross (ICRC) as well as international human rights groups from visiting Papua. Israel prevented Israeli and international human rights defenders as well as journalists from entering Gaza during the December 2008-January 2009 conflict, and has kept human rights activists out ever since (although it has been possible to gain access via Egypt since the conflict, and Gaza-based defenders have been able to work throughout the period). Sri Lanka blocked local and international human rights groups and independent journalists from most of the region in which the armed conflict that climaxed in 2009 was taking place, as well as access to internally displaced persons held in camps.

A number of governments block access to independent experts and rapporteurs from the UN human rights machinery. The governments of Uzbekistan, Turkmenistan, and Vietnam each continue to refuse access to more than a half-dozen UN special procedures, including on torture and human rights defenders, despite longstanding and repeated requests for invitations to visit the countries. Other similarly offending governments include Egypt, Eritrea, Ethiopia, Pakistan, and Saudi Arabia. At the end of October 2009, Zimbabwe prevented the special rapporteur on torture from entering the country, despite having invited him and agreed to the dates of the visit, while Russia has steadfastly refused to guarantee the conditions required for him to conduct a mission.

Certain governments seem to have no qualms about simply shutting down human rights organizations:

- Following the International Criminal Court's issuance of an arrest warrant for President Omar al-Bashir in March 2009, the Sudanese government closed three local human rights organizations, as well as expelling 13 international humanitarian NGOs working in Darfur.

- In July, the Chinese government shut down the Open Constitution Initiative, the country's leading nongovernmental legal aid organization, which has worked on issues such as the background causes of the 2008 Tibet protests and the scandal of melamine-poisoned milk that sickened hundreds of thousands of children.

- In Azerbaijan, after denying registration six times to the Election Monitoring Center, the government briefly registered it in February 2008, only to shut it down three months later, ostensibly for giving false information about its founder and legal address and for opening regional offices without informing the government. In 2009, the group reformed under a new name—the Election Monitoring and Democracy Studies Center—and applied for registration, but the Ministry of Justice refused in May and August to register it.

Detention, Harassment, Threats, and Other Attacks

Other governments openly harass or detain human rights defenders:

- The Cuban government refuses to recognize the legitimacy of any independent human rights organization. Local defenders are subjected to regular harassment, threatened with beatings and imprisonment if they do not abandon their work, and sentenced under broad laws that criminalize virtually all forms of dissent. Dozens of human rights defenders are currently imprisoned in Cuba, including several sentenced under an Orwellian "dangerousness" law, which allows individuals to be sentenced not because they have committed a crime but to prevent them from committing one in the future.

- The Vietnamese government bans independent human rights organiza- tions, which it considers part of subversive plots to undermine the Vietnamese Communist Party through "peaceful evolution." Human rights defenders are often imprisoned for national security crimes, such as "abusing democratic freedoms" of expression, assembly, and association to "infringe upon the interests of the State." Lawyers seeking to defend Vietnamese human rights activists also face threats, harassment, disbar- ment, physical assault, and arrest. In June 2009, for example, police arrested defense lawyer Le Cong Dinh and accused him of using his repre- sentation of democracy and religious-freedom activists to "propagandize against the regime and distort Vietnam's constitution and laws." Rights lawyer Bui Kim Thanh was involuntarily committed to a mental institution in 2008 because of her defense of farmers seeking redress for confiscation of their land.

- In Iran, security forces in December 2008 ransacked the offices of Nobel Peace Prize laureate Shirin Ebadi, removed files and computers, and arrested some staff members, in advance of a planned celebration of the 60th anniversary of the Universal Declaration of Human Rights. In November 2009, the authorities confiscated Ebadi's Nobel medal and opened legal proceedings for "back taxes" on the financial component on the prize. Prominent human rights lawyers were arrested to prevent them from representing supporters of reform following Iran's disputed June 2009 presidential elections.

- In Saudi Arabia, the secret police arrested rights activists Muhammad al-'Utaibi and Khalid al-'Umair as they planned to attend a peaceful Gaza sol- idarity rally. The security forces have kept them in pretrial detention beyond the six-month limit allowed under Saudi law and despite the fact that the prosecutor's office decided not to press charges. When the authorities in November 2009 suspected al-'Umair of informing fellow rights activists via an illegally held mobile phone about prison conditions in al-Ha'ir prison, including guards beating prisoners and prisoners dying from lack of healthcare, they transferred him to solitary confinement.

- In October 2009, Syrian State Security detained Haytham al-Maleh, 78, a prominent human rights lawyer, following his appearance on an opposition television station in which he criticized the ongoing repression of freedom of expression in Syria. In November, a military judge charged him with "spreading false or exaggerated information that can weaken national sentiment." His trial is ongoing.

- In Cambodia, more than 60 community activists were imprisoned or awaiting trial during 2009—often on spurious charges—for helping to organize and represent fellow community members facing eviction or illegal confiscation of their land by private companies linked to high-ranking government and military officials.

- Yemen remained notorious for its forced disappearances, including that of Muhammad al-Maqalih, a journalist for the opposition Yemeni Socialist Party's online party organ, Eshtiraki.net. A group of men grabbed Maqalih in September 2009 in the capital San'a, shortly after he had criticized the government over its bombing campaign against northern rebels. His associates said sources had identified him at the Political Security Organization prison, then at a Ministry of Defense prison, and, in November, in a prison in Aden.

Some governments use threats of violence, whether explicit or coded, to deter or punish human rights defenders. For example:

- In Colombia, President Álvaro Uribe and senior government officials have made baseless accusations linking human rights defenders as well as journalists and trade union activists to the FARC guerrillas. In the context of a long history of illegal armed groups murdering human rights defenders for their work, such charges can be extraordinarily dangerous. The Colombian intelligence agency, which answers directly to Uribe, has also closely monitored human rights groups through illegal wiretapping, email interception, and surveillance.

- The government of the Democratic Republic of Congo accused human rights workers of being "humanitarian terrorists"—adding considerably to the danger they already face working in the war zone of eastern Congo.

- A number of Sri Lankan activists fled the country because of threats and harassment. In August 2009, Dr. Paikiasothy Saravanamuttu, the executive director of the Centre for Policy Alternatives, a Sri Lankan think-tank often critical of the government, received a death threat in an anonymous letter, blaming him for Sri Lanka's possible loss of EU trade privileges because of its poor human rights record. Two weeks later, police briefly detained and questioned him at the airport upon his return to Sri Lanka from abroad.

- In Nicaragua, women's rights advocates campaigning against an absolute ban on abortion enacted in 2006 faced official investigations into their work as well as threatening calls and acts of vandalism from unknown assailants.

Despite broad recognition of reproductive rights and sexual rights under international law, these rights remain socially and politically under attack in many parts of the world. Discrimination and extreme violence sometimes rising to the level of murder persist against those asserting claims to these rights. Advocates working to combat HIV/AIDS, those who promote women's access to safe and legal abortion, or NGOs that promote lesbian, gay, bisexual, and transgender rights are frequently attacked because of the social and political controversy surrounding these issues. For example, Uganda's proposed "Anti-homosexuality Law" would make it a crime to "promote" homosexuality, on pain of criminal prosecution and dissolution of the offending NGO.

Restrictive Regulations

The above methods for trying to silence the human rights movement are hardly subtle. But because of their transparency they also carry a more direct price in terms of damage to the abusive government's reputation and international relations. As a result, abusive governments often resort to less obvious techniques. One method seemingly in the ascendancy is the adoption of intrusive laws and regulations—designed not to provide a framework to facilitate the creation and operation of NGOs, but to control and muffle them. In 2006, the UN special rap-porteur on human rights defenders noted that "while a few States have adopted national laws reflecting the international obligations contained in the Declaration [on Human Rights Defenders], the overall trend has been for States to adopt new laws restricting the space for human rights activities." Governments that adopt this approach try to pretend that it is no more than ordinary oversight of an important sector, but the intent and effect are to prevent these groups from hold-ing governments accountable to international human rights standards.

Russia reinvigorated this regulatory approach when it adopted a controversial law governing NGOs in 2006. The authorities also deploy tax, fire-safety, and soft-ware-piracy codes to the same effect. NGOs involved in noncontroversial work have felt relatively little impact, but human rights organizations and others seek-ing to promote government accountability have faced burdensome regulations, close oversight, selectively imposed audits and inspections, and the threat of clo-sure for failing to comply. At best, these organizations must waste their time responding to government overseers rather than carrying out their work; accord-ing to one study, registration for NGOs had become 40 percent more expensive than for commercial enterprises. At worst, these organizations are subject to liq-uidation or suspension for relatively minor, technical violations or otherwise pre-vented from doing their core work because of the demands of inspections. In 2009, courts cited technical violations to order the liquidation of two regional offices of the For Human Rights Movement. Agora, a regional human rights asso-ciation, has been prevented from doing its substantive work since July because of a series of harassing inspections.

Ethiopia's new law on civil society organizations, adopted in January 2009, has had an even more devastating effect. It has essentially shut down most domestic human rights monitoring. The law bars "foreign organizations," defined as any group that receives more than 10 percent of its funding from abroad, from con-ducting any activities related to the issues of human rights, women's rights, chil-dren's rights, or good governance. The lack of domestic donors has meant that NGOs have had to avoid these sensitive areas. The Ethiopian government justifies the law by noting that many governments, such as the United States, prohibit for-eign funding of political candidates, but political campaigns are very different from civil society organizations exercising their rights to freedom of expression, association, and peaceful assembly. The Ethiopian government also notes that it permits foreign funding of development activities (a major source of revenue to the government), but the best way of ensuring that development efforts address the greatest public needs is to allow the kind of independent monitoring that the civil society law restricts. Its constricting effect is compounded by a new anti-terrorism law, which can be used to criminalize peaceful public protest and expression under an overbroad definition of promoting terrorism.

India's Foreign Contribution (Regulation) Act, while initially enacted to prohibit political parties, politicians, and electoral candidates from accepting foreign financial support in order to ensure that Indian elections were not affected by foreign interests, has been used instead to block funding of and harass organizations for criticizing government policies and practices. Proposed amendments to the law will further undermine the right of NGOs to seek and receive financial support for any activity deemed detrimental to the "national interest."

In Israel, Prime Minister Benjamin Netanyahu used the power of his position rather than the law to attack the funding base of a key human rights group. In August, he publicly urged European governments to cut their funding to the Israeli veterans' group Breaking the Silence, shortly after it had issued a highly critical report on the Israel Defense Forces' conduct in Gaza. The report included the testimonies of 26 soldiers who had participated in the Gaza military operation. A senior official in Netanyahu's office stated publicly, "We are going to dedicate time and manpower to combating these groups; we are not going to be sitting ducks in a pond for the human rights groups to shoot at us with impunity."

Other governments with restrictive laws on NGOs and associations include:

- Egypt, where the law governing associations provides criminal penalties that stifle legitimate NGO activities, including for "engaging in political or union activities," and allows NGOs to be dissolved by administrative order. Egypt also continues a host of intrusive administrative practices that restrict the natural development of civil society and provide ample means for political or bureaucratic interference. Security services routinely review and reject NGO registrations and scrutinize their leaders, activities, and funding.

- Jordan, where a 2009 law allows the government to remove an NGO's management and replace it with state functionaries. The law now also obliges NGOs to seek official approval for any foreign donation.

- Uganda, where a 2007 law requires NGOs to give seven days' notice of any intention to make "direct contact with people in any rural area of Uganda."

- Turkmenistan, which makes no pretence of respecting NGOs' independence. Under its law, NGOs must secure the support of a government agency to be registered. They must also allow government representatives to attend all meetings and register each grant with the Ministry of Justice.

- Libya, where a law on associations requires a political body to approve all NGOs and allows for continuous governmental interference in running them. Any group deemed to oppose the ideology of the 1969 Libyan revolution is criminalized—potentially a capital offense.

This regulatory approach to restricting human rights monitoring has proved so handy that a number of governments—not limited to traditionally repressive ones—have proposed similar laws. Among the countries where bills are pending are:

- Venezuela, where a bill before the National Assembly since 2006 would subject NGOs that receive foreign assistance to vague registration requirements and the duty to answer intrusive government questions about their activities, funding, and expenses.

- Peru, where a congressional committee has taken steps to reinstate a law allowing a governmental agency to supervise NGOs despite the Constitutional Tribunal of Peru having struck the law down.

- Cambodia, where Prime Minister Hun Sen declared in November 2009 that an NGO law would soon be passed to weed out "bad NGOs" who "speak too loud," are used as fronts for political or terrorist activities, or receive funding from foreign countries to oppose the Cambodian government. A draft law is expected to be taken up by the National Assembly soon, even though civil society groups have not been provided the bill for review and comment.

- Rwanda, where the government is proposing to tighten already intrusive requirements that NGOs provide the government detailed financial information, lists of staff and assets, and yearly activity reports.

- Kyrgyzstan, where a draft law would impose onerous reporting requirements for NGOs, forbid them from engaging in "political" activities, and set out a new regime of government inspections and warnings. Parliamentary hearings on the bill were postponed after local and international outcry.

Disbarring Lawyers

Because lawyers often play a prominent role in defending rights, they frequently face special attack. Both China and Iran have disbarred lawyers on political grounds to prevent them from representing victims of human rights abuses.

- In China, the government silenced activist lawyers by refusing to renew their professional licenses, pressuring the law firms that employ them, and restricting the type of cases that they are permitted to take on. In the largest retaliatory move to date, up to 30 lawyers in Beijing have been deregistered. The disbarred lawyers were all involved in high-profile cases challenging local or central authorities: the Sanlu contaminated milk scandal, allegations of corruption in the construction of schools that collapsed in the 2008 Sichuan earthquake, a challenge over government control of the official Beijing Bar Association, and an alphabet soup of human rights cases ranging from forced evictions of tenants and farmers to politically motivated prosecutions of dissidents and religious dissenters.

- In June 2009, following the disputed presidential elections, the Iranian government adopted new regulations that severely limit the independence of the Iranian Bar Association, giving the government control over a lawyer's right to practice. Until then, the Bar Association, which has the exclusive power to grant or deny licenses to practice, had resisted government efforts to rein in lawyers who defend human rights.

- In July, Syrian State Security detained Muhannad al-Hasani, president of the Syrian Human Rights Organization (Swasiah). An investigating judge charged him with "weakening national sentiment" and "spreading false or exaggerated information" in connection with his monitoring of trials before the Supreme State Security Court. His trial is ongoing. In November, the Syrian Bar Association issued a decision to permanently disbar him.

Criminal Charges

Many governments have used trumped-up criminal charges to silence human rights defenders. For example:

- In their effort to crush China's foremost independent legal aid organization, the Open Constitution Initiative, Beijing authorities detained its founder, Xu Zhiyong, and another staff member for three weeks in August 2009 on suspicion of "tax evasion." The stated grounds: not having paid taxes on a charitable grant received from Yale University. The group was also deregistered. A domestic and international outcry helped to secure Xu's release, but China's leading public interest law NGO remains shuttered.

- In November, China convicted veteran human rights activist Huang Qi of "possession of state secrets" and sentenced him to three years in prison after a closed trial and without ever publicly disclosing what secrets he allegedly possessed. Huang's prosecution followed his investigation into allegations that shoddy construction contributed to the collapse of schools in the Sichuan earthquake zone in May 2008. The government also prosecuted Tan Zuoren, a literary editor and environmental activist, who was tried in Chengdu in August 2009 on charges of "subversion" related to his compilation of a list of children killed in the Sichuan earthquake.

- Uzbekistan has repeatedly used trumped-up criminal charges against human rights activists, especially those working on the rights of farmers.

For example, Ganikhon Mamatkhanov, a human rights defender and farmers' rights activist who regularly provided commentary on the human rights situation in the country to Radio Ozodlik, the Uzbek branch of Radio Free Europe/Radio Liberty, was sentenced in November 2009 to five years' imprisonment on charges of fraud and bribery after he was detained the previous month following an apparent attempt to frame him. Mamatkhanov received a call from an unidentified man asking to meet him at a market. When he showed up, the man reportedly started to hit him and shoved something into his bag. Mamatkhanov tried to stop him and, realizing that it was a set-up, tried to throw the item away. However, he was immediately detained by the police who confiscated the item, subsequently found to be 500,000 Uzbek som (about US$330) in banknotes. Mamatkhanov reported that he had never seen his assailant before.

- Rwanda has used its criminal law against "genocide ideology" to silence individuals critical of current government policies or those who challenge past abuses committed by the Rwandan Patriotic Front. It has also employed its informal gacaca courts—a form of popular justice devoid of many fair trial guarantees—to falsely accuse government critics of complicity in the 1994 genocide. Ironically, these steps, taken in the name of national reconciliation, have undermined the formation of independent civil society groups that could bridge ethnic divides and ease ethnic tensions.

- The Iranian government has arrested scores of NGO activists and sentenced them to prison on the grounds that their work or speech allegedly "harms national security" or that they are "foreign agents." Members of Kurdish rights organizations have faced even worse, with lengthy prison sentences, including the death penalty, for their work reporting on rights violations affecting the Kurdish community. In 2008, the government sentenced to death Farzad Kamangar, a member of the Organization for the Defense of Human Rights in Kurdistan, claiming without proof that he was a member of the banned Kurdistan Workers Party (PKK). It also sentenced Sadigh Kaboudvand, who headed the group, to 11 years in prison for his NGO activities, along with prison terms for 12 of his colleagues.

In a twist on the use of questionable charges, Evgeniy Zhovtis, founding director of the Kazakhstan International Bureau for Human Rights and the Rule of Law and the country's most prominent human rights defender, was found guilty in September 2009 of manslaughter following a motor vehicle accident in which a young man was killed. The investigation and trial leading to his conviction were marred by serious procedural flaws that denied him the right to present a defense, and gave rise to concern that this human tragedy was being politically exploited.

Criminal libel laws have also become a favorite tool to silence human rights criticisms.

- In Morocco, a court in June imposed a three-year sentence on Chekib el-Khayari, president of the Human Rights Association in the Rif, on the grounds that his criticism of officials allegedly complicit in drug-trafficking had "gravely offended" state institutions; the court also convicted him of minor currency violations.

- Chechen President Ramzan Kadyrov filed a civil libel suit and a criminal libel complaint against Oleg Orlov, the head of the human rights group Memorial, for accusing Kadyrov of responsibility in human rights activist Natalia Estemirova's murder. A court ruled in Kadyrov's favor on the civil suit in October, before the investigation of Estemirova's murder was completed. Police are investigating Orlov for criminal libel.

- Natasa Kandic, the director of the Humanitarian Law Center and a prominent critic of Serbia's failure to fully confront its role in wartime abuses in the Balkans during the 1990s, is currently the subject of a dozen civil and criminal lawsuits initiated in 2009 by Serbian public officials. The plaintiffs include officials of the Ministry of Interior and high-ranking members of the police, all of whom Kandic has accused of having participated directly or indirectly in war crimes. The Serbian government has not officially reacted to these cases.

- In Indonesia, Usman Hamid, director of Kontras, one of the country's leading human rights organizations, faces criminal defamation charges pressed by Muchdi Purwopranjono, former Special Forces commander and deputy director of National Intelligence. Hamid had criticized the not-guilty verdict in the deeply flawed trial of Muchdi for the arsenic-poisoning murder of Munir Said Thalib, the founder of Kontras.

In a slight variation on the same theme, Sri Lanka detained four government doctors for several months for allegedly "disseminating false information," based on their reports about indiscriminate government shelling of hospitals in areas controlled by the Tamil Tigers during the final weeks of the armed conflict with the Tigers.

* * *

Despite the variation and inventiveness of government efforts to restrict or punish human rights defenders, the motives are largely the same. In today's world, human rights abuse does carry a price. One would hope that for most governments, that price would provide yet another reason to respect their legal obligations and uphold human rights. But some governments, as described, cannot resist trying to minimize the price by attacking or restricting the messengers. Whether that cynical approach succeeds will depend on the vigor of the response from those governments that are committed to protecting human rights. Human Rights Watch hopes that by highlighting this disturbing trend, we will mobilize a strong response.

Attacks on Human Rights Institutions

International Criminal Court

The reaction to a strong defense of human rights has not been limited to human rights defenders. Perhaps the greatest recent victory of the human rights movement has been its contribution to erecting a new international system of justice for the worst human rights offenders, most notably with the launching in 2002 of the International Criminal Court in The Hague. Before the emergence of an international system of justice, highly abusive governments could reasonably calculate that they could get away with mass murder by using violence or threats to cripple their national justice system. The ICC and its brethren institutions, such as the tribunals for Rwanda, Sierra Leone, and the former Yugoslavia, represent the possibility of justice, beyond the reach of tyrants and dictators to compromise it.

Those institutions are still at a rudimentary stage and they will never have the capacity to prosecute all alleged perpetrators. Moreover, with deeply rooted disparities of power often determining which abusers come under scrutiny, officials from or supported by certain states are less vulnerable to international prosecution. These shortcomings mean that many atrocities remain unaddressed. But the fact that sometimes international justice is available when national justice efforts fail is a development of major significance. Bringing perpetrators to justice pays respect to their victims. And threatening would-be perpetrators with justice offers the prospect of deterring atrocities and saving lives.

But just as those developments are welcome from the perspective of the victims and survivors of atrocities, so they are a threat from the perspective of the perpetrators. And just as abusive governments have attacked human rights defenders for exposing abuses and generating pressure for change, so they have begun to attack the international system of justice for threatening the impunity that they still enjoy.

The trigger for this new assault on international justice was the ICC prosecutor's July 2008 request for an arrest warrant for Sudanese President Omar al-Bashir for crimes committed by Sudanese forces and allied militia against the civilian population of Darfur. In March 2009, al-Bashir became the first sitting head of state to be sought by the ICC for war crimes and crimes against humanity.

One would have wanted African leaders to applaud the move. After all, the world had dithered for more than five years as the people of Darfur faced mass murder and forced displacement. Finally, someone was taking decisive action. Unfortunately, some African leaders seemed less troubled by the slaughter of ordinary African people than by the audacious prospect that a sitting African leader might actually be brought to justice for these horrendous crimes.

The nadir came during the African Union summit held in July 2009 in Sirte, Libya. Under pressure from Libyan leader Mu'ammar al-Gaddafi and the governments of several other North African states, the AU adopted a resolution urging African states not to cooperate with the ICC in its efforts to execute the arrest warrant for al-Bashir. Some governments, notably Botswana and South Africa, later rejected that position, but the sad spectacle remains that the AU, an institution built around principles of human rights and the rule of law, had sided with an alleged mass murderer over his victims.

The AU offered various reasons for its position, none of which bore scrutiny. One was that the UN Security Council had not formally responded to the AU's request that the case against al-Bashir be deferred. But that request was controversial to say the least, premised as it was on the dubious proposition that a leader who had sponsored large-scale slaughter in Darfur would suddenly become a man of peace if only given a second chance. The Security Council was split on how to respond, and without the consent of the five permanent members, was incapable of responding.

That claimed procedural sleight aside, some African leaders objected that the ICC was pursuing justice selectively because all of the four situations on which the ICC had then focused were in Africa. (The ICC prosecutor has since sought authorization to open an investigation in a fifth situation, involving Kenya.) In fact, this focus should have been reason for Africans to celebrate: for the first time an international court was addressing serious crimes on the continent. And African leaders had not objected when the court indicted several warlords.

But the tone changed when the ICC issued a warrant for Sudan's al-Bashir in 2008. The AU, led by some of the continent's worst autocrats, began accusing the court of unfairly targeting Africans. In reality, these leaders were cynically trying to protect one of their own. They knew full well that, in three of the four situations, African governments themselves had invited the court to open investigations. The fourth—Darfur—was the product of a referral from the Security Council, after a vote supported strongly by Benin and Tanzania, the African members of the Security Council at the time. Even the AU's own high-level panel on Darfur, established in 2009 and led by former South African President Thabo Mbeki, highlighted the need for prosecutions for crimes committed in Darfur. African civil society and progressive African states saw through these blatant attempts to perpetuate impunity on the continent and focused rightfully on the legal obligations of all governments to respect the rule of law and of ICC member states to cooperate with the court.

That is not to deny that there have been problems with the ICC's reach. The prosecutor has conducted preliminary inquiries elsewhere—most notably in Colombia, Afghanistan, Georgia, and Gaza—but he has yet to conduct formal investigations outside of Africa. In part that appears to be because of his general reluctance to seek to open investigations on his own initiative (as opposed to on the basis of a referral, although the recent action on Kenya was on his initiative) or to pursue cases that might give rise to complex legal issues. A demonstrated willingness to go after anyone responsible for large-scale atrocities would greatly enhance the ICC's perceived legitimacy.

Another problem is the lack of comprehensive ICC ratification. Some of the clearest cases for ICC involvement—Sri Lanka, Iraq, Gaza, Chechnya—are made difficult by the responsible government's failure to have ratified the ICC's treaty. Rather than attacking the ICC for this deficiency, those interested in a broader reach for the ICC would do better to promote widespread ratification.

There is also a larger problem of double standards and inconsistencies by the major Western powers. The West's eagerness to see prosecutions for, say, atrocities in Guinea, Kenya, or Darfur contrasts pointedly with its reluctance to press Israel even to bring to justice in its own courts those who may be responsible for war crimes in Gaza. That tendency to protect abusive friends only encourages a closing of the ranks on the part of the AU.

Yet the AU must still bear primary responsibility for its solidarity with al-Bashir. That the pleas of non-African victims of international crimes have gone unanswered is no reason to ignore African victims' quest for justice. But the West should stop facilitating the AU's callousness toward its own people. A more principled defense of justice, even when one's friends are implicated, is the best way to encourage emulation and justice no matter where serious crimes are committed.

UN Human Rights Council

The Human Rights Council is a troubled institution. While repeatedly criticizing the Israeli government for human rights violations, it has neglected or downplayed comparable and more serious situations. For example, in May 2009 a small group of traditionally pro-human rights governments succeeded in holding a special session to address the grave situation in Sri Lanka, where the government had just shelled and killed several thousand civilians who had been forcibly held by the Tamil Tigers, and had then interned nearly 300,000 civilians when the fighting ended with a government victory. Rather than press for an independent investigation into war crimes by both the government and the Tamil Tigers, the Council largely commended the government while ignoring its rights violations, and focused on abuses committed only by the Tigers.

As in the Council's other disappointing actions, this embarrassing resolution was by no means preordained by the Council's membership. A majority of the Council's members are democracies that might have been expected to vote in the Council according to the same principles to which they subscribe domestically. Their repeated failure to do so reflects the ability of some of the world's most repressive governments to convince them to vote according to a perverse sense of regional or Southern solidarity rather than the human rights principles that they endorse at home. That is, as in the case of the ICC and the AU, the repressive leaders at the Council have succeeded in convincing these democracies to value solidarity with abusive Southern leaders rather than their Southern victims.

Again, their position has been facilitated by the West's own bloc tendencies and misplaced solidarity. When the European Union spends so much time devising a common position that it has little energy to engage with anyone else, or when the United States, reflexively protecting Israel, attacked the September 2009 report of the UN fact-finding mission on Gaza led by former South African Justice Richard Goldstone, they make it easier for repressive leaders to build a common stance behind their own favorite abusers.

But these repressive leaders have not been content to settle for a series of political victories. The Council is a body of governments, but one of its virtues is that its traditions allow many opportunities for independent voices to be heard. Independent experts and rapporteurs routinely report. NGOs add their views. The Office of the High Commissioner for Human Rights has a say. All of these are important antidotes to a system that is currently dominated by many of the very abusers who should be the subject of Council action.

23

The repressive leaders at the Council now seem determined to silence these voices whenever possible. They have offered a series of techniques, from "codes of conduct" to restrictive rules and oversight, to limit the ability of these voices to be heard. That would undermine some of the most important ways in which the Council continues to be useful despite the current dominance of its repressive leadership. As the Council approaches a mandated five-year review in 2011, there is a danger that this scheme will succeed unless traditional defenders of human rights can be mobilized.

Cuba provides a good illustration of the manipulative tools used by abusive governments to block independent voices from being heard. Its target was the procedure known as Universal Periodic Review—an important innovation of the Council by which the human rights record of every government, even the most powerful, is scrutinized every four years. Because those doing the reviewing are largely governments, Cuba went out of its way to ensure that many friendly governments would line up to speak during the review in support of its record, reducing the opportunity during the limited time allocated for critics to take the floor. When the time came for NGOs to speak, the Cuban government sought to dilute that independent voice by encouraging dozens of government-organized associations to make uniformly positive submissions about the Cuban government's rights record. These efforts to stifle independent commentary facilitated the Cuban government's ability to deny, implausibly, that it holds any political prisoners or restricts freedom of speech. In addition, there is no evidence that in preparing its submission the government consulted with any independent figures within Cuba, as it is encouraged to do.

UN NGO Committee

This attack on independent NGO voices at the United Nations extends beyond the Council. To gain the right to speak before UN bodies an NGO must obtain "consultative status" from the UN's NGO Committee, another collection of governments. As in the case of the Council, governments that tend to have restrictive policies toward NGOs seem to actively seek membership and are overrepresented. The current membership includes Angola, China, Cuba, Egypt, Russia and Sudan. Among the NGOs that the committee has rejected are a Christian group from China (for refusing to provide a list of its members in China—a revelation that would have invited retaliation against them by Beijing), the Ethiopian Human Rights Council (because the group supposedly had not complied with Ethiopia's new, restrictive civil society law), and the US-based Democracy Coalition Project (because China, Cuba and Russia objected to its supposed discrimination against them, although this rejection was later overturned by a higher UN body). Groups defending the rights of gays and lesbians have had a particularly difficult time obtaining consultative status because committee members substitute their own moral preferences for the right of NGOs to advocate freely on behalf of the human rights of anyone.

European Regional Mechanisms

UN institutions are not alone in facing a backlash from rights abusers. The European Court of Human Rights has been the international institution that most consistently holds the Russian government to account for its highly abusive conduct in Chechnya. The Court has issued more than 100 rulings against Russia for the abduction, torture, and execution of people in Chechnya, and for failing to properly investigate these crimes. Russia complies with orders that it pay compensation, but consistently refuses to implement the structural reforms ordered, such as the mandate to end the impunity that underlies so many of these abuses by conducting effective investigations and prosecutions. That failure is particularly glaring when the identity of the offending commander or security-force unit is known, as it sometimes is. In some 40 of the cases, the Russian government also violated its obligation to share relevant documents with the court. In addition, Russia stands alone among Council of Europe member states in blocking Protocol 14, a revision of the European Convention on Human Rights that would allow an intergovernmental ministerial committee to sue a government before the European Court for refusing to comply with the Court's judgments.

The Russian government also continues to postpone a long-planned visit by Dick Marty, the rapporteur of the Parliamentary Assembly of the Council of Europe on the human rights situation in the North Caucasus.

ASEAN Commission on Human Rights

The one potentially positive institutional development in 2009 turned out to merit little fanfare. In October 2009, the 10-member Association of Southeast Asian Nations (ASEAN) launched the Intergovernmental Commission on Human Rights— an institution that had been years in the making. Judging by its debut, it was not worth the wait. It has vowed to adopt a "constructive," "non-confrontational," and "evolutionary" approach to human rights. Although its terms of reference include the promotion and protection of "human rights and fundamental freedoms of the peoples of ASEAN," its reach is limited by its commitment to "non-interference in the internal affairs of ASEAN member states," its mandate to reach decisions through "consultation and consensus," and its admonishment to be aware of "national and regional particularities and mutual respect for different historical, cultural and religious backgrounds and taking into account the balance between rights and responsibilities." Together, these principles give veto power to any member state, and deny member states the power to receive complaints, to monitor and investigate an alleged abusive state, to impose sanctions, or to expel a recalcitrant member.

Thai Prime Minister Abhisit Vejjajiva, acting as ASEAN chairman, explained that in ASEAN's view "the issue of human rights is not about condemnation, but about awareness," adding that improving human rights is an "evolutionary process." Given that ASEAN members include Burma, led by a ruthless military government that shows no sign of respecting the rights of its people, and entrenched dictatorships in Vietnam and Laos, that no-pressure form of evolution is likely to take a long time.

The new Commission was expected to engage with civil society. But at the first "interface meeting," the Thai chair rejected five of ten planned participants—from Burma, Cambodia, Laos, the Philippines and Singapore—leading three of the remaining five to walk out. At an earlier meeting of foreign ministers, ASEAN members had decreed that each state would choose the civil society organization it wished to be part of the interface, suggesting that independence was hardly an important criterion.

Conclusion

The human rights movement could do without the back-handed compliment represented by the attacks on its activists and institutions. Nice as it is to know that the targets of pressure are feeling the heat, their backlash can cause great harm to those who face it. The movement as a whole remains impressively resilient, capable of fighting back against this reactionary effort. But individual parts of the movement—particular defenders and organizations—remain vulnerable, in need of support.

It is one thing to note that many repressive governments are intent on lowering the cost of their abuse, on crippling the movement's capacity to exact a toll for violating human rights and changing the cost-benefit calculus. It is another thing to do something about it. The success of these efforts should not depend solely on the courage of individual human rights activists. The human rights movement should also be able to benefit from the backing of its ostensible governmental supporters. The retaliatory techniques described in this introduction, while often more refined than in years past, are plain for all to see. Will the governmental supporters of human rights parry those techniques, or will they conveniently close their eyes to the thrust? The answer may well determine the success of the abusers' reaction.

It is time for a more vigorous governmental defense of human rights activists and institutions throughout the world. That requires standing up more firmly for the people and principles under attack, even when the attacker is an ally. It also requires seeing through these acts of retaliation to recognize and condemn them for what they are. It is no ordinary abuse to kill or arbitrarily detain a human rights defender, deregister a human rights organization, or attack an international human rights institution. It is a tacit confession of still greater abuse. Governments try to silence the messenger because they do not want the message heard. The surest way to reverse that censorship is to redouble efforts to redress the very abuses that these governments are seeking to hide from scrutiny.

This Report

This report is Human Rights Watch's twentieth annual review of human rights practices around the globe. It summarizes key human rights issues in more than 90 countries and territories worldwide, drawing on events through November 2009.

Each country entry identifies significant human rights issues, examines the freedom of local human rights defenders to conduct their work, and surveys the response of key international actors, such as the United Nations, European Union, Japan, the United States, and various regional and international organizations and institutions.

This report reflects extensive investigative work undertaken in 2009 by the Human Rights Watch research staff, usually in close partnership with human rights activists in the country in question. It also reflects the work of our advocacy team, which monitors policy developments and strives to persuade governments and international institutions to curb abuses and promote human rights. Human Rights Watch publications, issued throughout the year, contain more detailed accounts of many of the issues addressed in the brief summaries collected in this volume. They can be found on the Human Rights Watch website, www.hrw.org.

As in past years, this report does not include a chapter on every country where Human Rights Watch works, nor does it discuss every issue of importance. The failure to include a particular country or issue often reflects no more than staffing limitations and should not be taken as commentary on the significance of the problem. There are many serious human rights violations that Human Rights Watch simply lacks the capacity to address.

The factors we considered in determining the focus of our work in 2009 (and hence the content of this volume) include the number of people affected and the severity of abuse, access to the country and the availability of information about it, the susceptibility of abusive forces to influence, and the importance of addressing certain thematic concerns and of reinforcing the work of local rights organizations.

The World Report does not have separate chapters addressing our thematic work but instead incorporates such material directly into the country entries. Please consult the Human Rights Watch website for more detailed treatment of our work on children's rights, women's rights, arms and military issues, business and human rights, health and human rights, international justice, terrorism and counterterrorism, refugees and displaced people, and lesbian, gay, bisexual, and transgender people's rights, and for information about our international film festivals.

Kenneth Roth is executive director of Human Rights Watch.

Civilian Protection and Middle East Armed Groups: In Search of Authoritative Local Voices

By Joe Stork

The Middle East has over many years been wracked by political violence and armed conflicts in which governments and armed groups alike have shown a pernicious disregard for the lives of civilians. When they do so during armed conflict, they violate the core principle of international humanitarian law—civilian immunity—which requires a warring party to distinguish between the civilian population and military targets, and to direct attacks only against military targets. Outside of armed conflicts, such attacks on civilians may amount to crimes against humanity.

Many of the armed groups in the Middle East responsible for breaching this core principal by deliberately or indiscriminately killing civilians assert an Islamic identity, and some justify their decision to take up arms in Islamic terms. Exception to the principle of civilian immunity is invoked on political and sometimes religious grounds.

It would be hard to exaggerate the impact of the Israeli-Palestinian conflict on the evolution of popular views of political violence and armed conflict in the region, including attitudes toward civilian protection. And owing in large measure to the prominent international dimension of the conflict, human rights proponents as well as governments and groups resistant to human rights criticism have scrutinized the stance of outside actors, particularly the United States, for evidence of partisanship and double standards in monitoring and protesting violations of international law.

Against this backdrop, what prospects exist for identifying authoritative voices in majority Muslim countries of the Middle East who can advance civilian protection, by discussing these issues openly and in ways that demonstrate the shared prohibition in Islamic ethics and international humanitarian law against targeting persons not participating in armed hostilities?

Civilian Protection in Human Rights and Humanitarian Law

International humanitarian law (IHL), or the laws of war, does not address whether a decision to take up arms is legal or justified. Instead, it is concerned with the methods and means of military operations and the treatment of non-combatants (civilians, prisoners-of-war, wounded fighters, etc). A critical feature of IHL is that it applies to all parties to an armed conflict, that is, both states and non-state armed groups. Were the laws of war to apply to only one side to an armed conflict, be it the military aggressor or only a recognized state, then compliance would quickly fall apart. Likewise, violations by one side's forces do not permit or justify violations by their adversary.

The principle of civilian immunity prohibits attacks that target civilians, as well as attacks that indiscriminately harm civilians—that is, in which the attacking party does not or cannot distinguish between civilians and military objectives. States and non-state armed groups responsible for such attacks are committing violations of IHL. War crimes are serious violations of IHL committed with criminal intent—that is, deliberately or recklessly—by individuals. Crimes against humanity are serious criminal acts committed during peacetime or armed conflict that are part of a widespread or systematic attack against a specific civilian population. In the Middle East, the disregard for civilian immunity has resulted in war crimes and crimes against humanity by members of both national armed forces and opposition armed groups.

Attitudes toward Civilian Harm

For some Middle Eastern governments, the path to power was exceedingly violent. The conduct of liberation wars such as Algeria's in the 1950s in turn helped to shape the guerrilla movements that developed in the Middle East, particularly among Palestinians.[1] With such legacies, habits of unrestrained assault on adversaries and their populations were ingrained in the conduct of thoroughly secular parties to various conflicts. When in the 1980s and 1990s new political movements claiming Islamic legitimacy emerged, the armed groups they spawned—in Egypt and Algeria, for example—soon adopted similarly unbounded tactics in their conduct of armed violence, initially directed at the often-brutal security apparatuses of the states they were fighting, but soon also at "soft" civilian targets. Although these groups invoked to varying degrees a discourse they claimed to be grounded in religious doctrine, the violence they perpetrated against civilians and other non-combatants reflected and extended the illegal and murderous practices of secular actors.

Since the Palestinian Islamist groups Hamas and Islamic Jihad initiated suicide bombing attacks against Israeli civilians in 1995-96, Middle East human rights activists and society until recently had little to say on the issue, reflecting a general perception in the Middle East that illegal Israeli occupation practices, for the most part enjoying international tolerance if not support, made such violence unavoidable and even legitimate.[2] To be sure, human rights proponents did not endorse suicide bombings against civilians, but neither did they criticize them, either because they shared the approving sentiments of opinion-shapers in those countries or because they did not feel secure enough to challenge those sentiments.

One discussion of the issue in the late 1990s, called "The Operations of Hamas from a Human Rights Perspective," appeared as part of a booklet produced by the Cairo Institute for Human Rights Studies.[3] In his introductory remarks, institute director Bahey el-Din Hassan observed that the Hamas bombings had stirred up considerable controversy within Egyptian human rights circles and "particularly in the human rights movement in Palestine." While a number of participants were critical of the bombings, only the comments of political analyst Muhammad al-Sayed Sa'id showed awareness of international humanitarian law and the core principle of respecting civilian immunity. One of the few human rights activists recorded as participating in the discussion endorsed the view that because of Israel's illegal occupation "there is no such thing as 'an Israeli civilian.'" Political analyst Usama al-Ghazali Harb was sharply critical of Hamas's attacks but on a strictly instrumentalist basis: the question of whether the attacks violate human rights, he said, "does not interest me.... Did these operations advance [Palestinian] interests?" Because they do not, "I say that—regardless of the issue of human rights— they are operations worthy of condemnation."

In late 2000, after already limited Palestinian-Israeli negotiations collapsed and the Al Aqsa intifada erupted, Hamas and Islamic Jihad initiated suicide bombings against civilians in Israel in January 2001, joined by the Fatah-affiliated Al Aqsa

Martyrs Brigade in late 2001.[4] The number of attacks and number of victims spiked in 2002, but attacks and civilian deaths continued through early 2007.

Palestinian criticism of suicide bombings targeting civilians surfaced publicly at the end of 2001. Critics argued that these actions were ineffective and counter-productive. In one public intervention, Birzeit University professors Rema Hammami and Musa Budeiri wrote that the bombings were "isolated from a strategic reading of Israeli society's reaction to and understanding of the uprising and of Palestinian resistance in general."[5] That criticism grew considerably when Prime Minister Ariel Sharon ordered the Israel Defense Forces (IDF) to reoccupy the West Bank after a Hamas suicide bombing at a Passover celebration in Netanya killed 29 Israelis. On June 19, 2002, and on several subsequent days, the daily *Al-Quds* carried a full-page petition initially signed by 55 academics, writers, and prominent figures, which called on the armed groups to cease "military oper-ations targeting civilians in Israel" on the grounds that they deepen hatred between Palestinians and Israelis while strengthening "the enemies of peace on the Israeli side" and "pushing the area toward an existential war" between Israelis and Palestinians.[6]

Signatories to the petition included human rights activists Iyad al-Sarraj and Khader Shrikat, but Arab and Palestinian human rights groups as such largely remained silent, reflecting the extent of division among members on the issue. One element in this was a tendency to conflate the question of armed resistance against legitimate military targets and attacks against Israeli civilians, as well as frustration with the persistent failure of Israel's supporters internationally to hold Israeli leaders accountable for numerous killings of Palestinian civilians in the West Bank and Gaza Strip by the Israeli military. The silence may also have reflected uneasiness among human rights activists about their sometimes thin support in society and among political elites, and wariness about testing that support with a public stance that would surely attract public criticism from the armed groups and their partisans. Palestinian rights activist Fateh Azzam, review-ing the record of the leading Palestinian human rights group, Al-Haq, wrote in 2004 that "a serious gap" in its "honorable human rights record" was its "failure to take a clear public position on the problem of armed attacks against civilian targets inside Israel during the first three years of the current intifada."[7]

Human Rights Watch, when it released a highly critical investigative report on Palestinian suicide bombings against Israeli civilians in November 2002, encountered condemnations from some human rights activists in the region. There were indications, however, that this initial hostility moderated in the following period. The Gaza-based Palestinian independent legislator (and briefly Minister of Foreign Affairs in a Palestinian Authority unity government) Ziad Abu Amr said that the report "helped define the public debate, allowing people to speak critically about these attacks," although in his view the perpetrator groups remained "trapped by their own past positions and rhetoric."[8] Palestinian journalists in the West Bank agreed that the report "helped raise questions about the [suicide] bombings."[9]

Arab human rights groups, for their part, did move on the issue as well, initially in a collective fashion. The "Rabat Declaration" from a meeting of Arab civil society NGOs in December 2004 criticized "the silence or the collaboration of the majority of Arab governments with a religious discourse and *fatwa* justifying terrorism issued by [Islamic] jurists, some of them working for religious institutions subject to the state." The declaration also spoke against "terrorist groups in Iraq" that "bombarded civil institutions, abducted and murdered police officers as well as Iraqi and non-Iraqi civilians." Most significantly, with regard to the Palestine-Israel conflict, "The conference condemns targeting and terrorizing civilians on both sides."[10] In 2006 several human rights organizations in the region did make public statements critical of armed attacks against Israeli civilians by Palestinian and Lebanese armed groups. In July Al-Haq issued a public appeal stating that the armed groups "may not resort to reciprocity as a legal justification" for violations of humanitarian law.[11]

Over the past several years, I and colleagues from Human Rights Watch met in various Arab countries with civil society activists, editors, and religious leaders to discuss attacks against civilians as serious human rights abuses and violations of humanitarian law.[12] With what we called the Civilian Protection Initiative, Human Rights Watch sought to engage with activists and opinion-shapers across the region on the question of attacks targeting civilians, and to encourage them to criticize publicly such attacks when they occur, even when the perpetrators espouse a cause that enjoys widespread popular support, such as ending Israel's military occupation of the West Bank and Gaza Strip. Our previous experience investigating and reporting on such violence in the Occupied Palestinian Territories, Iraq, and Egypt suggested that greater engagement around these issues by local human rights activists and sympathizers would be essential in any effort to persuade the perpetrators to cease such attacks.[13] The views of our interlocutors provide a complicated portrait of the state of elite opinion regarding civilian protection.

First, virtually every interlocutor stressed the need to appreciate the context of military occupation in terms of killings in Israel and Iraq. For some, this context was everything: end the occupation and the violence will end. "Stop the injustice that makes me tolerate [attacks against Israeli civilians]" was how one former high-ranking Jordanian official put it. "We are fighting an occupation that violates [international humanitarian] law every day," said a West Bank leader of the reformist wing of Fatah. International humanitarian law, however, obliges all parties to an armed conflict to respect civilian immunity, including in resisting military occupation.[14]

Second, almost all interlocutors made a point of distinguishing between the attacks on civilians in Iraq, which they condemned, and attacks by Palestinians against Israeli civilians. "Denunciations of Iraqi attacks have been clear, no one justifies them," said a Dubai-based Islamist lawyer and human rights activist, "but Palestine remains outside of such a critique." Perhaps the most common refrain in these discussions is the notion that the Palestine/Israel conflict is "unique": for persons who agreed with the basic principle that civilians should be immune from attack, Palestine is the "but" that almost invariably follows. On this point, there is no discernible difference between Islamists or Islamic leaders, on the one hand, and secularists and leftists, on the other. This Palestine exceptionalism takes several forms. A common one is the assertion that Israeli society is militarized to the point that "there are no civilians there." Another is that the disparity of arms between Israel and Palestinian armed groups gives the latter leeway to use whatever means they can devise. Neither of these rationales can justify targeting civilians.[15]

The greatest readiness to criticize Palestinian attacks against Israeli civilians, perhaps not surprisingly, was among Palestinians themselves. Journalists and writers in the West Bank appeared to have no problem accepting that targeting civilians was wrong in all circumstances. They indicated interest in being part of a public service campaign to promote awareness of this humanitarian principle, its history, and what it means in the Palestinian context—although they were emphatically not proposing to initiate such an effort. Several spoke of a "culture of fear" of running afoul of the armed groups and their partisans.

This vulnerability is even more pronounced in nearby countries where solidarity with Palestinians has taken on a doctrinaire quality, notably Egypt and Jordan. An Egyptian political activist from an Islamist background and well disposed toward human rights concerns said he condemned Palestinian attacks against civilians, but "I can't convince other intellectuals to join me, and the broader public is more difficult yet. We need a package solution. In our environment I or others can easily be isolated as a traitor or agent. We need to emphasize abuses by the superior power."[16]

In the view of many with whom we spoke, Western human rights groups also betray elements of double standards. Human Rights Watch, they said, criticizes Israeli violations, to be sure, but in their view the language tends to be more restrained than when discussing Palestinian violations. "We don't feel justice in the way international human rights organizations view conflict in our region," one Egyptian activist said.[17]

Probably the most difficult challenge to efforts to promote public criticism of Palestinian attacks on Israeli civilians was what many interlocutors argued was Israeli impunity in the face of its considerably more extensive (and in their view more egregious) violations of international humanitarian law, and the failure of those states that proclaim their fidelity to human rights to hold Israel—or, in the case of Iraq, the United States—accountable. "Show me that international humanitarian law matters" was their bottom line. In the words of a West Bank Hamas spokesperson, "We will follow [IHL] if we have a guarantee" that Israel will also abide. At present, he said, Israel left Palestinians with few options.[18]

The intense international attention focused recently on the report of the United Nations Fact-Finding Mission on the Gaza Conflict ("the Goldstone report"), with its findings of serious laws of war violations by Israel and Palestinian armed groups and its call for their referral to international justice mechanisms if they do not mount credible domestic investigations, has highlighted in an unprecedented way the importance of accountability for war crimes and crimes against humanity. Much will hinge on whether and to what extent the international community uses this opportunity to promote respect for international humanitarian law principles by addressing the important element of accountability. As discussed below, the laws of war prohibition against targeting civilians is absolute, and does not rest on compliance by an adversary.[19]

Human rights organizations in the region put forth one further argument for remaining silent on this issue. Their focus is on abuses committed by their own governments, which are all too ready to pounce on any opportunity to discredit these groups. Those governments and their cronies dominate the media. If, say, the Tunisian League for Human Rights were to condemn Palestinian armed groups for attacks on Israeli civilians, the Tunisian government-controlled media would depict their action as proof of their "Zionist" or at least pro-Western agenda and their betrayal of the Palestinian cause. If the Tunisian media were free, a group like the League might be able to fight back, but it is not. In this situation, these organizations are protective of their credibility and carefully monitor their political capital so that they can continue to monitor abuses by their own governments, and they would find the risks too high in coming out with statements criticizing Hamas or other Palestinian groups.

Our meetings also involved conversations with groups perpetrating violations. Members of groups that have carried out attacks against Israeli civilians knew basic IHL standards and claimed to have no quarrel with them. Sometimes they excuse the harm to civilians as unavoidable, in terms not that different from IHL notions of "collateral damage." But in reality these groups have a major quarrel with those standards, particularly regarding non-reciprocity—the principle that violations by one party to a conflict do not permit or justify violations by the other. The groups are familiar with the prohibition against indiscriminate attacks or those that target civilians, but they made clear that they were willing to spare civilians only to the extent that their adversary—Israel—did so as well. "Targeting civilians is utterly unacceptable," a Hezbollah leader told us in early July 2006. But in the same conversation, this spokesman acknowledged that Hezbollah did carry out such attacks as reprisals for Israeli attacks that killed Lebanese civilians. "How can you counter Israeli targeting of your civilians? You have to punish

[them]," he said.[20] Discussing Iraq, however, he was unequivocal: "What we consider resistance there targets only military occupiers," he said. "Those who target civilians are terrorists." A week after this interview, the war in Lebanon erupted and Hezbollah and Israel systematically traded indiscriminate attacks that killed and wounded civilians on the other side.

Some Hamas leaders have been more blunt in asserting that it is permissible to target an adversary's civilians in reprisal. Under IHL, a belligerent reprisal is an otherwise unlawful action permitted in exceptional circumstances as an enforcement measure against unlawful acts by an adversary. Reprisals against civilians are broadly if not universally condemned by states. As a matter of customary IHL, reprisals are never permitted in non-international armed conflicts—those not between states.[21]

"It's not targeting civilians," Ismail Abu Shanab told Human Rights Watch. "It is saying if you attack mine I'll attack yours." Abu Shanab continued: "If you ask us to comply [with IHL], that is not difficult. Islamic teachings support the Geneva Conventions. They are accepted. When it comes to the other side, if they don't abide, we cannot be obliged to them, except insofar as we can achieve something."[22] In Beirut, Human Rights Watch also met with Usama Hamdan, who represents Hamas in Lebanon. His comments demonstrated that the policy of reprisal went hand in hand with a tendency to erase the operative distinctions between civilian and combatant in the case of Israel: "Israel is a democratic state and popular pressure on this issue could change policies, but those civilians are supporting [IDF] attacks on our civilians."[23] In addition to justifying attacks against civilians, which international humanitarian law absolutely prohibits, this is a recipe for collective punishment, which is also a serious violation of the laws of war.

Myths and Realities of Islamist Motivation

Few of those we have met with to discuss these issues, including Islamists and Islamic scholars or representatives of Islamist groups that have been responsible for targeting civilians, suggested that Islamic law differed significantly from international humanitarian law when it comes to prohibiting attacks on civilians. Typical was the comment of an Egyptian Muslim Brotherhood leader. "One crime does not justify another," he said. "Muslims are being diverted from Islam, including the rules of war."[24]

This is not to argue that religion, religious history, and religious symbols play no role in facilitating attitudes of disregard for humanitarian principles. Invocations of religious doctrine are important in recruitment of fighters (or "martyrs") and enlisting them in attacks against civilians. But we encountered little or no effort on the part of our interlocutors, even those who were Islamist activists or religious leaders, to justify violations of the principle of civilian immunity from attack on grounds that such attacks are permitted, or not prohibited, under Islamic law. In an investigation into Hezbollah's firing of rockets into civilian areas in Israel, Human Rights Watch encountered no instance in which Hezbollah leaders cited religious justifications for those attacks.[25] But at the same time, in an environment of Islamist revivalism, the imprimatur of Islamic authority is important. Thus, Khalid Mishal, the head of Hamas's political bureau, claimed that "martyrdom operations [are] one of the many forms of resistance, indeed it is the highest and noblest form of resistance and one that is most effective. Most of the scholars in our Islamic nations have ruled that it is permissible and, indeed, one of the best forms of jihad and resistance."[26] It would appear from the videotaped messages that suicide bombers typically leave, as well as other statements, that this Islamic legitimation is an important factor in their recruitment and motivation.

The role of Islamic doctrine and Islamist ideology is much more pronounced in the other main category of movements that have taken up arms and employed violence against ordinary people as well as agents of the state, namely political movements that aim to overthrow or radically alter an existing government that itself claims Islamic legitimacy. The Gama`a Islamiyya and Islamic Jihad movements in Egypt in the 1980s and 1990s, influenced by the writings of Sayyid Qutb, and the jihadist *salafiyya* movement in Saudi Arabia, led by veterans of the anti-Soviet campaign of the 1980s in Afghanistan, illustrate this.[27]

Such insurgencies raise serious legitimacy issues: Muslim polities, like others, do not look kindly on armed insurgencies and would-be usurpers, and this resistance to rebellion is encoded in the opposition to *fitna*, or disorder. In Islamic terms, it is essential for a rebel or insurgent movement to make a credible claim that the government in question is not, and in some versions never was, genuinely or sufficiently Islamic in its practices, or has betrayed Islam in some serious manner. In the eyes of the insurgents, such governments are no longer Muslim and must be fought as apostates and non-believers (*kufar*). This can be self-evident where the ruling party is foreign and non-Muslim. With regard to existing Arab governments, rebels and insurgents justify in Islamic terms their recourse to armed violence by declaring the leaders of the state in question, and those who support those leaders, to be *kufar*.

Although the Egyptian government ruthlessly suppressed the Islamist insurgency in the 1990s, an element of its defeat (at least as significant in the opinion of many Egyptian observers as the repressive capacity of the state) was the political isolation that Gama`a Islamiyya had brought on itself by its tactic of attacks that indiscriminately killed civilians, many of them directed at the tourist industry, an important source of income for many citizens as well as for the government. In the aftermath of this defeat, many leaders of the Gama`a Islamiyya renounced the use of violence. However, in the view of Hugh Roberts, who wrote an exceptionally lucid series of analytical pieces on contemporary Islamism for the International Crisis Group, the "recantations" written by Karam Zuhdi and others disavowing the group's recourse to violence "left unanswered the critical question of whether Egyptian Islamic radicalism has genuinely and comprehensively come to terms with the bankruptcy of its *jihadi* strategy and settled its intellectual accounts with the thinking that inspired it."[28] Islamic Jihad responded to the defeat of the insurgency in Egypt by reorienting itself to the international arena, joining with al Qaeda in the late 1990s. Only in late 2007 did one of the group's founders and chief ideologues, Sayid Imam Sharif, issue a similar "reinterpretation" of jihad, specifically ruling out the denunciation and condemnation of persons as *kufar* in order to justify harming them, as well as the killing of non-Muslims in Muslim countries or Muslims belonging to other sects, such as Shia.[29]

The targeting of civilians by Islamist armed groups became particularly controversial among Islamist militants themselves in the context of the bloodbath in Iraq in the years after the US invasion. Some, with impeccable militant credentials, have condemned such attacks in no uncertain terms. The Palestinian-Jordanian Islamist ideologue Abu Muhammad al-Maqdisi unreservedly denounced as *kufar* governments that do not institute rule based on Sharia (Islamic law), and dismissed democracy as tantamount to changing one's religion—that is, committing apostasy.[30] In 2005, however, he criticized his former comrade Abu Musab al-

Zarqawi for his brutal campaign of attacks targeting civilians in Iraq's Shia communities. "My project is not to blow up a bar, my project is not to blow up a cinema," al-Maqdisi told an Al Jazeera interviewer in July 2005:

> My project is to bring back to the Islamic Nation its glories and to establish the Islamic state that provides refuge to every Muslim, and this is a grand and large project that does not come by small vengeful acts…. Since when did we speak of killing women and children? Since when did we speak of killing the laymen of the Shia?

The Iraq experience, with its multiplicity of actors and unrelenting reign of terror against civilians, often solely on the basis of their being Sunni or Shia, in some ways reprises the massacres of civilians that characterized the Algerian civil war in the mid-1990s. In both cases the insurgent forces included at the leadership level Arab veterans of the war in Afghanistan who, among other things, put great store in imposing what they regarded as "correct" Islamic practices.

The armed insurgents in Saudi Arabia appear to present a case of Islamist political violence most directly and unambiguously rooted in doctrine and religious ideology. In part this probably reflects the near-total hegemony of religious discourse in Saudi Arabian discussions of political and social issues, fostered by the free hand Saudi rulers have given to Islamist ideologues along with their systematic silencing of dissenting liberal views. Many of the perpetrators of political violence in Saudi Arabia are the political and ideological heirs of those whom the Saudi state had encouraged and enabled (with fulsome support from Washington) to fight against the former Soviet-supported government in Afghanistan. Their shift of focus to Saudi Arabia and the Western presence there seems to be doctrinally inspired. In Nasir al-Fahd's pamphlet "Revealing the Blasphemy of Those Who Help Americans" it would be difficult to find a more succinct statement of the rationale for insurgent violence directed not just at Americans and other Westerners in the kingdom, but against the indigenous (and religiously-sanctioned) political authority. Al-Fahd's pamphlet, according to Saudi scholar Madawi al-Rasheed, describes a "legitimizing narrative of violence" that draws on the Quran and Hadith (sayings of the Prophet Mohammed), with "its own religious codes, meanings, politics and poetics."[31]

Human Rights Watch had the opportunity to raise these issues with Saudi dissidents during a visit to the country in December 2006.[32] There seemed to be full agreement on two points. First, public support for violent opposition groups, or at least reluctance to condemn such violence, is motivated primarily by the close Saudi government relationship with the United States, without regard for what they consider to be Washington's unacceptable policies in Iraq and the Israeli-Palestinian conflict. Second, they argued, the Saudi government must end its systematic suppression of basic civil and political rights, especially freedom of expression, to allow peaceful challenges to the status quo. To the extent that these views are representative, the basis for whatever popular support exists for the armed attacks against civilians is grounded in politics rather than religion. There was also widespread agreement, though not consensus, on a third point, which underscores a religious dimension to the violence: that the Saudi ruling family's accommodation of a religious establishment whose intolerance toward non-Muslims and Muslims who do not subscribe to the official Wahhabi interpretation of Islam has also contributed to support for attacks against foreigners, and any successful political liberalization requires religious reform as well.

Our interlocutors largely agreed, as noted, that "behind the violence is oppression, injustice, and occupation," referring to conditions in the Arab world. With regard to Saudi Arabia itself, they stressed as well the "zero framework for civil society and no independent judiciary," in the words of Matrook al-Faleh, a political science professor at King Saud University who has been jailed for his reformist activism and remains banned from traveling. The state, he and others said, was just as hostile to their peaceful criticisms as to the challenge of the violent groups. "A nine-year prison term for suggesting a constitution!" said Abdullah al-Hamid, a former professor of literature and reform activist, referring to prison terms handed down to himself, al-Faleh, and another activist.[33] "Proponents of violence point to that and say, see what your peaceful petitions get you."

A Way Ahead?

The concept of *jihad*, or struggle, is integral to Islamic doctrine and tradition, but, in addition to incorporating many different meanings of struggle, it has been quintessentially rule-bound, particularly as it applies to combat and use of force.[34] Rules, of course, are part of the field of contestation, not just in terms of legal or juridical understandings but ethical imperatives as well. The questions at stake now include who can speak with authority regarding core elements of Islamic tradition, at a time when authority is contested and fragmented.

More important than identifying authoritative voices, who are likely to be contested in any event, is the need for opinion-shapers in majority Muslim countries of the Middle East to discuss these issues in ways that incorporate the shared parameters of Islamic ethics and international humanitarian law principles. The underlying element in both systems is the understanding that, in warfare, there are limits as to the means and methods that warring parties may employ.[35] The limits spelled out in the Islamic tradition include prohibitions against treachery and mutilation, and specify categories of enemy persons who are immune from attack, including children, slaves, women, and the lame and blind.[36] This requires attention to areas of divergence as well, but with the purpose of building a broad and encompassing framework for identifying the most effective ways of ensuring respect for those shared principles. Humanitarian law principles address not whether states or non-state groups should take up arms in a particular struggle, but how they deploy and use those arms in the conduct of a particular conflict. In Islamic terms, the issue is not whether jihad is permissible, compulsory, or prohibited (though these are certainly important questions about which Islamic law and more generally international law have much to say), but how that struggle is conducted when it assumes an armed dimension.

Whether religious or political in character, groups perpetrating attacks that target or indiscriminately harm civilians frequently justify those attacks as reprisal for attacks by an adversary that harms their civilians—a justification that is not permitted under international humanitarian law, but also not an impulse limited to Muslims. The reprisal argument, while not acceptable, does point to a factor that proponents of international humanitarian law must address in any effort to get traction for their advocacy in Muslim societies today—namely, the apparent absence of political will internationally to address such killings by all parties, including powerful states. From their perspective, IHL is a legal regime that favors states: states can afford precision weapons and appear respectful of IHL even when their attacks kill many civilians, but insurgent groups often only have access to weapons that are crude and inaccurate. (States, for their part, argue that IHL favors insurgent groups by making it easy for their fighters to blend in with the civilian population, increasing civilian casualties that are blamed on state armed forces.) Here one cannot overstate the place of the Israeli-Palestinian conflict, and the deep and widespread sympathy that most Muslims share towards Palestinian goals and grievances.

This, rather than any fundamental incompatibility of humanitarian law principles with Islamic ethics and law, constitutes a major obstacle to constructing a viable and effective body of public opinion ready to speak out against such attacks by groups with whose goals they sympathize. When it comes to the most serious violations of international humanitarian law, such as targeting civilians, the prohibitions are not contingent on reciprocal behavior by one's adversary. However, if the more powerful adversary encounters no consequences for its own serious violations, it is more difficult to persuade others that it is in the interest of all parties to uphold and respect international humanitarian law.

In the process of promoting respect for core international humanitarian law principles and effective accountability mechanisms in Arab societies, there is clearly a role for persons who are able to articulate those principles in language that will persuade other Muslims, including Islamists and nationalists who use primarily Islamic idioms and doctrinal references. There is a need in particular for persons who have credibility and who are not merely religious authorities speaking on behalf of the government, particularly if that government's own compliance with these principles is questionable.

Human Rights Watch's effort to promote this conversation in the region, with its Civilian Protection Initiative, has had resonance among human rights and other civil society activists in the region, and it is no longer unusual to find columns and editorials in Arab media criticizing attacks against civilians by armed groups in the Arab region or in other Muslim contexts. Eliciting broader commitment to the core principle of civilian immunity from opinion-shapers, not to mention society more broadly, will require further initiatives from regional as well as international activists. This is why it is critical for political and religious leaders and influential media, as well as human rights and other social movement activists, to speak out forcefully against such atrocities, even when—indeed, especially when—they are perpetrated by a government in their name or a movement whose goals they broadly support.

Joe Stork is deputy director of the Middle East and North Africa Division at Human Rights Watch.

1 On the Palestinians, see Yezid Sayigh, *Armed Struggle and the Search for State* (Oxford: Oxford University Press, 1997); on atrocities by all parties in the Algerian war of independence, see Alistair Horne, *A Savage War of Peace: Algeria 1954-1962* (New York: Viking Press, 1977)

2 In this essay I use the term "Islamist" to refer to politically engaged persons or groups who assert and promote policies and political programs that they believe are consistent with Islamic traditions and teachings and advance what they consider to be Islamic interests. There are many different Islamist organizations and tendencies that share this orientation, though their own understandings of what those traditions, teachings, and interests may be vary considerably. Here I am mainly concerned with that subset of Islamist groups that use or promote the use of armed violence.

3 *The Peace Process: Implications for Democracy and Human Rights* Ibn Rushd Booklets Series, 3 (1997), pp. 75 - 128.

4 Ariel Sharon's provocative visit to the site of the Al Aqsa mosque in East Jerusalem on September 29, 2000, and the response of Israeli security forces to Palestinian protestors, led to sustained clashes involving Israeli forces and armed Palestinians in what became known as the Al Aqsa intifada, or uprising. For details on Palestinian suicide bombings through late 2002, and analysis of such attacks from a human rights perspective, see Human Rights Watch, *Erased in a Moment: Suicide Bombing Attacks against Israeli Civilians* (New York, Human Rights Watch, 2002), http://www.hrw.org/legacy/reports/2002/isrl-pa/.

5 Cited in Lori Allen, "Palestinians Debate 'Polite' Resistance to Occupation," in Joel Beinin and Rebecca Stein, *The Struggle for Sovereignty: Palestine and Israel 2003-2005* (Stanford: Stanford University Press, 2006), p. 289.

6 Ibid., pp. 301-02.

7 "Al-Haq in 2004: A Twenty-five Year Retrospective," in *Waiting for Justice: Al-Haq Annual Report 2004* (Ramallah, 2005), pp. 12-13. Azzam worked with Al-Haq from 1987 to 1995.

8 Human Rights Watch interview with Ziad Abu Amr, Washington, DC, June 2006.

9 Human Rights Watch discussion with Palestinian journalists in Ramallah, August 2005.

10 "Rabat Declaration: Towards an Equal Partnership for Democracy, Human Rights, Fair Peace and Economic and Social Development," Statement of the Civil Society NGOs and Actors to the Forum for the Future[summit meeting of G-8 and Arab foreign ministers], December 8-9, 2004. The NGO assembly was sponsored by the Euro-Mediterranean Human Rights Network, the Moroccan Organization for Human Rights, the Cairo Institute for Human Rights Studies, and the International Federation for Human Rights.

11 "Al-Haq's Appeal to Palestinian Political Parties and Armed Factions," Al-Haq Press Release REF: 21.2006E, 3 July 2006). A year earlier, in August 2005, Al-Haq activists told Human Rights Watch that the group had drafted talking points to use in a Beirut meeting on armed groups sponsored by Amnesty International, but then decided not to partici-pate in the meeting before getting full agreement of the group's staff and board. "We need to be courageous, but it's difficult," one person said, noting that many of those who had signed the public petitions had been "harassed by the community."

12 These meetings took place in Cairo, Ramallah, Bethlehem, Amman, Rabat, Tunis, Kuwait, Dubai, Riyadh, Beirut, and Bahrain.

13 On Palestinian attacks, see Human Rights Watch, *Erased in a Moment,* http://www.hrw.org/legacy/reports/2002/isrl-pa/; on Iraqi attacks, see *A Face and a Name: Civilian Victims of Insurgent Groups in Iraq,* vol, 17, no. 9(E), October 2005, http://www.hrw.org/en/reports/2005/10/02/face-and-name-0; on Egypt see *Egypt: Mass Arrests and Torture in Sinai,* vol. 17, no. 3(E), February 2005, http://www.hrw.org/en/reports/2005/02/21/egypt-mass-arrests-and-torture-sinai-0.

14 For instance, the First Additional Protocol of 1977 to the Geneva Conventions (Protocol I), which prohibits attacks against civilians, expressly covers "armed conflicts in which people are fighting against colonial domination and alien occupation and racist regimes in the exercise of their right of self determination...." Protocol I, article 1(4).

15 Under IHL, anyone who is not a combatant is a civilian, and civilians lose their immu-nity only when and for such time as they directly participate in hostilities. Under IHL, reserve soldiers, when they are not subject to the integrated disciplinary command of the armed forces, are considered civilians. Most wars are between forces of unequal means, and an exception to IHL on these grounds would completely undermine the principle of civilian immunity.

16 Human Rights Watch interview, Cairo, April 9, 2006.

17 The comment was made at a roundtable in Cairo co-hosted by Human Rights Watch and the Cairo Institute for Human Rights Studies, June 26, 2005.

18 Human Rights Watch interview, Ramallah, August 2005.

19 See, e.g. article 51(6) of Protocol I, which states: "Attacks against the civilian population or civilians by way of reprisals are prohibited."

20 Human Rights Watch interview, Beirut, July 1, 2006.

21 International Committee of the Red Cross (ICRC), *Customary International Humanitarian Law,* pp. 513-29.

22 Human Rights Watch, *Erased in a Moment,* http://www.hrw.org/legacy/reports/2002/isrl-pa/, p. 52.

[23] Human Rights Watch interview, Beirut, July 2, 2006.

[24] Human Rights Watch interview, Cairo, April 9, 2006.

[25] Human Rights Watch, *Civilians Under Assault: Hizbollah's Rocket Attacks on Israel in the 2006 War,* vol. 19, no. 3(E), August 2007, at http://hrw.org/reports/2007/iopt0807/.

[26] Cited in Mohamed M. Hafez, "Rationality, Culture, and Structure in the Making of Suicide Bombers: A Preliminary Theoretical Synthesis and Illustrative Case Study," *Studies in Conflict & Terrorism* 29, pp. 165-185.

[27] The Egyptian Muslim Brotherhood activist Sayyid Qutb spent 10 years in prison for his alleged involvement in a coup against President Gamal Abdel Nasser, where he was subjected to torture. Released in 1964, he was jailed again in 1965 in connection with another alleged plot and hanged in August 1966. His *Signposts on the Road* (Ma`alim fi'l-tariq), in the view of Malise Ruthven, "more than any other text, articulates both the rage and revolutionary energy underpinning the Islamist movement." Malise Ruthven, *A Fury for God* (London: Granta Books, 2002), p.85.

[28] Hugh Roberts, "Islam in North Africa II: Egypt's Opportunity," International Crisis Group Middle East and North Africa Briefing, April 20, 2004, p. 9.

[29] Imam Sharif, also known as Dr. Fadl, was the author of *Basic Principles in Making Preparations for Jihad (Al-umda fi e'dad al-udda)*. His revision, entitled "Rationalizing Jihad in Egypt and the World," appeared as a series of articles in November 2007 in the Egyptian daily, *Masri al-Yom*. See Jailan Halawi, "Bidding Violence Farewell," *Al-Ahram Weekly*, November 22-28, 2007, and Marc Lynch's commentary in his Abu Aardvark blog of November 27, 2007, available at http://abuaardvark.typepad.com/abuaardvark/2007/11/dr-fadls-review.html.

[30] Nibras Kazimi, "A Virulent Ideology in Mutation: Zarqawi Upstages Maqdisi," in Hillel Fradkin, et al., eds., *Current Trends in Islamist Ideology* (Washington: The Hudson Institute, 2005), also available at http://www.futureofmuslimworld.com/research/pubID.24/pub_detail.asp. (accessed March 22, 2007).

[31] The interview, dated July 5, 2005, is cited in Kazimi. Al-Maqdisi, who in the late 1990s had been imprisoned with al-Zarqawi, was detained again on terrorism-related charges in 2000 but released after a Jordanian State Security Court found him innocent of the charges on December 28, 2004. He was rearrested the day after the Al Jazeera interview, apparently for not denouncing al-Zarqawi more forcefully. The case of al-Maqdisi is one of those discussed in Human Rights Watch, *Suspicious Sweeps: The General Intelligence Department and Jordan's Rule of Law Problem* (New York, September 2006), available at http://hrw.org/reports/2006/jordan0906/.

32 Madawi al-Rasheed, *Contesting the Saudi State: Islamic Voices from a New Generation* (Cambridge, UK: Cambridge University Press, 2007), pp. 135-36.

33 Joe Stork, "Violence and Political Change in Saudi Arabia," *ISIM Review* 19, Spring 2007, pp. 54- 55, http://www.isim.nl/files/Review_19/Review_19-54.pdf.

34 Al-Faleh, al-Hamid, and writer Ali al-Dumaini were detained in March 2004 after they refused to sign a pledge to cease all public criticism of the government. Following an unfair trial a court sentenced them in May 2005 to six, seven, and nine years respectively. In August 2005 King Abdullah pardoned them but they still are banned from travel and from access to Saudi media.

35 For an illuminating analysis of the evolution of the concept of jihad in Islam's first centuries, see Roy Parviz Mottahedeh and Ridwan al-Sayyid, "The Idea of the *Jihad* in Islam before the Crusades," in Angeliki E. Laiou and Roy Parviz Mottahedeh, *The Crusades from the Perspective of Byzantium and the Muslim World* (Washington, D.C.: Dumbarton Oaks Research Library and Collection, 2001), available at www.doaks.org/etexts.html.

36 Sohail Hashemi, who notes that "jus in bello issues receive very little attention" in contemporary Muslim discourses on war, cites the Quranic injunction to "not transgress limits" in the course of fighting "God's cause," and enumerates restraints based in the *sunna* (practices) of the Prophet Muhammad and his earliest ("rightly guided") successors as leaders of the Muslim community. See his "Interpreting the Islamic Ethics of War and Peace," in Sohail H. Hashmi, ed., *Islamic Political Ethics: Civil Society, Pluralism, and Conflict* (Princeton: Princeton University Press, 2002).

37 John Kelsay, *Arguing the Just War in Islam* (Cambridge, MA: Harvard University Press, 2007), especially chapter 3: "Politics, Ethics, and War in Premodern Islam." There Kelsay writes: "The point is not simply that the Prophet identified, women, children and others as protected groups. Rather, these persons are listed because, as a general matter, they 'do not fight'" (p. 114).

ABUSING PATIENTS:
HEALTH PROVIDERS' COMPLICITY IN TORTURE AND CRUEL, INHUMAN OR DEGRADING TREATMENT

By Joseph Amon

In 2002 Human Rights Watch documented a network of Chinese psychiatric facilities where dissidents were detained alongside the mentally ill. One "patient," Tan Guihua, was detained on September 12, 1999. She was sent to the Jiaozhou Mental Hospital in Shandong province for supporting and practicing Falungong, a form a spiritual meditation. Because she refused to renounce her beliefs she was repeatedly tortured by medical personnel using electroshock therapy, and was force-fed antipsychotic medicines.[1]

The human rights community's attention to the complicity of doctors and other health workers in torture or cruel and inhuman treatment has generally been focused on cases like that of Tan Guihua and other political prisoners in detention settings. Most notorious was the "Doctor's Trial" of Nazi physicians at Nuremberg in 1946-47. More recently, the participation of US military psychiatrists and psychologists in "Behavioral Science Consultation Teams" to prepare and provide feedback to interrogators at the Guantanamo Bay detention facility has drawn attention and controversy.

Yet torture and cruel, inhuman, or degrading treatment conducted by medical providers is not confined to political prisoners or counterterrorism efforts. Increasingly, attention has focused on the complicity of medical personnel in such abuses in medical or rehabilitation settings. In healthcare facilities, juvenile detention centers, orphanages, drug treatment centers, and so-called social rehabilitation centers, health providers unjustifiably, discriminatorily, or arbitrarily withhold treatment, or engage in treatment that intentionally or negligently inflicts severe pain or suffering and has no legitimate medical purpose. These actions—and inactions—may be done in compliance with state medical policies, in contradiction to them, or in their absence, but when they do occur they can be described as torture or cruel, inhuman, or degrading treatment (CIDT), in which case both the medical provider and the state must be held accountable.

A precise definition of CIDT has yet to be articulated, but the possibility of CIDT being inflicted in health settings has been clearly anticipated. The International Covenant on Civil and Political Rights (ICCPR), the first international treaty to explicitly address torture and CIDT, provides, in article 7, that "no one shall be subjected to torture or to cruel, inhuman or degrading treatment or punishment. In particular, no one shall be subjected without his free consent to medical or scientific experimentation." Article 16 of the Convention against Torture and Other Cruel, Inhuman or Degrading Treatment or Punishment (Convention against Torture), and interpretations by the European Court of Human Rights and the United Nations special rapporteur on torture and other cruel, inhuman or degrading treatment or punishment suggest that, at a minimum, CIDT covers "treatment as deliberately caus[ing] severe suffering, mental or physical, which in the particular situation is unjustifiable."[2] The special rapporteur, Manfred Nowak, suggests that CIDT is distinguished from torture in that CIDT may occur out of intentional and negligent actions.[3]

The ethical guidelines of health providers also uniformly prohibit providers from any form of participation in torture or CIDT. The World Medical Association's Declaration of Tokyo expressly condemns medical participation in torture, cruel and inhuman or degrading treatment, or "any act to diminish the ability of the victim to resist such treatment."[4] The Hippocratic Oath declares that physicians must treat all patients to the best of their abilities, respect patient privacy, and do them "no harm or injustice."

Despite these declarations and oaths, and calls for a permanent "International Medical Tribunal" to prosecute medical personnel who violate human rights, the complicity of medical providers in torture or CIDT is routinely reported, and states and professional associations have shown little interest in or ability to ensure accountability. Where specific medical practices are questioned, courts have traditionally shown deference to medical "expertise" or been reluctant to evaluate competing claims of appropriate medical practice. International human rights bodies like the European Court of Human Rights have had few opportunities to adjudicate on whether particular acts by medical practitioners constitute torture or CIDT.

What, then, can be done?

Recognize Abuses of Patients as Torture and Cruel, Inhuman, or Degrading Treatment

Human Rights Watch has reported on a wide range of abuses against patients and individuals under medical supervision, including the practice of forcible anal and vaginal exams, female genital mutilation, and the failure to provide life-saving abortion, palliative care, and treatment for drug dependency. While these abuses are sometimes understood as torture or CIDT, too often the denial of care resulting in torture or CIDT is understood more narrowly—both by the human rights community and the medical community—as abuses interfering with the "right to health." This interpretation puts these abuses within a context of the vast demands upon the state, and undermines the absolute prohibition required of states to prevent and protect individuals from torture and CIDT. Health providers, their respective professional associations, and human rights actors therefore too rarely act forcefully to stop provider abuse and end abusive state policies.

As a first step toward addressing these abuses, human rights advocates and medical practitioners and associations need to recognize how medical provider behaviors and state health policies can constitute torture or CIDT. The following represent just a few examples from Human Rights Watch's own research.

Forcible Anal and Vaginal Exams

State-sponsored forcible anal exams have been recognized as torture by the United Nations Committee against Torture, and invasive virginity exams have been recognized as torture by the Inter-American Court of Human Rights. Human Rights Watch found that medical providers in Egypt, Libya, and Jordan have engaged in such procedures with impunity.

In Egypt, men arrested on suspicion of engaging in homosexual activity in violation of that country's legal codes banning "debauchery" are subject to forcible anal exams by physicians. Exams involve anal probing, dilating, and penetration. While prosecutors describe the exams as integral to establishing criminality, examining physicians have admitted that the exams do not determine whether sexual activity took place. In 2003 Human Rights Watch documented the use of such exams by police officials and medical personnel in a report entitled "In a Time of Torture."[5] One man, Ziyad, described the humiliation and abuse he suffered during such an exam. Ziyad said that upon entering the examination room the "head man" commanded him to strip and kneel. The man shouted at Ziyad, commanding him to bend over, and to raise his buttocks into the air. While Ziyad cried and protested, the head man and six other doctors forcibly pulled his buttocks apart and examined him using fingers and other objects.

In both Libya and Jordan Human Rights Watch documented how medical providers conduct "virginity exams" without consent. In Libya these took place in "social rehabilitation" centers, where women and girls were detained under suspicion of transgressing moral codes, sometimes indefinitely.[6] In Jordan Human Rights Watch research found that police referred women, including in cases where no evidence of a crime was present, to medical providers who conducted such tests, upon the request of their families.[7] In both countries, medical personnel play an indispensable role in establishing these women's "culpability." Although they have no medical accuracy, the exams were performed to establish virginity for prosecutorial purpose or to inform the family's decision on whether to abandon, institutionalize, or harm the woman.

Female Genital Mutilation (FGM)

In 2009 Human Rights Watch found that health providers in Iraqi Kurdistan were involved in both performing and promoting misinformation about the practice of female genital mutilation. FGM is defined by the World Health Organization (WHO) as all practices "involving partial or total removal of the external female genitalia or injury to the female genital organs for non-medical reasons."

The investigation found that FGM was practiced by midwives, but that its prevalence and harm were routinely minimized by physicians and government medical officials. For example, one physician explained to Human Rights Watch that she counselled patients that "circumcision is nothing; it does not influence life because a woman is sensitive in all her parts."[8] Government medical providers routinely told Human Rights Watch that FGM was uncommon—despite surveys finding nearly half of all girls to be circumcised—and promoted false information in media campaigns. One woman told Human Rights Watch that on television "a [government] doctor explained that FGM is normal.... The doctor said, 'If you do it or not it's still the same.'"

The UN Human Rights Committee has said that FGM violates protections against torture or cruel, inhuman, or degrading treatment found in the ICCPR. The UN Committee against Torture has repeatedly said that practices such as FGM violate the physical integrity and human dignity of girls and women. In Iraqi Kurdistan, medical personnel are both complicit in action, performing FGM or providing patients patently false information about it, and inaction, failing to halt the practice in their role as government officials.

Drug Dependency Treatment

The withholding of medical treatment for drug dependency and withdrawal has also been identified by some medical professionals and human rights experts and courts as amounting to CIDT. Yet, as with FGM, medical providers often minimize or dismiss the suffering that can result from this denial of care.[9] Government policies that prohibit effective treatment for individuals who use drugs, and instead endorse forced labor and detention, can meet the specific criteria of torture as set out in article 1 of the Convention against Torture: the intentional infliction of severe pain and suffering by government officials as punishment for addiction, or based upon discrimination due to a characterizing feature (in these cases, drug use).

In China our research has found that alleged drug users could be forcibly confined to drug detoxification centers for up to seven years under administrative law for a single "dirty urine." As in Cambodia, where we have also investigated government-run compulsory drug detention centers, the purpose of detention is supposedly for "treatment." Yet there is no need for treatment for many individuals in these centers who are not actually dependent upon drugs, and no treatment available for those who are. In both countries, we found that drug detention centers typically provide neither medicated withdrawal nor evidence-based, effective drug dependency therapy.[10] Instead, individuals in these centers are physically and sometimes sexually abused, and forced to work long hours without pay.

Abortion

Absolute prohibitions on abortion, even in life-saving emergencies, further illustrate the potentially harmful and coercive effects of state medical policies. Nicaragua is one of the few remaining countries in the world where abortion is unlawful under all circumstances, including to save the life of the mother. Human Rights Watch found in 2007 that a blanket ban on abortion (and the criminalization of doctors who perform abortions) results in the denial of life-saving care and avoidable death.[11] A physician in Managua told us, "It was clear that [a woman] needed a therapeutic abortion. No one wanted to carry out the abortion because the fetus was still alive. The woman was here two days without treatment until she expulsed the fetus on her own. And by then she was already in septic shock and died five days later."

The Human Rights Committee has found that criminalization of abortion, including in cases of rape, violates the prohibition against cruel, inhuman, and degrading treatment in article 7 of the ICCPR. Some human rights groups have argued that Nicaragua's enactment of the ban despite forewarning of the law's detrimental effect on women's health constitutes intent by the government to inflict harm for discriminatory purpose—meeting the Article 1 definition of torture.

Palliative Care

In 2009 Human Rights Watch documented the failure of the government of India to take steps to ensure that patients suffering from severe, treatable pain were able to access adequate pain medication.[12] Our report found that fewer than 4 percent of the roughly 1 million terminal cancer patients in India who suffer severe pain every year were able to receive adequate treatment. Even though the majority of patients who arrive at regional cancer centers come at an advanced stage of cancer, and in severe pain, most cancer hospitals have no palliative care departments, do not offer any palliative care services, and do not even stock morphine—globally recognized as an inexpensive and effective drug for pain relief.

HIV and tuberculosis (TB)-infected patients also spoke to Human Rights Watch of the pain they experienced. In the case of one patient we met, TB had infected his spine and caused his legs to twist abnormally, forcing his toes up and causing excruciating pain. Despite the fact that TB requires lengthy, sustained treatment, his doctors prescribed only a weak painkiller and assured him that the pain would subside on its own as his TB improved. The pain continued, unabated, for six months.

The UN special rapporteur on torture recently recognized that outdated and unnecessarily restrictive drug control laws contribute to widespread failures of states to provide pain relief to patients in moderate and severe pain. The special rapporteur further categorized the "de facto denial of access to pain relief, where it causes severe pain and suffering" as CIDT, saying that "all measures should be taken to ensure full access and to overcome current regulatory, educational and attitudinal obstacles to ensure full access to palliative care."[13]

Empower Medical Providers to Challenge Abusive State Policies

After recognizing the forms of abuse described above—both the specific acts and the denial of care—as torture or CIDT, a crucial next step is eliminating laws and policies that require, condone, or facilitate these abuses. Empowering medical providers and their professional associations to challenge these laws and policies is essential to reform efforts.

Healthcare providers are naturally caught in a difficult bind when there is conflict between their obligations to their patients and abusive laws and policies that restrict their actions. In Nicaragua, as noted above, providers may face criminal charges if they perform life-saving abortions. In settings with repressive drug laws, medical providers can also be harassed or prosecuted for simply trying to comply with patients' medical needs—whether for pain relief or effective drug dependency treatment.

In Ukraine Human Rights Watch interviewed physicians specializing in drug dependency treatment who had been harassed by drug control authorities. One physician reported, "They inspected me every week. My name was discussed at meetings. They said that I was giving out drugs to drug users... [The] Department for Combating Illegal Drug Circulation told me not to play tricks. They said if they had found any violations, they would have put me in jail." He said his patients had also been harassed, driving some away from treatment and back to illicit drug use.[14]

But laws and policies can also be used as a shield by health providers to evade their responsibility to protect their patients from harm, discrimination, torture, or CIDT. In these cases, outspoken advocacy from professional organizations is critical—to support those providers refusing to be complicit, to shame or stigmatize those who are, and to engage governments in the reform of abusive laws or policies. In advocating against conducting FGM in hospitals in Egypt or virginity exams by physicians in Turkey, advocacy by medical societies has been influential.

At a global level, the World Medical Association has encouraged doctors to "honour their commitment as physicians to serve humanity and to resist any pressure to act contrary to the ethical principles governing their dedication to this task; to support physicians experiencing difficulties as a result of their resistance to any such pressure or as a result of their attempts to speak out or to act against such inhuman procedures." The organization has also explicitly criticized governments for "any involvement of, or any pressure to involve, medical doctors in acts of torture or other forms of cruel, inhuman or degrading treatment or punishment."[15] At the national level, healthcare providers and human rights advocates should encourage—and hold accountable—professional organizations to speak out about abusive laws and policies and the ethical and international legal obligations of their members.

Develop Stronger Accountability Mechanisms

Beyond the actions of healthcare providers, other actors—for example, victims, patients' rights, and broader human rights organizations, and the international human rights protection system—must also be empowered to combat abuses occurring in health settings. Prohibitions against torture and CIDT in international human rights treaties open multiple, largely underused, international avenues of redress for victims of such abuses. In addition, stronger systems of accountability, especially at national and regional levels, that address abusive government health policies should be developed.

The UN Human Rights Committee emphasizes that article 7 of the ICCPR "protects, in particular ... patients in teaching and medical institutions."[16] The UN Manual on Reporting also notes, "Article 7 protects not only detainees from ill-treatment by public authorities or by persons acting outside or without any official authority but also in general any person. This point is of particular relevance in situations concerning ... patients in ... medical institutions, whether public or private."[17]

Focusing attention on the absolute and non-derogable nature of torture and CIDT in examining health-related abuses strengthens the opportunity for accountability beyond mechanisms related to the right to health. Claims under the Convention against Torture provide aggrieved individuals with a specific forum to seek a remedy; and the treaty obligates states to take specific steps to prevent torture and CIDT from occurring. The Convention against Torture also contains a mechanism to permit the Committee against Torture to investigate systematic torture, and states must submit periodic reports for Committee review. Further, the Optional Protocol to the Convention against Torture (OPCAT) has a Sub-Committee for the Prevention of Torture, which can conduct its own country visits to signatory countries, and mandates that states that adopt OPCAT establish an independent body to monitor places of detention. The Human Rights Committee reviews reports concerning compliance with the ICCPR, including its prohibitions against torture, and the UN special rapporteur on torture is another mechanism to investigate and report on torture and CIDT. Increased recognition of the role of abuses in health-care settings constituting torture or CIDT contrary to the Convention against Torture and ICCPR provisions therefore opens a range of expanded options for redress available to victims of such abuses.

In addition to capitalizing on the opportunities for redress under international human rights law, victims of health provider abuses also need to have available to them strengthened accountability mechanisms at the domestic level. Professional association ethical codes and state criminal codes should contain explicit prohibitions on the types of practices described above if they do not already, and disciplinary committees and state courts should expand investigatory and prosecutorial capacity to target abuses occurring in healthcare settings or under the supervision of healthcare providers. Additionally, at the regional and international level, state law and health policies that contravene torture and CIDT provisions need to be routinely addressed.

Conclusions

The actions and inactions of health providers—whether consistent with, in conflict with, or unregulated by, state laws and policies—that result in the intentional, unjustifiable infliction of severe physical or mental pain must be recognized, condemned, and combated. Only by expanding recognition of these abuses, engaging in joint advocacy between health and human rights activists, and strengthening accountability and redress mechanisms, will abusive laws and policies be effectively addressed and torture and CIDT in healthcare settings be prevented. Perhaps then, the Hippocratic pledge that providers do no harm or injustice can be realized.

Joseph Amon is the director of the Health and Human Rights Division
at Human Rights Watch.

---

[1] Human Rights Watch and Geneva Initiative on Psychiatry, *Dangerous Minds: Political Psychiatry in China Today and its Origins in the Mao Era* (New York: Human Rights Watch, 2002), http://www.hrw.org/en/reports/2002/08/13/dangerous-minds.

[2] M. Nowak, "What Practices Constitute Torture?" *Human Rights Quarterly* 28(2006), p. 821, quoting from A. Boulesbaa, *The UN Convention on Torture and the Prospects for Enforcement* (Martinus Nijhoff Publishers, 1999).

[3] M. Nowak and E. McArthur, *The United Nations Convention Against Torture. A Commentary* (New York: Oxford University Press, 2008), p. 553.

[4] Declaration of Tokyo, World Medical Association G.A. Res (1975).

[5] Human Rights Watch, *In a Time of Torture,The Assault on Justice in Egypt's Crackdown on Homosexual Conduct* (New York: Human Rights Watch, 2003), http://www.hrw.org/en/reports/2004/02/29/time-torture-o.

[6] Human Rights Watch, *Libya – A Threat to Society? Arbitrary Detention of Women and Girls for "Social Rehabilitation,"* vol. 18, no. 2(E), February 2006, http://www.hrw.org/en/reports/2006/02/27/libya-threat-society.

7 Human Rights Watch, *Honoring the Killers: Justice Denied For "Honor" Crimes in Jordan*, vol. 16, no.1(E), April 2004, http://www.hrw.org/en/reports/2004/04/19/honoring-killers-0.

8 Human Rights Watch, *Iraq —They Took Me and Told Me Nothing* (publication pending).

9 See, for example: Human Rights Watch, *Rehabilitation Required: Russia's Human Rights Obligation to Provide Evidence-based Drug Dependence Treatment*, vol. 19, no. 7(D), November 2007, http://www.hrw.org/en/reports/2007/11/07/rehabilitation-required-0, p. 46.

10 Human Rights Watch, *An Unbreakable Cycle: Drug Dependency Treatment, Mandatory Confinement, and HIV/AIDS in China's Guangxi Province*, 1-56432-416-8, December 2008, http://www.hrw.org/en/reports/2008/12/09/unbreakable-cycle-0; and Human Rights Watch, *Cambodia – Skin on the Cable* (publication pending).

11 Human Rights Watch, *Over Their Dead Bodies: Denial of Access to Emergency Obstetric Care and Therapeutic Abortion in Nicaragua*, vol. 19, no. 2(B), October 2007, http://www.hrw.org/en/reports/2007/10/01/over-their-dead-bodies.

12 Human Rights Watch, *Unbearable Pain: India's Obligation to Ensure Palliative Care*, 1-56432-555-5, October 2009, http://www.hrw.org/en/reports/2009/10/28/unbearable-pain-0.

13 Report of the Special Rapporteur on torture and other cruel, inhuman or degrading treatment or punishment, Manfred Nowak to the Human Rights Council, A/HRC/10/44, January 14, 2009.

14 Human Rights Watch, *Rhetoric and Risk: Human Rights Abuses Impeding Ukraine's Fight Against HIV/AIDS*, vol. 18, no. 2(D), March 2006, http://www.hrw.org/en/reports/2006/03/01/rhetoric-and-risk-0.

15 World Medical Association Declaration Concerning Support for Medical Doctors Refusing to Participate in, or to Condone, the Use of Torture or Other Forms of Cruel, Inhuman or Degrading Treatment, Adopted by the 49th WMA General Assembly Hamburg, Germany, November 1997.

16 Committee on Economic, Social, and Cultural Rights, General Comment No. 20, UN Doc. A/47/40 (1992), paras. 5 and 7.

17 E. Rosenthal and C.J. Sundram, "International Human Rights in Mental Health Legislation," *New York Law School Journal of International and Comparative Law* 21/469 (2002), p. 515.

In the Migration Trap:
Unaccompanied Migrant Children in Europe

By Simone Troller

One might have thought that in Western Europe, where child mortality is close to zero, education and healthcare a given, and social services and institutions well developed, children's rights would be one of the most uncontroversial topics for policy-makers. Not, it seems, when the children in question are unaccompanied migrants.

All too often the thousands of unaccompanied children arriving without parents or caregivers find themselves trapped in their status as migrants, with European governments giving little consideration to their vulnerabilities and needs as children. Many end up without the humane treatment Europe claims to stand for. Instead they may face prolonged detention, intimidation and abusive police behavior, registration and treatment as adults after unreliable age exams, bureaucratic obstacles to accessing education, abuse when detained or housed in institutions and, too often, exploitation.

Compounding this, many suffer from a pervasive lack of legal defense that leaves them unable to claim their rights. They may be prevented from seeking redress in case of ill-treatment, from challenging their detention, from appealing a negative asylum decision, or simply from appointing a lawyer to protect their rights.

Unaccompanied migrant children represent a tiny fraction of all migrants entering Europe, and governments are unable to present reliable data.[1] Yet, officials across the continent speak about a "mass influx" or "avalanche" of children. Unsurprisingly, these children have now become the focus of regional concern, not least because they are perceived to be a resource burden.

Deliberate Legal Gaps

Within a given country, unaccompanied migrant children are typically dealt with under two different and often contradictory sets of laws: immigration legislation and child-protection legislation. All too often, authorities resort to immigration

legislation first and child-protection second, which has direct and dire consequences for children.

France presents one of the worst examples of what happens when unaccompanied migrant children are dealt with primarily as irregular migrants. It maintains
extra-territorial zones, the biggest at Roissy Charles de Gaulle airport near Paris,
where unaccompanied migrant children are treated as if they had not entered
France. Inside these zones, they are subject to a different legal regime. In practice, the legal fiction that they are not in France means they have fewer rights.

Up to 1,000 unaccompanied migrant children per year end up in the legal bubble
of the Roissy Charles de Gaulle airport transit zone, a zone that goes well beyond
the immediate surroundings of the airport to include places as far as 20 kilometers away, and which can be extended at authorities' discretion. The purpose of
that transit zone is simple: to insulate migrant children from the rights they would
be accorded on French territory, thereby greasing the legal skids for their speedy
removal from France.

Speedy removal includes removing these children to countries they merely transited on their journey to France. For example, French authorities attempted to
deport a Chadian boy to Egypt, an Egyptian boy to Madagascar, and in 2008 contemplated the removal of a five-year-old Comorian child to Yemen. Some of these
children resisted their deportation and risked police custody and criminal charges
as a result. Those who were removed—around 30 percent of all children who
arrived—almost always left without any record of what happened to them.[2]

Systems that prevent unaccompanied migrant children from accessing their rights
in Europe are not necessarily the result of sophisticated legal regimes. Legal gaps
that either target unaccompanied migrant children—or hit them as "collateral
damage"—may be blunt and discriminatory. European governments have all
signed the main United Nations treaty protecting the rights of children, the
Convention on the Rights of the Child (CRC). Still, some have excluded migrant
children from entitlements otherwise granted to children through reservations
and declarations to the CRC that give deference to immigration legislation. In
other words, children are first considered migrants, and only secondly children.

For years the United Kingdom was criticized for excluding migrant children from the full entitlements under the CRC due to their migration status until it lifted the reservation in 2008, announcing its move days before the United Nations was set to evaluate its children's rights record.[3]

Germany has a similar declaration, filed in 1990 by the federal government. While saying it does not object to withdrawing the declaration, the federal government argues it is powerless to lift it, despite explicit requests by parliament, because, it claims, several of the 16 German states object. Whatever it says, there are other signs that the government itself is reluctant to end the discrimination against migrant children: it argues, for example, that ending the reservation could act as a "pull-factor" leading to the arrival of large numbers of migrant children and create unpredictable costs.[4] Meanwhile, in Germany the declaration continues to have serious consequences for unaccompanied children who seek asylum. From age 16 these children may not be assisted by a guardian or lawyer when going through the complexities of an asylum procedure, and have to stay in reception centers with adults.

Perhaps the most egregious regime for children treated as irregular migrants is to be found in Greece, one of the major gateways for migrants into Europe. Children spend months in detention centers—often in the same cell with adults—in conditions that a European rights body termed "unacceptable."[5] Released from detention, they are served an order to leave the country. If they do not, they may find themselves back in detention, no matter how vulnerable they are. Even outside detention they are far from protected. Greece offers a mere 300 places in reception centers, which are full, for an estimated annual arrival of 1,000 children. With no safety net, even for trafficked children and others most at risk, they can end up in a daily struggle for survival and in a vicious cycle of exploitation.[6]

Government Coordination, or How to Pass the Buck

The fact of two sets of legislation applying to unaccompanied migrant children means that at least two government bodies are in charge of them. One would like to think this might mean double assistance and protection. But the reality is that children fall through the bureaucratic cracks. Social policy ministries and interior or immigration ministries, the two types of bodies typically in charge, have inherently different approaches.

Greek police officials, for example, pointed out to Human Rights Watch that they cannot release migrant children from detention because no other accommodation is available. Yet the Ministry of Health, responsible for providing care centers for these children, claims there is no need for more reception facilities since many children abscond shortly after their admission, a circumstance that should be worrying in itself. With both bodies pointing fingers at the other, neither takes responsibility for the children; the deadlock contributes to children's prolonged stay in detention.

Even when the overall number of unaccompanied migrant children in a given country may not be that significant, their presence can put a considerable burden on entry point regions, such as the Canary Islands in Spain, or the department of Seine-Saint-Denis in France which has Roissy Charles de Gaulle airport on its territory. When the primary responsibility within a country is devolved to regions, the central state, although bound by international law to make sure all children in the country can access their rights, may shirk responsibility by hiding behind such administrative arrangements.

The Canary Islands, by geographical circumstance is a first landing point for migrants from West Africa, Morocco, and Western Sahara, saw about 1,000 unaccompanied migrant children arriving at its shores in 2006. It rushed to set up emergency shelters in industrial sites and reopened a previously closed detention center to house several hundred children. Then it demanded that the government in Madrid take in or redistribute all but 300 children, its self-declared maximum capacity. The central government organized and paid for some children's transfer to other regions, but ongoing arrivals kept numbers stable and few other regions offered to accept children. While Madrid gradually withdrew its engagement, the temporary and substandard shelters turned into the children's permanent residences. Even when Human Rights Watch confronted Madrid with findings that children had been abused and continued to face risks in these centers, the central government maintained that it was powerless over the situation. The Canary Islands responded similarly, saying these centers would be closed as soon as the central government accepted responsibility for the children. So the buck kept being passed, with children left unprotected.[7]

Worse Off than Adults

Because migrant children are underage, many governments deem them incapable of making important decisions. As persons considered legally incapable, they are assigned a guardian (a person or institution) that is mandated to decide all matters on their behalf. Guardianship is intended to safeguard children's interests especially because children tend to be unaware of their entitlements. In reality, however, guardians too often are ineffective, lack the necessary powers or expertise, or worse, do not challenge government action and as a result fail to serve children's best interests. Children in these cases not only bear the full brunt of tough migration policies, but stripped from decision-making, they are even worse off than adults.

France, for example, provides that every unaccompanied migrant child arriving at Charles de Gaulle airport be represented by a guardian. Yet the role of these guardians may be redundant. If for any reason no guardian is available, or the guardian arrives "too late" to meet the child, this does not prevent authorities from detaining and deporting children. In 2008 around 30 percent of children never met with their appointed guardian, often because they were deported before their representative arrived. Yet, without that guardian, children cannot legally challenge their detention or deportation, as they are themselves considered "incapable" to file legal acts or even to appoint a lawyer. So the absent guardian turns into an obstacle that prevents the child from escaping his or her legal limbo.

Children may be powerless to object to guardians who do not act in their interest. Spain deported unaccompanied migrant children to Morocco until 2008 on the assumption that the child's return was in his or her best interest. Government institutions acted as the child's guardian, but officials did not consult with the child and they ignored consistent reports of children's ill-treatment and detention upon return.[8] Children, in turn, were unable to challenge their deportation. To do so, they would have needed their guardian, who initiated the decision in the first place, and therefore was not going to challenge it. The Spanish government fought hard to keep the system that way, tried to block lawyers from representing these children, and demanded the guardian's exclusive power in all decision-making over the child. Spanish national courts, in dozens of rulings that suspended governmental deportation orders, for the time being, put an end to this shameful practice.[9]

In Greece, children Human Rights Watch spoke to in 2008 and 2009 were unaware they had a guardian—and guardians were unable to tell us how many children they represented. Police in some cases did not even bother to inform guardians about a child's existence. In such situations, children below age 14 are barred from accessing the universal right to seek asylum because they need a guardian to do so. For example, a 10-year-old unaccompanied girl from Somalia who Human Rights Watch met in June 2008 could not file an asylum application because of the dysfunctional guardianship system. She remained an irregular migrant instead, and Greek police detained her multiple times.[10]

The Returns "Solution"

As European governments struggle with their response to unaccompanied children on their territory and the responsibility and costs they generate, the instinct of some European Union member states is to find a cheap and easy solution: the child's return. While return is only one of several possible lasting solutions for a child, it is too often the solution governments immediately favor, with little consideration as to whether repatriation is in the child's best interests.

In sending countries where social services barely exist and family tracing and reunification remains difficult, some European host governments are attracted by the idea of building reception centers to which they can swiftly return unaccompanied migrant children. International law does not forbid the child's return to a care institution in the country of origin, but it allows it only when it is in the child's best interests. It remains questionable to what extent the return to an institution is in the child's best interest when, for example, it is far from his or her family and local community, and when it is used as a way of ensuring the child's fast removal rather than the search for a permanent solution.

Investing in such a way in the returns of children may not only be a waste of money, with those returned leaving their countries soon again, but it may also put children back at serious risk. The construction of model care centers in countries where services for children are absent or inadequate may also have an unintended side-effect: they create disparities in countries of origin and could draw children into migration as the only way to get services that would not be available if they stayed home. Instead of seemingly quick and easy solutions that focus on returns, investments into services and institutions accessible to all children in their home countries are needed.

Finally, European governments are not simply off the hook once the child is returned. They are directly responsible if the child is ill-treated, detained, or disappears upon arrival if they ignored relevant information before returning a child and did nothing to mitigate such risks. The European Court of Human Rights' condemnation in 2006 of Belgium for returning a five-year-old unaccompanied Congolese girl by dumping her at Kinshasa airport was a much needed signal that such action is held to account. In a decision concluding that Belgium demonstrated "a total lack of humanity," the court maintains that governments are obliged to take "measures and precautions" against the inhuman treatment of a returned child.[11]

Enter the European Union

It is positive that the EU wants to address the situation of these children in the Stockholm Program, its five-year asylum and migration strategy, starting with an action plan in 2010. EU policy coherence and action is needed in light of legal provisions that require governments to remove a trafficking victim under one set of laws, and to protect the victim under another set. Additionally, EU legislation does not address the needs of those children who never file an asylum application—possibly a majority—including the needs of those who cannot file a claim because of practical or legal obstacles.[12]

The EU should be cautious, though, and make sure that before adopting an action plan it takes the time to understand the complexities behind children's migration and informs itself on the basis of existing and, where necessary, additional unbiased research. It should avoid falling back on myths and false pretexts put forward by some member states. Those include that detaining children protects them from traffickers, or that intercepting (and returning) migrants before they reach European soil prevents the unnecessary deaths of children. The EU should also avoid repeating broad generalizations that the best place for a child is always with the family, or that better services and laws in Europe will only lead to more children arriving.[13] Not only are such arguments dangerous and unsubstantiated, but they inevitably open up a race to the lowest standards and undermine the ultimate goal of better protection. The EU should also refrain from using its political and economic weight to put undue pressure on countries of origin to take children back.

Instead, the EU should ensure its policies and actions are truly rights-based and treat these children first and foremost as children, and not on the basis of their migration status. It should help member states adopt sound and transparent procedures to guarantee every child a fair, comprehensive, and individualized assessment that leads to a lasting and beneficial solution. All options for a child's durable solution should be considered on an equal basis, including the possibility of the child's stay in the host country, or transfer to another EU member state to join close relatives (such as siblings), alongside return to country of origin. The primary factors in such decision-making should be the child's best interests, informed by a number of elements including the child's personal history and his or her views.

The EU should put forward standards to ensure that children enjoy better safeguards, can defend their rights, and are able to challenge government decisions with the help of guardians and lawyers when they face detention, deportation, or go through an asylum interview. These standards should require guardians' to possess expertise on migrants and children's rights, undergo regular training, be independent from the body deciding on a child's return, and to be subject to independent review. Guardians who have a conflict of interest in representing the child should be excluded from taking on such a role. Guardians also need to be given the mandate and the power to represent the child's best interests, and they need to have a say in all decision-making, including decisions regarding a child's detention or deportation. Furthermore, in all administrative and judicial decisions children should be represented by lawyers in addition to guardians.[14]

Current methods to determine the age of a child are another area where EU guidance can make a positive contribution. Because some governments predominantly use unreliable age tests based on medical examinations only, an unaccompanied child risks being arbitrarily declared an adult. Minimum safeguards to prevent such scenarios include that the error margin in these examinations is acknowledged, that the child and guardian consent to the exam, and that the child is given the benefit of the doubt and has access to a lawyer and legal procedure to challenge flawed results. The EU should further support member states' adoption of comprehensive exams that also take into account a child's psychological maturity, life experiences, ability to interact with adults, and demeanor.

Spain, with its long-standing exposure to unaccompanied migrant children, is certainly well placed to lead the adoption of an action plan during its presidency in early 2010.[15] Spanish practices of not detaining unaccompanied migrant children and of regularizing their presence while on Spanish territory are powerful examples of good practice for other EU member states. But Spain also needs to critically and honestly examine its record and not repeat past mistakes. This includes recognition that readmission agreements lacking transparency and safeguards for children, and requiring sending countries to accept children back within an unrealistic timeframe, are not the way forward.[16] It should also reflect on why unaccompanied children in Spain almost never seek asylum—without resorting to the implausible explanation that none of them fit the profile. And it should candidly look at its record of returning unaccompanied Moroccan children to dangerous situations, with the result that many went straight back to Spain. These are important lessons that need to feed into discussion on EU action.

Last but not least, the EU needs to make sure its policies do not undermine but realize European governments' obligations under international human rights law and under the EU's Charter of Fundamental Rights. Its proposed children's rights strategy has the potential to contribute toward this aim and should make unaccompanied migrant children an integral part. Ultimately, though, the EU should also consider filling the existing gaps with a set of binding rules that harmonize member states' response to the common needs and vulnerabilities of all unaccompanied migrant children in Europe, whether they escape persecution or abuse, are smuggled into Europe for exploitation, or have left their homes in search for a better life. And the EU needs to underscore that its members must fulfill obligations under applicable human rights treaties while these children are on European territory, and that children are protected from return to abuse, ill-treatment, or neglect. Member states whose actions fall below European standards should be held to account.

Without such decisive action, unaccompanied migrant children likely remain trapped in their status as migrants, with the result that their protection and safety as children remain elusive aspirations.

Simone Troller is a researcher in the Children's Rights Division at Human Rights Watch.

---

[1] There are no reliable statistics on how many unaccompanied migrant children enter Europe every year. Asylum statistics, although they do not account for all children, are indicative of the proportion of unaccompanied children as compared to other asylum seekers in Europe. According to the United Nations High Commissioner for Refugees (UNHCR), over the past 10 years unaccompanied children have consistently made up 4 or 5 percent of all asylum applicants in the EU. "Addressing the Protection Gap for Unaccompanied and Separated Children in the European Union," Judith Kumin, director, UNHCR Bureau for Europe, Brussels, September 15, 2009. The presentation is on file with Human Rights Watch.

[2] Human Rights Watch, *France – Lost in Transit: Insufficient Protection for Unaccompanied Migrant Children at Roissy Charles de Gaulle Airport*, 1-56432-557-1, October 2009, http://www.hrw.org/sites/default/files/reports/france1009webwcover_0.pdf, pp. 49-54.

[3] United Nations Committee on the Rights of the Child, "Consideration of Reports Submitted by States Parties under Article 44 of the Convention, Concluding Observations, United Kingdom of Great Britain and Northern Ireland," CRC/C/GBR/CO/4, October 20, 2008, http://www2.ohchr.org/english/bodies/crc/docs/AdvanceVersions/CRC.C.GBR.CO.4.pdf (accessed September 28, 2009), para. 70.

4 Deutscher Bundestag (German Parliament), "Antwort der Bundesregierung auf die Grosse Anfrage der Abgeordneten Ekin Deligöz, Grietje Bettin, Volker Beck (Köln), weiterer Abgeordneter und der Fraktion BÜNDNIS 90/DIE GR NEN – Drucksache 16/4205 – R cknahme der Vorbehalte zur UN-Kinderrechtskonvention" ("Response by the German Government to the Extended Request of the members of Parliament Ekin Deligöz, Grietje Bettin, Volker Beck (Köln), other members and the parliamentary group BÜNDNIS 90/DIE GRÜNEN – Reference number 16/4205 – Withdrawal of Reservations to the UN Convention on the Rights of the Child"), July 13, 2007, p. 9. Deutscher Bundestag (German Parliament), "Antwort der Bundesregierung auf die Kleine Anfrage der Abgeordneten Rainer Funke, Dr. Werner Hoyer, Klaus Haupt, weiterer Abgeordneter und der Fraktion der FDP – Drucksache 15/1606 – Vorbehaltserklärungen Deutschlands zur Kinderrechtskonvention der Vereinten Nationen" ("Response by the German Government to the Request of the members of Parliament Rainer Funke, Dr. Werner Hoyer, Klaus Haupt, and others, and the FDP parliamentary group – Reference number 15/1606 – Reservations by Germany to the UN Convention on the Rights of the Child"), October 23, 2003, p. 3.

5 European Committee for the Prevention of Torture, "Report to the Government of Greece on the visit to Greece carried out by the European Committee for the Prevention of Torture and Inhuman or Degrading Treatment or Punishment (CPT) from 23 to 29 September 2008," http://www.cpt.coe.int/documents/grc/2009-20-inf-eng.htm (accessed November 1, 2009), para. 53.

6 Human Rights Watch, *Left to Survive: Systematic Failure to Protect Unaccompanied Migrant Children in Greece*, 1-56432-418-4, December 2008, http://www.hrw.org/en/reports/2008/12/22/left-survive, pp. 53-93.

7 Human Rights Watch, *Unwelcome Responsibilities: Spain's Failure to Protect the Rights of Unaccompanied Migrant Children in the Canary Islands*, vol. 19, no. 4(D), http://www.hrw.org/en/node/10817/section/5, pp. 55-69, 95-98.

8 Human Rights Watch, *Nowhere to Turn: State Abuses of Unaccompanied Migrant Children by Spain and Morocco*, vol. 14, no. 4(D), May 2002, http://www.hrw.org/en/news/2002/05/06/spain-and-morocco-abuse-child-migrants, pp. 28-37.

9 Ibid., pp. 8-14.

10 Human Rights Watch, *Left to Survive*, pp. 56-57.

11 *Mubilanzila Mayeka and Kaniki Mitunga v. Belgium* (Application no. 13178/03), October 12, 2006, www.echr.coe.int, para. 69.

[12] Human Rights Watch, *Left to Survive*, pp. 42-45; *Unwelcome Responsibilities*, pp. 49-54; *Lost in Transit*, pp. 39-41; and Human Rights Watch, *Returns at Any Cost: Spain's Push to Repatriate Unaccompanied Children in the Absence of Safeguards*, 1-56432-388-9, October 2008, http://www.hrw.org/en/reports/2008/10/17/returns-any-cost-0, pp. 18-19.

[13] Host states should trace the family or caregiver of unaccompanied children and seek reunification. In certain cases, however, particularly when the child was subjected to violence, exploitation, or neglect inside the family, or when the family was unable to protect the child from such abuse, a child's best interest may not be the return to parents or caregiver. A decision whether it is in a child's best interest to return to his or her family, therefore, must be subject to a careful assessment and cannot be generally assumed.

[14] EU standards on guardianship should be in line with those of the Committee on the Rights of the Child. UN Committee on the Rights of the Child, "Treatment of Unaccompanied and Separated Children Outside their Country of Origin," General Comment No. 6, UN Doc. CRC/GC/2005/6 (2005), paras. 33-38.

[15] Human Rights Watch joined Save the Children, UNHCR, UNICEF, and the Separated Children in Europe Programme in recommendations on necessary EU actions that should feature in an EU action plan. "General Recommendations for EU Action in relation to Unaccompanied and Separated Children of Third Country Origin," September 15, 2009, http://www.savethechildren.net/alliance/europegroup/europegrp_pubs.html (accessed October 21, 2009).

[16] Letter from Human Rights Watch to Prime Minister José Luis Rodríguez Zapatero, January 9, 2007, http://hrw.org/pub/2006/SpainMorocco010907.pdf; Letter from Human Rights Watch to Prime Minister José Luis Rodríguez Zapatero, April 2, 2007, http://hrw.org/english/docs/2007/04/02/spain15628.htm.

ZIMBABWE

Crisis without Limits

Human Rights and Humanitarian Consequences
of Political Repression in Zimbabwe

HUMAN
RIGHTS
WATCH

WORLD REPORT

2010

AFRICA

ANGOLA

More than one year after the September 2008 parliamentary elections—the first elections held in Angola since 1992—Angolans in 2009 were unable to vote, as planned, in a presidential election. The government postponed the vote pending the completion of a constitutional review that is ongoing at this writing. The review has been strongly influenced by the current president, José Eduardo dos Santos, who has been in power for 30 years. The Constitutional Commission dominated by the ruling Popular Movement for the Liberation of Angola (MPLA) followed the president's suggestions to propose a new parliament-based model for electing the president, rather than holding separate elections. It remains unpredictable when the new constitution might be adopted and what its implications for upcoming elections might be.

The 2008 legislative elections produced a landslide victory for the MPLA. No independent investigation into the numerous shortcomings of those elections has taken place.

Cabinda

Although Angola has been at peace since 2002, and a peace agreement was signed in Cabinda in 2006, an intermittent, armed separatist conflict has persisted in the enclave since 1975. The Angolan Armed Forces' (FAA) presence there continues to be stronger than elsewhere in the country, and the military has stepped up operations to wipe out remaining guerrilla forces in light of the forthcoming (January 2010) Africa Cup of Nations soccer tournament, some matches being slated to take place in Cabinda city.

Human rights scrutiny remains restricted in Cabinda, particularly in the interior. The government has not responded to calls for an independent investigation into allegations of torture and other serious human rights violations committed by the FAA, and perpetrators of torture are not prosecuted.

Since September 2007 the military has arbitrarily arrested more than 40 rebel suspects. Most of them claim to have been subjected to torture and mistreatment designed to extort confessions during lengthy incommunicado custody. They were

ANGOLA

Democracy or Monopoly?

Angola's Reluctant Return to Elections

H U M A N
R I G H T S
W A T C H

ANGOLA

"They Put Me in the Hole"

Military Detention, Torture and Lack of Due Process in Cabinda

HUMAN
RIGHTS
WATCH

eventually brought to a civilian prison and charged with "crimes against the security of the state" and other related crimes, but in several cases were denied due process rights.

In September 2008, in a trial that was patently unfair, a military court sentenced Fernando Lelo, a civilian and former Voice of America correspondent, to 12 years in jail, and five FAA soldiers accused along with him to 13 years' imprisonment, for alleged involvement in rebel armed attacks in 2007. In August 2009 the Supreme Military Court reviewed Lelo's conviction and acquitted him. But the court also re-sentenced three of his co-accused to 24 years' and the other two to 20 years' imprisonment, despite lack of evidence and serious torture allegations. In four trials between June and November 2009, the Cabinda civil court sentenced nine men accused of national security offenses to up to 20 years in jail, despite serious allegations of torture in initial military custody, while it acquitted 11 for lack of evidence.

Media Freedom

The media environment continues to be restricted, despite the emergence of a number of new media outlets since 2008. More than three years after a new press law was enacted in May 2006, the legislation required to implement crucial parts of the law, which would improve the legal protection of freedom of expression and access to information, has still not passed. Independent private radio stations cannot broadcast nationwide, while the government's licensing practices have favored new radio and television stations linked with the MPLA. The public media remain strongly biased in favor of the ruling party.

Defamation remains a criminal offense in the new press law. Other vague offenses, such as "abuse of press freedom," are open to official manipulation. Since 2007 government officials have increasingly pressed charges against private media editors and journalists for libel and related offenses. This trend continued in 2009. In July a court sentenced Eugénio Mateus, a journalist with the private weekly *O País*, to three months in prison for libel and "abuse of press freedom," suspended for two years, following a complaint by the Angolan Armed Forces chief of staff. The lawsuit was based on a 2007 article published in the weekly *A Capital* that criticized the FAA for allegedly renting out state property. Also in July the editor of *A Capital*, Tandala Francisco, was informed of a libel lawsuit for an opinion article critical of President Dos Santos. In October, Welwitchia "Tchizé" dos Santos, the president's daughter and ,until recently, a member of parliament, pressed charges against the secretary-general of the Angolan Journalist Union (SJA), Luísa Rogério, as well as Vítor Silva, director of the private weekly *Novo Jornal*, and Ana Margoso, a journalist of the same weekly, for libel. Luísa Rogério had criticized "Tchizé"'s appointment to the state television channel TPA's management commission as incompatible with her role as an MP, while *Novo Jornal* had reported about the controversy. At this writing the proceedings are ongoing.

Such litigation, in an increasingly difficult economic environment for the private media, perpetuates a widespread culture of self-censorship that restricts the public's access to independent information.

Housing Rights and Forced Evictions

Angola's laws do not give adequate protection against forced eviction, nor do they enshrine the right to adequate housing. In 2009 the government stepped up forced evictions and house demolitions in areas that it claims to be reserved for public construction in the capital, Luanda, and increasingly also in provincial towns. In July, in the largest-scale demolition operation ever in Luanda, armed police and military destroyed 3,000 houses in the Iraque and Bagdad neighborhoods, leaving an estimated 15,000 residents destitute of their homes and belongings. Immediately following the forced evictions, security forces prevented residents from demonstrating in front of the president's palace, and in August the provincial government repeatedly delayed permission to hold a public protest demonstration organized by local human rights organizations.

The new government in 2008 announced its intention to allocate more resources for public housing over the next five years and to construct one million houses in the country. However, many of the people forcibly evicted in recent years continue to await compensation and alternative housing.

Mass Expulsion of Foreign Migrants

In 2009 the Angolan authorities expelled tens of thousands of allegedly irregular migrants and their families—most of them from the Democratic Republic of Congo (DRC). Mass expulsion operations were carried out in the eastern diamond-rich provinces in the first half of 2009 and in the northern provinces of Cabinda and Zaire in September. The United Nations Office for the Coordination of Humanitarian Affairs (OCHA) reported that Angolan military and police committed serious abuses, including rape and pillage, during these mass expulsions. Refugees and asylum seekers in Nzage, Lunda Norte, told Human Rights Watch that military temporarily arrested them in door-to-door operations, pillaged their houses, and raped several women during a mass expulsion operation in May. In Cabinda, both migrants and Cabindans told Human Rights Watch that border police beat and injured people whom they assumed to be irregular migrants and transported and held them in inhumane and degrading conditions during mass expulsions in September and October.

Mass expulsions of foreigners, particularly from the diamond exploration areas, have taken place repeatedly since 2003 amid allegations of serious rights abuses by Angola's military and police. In October 2009 the DRC authorities ordered the unprecedented reciprocal expulsion of Angolan irregular migrants from Bas-Congo, as a result of which tens of thousands of Angolans were forced to return to Angola.

Human Rights Defenders

The environment for human rights defenders remains restricted. Threats by government officials in 2007 to ban several national and international civil society organizations have not materialized, and the government's long-announced review of the legislation concerning civil society organizations has remained pending. However, some of the most outspoken human rights organizations have continued to struggle with unresolved lawsuits against banning orders and threats. An appeal against the 2006 Cabinda provincial court ruling banning the civic association Mpalabanda is still pending in the Supreme Court. Legal proceedings to ban the Association Justice Peace and Democracy (AJPD), going back to a lawsuit initiated in 2003, have not seen any development since the Supreme Court took charge of the case in May 2009.

In August the coordinator of the housing rights organization SOS Habitat, Luiz Araújo, claimed to have been subjected to intense surveillance and an assault attempt against his office premises and his life.

Key International Actors

Angola is one of Africa's biggest oil producers, served as chair of the Organization of the Petroleum Exporting Countries (OPEC) in 2009, and is China's second most important source of oil and most important commercial partner in Africa. This oil wealth, and Angola's regional military power, have greatly limited leverage of partners and international organizations pushing for good governance and human rights. Commercial partners remain reluctant to criticize the government, to protect their economic interests.

However, falling oil and diamond prices and the global economic crisis have hit Angola's fast-growing economy. In 2009 the government invested more efforts to seek support from international partners, including from the International Monetary Fund, to cope with budget shortfalls.

On his first visit to Angola, in March 2009 at the invitation of President Dos Santos, Pope Benedict XVI publicly raised important human rights issues, such as the urgent need for good governance and better distribution of the country's wealth to benefit the poor majority. The Vatican's diplomatic efforts were not successful, however, in unblocking the Roman Catholic Church-owned *Rádio Ecclésia*'s long-awaited signal extension beyond Luanda.

BURUNDI

Burundi's 16-year civil war ended in April 2009 after the government and the last active rebel movement, the National Liberation Forces (FNL), resolved most issues that had impeded the implementation of a September 2006 ceasefire agreement. The FNL laid down its arms and became a political party. FNL fighters and political leaders were integrated into the security forces and government.

Several politically motivated murders and assaults occurred in early 2009, generally pitting supporters of the ruling party, the National Council for the Defense of Democracy—Forces for the Defense of Democracy (CNDD-FDD), against supporters of the FNL and other opposition parties, particularly the Front for Democracy in Burundi (Frodebu). Advances in the peace process did not appear to terminate such violence, as parties strove to dominate the political terrain in preparation for general elections due in 2010.

Progress in Peace Negotiations and Demobilization

Negotiations between the government and the FNL, which had resumed in May 2008 after a long hiatus, picked up speed in early 2009. The government offered 33 political posts to FNL leaders (although only 24 had been concretely offered and filled by October 2009), and the FNL registered as a political party after turning in approximately 700 weapons. Some 3,500 FNL members were integrated into the security forces, while 5,000 adults and 340 former child soldiers participated in World Bank-funded demobilization programs. Ten thousand "militant-combatants" (men associated with the FNL who had not necessarily participated in regular combat) and a thousand "associated women" received small "reinsertion packages."

Political Violence

Despite advances in the peace process, political violence continues. In January 2009 a CNDD-FDD activist in Ngozi province, Anthère Ntarundenga, was killed. Two FNL members were arrested but then given "provisional liberty" under a provision of the peace agreement. In Bujumbura Rural, in April, FNL members killed

BURUNDI

Pursuit of Power

Political Violence and Repression in Burundi

HUMAN
RIGHTS
WATCH

prominent CNDD-FDD member Antoine Baransekera. Police arrested the former communal administrator of Isale, a Frodebu member, who was charged with having ordered the killing and is awaiting trial at this writing.

In February FNL combatants killed one of their own civilian members, Abraham Ngendakumana, after he publicly criticized FNL policies. They abducted and tortured another, Jean Baptiste Nsabimana, in late January for similar reasons. Police failed to investigate, qualifying the incidents as "internal FNL matters."

Four Frodebu members were assassinated in Bujumbura, the capital, between January and April. Three were former CNDD-FDD combatants who had been recruited by Frodebu in a public ceremony in January; at least two of these were killed by other ex-combatants linked to the CNDD-FDD and to the intelligence service (SNR). Police investigations were inadequate, and no arrests were made. The fourth victim from Frodebu was Emmanuel Minyurano, a local official who also had close ties to the FNL. Police and prosecutors identified an SNR agent, Olivier Ndayishimiye, as the primary suspect, and issued an arrest warrant, but failed to execute it. Witnesses told Human Rights Watch that Ndayishimiye is protected by the SNR, which for months following the killing denied that Ndayishimiye was in its service. In October Ndayishimiye was finally summoned for questioning but was not arrested.

The CNDD-FDD's youth league, Imbonerakure, engages in acts of intimidation. In Muyinga, Kirundo, Ngozi, and Makamba provinces, Imbonerakure members paraded through the streets, armed with sticks and clubs and chanting slogans that threatened the opposition. Imbonerakure members and demobilized CNDD-FDD combatants illegally arrested opposition members and shut down party meetings. In Muyinga in July, a CNDD-FDD official slashed an FNL member in the head with a machete in an attempt to break up a meeting. Police opened investigations but did not arrest the suspect.

The impunity for these apparently politically motivated crimes caused opposition activists to express concern for their own safety as Burundi approaches general elections in mid-2010.

Repression of Political Opposition

Opposition parties met with obstacles in carrying out activities. Human Rights Watch documented 120 politically motivated arrests between July 2008 and April 2009, and arrests continue unabated. Many opposition members are arrested for "attending unauthorized meetings"—not a criminal offense under Burundian law. While police conduct some arrests, others are carried out by local administrative officials, who have no mandate to do so.

Alexis Sinduhije, founder of the Movement for Solidarity and Democracy (MSD), was acquitted in March of "insulting the president." Following the acquittal, a judge was abducted and beaten by men in police uniform, who accused him of influencing the decision. The judge subsequently fled the country.

A law requiring parties to inform local authorities of their intent to hold meetings was frequently abused, with communal administrators and governors arbitrarily prohibiting dozens of opposition meetings throughout the country.

In May, Hussein Radjabu, the former CNDD-FDD party leader expelled from the party in 2007 and convicted in 2008 (along with seven others) of "threatening state security," lost an appeal. Judges refused to hear several witnesses proposed by the defense, and admitted into evidence a confession extracted under torture. Radjabu took his case to the cassation court, the final appeals stage. Two of Radjabu's allies, Pasteur Mpawenayo and Gérard Nkurunziza, arrested in 2008 on similar charges, remain in prison awaiting trial.

Human Rights Defenders and Journalists

Trade union leader Juvenal Rududura and journalist Jean-Claude Kavumbagu, both imprisoned in September 2008 pending trial on defamation charges after accusing government officials of corruption, were released: Kavumbagu was acquitted in March 2009, while Rududura was "provisionally released" in July after the Anti-Corruption Court declared itself not competent to hear his case.

On April 9, civil society activist Ernest Manirumva, vice-president of the Anti-Corruption and Economic Malpractice Observatory (OLUCOME), was murdered. The government established an investigatory commission and accepted an offer from the United States to provide FBI technical support, but failed to provide the commission with resources and named as its head a prosecutor known to be close to the SNR, which some Burundian civil society groups suspected of playing a role in the killing. Under pressure from Burundian civil society organizations, the government disbanded the commission and named a new one in October, and investigations appeared to move forward. Civil society organizations were refused permits on two occasions for a planned march to protest Manirumva's assassination.

In November, Pacifique Nininahazwe, a representative of Forum for the Strengthening of Civil Society (FORSC), was subjected to death threats and surveillance by the SNR, seemingly because of his outspoken role in calling for justice for Ernest Manirumva. On November 23, FORSC's registration was revoked by the Minister of Interior, marking the first time that the government of Burundi has outlawed a civil society organization.

Criminal Justice System and Transitional Justice

In April 2009 President Pierre Nkurunziza signed into law a new criminal code. It contains many human rights advances: it abolished the death penalty, prohibits torture, increased penalties for most forms of sexual violence, and raised the age of criminal responsibility from 13 to 15. However, the new code criminalizes homosexual conduct for the first time in Burundi's history.

Although a number of police and soldiers have been arrested for common crimes such as rape and assault, members of the security forces continue to enjoy impunity for the abuse of detainees. Three police officers charged in 2007 with torturing at least 13 detainees have not yet been tried; two remain on active duty despite the gravity of the charges against them, and the third was imprisoned after a May 2009 incident in which he ordered police to fire on a group of boy scouts. Human Rights Watch received several other allegations of mistreatment of detainees in 2009, none of which were followed by arrests. On November 5, Salvator Nsabiriho died after being brutally beaten in October. Before his death he told Burundian human rights activists that he was beaten by police on orders of the governor of Kayanza, who had a land conflict with Nsabiriho. The governor was questioned the following week but was not arrested.

After months of delays, a tripartite committee including the government, the United Nations, and civil society initiated in July a series of national consultations on transitional justice, financed by the UN Peacebuilding Fund. The consultations

seek to solicit Burundians' opinions on aspects of a proposed Truth and
Reconciliation Commission and a special chamber in Burundi's judicial system.
The latter, potentially composed of both Burundian and international judges,
would be dedicated to prosecuting war crimes, crimes against humanity, and
genocide. No timeline is in place for the establishment of either mechanism, however. Serious war crimes by the FNL, the CNDD-FDD, and the former Burundian
army remain unpunished.

Key International Actors

In September 2008 the UN Human Rights Council renewed the mandate for the
independent expert on the situation of human rights in Burundi. The Burundian
government agreed to extend the mandate until a proposed national human
rights commission (CNIDH) begins operating. However, as of late 2009 the CNIDH
had not been established. The UN determined that the independent expert would
not report at the September 2009 Council meeting because of a provision insisted on by the Burundian government that the expert would report to the Council
"at the session following the establishment of the above-mentioned commission," rendering his mandate essentially meaningless given the evident lack of
political will by the Burundian government to establish the commission.

South African facilitators and the UN Integrated Office in Burundi (BINUB) were
instrumental in advancing negotiations between the government and the FNL. A
"Political Directorate" including representatives of the government, the FNL, and
key international partners remained in place to follow loose ends in the peace
process through the end of 2009.

In August South Africa, Tanzania, the European Union, the US, and the UN jointly
expressed concern over the lack of dialogue between political parties concerning
a proposed Electoral Law. The statement sent a strong message that international
actors were closely watching the preparations for the 2010 elections, and several
days later a compromise bill was adopted.

While international actors vigorously condemned the murder of OLUCOME vice-
president Manirumva, they were less outspoken in response to the murders and
harassment of low-level political activists.

CHAD

Chad continues to be destabilized by its ongoing proxy conflict with neighboring Sudan, although the government was bolstered by the defeat of Chadian rebels backed by Khartoum in combat in eastern Chad in May. Reports indicate that during the fighting government forces carried out extrajudicial executions of rebels, acts of gender-based violence, and used child soldiers. These have also been features of previous counterinsurgency efforts since the start of hostilities in late 2005. The government's Chadian rebel adversaries and Sudanese rebel allies have also been responsible for serious human rights violations, particularly the recruitment and use of child soldiers.

Civilians suspected of harboring sympathies for Chadian rebels, and members of ethnic groups associated with rebel groups, were subject to arbitrary arrest, torture, and enforced disappearance at the hands of Chadian government security forces. The government generally failed to ensure accountability for war crimes and other serious rights abuses, particularly in cases involving government officials and members of the armed forces.

This impunity raises concerns about the legislative elections scheduled to take place in 2010, as well as the presidential election slated for 2011. In the current climate, where security forces are free to abuse civilians without sanction, often on the basis of ethnicity, the ability of individuals to associate freely and the ability of political parties to campaign are highly questionable.

Combat near Sudan Border

Government security forces were responsible for serious violations of international humanitarian law during and after combat with Chadian rebels in the town of Am Dam, in the Dar Sila region near the border with Sudan. On the morning of May 7, 2009, members of the Chadian National Army (ANT) summarily executed at least nine rebel combatants and were responsible for indiscriminate attacks on civilians, several of whom were crushed to death when government tanks flattened homes where rebels were thought to be hiding.

Refugees and Internally Displaced Persons

Eastern Chad hosts more than 250,000 refugees from conflicts in Sudan and the Central African Republic, as well as at least 167,000 internally displaced Chadians who abandoned their homes between 2005 and 2007. Refugees and IDPs are exposed to rights abuses in the camp environment, particularly vulnerable groups such as women, who suffer from sexual- and gender-based violence, and children, who are targeted for recruitment into armed groups.

In an effort to restore the civilian character of Oure Cassoni camp, which is situated on the border in close proximity to a military base of the Darfur rebel group the Justice and Equality Movement (JEM), the United Nations revived calls to relocate the camp 40 kilometers to the west. Refugees refused to comply with similar efforts in 2007.

Nearly 30,000 internally displaced persons returned to their areas of origin in southeastern Chad in 2009, primarily to cultivate crops or to reassert land claims. Information about security conditions outside the camps was scarce, and some IDPs were killed by unidentified gunmen during these temporary returns; other civilians returned to find that their land had been confiscated by former neighbors. The Chadian government failed to restore security to the rural areas where many of these returns took place.

Sexual Violence

Owing to chronic insecurity related to the ongoing conflict and an entrenched culture of impunity, women and girls in eastern Chad face high levels of sexual violence. Despite the presence of UN troops and UN-trained Chadian police units, refugee and IDP women and girls are exposed to sexual abuse both inside the camps and when they venture outside for water and firewood. The proximity of Chadian government soldiers constitutes a risk factor for sexual- and gender-based violence. Human Rights Watch documented numerous instances of rape and attempted rape by government soldiers following military mobilizations and clashes with rebel forces in border areas of eastern Chad.

During the May hostilities government soldiers sexually assaulted women and girls in Am Dam and in surrounding areas, which in conflict constitutes a war

CHAD

The Risk of Return

Repatriating the Displaced in the Context of Conflict
in Eastern Chad

HUMAN
RIGHTS
WATCH

crime. Women and girls abandoned the village of Galbassa, 2 kilometers east of Am Dam, after ANT soldiers sexually assaulted two sisters, ages 14 and 19, on the night of May 7; they returned only after government security forces had withdrawn from the area.

Child Soldiers

Government security forces continued to recruit and use children, including the ANT, the *gendarmerie*, and the Office of Security Services for State Institutions (DGSSIE), an elite fighting force that answers directly to President Idriss Deby Itno. The JEM, which receives backing from the Chadian government, actively and openly recruited children from refugee camps in eastern Chad, in some cases threatening refugees and child protection officials for attempting to intervene.

Since May 2007, when the Chadian government reached an agreement with the United Nations Children's Fund (UNICEF) to release all children from the armed forces, 654 child soldiers have been released from the army. However, fewer than 10 percent of those demobilized came from the government ranks; most were from former rebel groups that had joined forces with the government in peace accords. UNICEF is allowed to inspect ANT bases for the presence of children, but access to DGSSIE positions, many of them situated in frontline areas, was routinely denied. DGSSIE soldiers contacted by Human Rights Watch reported the presence of children under age 15 in their units. A member of the officer corps estimated that as much as 5 percent of the 8,000 to 10,000 soldiers in the DGSSIE were under 18.

United Nations Mission in Chad

The United Nations Mission in Central African Republic and Chad (MINURCAT), established by the UN Security Council in September 2007 to protect civilians at risk in eastern Chad, struggled to implement its protection mandate, with just over half of its 5,200 troops deployed to the field. MINURCAT also failed to exercise elements of its mandate allowing for reporting on human rights violations; its human rights unit has not issued any reports on rights abuses in Chad since the mission was established. MINURCAT forces were able to provide limited escorts to humanitarian actors, as well as area security for refugee and IDP camps in eastern Chad.

The Integrated Security Detachment (DIS), a component of MINURCAT comprised of 850 Chadian police officers trained by the UN, has been implicated in serious abuses against civilians since being deployed to eastern Chad in June 2009. In response to abuses including unlawful killings of civilians, MINURCAT has withdrawn the certification of DIS officers implicated in abuses, but the UN has encountered difficulties ensuring that Chadian authorities launch criminal proceedings against the accused. MINURCAT human rights officers can monitor abuses committed by members of the DIS but are prevented by mandate from public reporting on such abuses. As a result, the DIS is allowed to operate with scant accountability for crimes committed.

Hissène Habré Trial

Government officials in Senegal continued to stymie judicial proceedings against former Chadian president Hissène Habré, who stands accused of crimes against humanity and torture during his 1982-90 rule. Senegalese President Abdoulaye Wade publicly suggested that Habré could be expelled from Senegal if international donors did not assume the full expense of organizing a trial, which Senegal estimated at US$40 million. In February 2009 Belgium asked the International Court of Justice (ICJ) to order Senegal to prosecute or extradite Habré, and to keep Habré in Senegal pending a final ICJ decision. In May the ICJ accepted Senegal's formal assurance that it would not let Habré leave while the case was being heard. Belgium was given until July 2010 to file pleadings in the case, while Senegal was ordered to file its response by July 2011.

Key International Actors

France was instrumental in pushing the Chadian government to agree to an international inquiry into serious abuses by government forces during and after fighting with rebel forces in February 2008, and in 2009 French diplomats quietly urged the government to shed light on the fate of opposition leader Ibni Oumar Mahamat Saleh, who was "disappeared" by government security forces in February 2008 and is presumed dead. However, France has done little to ensure the independence of a follow-up body established in January 2009 to carry forward investigations into crimes committed in February 2008. France historically has provided crucial military support to the government, but it signaled its displeasure with the government's reluctance to negotiate an end of hostilities with Chadian rebel groups by sending French military aircraft out of the country during the May 2009 hostilities.

The United States maintains interests in Chad's petroleum sector, partners with the Chadian government in counterterrorism efforts, and it is the single largest contributor to humanitarian operations in the east of the country. On September 15 the US State Department Office of Trafficking in Persons imposed sanctions on the Chadian government, including the withdrawal of all US military assistance, for failing to make adequate efforts to combat the recruitment and use of child soldiers and other instances of child trafficking. That same day President Barack Obama waived the sanctions, citing US national interests.

CÔTE D'IVOIRE

Modest progress in implementing a March 2007 peace accord between the government and northern-based New Forces rebels resulted in minimal improvement in respect for human rights in Côte d'Ivoire in 2009. The ongoing political stalemate, further delays in election preparations and the disarmament of combatants, and ongoing conflicts over land and citizenship rights continued to threaten long-term stability.

The redeployment of judicial officials and the handover of power from rebel authorities to civil administrators in the north offered some hope but few concrete gains in respect for the rule of law. Government forces and New Forces rebels continue to engage in predatory and abusive behavior, including widespread extortion at checkpoints and sexual violence against girls and women, with near-total impunity. The judicial system remains plagued by corruption, a lack of independence, and insufficient resources.

Côte d'Ivoire's key partners, including the United Nations, the Economic Community of West African States (ECOWAS), and France, increasingly criticized the Ivorian government for delays in organizing a presidential election (postponed a fourth time and now likely to be held by early 2010), but remained reluctant to criticize the country's human rights record.

Political-Military Stalemate

Throughout 2009 the government of President Laurent Gbagbo missed important deadlines for the full restoration of state authority to the rebel-held north and for the disarmament and reintegration of former combatants, as set forth in the December 2008 supplementary agreement to the March 2007 Ouagadougou Agreement (the first to have been directly negotiated by the country's belligerents). While the Ivorian government announced in May that an oft-postponed presidential election would take place on November 29, 2009, continued delays in completing the voter identification and registration process and publishing the voter list resulted in another postponement to early 2010. More than four years after the October 2005 expiry of President Gbagbo's mandate, Ivorians were still denied the right to freely elect their representatives.

After months-long delays, the redeployment of civil authorities throughout the country in May—including judicial, police, and financial administrators—remained incomplete, and was seriously undermined by rebel commanders who continued to exercise near-complete control over economic, security, and, to a lesser extent, judicial affairs within their zones.

Meanwhile, the widespread presence of arms due to largely unsuccessful demobilization and disarmament efforts through 2009 led to concern about the ability of citizens to exercise their right to campaign and vote free of intimidation and violence. At this writing, more than 18,000 rebels and 25,000 pro-government militia members have yet to be disarmed or demobilized. Some 12,000 rebels participated in demobilization programs as of October 2009, but only one weapon per an estimated 200-300 "disarmed" combatants was collected. In addition, the UN Group of Experts monitoring sanctions against Côte d'Ivoire reported in October that the government and northern rebel commanders are importing additional arms, in violation of a 2004 UN arms embargo.

Rule of Law and Land Rights

While the redeployment of a number of judges and prosecutors to the north in January 2009, after an absence of seven years, was a crucial first step toward restoring the rule of law, inadequate financial support and persistent delays in the redeployment of police, corrections officers, and magistrates left many courts in the north ineffective. The judicial system countrywide, but particularly in the south, remained fraught with corruption and a lack of independence that served to further entrench a culture of impunity.

Violent conflicts over land rights, particularly in the north and west, were exacerbated by the chronic failure of the judicial system to resolve disputes, and persistent xenophobia toward those perceived as non-Ivorian nationals. In the west, perpetrators of violence often targeted non-indigenous internally displaced persons returning to their land.

Extortion and Racketeering

The government took no meaningful steps in 2009 to address the problem of widespread extortion and racketeering by government security forces—including the police, gendarmerie, military, and customs officials—as well as by government militia and New Forces rebels. Individuals who refused to pay bribes to corrupt officials were often beaten or arbitrarily detained. Although checkpoints remained throughout the country, extortion was most severe in the north, where New Forces rebels continued to exert almost complete economic control, extorting the equivalent of millions of US dollars annually at checkpoints and through other rackets.

Political Violence

Politically motivated violence by pro-government groups, such as the Young Patriots and the Student Federation of Côte d'Ivoire (FESCI), declined compared to previous years, but continued impunity for violent crimes fuels fears of unrestrained intimidation and violence at the time of elections. The voter registration process was on several occasions disrupted by attacks, particularly in the west, in which armed men intimidated those standing in line at registration centers, or confiscated briefcases of registration papers.

Members of FESCI and other pro-government groups continue to enjoy impunity for common acts of racketeering, vandalism, and intimidation of perceived opponents. Dozens of armed FESCI members gathered in January to launch an assault on a rival student union, and in August several hundred FESCI members caused property damage and threatened the mayor of an Abidjan suburb.

Media outlets allied to either the government or rebel forces on occasion published provocations to intolerance and violence, but the overall prevalence of hate speech was significantly lower than during the worst years of the crisis.

Sexual Violence

As in previous years, there were frequent incidents of sexual violence against women and girls, particularly in the north and west, and incidents of harassment and rape persisted at checkpoints run by government security forces and rebels. Survivors' access to health and legal services is extremely limited. Efforts at investigating and prosecuting cases of sexual violence are hampered by a lack of political will among police and court officials, and aggravated by severe deficiencies in the justice system, particularly in the north.

Early in 2009 a New Forces action plan, developed in cooperation with the UN Security Council Working Group on Children and Armed Conflict, to combat sexual violence committed by its troops and in its region showed some promise. However, the New Forces failed to implement it. The Ivorian government, for its part, failed to adopt a similar national action plan to combat sexual violence in government-held areas, despite pressure from the UN and other actors.

Child Labor

The Ivorian government only recently acknowledged the longstanding problem of child labor in its cocoa industry and has slowly begun implementing, often in partnership with nongovernmental organizations, programs to help children return to school. Few are currently benefiting from these programs, however, and many children continue to perform child labor, including the worst forms of child labor, in violation of Côte d'Ivoire's commitments under international law.

Accountability for Past Abuses

Although they were handed to the UN secretary-general in November 2004, the UN Security Council has still not made public the findings of the UN Commission of Inquiry into serious violations of human rights and international humanitarian law in Côte d'Ivoire since September 2002. In 2003 the Ivorian government accepted the jurisdiction of the International Criminal Court over serious crimes. While ICC officials visited the country in July 2009 at the invitation of civil society, as in previous years the government was not forthcoming in helping the ICC mission assess the existence or prospects of genuine national efforts at seeking accountability for such crimes.

The National Human Rights Commission, which began work in July 2008, submitted its first annual report in June 2009, but its capacity to fully investigate and report on serious abuses was limited by inadequate funding and support from the government.

April marked the fifth anniversary of the disappearance of Guy-André Kieffer, a journalist of dual French-Canadian nationality who was researching alleged illicit practices involving Ivorian government officials and the cocoa industry. French investigations into Kieffer's disappearance have been consistently stymied by a lack of cooperation from high-level Ivorian authorities.

Key International Actors

Many of Côte d'Ivoire's key partners, including the UN, ECOWAS, and France, remained reluctant to publicly criticize the government for its human rights record or to push for those responsible for war crimes or political violence to be held accountable, but they increasingly expressed frustrations at the lack of political will within the government and rebel leadership to organize free and fair elections. In January 2009 the UN Security Council demanded that Ivorian leaders set a realistic timeline and, after numerous delays, threatened in September to impose targeted sanctions against individuals who obstructed election preparations.

The UN Operation in Côte d'Ivoire (UNOCI) remained engaged to monitor the human rights situation, focusing on child protection and sexual violence, along with 8,400 military and police personnel to assist with security in the run-up to elections. France continued its drawdown of troops in Côte d'Ivoire that support UNOCI, reducing its total to 900 by the end of the year from a high of more than 4,000 in 2006.

The Security Council extended through October 31, 2010, a sanctions regime that included an arms embargo and a ban on the importation of Ivorian diamonds, as well as a travel ban and assets freeze on three individuals—two of whom were implicated in attacks against UN personnel in 2006.

The UN Human Rights Council reviewed Côte d'Ivoire under its Universal Periodic Review mechanism in December 2009.

DEMOCRATIC REPUBLIC OF CONGO (DRC)

Violence and brutal human rights abuses increased in the Democratic Republic of Congo throughout 2009. Two military campaigns by the Congolese army, in the east and north, resulted in a dramatic increase in violence against civilians by both rebel and government forces. At least 2,500 civilians were slaughtered, over 7,000 women and girls were raped, and more than 1 million people were forced to flee their homes. This pushed the total number of displaced people to over 2 million, the vast majority with limited or no access to humanitarian assistance, often forcing them to return to insecure areas to find food. United Nations peacekeepers supported Congolese army military operations and struggled to give meaning to their mandate to protect civilians.

Impunity, already endemic, was further entrenched with the promotion of Bosco Ntaganda to the rank of general, despite a warrant for his arrest from the International Criminal Court. In July the government announced a policy of "zero tolerance" for human rights abuses committed by its soldiers, but only made a handful of arrests. Violent attacks against human rights defenders and journalists continued throughout the country.

Violence in Eastern and Northern Congo

In January 2009 the political landscape changed dramatically in eastern Congo. Congolese President Joseph Kabila and Rwandan President Paul Kagame struck a deal to rid each other of their enemies. Rwanda put a stop to the rebellion of the Congolese Tutsi-led National Congress for the Defense of the People (CNDP) by arresting its leader, Laurent Nkunda, and forcing its fighters to integrate into the Congolese army. In exchange, the Congolese government agreed that Rwandan soldiers could enter eastern Congo for five weeks of joint military operations against the Democratic Forces for the Liberation of Rwanda (FDLR), a Rwandan Hutu rebel group, some of whose leaders had participated in the 1994 genocide. Following the brief operation, both governments pressed UN peacekeepers to support a second phase of military operations to finish the job. Under pressure and believing they could better protect civilians by being part of the operations, the UN agreed.

DEMOCRATIC REPUBLIC OF CONGO

Killings in Kiwanja

The UN's Inability to Protect Civilians

HUMAN
RIGHTS
WATCH

Democratic Republic of Congo

"You Will Be Punished"

Attacks on Civilians in Eastern Congo

HUMAN
RIGHTS
WATCH

The military operations were disastrous for civilians. The FDLR launched deliberate and targeted retaliatory attacks on civilians, killing and raping to punish the population for their government's change in policy toward them. In the worst single incident, the FDLR massacred at least 96 civilians in the village of Busurungi in North Kivu province on the night of May 9-10 by chopping them with machetes or burning them to death. The Congolese army failed to protect its own citizens from such attacks and itself targeted civilians who it perceived as FDLR collaborators, as well as Rwandan Hutu refugees. In one incident between April 27 and 30, Congolese army soldiers attacked camps in the Shalio Hill area and deliberately killed at least 129 refugees. Many of the victims were clubbed to death.

MONUC, the UN peacekeeping force in Congo, struggled to balance its mandate for civilian protection with its support to the Congolese military operations. Although the peacekeepers made some notable efforts to protect civilians, which undoubtedly saved lives, in many cases they arrived too late or not at all.

By October 2009 the military operations had succeeded in demobilizing 1,100 combatants from the ranks of the FDLR's estimated strength of 6,000. But it came at a high price: between January and September over 1,300 civilians had been slaughtered in North and South Kivu, the majority of them women, children, and the elderly; thousands of civilians were abducted and pressed into forced labor; and more than 900,000 people fled for their lives. The FDLR and Congolese soldiers pillaged their belongings and then burned an estimated 7,000 homes to the ground. Already poor, civilians were left with nothing.

Attacks in northern Congo by the Ugandan rebel group Lord's Resistance Army (LRA) also caused immense harm to Congolese civilians. When the Ugandan army scaled back military operations in Congo against the LRA in March 2009, civilian protection was largely left to the Congolese army and UN peacekeepers. LRA killings and abductions of civilians continued, leading to the displacement of over 200,000 people throughout the worst affected areas of Haut and Bas Uele districts of Orientale province. (See also Uganda chapter.)

Sexual Violence

The military operations in eastern Congo were accompanied by brutal rape. In a region already labeled "the worst place in the world to be a woman," the situation deteriorated further. An estimated 7,000 cases of sexual violence against women and girls were registered at health centers across North and South Kivu in the first seven months of 2009, nearly double the number of cases in 2008. In April 2009 the Congolese government and MONUC adopted a strategy to combat sexual violence, but it did not halt the increase in rape.

Sexual violence cases tried at military courts did increase during 2009, although only four officers were held to account. Funds aimed at efforts to protect women from rape remained shockingly low. In May UN Security Council ambassadors on mission to Congo handed the government a list of five senior officers they said were responsible for rape, including a general, Jerome Kakwavu, and demanded the officers be held to account. By October two had been arrested.

Threats to Journalists and Human Rights Defenders

On August 23, 2009, Bruno Koko Chirambiza, a journalist for Radio Star, was murdered by a group of eight armed men some 150 meters from a police post in Bukavu, eastern Congo. He was the third journalist killed in the city since 2007. Three female journalists in Bukavu received death threats in September 2009, prompting MONUC to publicly call on the Congolese authorities to take action to guarantee the safety of journalists.

On July 26 the Congolese government suspended Radio France International (RFI) after it broadcast a program detailing problems within the Congolese army. The minister of communications and the media said RFI was inciting soldiers to revolt. In August three local radio stations were threatened with closure if they continued to retransmit RFI's programming.

In May armed men threatened to kill Anicette Kabala, the executive secretary of Parliament of the Young Girl (PAJEF), a women's organization in Kalemie, if she did not drop cases of girls who had filed rape complaints. Her brother was shot and killed when he tried to intervene. On October 1, armed men raided the home

of another female human rights defender in Bunia and threatened to rape and kill her and her daughter for their role in trials taking place at the ICC.

In July Golden Misabiko, the Katanga provincial president of the National Association for Human Rights (ASADHO), was arrested by the National Intelligence Agency (ANR) after publishing a report about illegal exploitation at a uranium mine. He was tried and sentenced for spreading false information and threatening state security. He fled into exile. Four of his colleagues received death threats. Robert Ilunga Numbi, the president of the Friends of Nelson Mandela for the Defence of Human Rights (ANMDH) was also arrested by ANR agents in Kinshasa on August 31. He was detained incommunicado for nine days before being charged with disseminating false information, for a press conference he gave denouncing abuses of workers' rights.

Justice and Accountability

The fight against impunity was seriously undermined by the promotion of Bosco Ntaganda to the rank of general, despite an ICC arrest warrant for war crimes he committed in Ituri between 2002 and 2004. Other known human rights abusers were also integrated into the army, including Jean-Pierre Biyoyo, who previously had been convicted by a military court for the recruitment of child soldiers but had escaped from custody soon afterwards. The government justified its failure to make arrests of senior army officers by claiming it prioritized peace over justice. Local and international human rights groups protested the policy.

A few crucial cases helped to buck this somber trend. On March 5, 2009, the Mai Mai commander Gedeon Kyungu Mutanga, along with 20 co-accused, was convicted by a military court in Katanga for crimes against humanity and other charges. Also in March, 11 soldiers in Walikale, North Kivu, were convicted of rape as a crime against humanity. On July 27, in a rare case against an officer, Col. Ndayanbaje Kipanga was sentenced in absentia to life imprisonment for crimes against humanity relating to rape charges. He escaped custody before the trial.

On January 26, 2009, the ICC began its first-ever trial. Former Congolese warlord Thomas Lubanga Dyilo faced charges of war crimes for his use of child soldiers in the conflict in Ituri. The opening day's proceedings were broadcast across Congo.

The trial of two other Ituri warlords, Germain Katanga and Mathieu Ngudjolo Chui, commenced on November 24.

Key International Actors

Encouraged by the historic rapprochement between Congo and Rwanda, governments and international donors were reluctant to raise concerns that might upset the new relationship. Some privately raised concerns about Ntaganda's promotion, but few pressed effectively for his arrest. A number of diplomats, notably United States Secretary of State Hillary Clinton and UN Secretary-General Ban Ki-moon, visited eastern Congo and raised human rights concerns, especially on sexual violence. But they all stopped short of putting pressure on the Congolese government or MONUC to suspend military operations until measures for civilian protection were in place. In October, following a mission to Congo, the UN special rapporteur on extrajudicial executions became a rare voice loudly raising concerns about abuses committed during the military operations. In November the US special envoy for the African Great Lakes region marked a change of approach by calling the human cost of the military operations "unacceptable."

MONUC provided logistical and operational support to Congolese military operations. But contrary to the UN's own legal advice and its mandate from the Security Council, it did not put in place conditions to ensure respect for human rights before operations began. In November 2009 MONUC suspended its support to one army unit in North Kivu that it said had committed serious violations, but continued its support to other units. MONUC's ongoing support to the military operations raised serious questions about its implication in the abuses.

EQUATORIAL GUINEA

Despite Equatorial Guinea earning tens of billions of dollars as the fourth-largest Sub-Saharan African oil producer, the vast majority of its people remain impoverished due to corruption and mismanagement. The discovery of oil in the mid-1990s has enriched the country's elites and helped to further entrench an already autocratic regime. Free and fair elections are denied to the citizens of Equatorial Guinea, and arbitrary detention and torture continue to be widespread. The government severely restricts the media and almost no independent news information exists within the country.

President Teodoro Obiang Nguema, who celebrated his 30th year in power in August 2009, announced in October that Equatorial Guinea would hold its next presidential election on November 29, giving six weeks' notice. Opposition leaders condemned this announcement, saying they had expected the poll to be held later and were thus at a disadvantage to prepare their campaigns. The election year saw an increase in militarization, a common practice of the Obiang government. In previous years, allegations of coup attempts before elections provided justification to increase military presence in the streets and limit freedom of movement.

Economic and Social Rights

The gross domestic product (GDP) of Equatorial Guinea increased over 5,000 percent since 1992. Given its enormous oil wealth and its relatively small population of approximately 527,000 people, the country should be a model of development. However, underfunding of essential social services—far lower than the regional average—compels the conclusion that funds have been needlessly diverted from services and institutions critical to the fulfillment of Equatoguineans' economic and social rights. GDP per capita is among the highest in the world and the highest in Sub-Saharan Africa. However, nearly 77 percent of the population lives below the poverty line, and levels of severe poverty are on par with those of Haiti. Life expectancy is low, at 52 years, and infant mortality is high at 124 deaths per 1,000 live births. The 2009 United Nations Human Development Report showed that, of all the countries listed, Equatorial Guinea had the largest gap between its per capita GDP ranking and its Human Development Index ranking, which stood at 118 out of 182 countries. President Obiang is callous toward his obligations to fulfill socioeconomic rights, saying that most people in his country "are living very well" and that lazy citizens who "don't want to work" should "sweat a bit" to earn money. Most Equatoguineans live on less than a dollar a day.

Freedom of Expression and Association

Reporters Without Borders ranked Equatorial Guinea the 158th worst out of 175 countries for press freedom in 2009. A small number of non-state-controlled publications appear sporadically, none of which can report critically on government activity. Aside from the print media, there is only state radio, one state television station, and one private television station owned by the president's son. In a particularly stark example, a journalist for Agence France-Presse was imprisoned in Malabo's Black Beach Prison for four months after being charged with libel for a mistaken report that he wrote (and quickly corrected) about the head of the national airline. The government attacks its critics, even alleging that the 2009 reports on Equatorial Guinea by Human Rights Watch and the Center for Economic and Social Rights were attempts at "blackmail."

Freedom of association and assembly are severely curtailed, limiting the growth of a civil society capable of monitoring government action. There are no legally registered independent human rights organizations in the country.

Political Parties and Political Opposition

While Equatorial Guinea is nominally a multiparty democracy, in reality the Democratic Party (PDGE) maintains a monopoly over political life, and opposition parties are silenced through the use of criminal prosecution, arbitrary arrest, and harassment. Additionally, not all parties are legally registered. Only two, the Convergence for Social Democracy (CPDS) and the People's Union (UP), are actively opposed to the PDGE and to Obiang.

Arbitrary Detention, Torture, and Detention Conditions

Arbitrary detention and arrests without legal due process are common; numerous detainees were held for indefinite periods without knowing the charges against them. Following an attack on the presidential palace in February, 10 UP members were arbitrarily arrested without warrant and held without charge; at least two were tortured. At this writing, two of the 10 detainees, Marcelino Nguema and Santiago Asumu, remain in Black Beach prison.

Though national law prohibits torture, it remains a serious problem. In July Obiang commented to Spanish press that "there is no torture" in Equatorial Guinea, but the UN special rapporteur on torture and other cruel, inhuman or degrading treatment or punishment, Manfred Nowak, found in a January 2009 report on Equatorial Guinea that torture is regularly used to obtain confessions. Torture is often utilized against political opponents, common criminals, and perceived critics of the government. Epifanio Pascual Nguema Algo was arrested on February 22, after an anonymous tip alleged that he had made disparaging comments about the president. On March 2 he was severely tortured for hours—he suffered wounds to his genitals and was unable to walk or stand for several days. He was left without medical attention until March 23.

Torture is particularly problematic in detention centers. The US Department of State cited "systematic torture of prisoners and detainees by security forces" in its May 2009 *Advancing Freedom and Democracy* report. Nowak also addressed this problem in August 2009, stating, "In Equatorial Guinea, detainees spend several weeks or even months in overcrowded, often dark and filthy police cells with virtually nothing but a concrete floor where they are kept for 24 hours a day." Prisons do not feed detainees, leaving prisoners to rely on family members for food. Prisoners are forced to collect their bodily waste in bottles and bags, as there are no toilets, and sleep in shifts due to severe overcrowding. There are no separate detention facilities for female and child prisoners, who frequently are held in overcrowded cells with male prisoners and are vulnerable to abuse.

The notorious Black Beach prison held British coup plotter Simon Mann and his South African co-conspirators, until they received a presidential pardon on November 3, 2009. Although Mann's release was ostensibly for medical reasons, he had shared information on the alleged coup backers and the government felt that he had "genuinely repented."

Key International Actors

The United States is Equatorial Guinea's main trading partner and US companies dominate the country's oil sector. The Bush administration sought to improve relations with Equatorial Guinea, in part due to heavy lobbying by the US oil industry, and this "business first" relationship came at the expense of engaging Equatorial Guinea on human rights and democracy issues. President Obiang highly values a close relationship with the United States, giving the Obama administration an opportunity for a new relationship that prioritizes human rights and good governance. In a July address in Ghana, President Barack Obama criticized "leaders [who] exploit the economy to enrich themselves," and offered support to those working to promote good governance and combat corruption. The Obama administration nominated a new ambassador to Equatorial Guinea in July, who echoed the same theme at his confirmation hearings in November. It remains to be seen how this administration will hold Equatorial Guinea to these standards. Following revelations in November that a US government investigation identified nearly $80 million spent in the US by Teodorin Obiang, the president's son and minister of agriculture and forestry, the Obama administration was under increased pressure to deny entry to the US to Equatoguinean officials credibly accused of corruption, and to seize assets purchased with proceeds of corruption.

Spain's foreign minister, Miguel Ángel Moratinos, led a large, high-profile delegation to Equatorial Guinea in July 2009. Rather than press vigorously on human rights issues, the trip instead was meant to improve diplomatic relations and explore economic opportunities.

Internationally, there are several ongoing legal challenges alleging misuse of Equatorial Guinea's oil funds. In Spain a human rights organization has accused President Obiang and other government officials of siphoning money from a state-owned oil company and using it to buy houses. Together with other groups, it also filed a complaint to the African Commission on Human and Peoples' Rights on March 19, 2008, arguing that Obiang's diversion of the country's oil wealth violates the African Charter on Human and Peoples' Rights. In France, Transparency International and the rights group Sherpa brought a case against President Obiang, accusing him of using public funds to buy luxury homes and cars in France. The court ruled on October 29, 2009, that the groups did not have legal standing to bring a case; that decision is expected to be appealed.

While Equatorial Guinea has sought admission to the Extractive Industry Transparency Initiative (EITI), real progress in revenue transparency has been slow. The government has taken some steps in 2009 toward meeting objectives required to join the EITI, but its validation as a compliant country is due in March 2010 and there are concerns about its ability to meet EITI requirements, particularly regarding the lack of meaningful civil society participation.

The country was reviewed under the Universal Periodic Review mechanism of the United Nations Human Rights Council in December 2009.

EQUATORIAL GUINEA

Well Oiled

Oil and Human Rights in Equatorial Guinea

HUMAN
RIGHTS
WATCH

ERITREA

Eritrea remains a country in shackles. Arbitrary arrests and detention, torture, extrajudicial killings, severe restrictions on freedoms of expression and worship, and forced labor are routine. Despite government efforts to veil abuses from scrutiny, Eritrean refugees provided consistent firsthand accounts of widespread abuses. Thousands of people fled the country in 2009 due to Eritrea's serious human rights violations and indefinite military conscription.

Arbitrary Detention, Enforced Disappearances, and Deaths in Custody

Thousands of Eritreans are estimated to be incarcerated in known and secret detention facilities.

In September 2001 the government arrested eleven high-ranking government officials who had publicly criticized President Isayas Afewerki's leadership and called for democratic reforms in the wake of the 1998-2000 border war with Ethiopia. Simultaneously, the government closed all private newspapers and arrested their editors and publishers. None of those prisoners has been charged or brought to trial. The government ignored two judgments from the African Commission on Human and People's Rights and a finding by the United Nations Working Group on Arbitrary Detention criticizing the detentions and ordering the detainees' release. The leaders and journalists were reported to be held in incommunicado detention in remote prisons. In 2009 an opposition website published purported electronic copies of death certificates (but without official seals) for nine of the eleven leaders; four of the journalists have been presumed dead.

These prominent cases represent only a fraction of the number of people arbitrarily detained since September 2001. Thousands of less prominent people have been arrested and incarcerated without charge, trial, or opportunity to appeal and without access to family, lawyers, or independent prison monitoring organizations. A few prisoners were freed without explanation and warned not to speak to anyone about their detention. Most prisoners, however, remain in jail indefinitely. Among those reported to have been arrested in 2009 were five members of the staff of Radio Bana, a radio station sponsored by the Ministry of Education, two

ERITREA

Service for Life

State Repression and Indefinite Conscription in Eritrea

HUMAN
RIGHTS
WATCH

journalists for the government radio system, and twelve residents of a town who allegedly helped their children escape to Ethiopia to avoid conscription.

Deaths in custody are common as a result of ill-treatment, torture, starvation, and denial of medical care. Many other detainees have "disappeared," their whereabouts unknown. In 2009 a reliable website reported the deaths of four prisoners held because of their religious beliefs; three died after torture, the fourth after denial of treatment for malaria.

The Eritrean government is also responsible for extrajudicial killings. Some deliberate killings occurred during detention, others when prisoners attempted to escape confinement or flee the country. The government maintains a "shoot-to-kill" policy for anyone caught trying to cross the country's borders. Five teenage boys were reportedly shot at close range after having been captured trying to cross the border to Ethiopia in December 2008. Four were killed; the fifth managed to escape to Ethiopia after the others fell on him and he faked death.

Torture and Ill-Treatment

Torture and ill-treatment in detention are routine in Eritrea. Former detainees told Human Rights Watch that detention almost always included severe beatings, often leading to permanent physical damage. In addition to beatings, punishment entailed being hung up by the arms from trees, tied up in the sun in contorted positions for hours or days, and subjected to mock drowning.

Poor detention conditions often amount to cruel, inhuman, and degrading treatment. Prisoners were held in a variety of known and secret detention facilities, in unlit underground bunkers, or in shipping containers where they were subjected to extreme temperatures of well over 40°C (104°F) during the day and freezing conditions at night. People who escaped detention reported poor nutrition and starvation rations in most facilities. Medical care is minimal at best. In December 2008, 27 political prisoners, including three journalists arrested in 2001, were moved to the Dahlak archipelago in the Red Sea where prisoners were held in searing heat in subterranean isolation cells. In 2009 four prisoners held in underground cells for five years without access to daylight because they were "unrepentant" for their religious beliefs were reportedly blinded by sudden glare when they were brought to the surface; over the years there have been similar reports about other prisoners released from underground cells.

Freedom of Expression and Association

Since the private press was destroyed in 2001 no independent newspaper has been allowed to publish. No political organization other than the ruling People's Front for Democracy and Justice (PFDJ) was permitted. Eyewitnesses told Human Rights Watch that actions as innocuous as signing a petition for changes in educational policy result in imprisonment and beatings. Asking a critical question at a government-convened forum could have the same consequences. According to an expatriate website security officials arrested three internet users in late 2008 for allegedly connecting with opposition sites, and internet café owners were warned that they must control internet use.

The government prohibits the formation of private associations not under its leadership and control, including labor unions and self-help organizations.

Freedom of Religion

Since 2002 it is unlawful to practice any religion except the four official faiths: Eritrean Orthodox, Islam, Catholic, and Lutheran. Despite government statements that other religious groups could apply for registration, no applications have ever been granted.

Security forces indefinitely detain members of "illegal" religions. Persons arrested for their religious affiliations and practices suffer the same torture and abuse as other prisoners, usually with the expressed intent of compelling them to renounce their faith. In late 2008 and June 2009 the government arrested 25 Jehovah's Witnesses, some in their 70s and 80s, bringing the number of Jehovah's Witnesses in detention to 61, three of whom have been detained since 1994. In December 2008 members of unrecognized churches and of a modernizing wing of the Orthodox Church were victims of a wave of arrests. The patriarch of the Orthodox Church, deposed by the government in 2006, remained under house arrest.

Forced Labor

Eritrea's population is the world's second most militarized according to the International Institute of Strategic Studies. By law, all able-bodied adult Eritreans are required to perform 18 months of national service; in practice national service is prolonged indefinitely. National service conscripts are paid a pittance and are often used as cheap, involuntary labor on projects for the personal benefit of ranking civilian and military leaders: they are also sometimes used to provide forced labor to implement development projects. Abuse of conscripts, including torture, is common.

Relations in the Horn of Africa

Relations with Ethiopia remain tense. Ethiopia refused to accept the border demarcated by a Border Commission established under an armistice agreement ending the countries' 1998-2000 war. Although the commission demarcation was to be binding, Ethiopia still occupies Badme, the village where the war started, which falls on the Eritrean side of the demarcated border. In 2009 a Claims Commission established under the armistice agreement awarded Ethiopia US$174 million and Eritrea US$161 million in war-related damages. The Commission found both sides had raped civilians, imprisoned civilians under harsh conditions, mistreated prisoners of war, and engaged in other violations of international law. It also reaffirmed its earlier holding that Eritrea had violated international law in 1998 by attacking Badme, then under Ethiopian administration.

Eritrea continued to occupy a portion of Djibouti, which it entered in 2008, despite a unanimous UN Security Council resolution demanding that it withdraw its forces by the end of February 2009. The Security Council had taken no further action by late 2009.

A UN team monitoring a UN arms embargo on Somalia accused Eritrea of smuggling weapons and up to US$500,000 per month to insurgents fighting the transitional Somali government. Eritrea denied violating the embargo.

Key International Actors

Foreign aid, while modest, grew in importance as expatriate Eritreans increasingly protested government repression by refusing to remit Eritrea's two percent tax on foreign incomes. One of Eritrea's few international investment projects, a mining development at Bisha in western Eritrea, jointly owned by a Canadian firm and the Eritrean government, is to begin production in late 2010.

Eritrea receives little development aid. In 2009 the European Commission agreed to provide €122 million between 2008 and 2013, principally for food production and "infrastructure rehabilitation." China in 2009 agreed to provide an undisclosed number of volunteers for a year in agriculture, information technology, and sports. UN assistance was about US$12 million. Abu Dhabi will lend US$19.9 million for unspecified infrastructure projects. In late 2008 Iran's Bank for Export Development reportedly extended US$35 million in credit. Eritrea was also the recipient of loans and grants in undisclosed amounts from Qatar and Libya.

The United States provided no direct assistance because President Isayas, angered by US support of Ethiopia, refused its aid, and because the United States accused Eritrea of providing arms to the al Shabaab insurgency in Somalia. The US threatened to place sanctions on Eritrea but to date had not implemented the threat.

The African Union called for sanctions on Eritrea in May as a result of its role in Somalia.

ETHIOPIA

Ethiopia is on a deteriorating human rights trajectory as parliamentary elections approach in 2010. These will be the first national elections since 2005, when post-election protests resulted in the deaths of at least 200 protesters, many of them victims of excessive use of force by the police. Broad patterns of government repression have prevented the emergence of organized opposition in most of the country. In December 2008 the government re-imprisoned opposition leader Birtukan Midekssa for life after she made remarks that allegedly violated the terms of an earlier pardon.

In 2009 the government passed two pieces of legislation that codify some of the worst aspects of the slide towards deeper repression and political intolerance. A civil society law passed in January is one of the most restrictive of its kind, and its provisions will make most independent human rights work impossible. A new counterterrorism law passed in July permits the government and security forces to prosecute political protesters and non-violent expressions of dissent as acts of terrorism.

Political Repression and the 2010 Elections

As Ethiopia heads toward nationwide elections, the government continues to clamp down on the already limited space for dissent or independent political activity. Ordinary citizens who criticize government policies or officials frequently face arrest on trumped-up accusations of belonging to illegal "anti-peace" groups, including armed opposition movements. Officials sometimes bring criminal cases in a manner that appears to selectively target government critics, as when in June 2009 prominent human rights activist Abebe Worke was charged with illegal importation of radio equipment and ultimately fled the country. In the countryside government-supplied (and donor-funded) agricultural assistance and other resources are often used as leverage to punish and prevent dissent, or to compel individuals into joining the ruling party.

The opposition is in disarray, but the government has shown little willingness to tolerate potential challengers. In December 2008 the security forces re-arrested Birtukan Midekssa, leader of the Unity for Democracy and Justice Party, which had begun to build a grassroots following in the capital. The government announced that Birtukan would be jailed for life because she had made public remarks that violated the terms of an earlier pardon for alleged acts of treason surrounding the 2005 elections. The authorities stated that there was no need for a trial as the move was a mere legal technicality.

In July the Ethiopian government passed a new anti-terrorism law. The law provides broad powers to the police, and harsh criminal penalties can be applied to political protesters and others who engage in acts of nonviolent political dissent. Some of its provisions appear tailored less toward addressing terrorism and more toward allowing for a heavy-handed response to mass public unrest, like that which followed Ethiopia's 2005 elections.

Civil Society Activism and Media Freedom

The space for independent civil society activity in Ethiopia, already extremely narrow, shrank dramatically in 2009. In January the government passed a new civil society law whose provisions are among the most restrictive of any comparable law anywhere in the world. The law makes any work that touches on human rights or governance issues illegal if carried out by foreign non-governmental organizations, and labels any Ethiopian organization that receives more than 10 percent of its funding from sources outside of Ethiopia as "foreign." The law makes most independent human rights work virtually impossible, and human rights work deemed illegal under the law is punishable as a criminal offense.

Ethiopia passed a new media law in 2008 that improved upon several repressive aspects of the previous legal regime. The space for independent media activity in Ethiopia remains severely constrained, however. In August two journalists were jailed on charges derived partly from Ethiopia's old, and now defunct, press proclamation. Ethiopia's new anti-terror law contains provisions that will impact the media by making journalists and editors potential accomplices in acts of terrorism if they publish statements seen as encouraging or supporting terrorist acts, or even, simply, political protest.

Pretrial Detention and Torture

The Ethiopian government continues its longstanding practice of using lengthy periods of pretrial and pre-charge detention to punish critics and opposition activists, even where no criminal charges are ultimately pursued. Numerous prominent ethnic Oromo Ethiopians have been detained in recent years on charges of providing support to the outlawed Oromo Liberation Front (OLF); in almost none of these cases have charges been pursued, but the accused, including opposition activists, have remained in detention for long periods. Canadian national Bashir Makhtal was convicted on charges of supporting the rebel Ogaden National Liberation Front (ONLF) in July, after a trial that was widely criticized as unfair; he was in detention for two-and-a-half years before his sentence was handed down, and he was unable to access legal counsel and consular representatives for much of that period.

Not only are periods of pretrial detention punitively long, but detainees and convicted prisoners alike face torture and other ill-treatment. Human Rights Watch and other organizations have documented consistent patterns of torture in police and military custody for many years. The Ethiopian government regularly responds that these abuses do not exist, but even the government's own Human Rights Commission acknowledged in its 2009 annual report that torture and other abuses had taken place in several detention facilities, including in Ambo and Nekemte.

Impunity for Military Abuses

The Ethiopian National Defense Force (ENDF) has committed serious abuses, in some cases amounting to war crimes or crimes against humanity, in several different conflicts in recent years. Human Rights Watch is not aware of any meaningful efforts to hold the officers or government officials most responsible for those abuses to account. The only government response to crimes against humanity and other serious abuses committed by the military during a brutal counterinsurgency campaign in Gambella in late 2003 and 2004 was an inquiry that prosecuted a handful of junior personnel for deliberate and widespread patterns of abuse. No one has been investigated or held to account for war crimes and other widespread violations of the laws of war during Ethiopia's bloody military intervention in neighboring Somalia from 2006 to 2008.

In August 2008 the Ethiopian government did purport to launch an inquiry into allegations of serious crimes in Somali Regional State, where the armed forces have been fighting a campaign against the rebel Ogaden National Liberation Front for many years. The inquiry was sponsored by the Ministry of Foreign Affairs, lacked independence, and concluded that no serious abuses took place. To date the government continues to restrict access of independent investigators into the area.

Relations in the Horn of Africa

In August the Eritrea-Ethiopia Claims Commission issued its final rulings on monetary damages stemming from the bloody 1998-2000 border war between Ethiopia and Eritrea. Nonetheless the two countries remain locked in an intractable dispute about the demarcation of the heavily militarized frontier. Eritrea continues to play a destabilizing role throughout the Horn of Africa through its efforts to undermine and attack the government of Ethiopia wherever possible. The government of President Isayas Afewerki hosts and materially supports fighters from Ethiopian rebel movements, including the Oromo Liberation Front. Eritrea has also pursued a policy of supporting armed opposition groups in Somalia as a way of undermining Ethiopia's support for the country's weak Transitional Federal Government.

Key International Actors

Ethiopia is one of the most aid-dependant countries in the world and received more than US$2 billion in 2009, but its major donors have been unwilling to confront the government over its worsening human rights record. Even as the country slides deeper into repression, the Ethiopian government uses development aid funding as leverage against the donors who provide it—many donors fear that the government would discontinue or scale back their aid programs should they speak out on human rights concerns. This trend is perhaps best exemplified by the United Kingdom, whose government has consistently chosen to remain silent in order to protect its annual £130 million worth of bilateral aid and development programs.

Donors are also fearful of jeopardizing access for humanitarian organizations to respond to the drought and worsening food crisis. Millions of Ethiopians depend on food aid, and the government has sought to minimize the scale of the crisis and restrict access for independent surveys and response.

While Ethiopia's government puts in place measures to control the elections in 2010, many donors have ignored the larger trends and focused instead on negotiating with the government to allow them to send election observers.

A significant shift in donor policy toward Ethiopia would likely have to be led by the US government, Ethiopia's largest donor and most important political ally on the world stage. But President Barack Obama's administration has yet to depart from the policies of the Bush administration, which consistently refused to speak out against abuses in Ethiopia. While the reasons may be different—the current government is not as narrowly focused on security cooperation with Ethiopia as was the Bush administration— thus far the practical results have been the same. The events described above attracted little public protest from the US government in 2009.

GUINEA

The bloodless coup in December 2008 by a group of young military officers following the death of Guinea's longtime authoritarian president, Lansana Conté, brought initial hope for improvement in Guinea's chronic human rights problems. However, this hope was dashed as the military government consolidated control of the country's political affairs, failed to hold free and fair elections as initially promised, and steadily and violently suppressed the opposition, culminating in a large-scale massacre of some 150 demonstrators in September 2009. The perpetrators of these abuses enjoyed near-complete impunity.

International actors—including France, the United States, the European Union, the Economic Community of West African States (ECOWAS), the African Union, and the United Nations—consistently denounced abuses by the coup government and, following the September violence, took concrete steps to both isolate the government and push for accountability for the violence, including through the formation of a UN-mandated international commission of inquiry.

Bloodless Coup and Reversed Promises

A group of Guinean military officers calling themselves the National Council for Democracy and Development (CNDD) seized power hours after the death, on December 22, 2008, of Lansana Conté, Guinea's president for 24 years. The coup leaders, led by a self-proclaimed president, Captain Moussa Dadis Camara, quickly suspended the country's constitution, and pledged to hold elections in 2009 and relinquish control to a civilian-led government.

With early public support, the CNDD committed to rooting out the high levels of corruption and involvement by officials in drug trafficking that plagued the country for years. However, the CNDD took few concrete steps to organize elections. Under mounting pressure from key international stakeholders, Dadis Camara, in August, set January 31, 2010, as the presidential election date. Shortly thereafter, he reversed his pledge not to run for office, saying that any member of the CNDD should be "free to put forward their candidacy for the national election if they so desire."

Dadis Camara's presumed candidacy, the appointment of military officers to all administrative posts country-wide, and CNDD control over most political and economic affairs of the state generated considerable domestic and international concern about the likelihood of free and fair elections.

Conduct of Security Forces

Throughout the year, Guinean soldiers were implicated in regular acts of theft, extortion, and violence against businesspeople and ordinary Guineans. Soldiers in groups numbering up to 20—nearly all heavily armed and in red berets typically worn by elite units—raided shops, warehouses, medical clinics, and homes in broad daylight and at night. Soldiers stole cars, computers, generators, medicine, jewelry, cash, mobile phones, and large quantities of wholesale and retail merchandise, among other items, from their victims, which included Guineans and foreigners. The victims were often also threatened or physically assaulted. Many of these abuses were committed within the context of the CNDD's crackdown against drug traffickers and corrupt practices. The CNDD undertook no efforts throughout the year to investigate or hold accountable soldiers implicated in these serious abuses.

Political Opposition and Freedom of Expression

Upon taking power, Dadis Camara quickly suspended the country's constitution, dissolved the parliament and government, and declared a ban on political and union activity. As opposition parties increased their campaign activities in anticipation of elections, the CNDD restricted freedoms of political expression and assembly through intimidation and attacks. At various times throughout the year, Dadis Camara lifted and reinstated the ban on political and union activity.

CNDD suppression of opposition supporters increased further in response to a wave of criticism and calls for mass demonstrations against the military that began in August. During a news conference on August 19, Dadis Camara warned political leaders not to protest publicly, saying, "Any political leader who makes trouble by organizing strikes or protests or any other form of mass mobilization will simply be removed from the list of candidates and will also be prosecuted." Opposition leaders who continued to criticize the CNDD were summoned to the

Alpha Yaya Diallo military camp—the ad hoc seat of government—and urged to desist from commenting on Dadis Camara's possible candidacy. In addition, the CNDD president imposed in late August a ban on mobile phone text-messaging and in September a ban on political discussions on popular radio-phone-in shows. Both bans were later lifted in response to domestic and international criticism.

September 28 Massacre

On September 28, 2009, tens of thousands of protestors gathered at the main stadium in the capital, Conakry, to demonstrate against continued military rule and Dadis Camara's presumed candidacy in the January 2010 presidential elections. In response to the peaceful demonstration, members of the Presidential Guard and some gendarmes working with the Anti-Drug and Anti-Organized Crime unit carried out a massacre that left some 150 people dead, many riddled with bullets and bayonet wounds, and others killed in the ensuing panic. The violence appeared to be premeditated and organized by senior CNDD officials. During the violence, the Presidential Guard fired directly into the crowd of protesters and carried out widespread rape and sexual violence against dozens of girls and women at the stadium and in the days following the crackdown, often with such extreme brutality that their victims died from the wounds inflicted. The armed forces then engaged in a systematic attempt to hide the evidence of the crimes during which they removed numerous bodies from the stadium and hospital morgues, allegedly burying them in mass graves. The CNDD claimed that opposition supporters had stolen arms from a police station, and that the 57 official dead had been mostly crushed to death after an altercation with the security forces.

Rule of Law

The rule of law in Guinea suffered serious setbacks in 2009. This was manifested in a further weakening of the judiciary due to meddling by the military, an official call for vigilante justice to be meted out against suspected thieves, and an attempt by the government to set up an informal, parallel judicial system run by the military from the Alpha Yaya Diallo military camp. Meanwhile, there were no attempts to investigate, much less hold accountable, those responsible for ongoing or past state-sponsored violations, most notably by members of the security services. This failure to act, coupled with a weak judiciary characterized by a lack of independence from the executive branch, inadequate resources, and corruption, has left ordinary Guineans with scant hope for redress.

Detention Conditions and Arbitrary Detention

Guinean prison and detention centers remain severely overcrowded and operate far below international standards. In 2009 the largest prison in Guinea housed over 1,000 prisoners in a facility designed for 300. Malnutrition and inadequate healthcare and sanitation led to numerous deaths in detention. Prison officials consistently fail to separate convicted and untried prisoners, and, in some centers, children from adults. Unpaid prison guards regularly extort money from prisoners and their families, exacerbating problems of hunger and malnutrition. Meanwhile, over 80 percent of those held in Guinea's largest prison have not been brought to trial; some have been awaiting trial for more than five years.

Prolonged arbitrary detention of perceived opponents of the CNDD government remains a serious human rights issue. From late December 2008 through October 2009, some 20 military personnel and an unknown number of men believed to be opposition supporters were detained without charge in several military detention centers in and around Conakry. Many of the military officers detained formed part of the late President Conté's Presidential Guard, while others were detained following an alleged coup attempt against the CNDD. Those in detention were subjected to various forms of mistreatment, including torture, and were often prevented from receiving family visits.

Key International Actors

The December 2008 coup, delays in organizing elections, and persistent abuses by the military, most notably those associated with the September violence, were met with consistent, strong, and unified condemnation by key international actors, including France, the United States, the European Union, ECOWAS, the African Union, and the United Nations. The international response was organized through an International Contact Group for Guinea, which consistently pressured the CNDD to respect human rights and organize elections without delay.

The September 28 violence was harshly denounced by Guinea's international partners, most notably by French Foreign Minister Bernard Kouchner and US Secretary of State Hillary Clinton. It also led to the imposition of arms embargos by ECOWAS and the EU, and travel bans and asset freezes of CNDD members by the EU, US, and AU, as well as the withdrawal or cancellation of economic and military assistance from the EU, US, and France.

The international community was equally definitive about the need for those responsible for the September violence, including Dadis Camara himself, to be held accountable. As a result, an AU and ECOWAS-proposed international commission of inquiry was established by the UN Security Council. The prosecutor of the International Criminal Court also initiated a preliminary examination—a move that may precede the opening of an investigation—of the situation in Guinea, which is a party to the court.

Unfortunately, continued economic and diplomatic support from Libya, Senegal, and China, which signed a large natural resources agreement just weeks after the September violence, threatened to undermine the otherwise united international response in favor of respect for rule of law and accountability.

KENYA

A damning United Nations report on widespread abuses by, and impunity of, the security forces was followed by the police commissioner's removal in August, but incidents of extrajudicial killings and excessive use of force by police and military continued unchecked in 2009. There were also renewed reports of systematic torture and mistreatment of civilians during disarmament operations. Kenya's coalition government, formed in the wake of the flawed 2007 general elections, made little progress in implementing promised reforms.

At least 50,000 new refugees fleeing the conflict in neighboring Somalia arrived in the dramatically overstretched Dadaab refugee camps in northeast Kenya in the first nine months of 2009, prompting urgent calls for additional donor aid and more land for new camps.

Accountability for Post-Election Violence

More than 1,000 people lost their lives and an estimated 300,000 were displaced from their homes in the violence that followed the December 2007 elections. The coalition government formed in February 2008 had agreed to implement the recommendations of a commission established to investigate the post-election violence (known as the Waki Commission for its chairperson, Justice Philip Waki). The commission recommended in October 2008 that the government establish a national tribunal to investigate and prosecute those most responsible for the violence, or refer the crimes to the International Criminal Court.

Instead of implementing these recommendations, the government dragged its feet throughout 2009. Government officials failed to fully support a national tribunal, and several attempts to introduce a bill to establish the tribunal failed to muster enough support in parliament. The government has not made a referral to the ICC at this writing, despite agreeing in a July 2009 meeting with ICC officials to do so if the national option failed to coalesce. In November the ICC prosecutor announced that he would seek authority from the ICC's pretrial chamber to begin investigations in Kenya. Even if the ICC does investigate a small number of those deemed most responsible for the crimes, Kenya will still require a national mechanism that is independent of the existing judicial system to investigate and pros-ecute other perpetrators.

Extrajudicial Executions and Enforced Disappearances

The police regularly targeted civilians for killings and other violence in 2009, as in previous years. Members of rival factions within the regular and administration police were also victims of extrajudicial killings. The UN special rapporteur on extrajudicial, summary or arbitrary executions, Philip Alston, investigated police abuses and other serious crimes in the course of the government's 2008 coun-terinsurgency campaign in Mt. Elgon, during a February 2009 visit to Kenya.

In his report to the UN Human Rights Council, Alston noted widespread extrajudi-cial killings by the police that "clearly implicated senior officials," including the police commissioner. He also found compelling evidence that at least 200 people had been killed or were "disappeared" by the security forces in Mt. Elgon. Alston called for Police Commissioner Hussein Ali to be replaced and for Attorney General Amos Wako to resign, singling them out as key individuals "with direct responsibility for the current state of affairs." Ali was replaced as police commis-sioner in August, but the government failed to investigate or prosecute security forces implicated in the Mt. Elgon abuses.

Torture and Ill-Treatment in Security Operations

Allegations of torture and ill-treatment of civilians by police and military in the course of an October 2008 joint police-military disarmament operation in Mandera district surfaced within days of the start of the operation. Human Rights Watch investigated the allegations in northeast Kenya in February 2009 and found that security forces tortured scores of men, beat and injured at least 1,200 people (including one man who died from his wounds), and raped at least a dozen women over the course of the three-day operation. Human Rights Watch called for an independent investigation into the abuses and for prosecutions of the officers responsible for directing the operation, neither of which occurred.

In February 2009 similar abuses were reported in Samburu when, in response to fighting between different groups, the Kenyan police and military confiscated cattle and beat civilians.

Human Rights Defenders

Bernard Kiriinya, a whistleblower from the Kenya police who had supplied information about police extrajudicial executions to the Kenya National Commission on Human Rights (KNCHR), was assassinated in October 2008. Witnesses who had provided information to the Waki Commission in 2008 were also threatened and some went into witness protection programs. Three human rights groups reported intimidation by state agents because of their persistent calls for justice and accountability.

Following the visit of the UN special rapporteur on extrajudicial executions, human rights defenders who had provided information to him were harassed and intimidated in Mt. Elgon and Nairobi; some fled the country for several months. The assassination, in Nairobi, of Oscar Kamau Kingara and John Paul Oulu of the Oscar Foundation Free Legal Aid Clinic on March 5 shocked Kenya's human rights community and highlighted the growing threats to Kenyan civil society activists in 2009. Kingara and Oulu had been prominent campaigners on the issue of police killings of members of the Mungiki, a criminal gang. Many suspected police involvement in the murders, and Prime Minister Raila Odinga publicly voiced this suspicion in a statement.

The killings of Kingara and Oulu followed the murder, on January 29, of Francis Nyaruri, a journalist who had written extensively about corruption and malpractice by the police in Nyanza province. The police officer assigned to investigate Nyaruri's murder also faced intimidation and harassment from his fellow police officers.

"Bring the Gun or You'll Die"

Torture, Rape and Other Serious Human Rights Violations
by Kenyan Security Forces in the Mandera Triangle

**H U M A N
R I G H T S
W A T C H**

Health Issues and the HIV/AIDS Epidemic

Children's access to health services, including HIV treatment, continues to pose serious challenges. While the number of children receiving antiretroviral treatmet rose significantly in 2009, to around 28,000, tens of thousands of children still remained without access to the life-saving drugs.

Criminalization of same-sex activities drives lesbian, gay, bisexual, and transgender young people and adults away from accessing HIV/AIDS prevention, treatment, and care.

The government health budget, an estimated 7 percent of total expenditure, fell far below the government's commitment to devoting 15 percent of the budget to health. The child protection system remained weak, and many children, including orphans, failed to get medical care because of neglect and abuse by their carers.

Somali Refugees

As of October 2009 the almost twenty-year-old refugee camps in Dadaab, northeast Kenya, held around 280,000 mostly Somali refugees, more than three times their initial planned capacity. At least 50,000 of the refugees were new arrivals in 2009. The massive overcrowding has resulted in appalling conditions, with insufficient shelter, water, and other services. By October donors had committed around US$40 million to Dadaab, about 45 percent of the estimated needs. The Kenyan government failed to provide more land for new camps, despite lengthy negotiations with the UN High Commissioner for Refugees.

Many of the new refugees from Somalia faced abuses at the hands of Kenyan police while crossing the officially-closed border.

As the Somali crisis intensified throughout 2009, there were growing reports that Somali refugees in Kenya were being targeted for recruitment by parties to the armed conflict in Somalia, including the Transitional Federal Government (TFG) and al Shabaab, an Islamist opposition group. The recruitment of refugees violates the fundamental principle in international law that refugee camps should be entirely civilian and humanitarian in character.

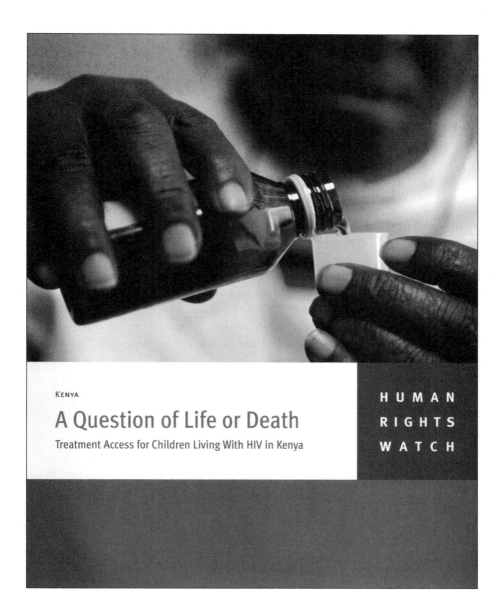

KENYA

A Question of Life or Death

Treatment Access for Children Living With HIV in Kenya

HUMAN
RIGHTS
WATCH

In October Human Rights Watch documented a recruitment drive, on behalf of the TFG and supported by the Kenyan authorities, that swept up Kenyan nationals alongside hundreds of Somali men and children from the Dadaab camps. The men and youths were often duped into enlisting by tales of high salaries and UN or international support for the force, and were then taken to a Kenyan military facility for training. Human Rights Watch also received credible accounts of al Shabaab forcibly recruiting men and boys, both within south/central Somalia (see Somalia chapter), and to a lesser extent, inside Somali refugee communities in Kenya.

Key International Actors

Most of Kenya's international partners, including the African Union, are united in putting pressure on Kenya's coalition government to deliver the reforms it agreed to implement in 2008. Accountability for the post-election violence is widely viewed as a crucial first step to ensure that the violence does not recur, particularly with elections scheduled for 2012. Former UN Secretary-General Kofi Annan, the chief mediator who negotiated the grand coalition, criticized the parties for failing to make progress when visiting in October 2009, stating that violence "is a serious risk if tangible reform is not achieved." The United States sent letters to key government officials warning that their future relationship with the US will be "tied to their support for implementation of the reform agenda and opposition to the use of violence." The US indicated in September that it would deny visas to senior officials implicated in post-election violence or who obstructed the reform process in Kenya, and in October denied Amos Wako a visa.

Regionally, the conflict in Somalia—and the growing strength of the al Shabaab faction of the insurgency—remains a key concern for Kenya. The Kenyan government has been strongly supportive of Somalia's TFG and has become increasingly apprehensive about the possibility of terrorist attacks on its soil carried out by al Shabaab.

KENYA

From Horror to Hopelessness

Kenya's Forgotten Somali Refugee Crisis

HUMAN
RIGHTS
WATCH

LIBERIA

Striking deficiencies within Liberia's rule of law sectors resulted in persistent human rights violations and undermined President Ellen Johnson Sirleaf's post-war recovery, anti-corruption, and development agendas. The increasing incidence of violent crime as well as protests by disgruntled youths, mob and vigilante justice, and bloody land disputes claimed numerous lives and exposed the systemic and persistent weaknesses within the police, judiciary, and corrections sectors. Concern about inadequate progress in strengthening the rule of law was exacerbated by several risk factors, notably the global economic crisis, high unemployment, and growing insecurity in neighboring Guinea and Côte d'Ivoire.

Sweeping changes in the leadership of the security and justice sectors in mid-2009 brought some hope of improvement and dispelled growing criticism at home and from donors. Meanwhile the government made tangible progress in creating the legislative framework for respect for human rights and improving access to key economic rights, including healthcare and primary education.

The June release of the draft concluding report of Liberia's Truth and Reconciliation Commission (TRC) generated considerable controversy about its recommendations to establish a tribunal to prosecute abusers and publicly sanction erstwhile supporters of the warring factions, including President Johnson Sirleaf.

Ongoing Insecurity, Police Conduct, and the Criminal Justice System

The security situation deteriorated in 2009 as evidenced in an increasing incidence of violent crime, including armed robbery and rape; violent protests over layoffs and employment disputes by youths and former combatants; and deadly land disputes. The undisciplined, poorly managed, and ill-equipped Liberian police were challenged to maintain law and order, on several occasions necessitating the intervention of United Nations peacekeepers deployed to Liberia since 2003. Lack of public confidence in the police and judicial system perpetuated the culture of impunity and led to mob attacks on alleged criminals, resulting in at least eight deaths.

Since 2004 the UN Mission in Liberia (UNMIL) has vetted and trained over 3,500 police officers, and, together with international donors, has set up numerous police stations and barracks. Nonetheless, Liberian police continue to engage in unprofessional and sometimes criminal behavior, including extortion, bribery, and armed robbery; frequent absenteeism; and failure to adequately investigate and later freeing alleged criminals. Lack of funding for transportation, communications, and forensic equipment further undermine the effectiveness of the national police, especially in rural areas.

The police did, however, show some progress in 2009 in their ability to detain and arrest alleged suspects and escaped criminals, and police leadership showed an increased willingness to investigate complaints of misconduct within the force.

Persistent deficiencies within Liberia's judiciary led to widespread abuses of the right to due process and undermined efforts to address impunity. Weaknesses are attributable to insufficient judicial personnel, including prosecutors and public defenders, limited court infrastructure and logistics, archaic rules of procedure, and poor case management. Unprofessional, corrupt, and, in a few cases, criminal practices by judicial staff continue to lead to rights abuses and undermine progress.

Because of the courts' inability to adequately process their cases, hundreds of prisoners continued to be held in extended pretrial detention in overcrowded jails and detention centers that lack basic sanitation and healthcare; in 2009 only 10 percent of the some 800 individuals detained in Liberia's prisons had been convicted of a crime. Meanwhile, hundreds of prisoners escaped in jailbreaks, illuminating the stark inability of the corrections sector to secure Liberia's prisons.

In June the president took concrete action to improve the weak leadership underpinning these problems by replacing the ministers of justice and national security, the solicitor-general, and the director of the Liberia National Police, among others. The president also ordered a review of pretrial detainees within Monrovia's central prison, resulting in the release of hundreds of prisoners detained on minor charges or who had already served sufficient time.

Harmful Traditional Practices

Serious abuses resulting from harmful traditional practices continued to occur in 2009, due in part to the absence or distrust of judicial authorities. These included the killing of alleged witches and "trials by ordeal," in which suspects are forced to swallow the poisonous sap of a tree or endure burning; their alleged guilt or innocence is determined by whether they survive.

Sexual Violence

The incidence of rape of women and girls continued to be alarmingly high in 2009, despite positive efforts by the government and UNMIL, including the establishment of a dedicated court for sexual violence. While public reporting of and police response to reports of rape improved somewhat, efforts to prosecute these cases are hampered by deficiencies in the justice system.

Corruption

Fighting endemic corruption was high on the president's agenda throughout 2009, but weaknesses within the judicial system undermined these efforts. The June acquittal of high-ranking public officials from the 2003-05 transitional government for the embezzlement of several million dollars was a blow to these efforts and in part led to the sweeping leadership changes in the Ministry of Justice. Over the course of the year the president sacked and referred for investigation scores of public officials, including high-level ministry personnel, county superintendants, and senior central bank officials. Corrupt practices have long undermined the provision of basic education and healthcare to the most vulnerable.

In July 2009 the president signed into law the Liberia Extractive Industries Transparency Initiative; Liberia is the first country in the world to include forestry and rubber into an EITI mandate.

Legislative Developments

During 2009 the government made further strides in creating the legislative framework for respect for human rights and good governance. Progress included the establishment of the Constitutional Review Task Force, the Law Reform Commission mandated to review Liberia's outdated laws, and the Land Commission to address the growing number of land disputes.

After a disappointing delay of four years, the proposed amendments holding up the establishment of the Independent National Commission on Human Rights were finally signed by the president, although at year's end the commission was yet to be constituted due to delays in parliamentary confirmation of its commissioners.

The Truth and Reconciliation Commission and Accountability

Liberia has not to date brought prosecutions against those allegedly responsible for serious crimes of international law committed during its armed conflicts. In June Liberia's TRC concluded its four-year mandate and began finalizing its report for submission to the legislature and president, as well as civil society and international partners. A published draft highlighted the role played by corruption and poor management of natural resources in giving rise to Liberia's armed conflicts, and concluded that all warring factions were responsible for gross human rights violations, including war crimes and crimes against humanity. The report's recommendations, which included the establishment of an extraordinary criminal tribunal to prosecute over 100 of the most notorious perpetrators and the barring from public office of some 50 former supporters of the warring factions, were greeted with considerable controversy and some threats by former faction leaders. The legislature's formal debate of the report was postponed until early 2010.

Throughout the year there was significant civil society support for prosecutions, although serious questions remain about the political will of both the Liberian government and the international donor community to establish the recommended accountability mechanism, which calls for the inclusion of foreign judges. Efforts at justice are further complicated by problems with the quality of the TRC's report, weaknesses within the Liberian judicial system, the potential for the legislature to block accountability efforts, and the existence of a 2003 act that granted immunity for war crimes committed from 1989 through 2003.

Disarmament of Former Combatants

Since the end of the war in 2003, 101,000 former combatants have been disarmed and some 97,000 have received vocational training or education in association with the demobilization program, which formally closed in July 2009. Violent demonstrations staged by former combatants, rising unemployment, and reports that many Liberian former fighters have joined Ivorian militia and rebel groups and Guinean security forces, remain a serious concern for sustained peace.

Liberian Army

The program funded and led by the United States to recruit and train a new 2,000-strong Liberian army completed its work in December 2009. During the exercise, implemented by the US contractor DynCorp, recruits were vetted for past abuses. Continued training of the officer corps will be conducted by the United States, the Economic Community of West African States, and the United Nations. The army is not expected to be fully operational until 2012.

Key International Actors

Threats to regional stability and weaknesses in security and rule of law institutions that could reverse hard-earned post-war gains generated considerable concern among Liberia's key international and development partners, most notably the UN and US. Visits by the UN Security Council, UN under-secretary-general for peacekeeping operations, and US Secretary of State Hillary Clinton pressed home these concerns.

The United States is Liberia's largest donor, and in fiscal year 2008-09 contributed more than US$200 million to support democratization, security, and reconstruction efforts.

In December 2008 the UN Security Council renewed for one year the arms and travel bans on associates of former President Charles Taylor, as well as the mandate for the panel of experts charged with monitoring the implementation of sanctions and resource exploitation. In September 2009 the Council renewed UNMIL's mandate for one year. In 2008 Liberia was declared eligible for US$15 million in funds administered by the UN Peacebuilding Commission.

NIGERIA

More than halfway through his term in office, President Umaru Yar'Adua and his administration have done little to improve Nigeria's poor human rights record. Bloody sectarian clashes claimed hundreds of lives in late 2008 and 2009, while the government failed to investigate, much less hold accountable, members of the security forces implicated in numerous incidents of extrajudicial killings, torture, and extortion. The government's amnesty for militants in the Niger Delta failed to address the root causes of the violence.

Despite limited gains from anti-corruption efforts, Nigeria's political leaders continued to enjoy near-total impunity for massive corruption and sponsoring political violence. The National Assembly failed again to pass legislation to improve transparency and good governance. Nonetheless, free speech and the independent press remain fairly robust. Foreign partners took some positive steps in confronting endemic corruption in Nigeria, but appeared reluctant to exert meaningful pressure on Nigeria over its human rights record.

Government Corruption

Nigeria's fledgling anti-corruption campaign produced mixed results in 2009. In October a powerful ruling People's Democratic Party (PDP) chieftain, Olabode George, was convicted for financial crimes, in the most significant conviction secured by Nigeria's anti-corruption body since Yar'Adua came to power. The new chairman of the central bank, Lamido Sanusi, sacked the chief executives of eight Nigerian banks due to financial mismanagement and fraud. Farida Waziri, the head of the Economic and Financial Crimes Commission (EFCC), promptly filed corruption charges against several of the bankers, but failed to indict key politicians credibly implicated in the massive looting of the state treasury, including former Rivers State governor Peter Odili. Several other high-profile corruption cases initiated by Waziri's predecessor at the EFCC have been effectively stalled. Meanwhile, the country's tremendous oil wealth, which could have been used to improve the lives of ordinary Nigerians, continues to be squandered and siphoned off by the governing elite, leaving poverty, malnutrition, and mortality rates among the worst in the world.

Intercommunal and Political Violence

Intercommunal, political, and sectarian violence have claimed the lives of more than 13,500 people during the past decade in Nigeria. Nigeria's politicians continue to manipulate ethnic and religious tensions by sponsoring violence for personal political gain, and widespread poverty and poor governance have created an environment where militant groups can thrive. Violent clashes in July between government security forces and a militant Islamist group in northern Nigeria known as Boko Haram left at least 800 dead; according to the government, most of those killed were militants. Members of the Boko Haram group also burned churches and attacked and killed Christians during the violence. In November 2008 more than 700 people were killed during two days of Christian-Muslim sectarian clashes following a disputed local government election in the central city of Jos. Intercommunal tensions are exacerbated by state and local government policies that discriminate against "non-indigenes"—people who cannot trace their ancestry to what are said to be the original inhabitants of an area.

Yar'Adua had pledged to reform Nigeria's broken electoral system, but in 2009 rejected core recommendations of his electoral reform committee. The Supreme Court, in December 2008, upheld Yar'Adua's own controversial 2007 election. The government has still not held accountable those responsible for the 2007 election violence that left at least 300 dead, while a closely fought gubernatorial election rerun in Ekiti State in April 2009 was again marred by violence, vote-rigging, and fraud. Nonetheless, Nigeria's judiciary continues to exercise a degree of independence in electoral matters: Since 2007 the courts have overturned one-third of the PDP gubernatorial election victories on grounds of electoral malpractice or other irregularities.

Conduct of Security Forces

The government demonstrated a lack of political will to reform the police, who were again implicated in numerous extrajudicial killings of persons in custody, torture of criminal suspects, and widespread extortion and corruption. On July 30, 2009, the police in the northern city of Maiduguri brazenly executed the Boko Haram leader Mohammed Yusuf in police custody. The following day his father-in-law, Baba Mohammed, and a former state government official suspected of funding Boko Haram, Buji Foi, were also reportedly killed in police custody. Yar'Adua promised to promptly investigate these killings, but at this writing no one has been held accountable.

In November 2008 the police and military were credibly implicated in more than 130 unlawful killings while responding to the election-related violence in Jos. At this writing a panel set up by Yar'Adua to investigate the Jos violence is scheduled to begin hearings in December 2009. The government has still not held members of the security forces accountable for past crimes, including the massacre of more than 200 people by the military in Benue State in 2001 and the military's complete destruction of the town of Odi, Bayelsa State, in 1999.

Violence and Poverty in the Niger Delta

An amnesty for armed militants in the oil-rich Niger Delta led several thousand men, including top militant commanders, to surrender weapons to the government. Since the latest escalation of violence began in early 2006, hundreds of people have been killed in clashes between rival armed groups vying for illicit patronage doled out by corrupt politicians, or between militants and government security forces. Armed gangs have carried out numerous attacks on oil facilities and kidnapped more than 500 oil workers and ordinary Nigerians for ransom during this period. The amnesty offer, announced in June 2009, followed a major military offensive in May against militants in the creeks of Delta State, which left scores dead and thousands of residents displaced.

The government's blanket amnesty, cash payouts to armed militants, and a proposal to give oil-producing communities a 10 percent stake in government oil ventures bought some respite from militant attacks, but further entrenched impunity and failed to address the government corruption, political sponsorship of violence, and environmental degradation that underlie the violence and discontent in the Niger Delta. A similar amnesty granted to rival armed groups in 2004 failed to end the Niger Delta violence.

Human Rights Concerns in the Context of Sharia

Twelve state governments in northern Nigeria continue to apply Sharia law as part of their criminal justice system. Sentencing provisions such as the death penalty, amputations, and floggings amount to cruel, inhuman, and degrading punishment. Although the death sentences appealed to date have been overturned, lower Sharia courts continue to hand them down. Serious due process concerns also exist in Sharia proceedings. Most defendants are tried without legal representation. Judges are poorly trained and, as is also common in Nigeria's conventional criminal courts, often rely on statements that were extracted by the police through torture. Evidentiary standards in the Sharia codes discriminate against women, particularly in adultery cases where standards of evidence differ for men and women.

Sexual Orientation and Gender Identity

Nigeria's federal criminal code punishes consensual homosexual conduct with up to 14 years in prison. In the states applying Sharia, consensual homosexual conduct among men is punishable by death by stoning, and by flogging in the case of women. Draft federal legislation that would criminalize anyone who enters into or assists a "same gender" marriage was introduced in the House of Representatives in December 2008.

Freedom of Expression and the Media

Civil society and the independent press openly criticize the government and its policies, allowing for robust public debate. However, journalists are still subject to intimidation and violence when reporting on issues implicating the political and economic elite. On September 20, 2009, Bayo Ohu, the deputy political editor of the *Guardian*, one of Nigeria's largest newspapers, was gunned down at the entrance to his home. During the April elections in Ekiti State, PDP members reportedly detained and assaulted three journalists inside the state government headquarters. Journalists working for local media outlets generally enjoy considerably less freedom than their national counterparts and are more often subjected to harassment by government officials.

Health and Human Rights

Health indicators, including those for infant and child mortality and women's reproductive health and maternal mortality, remain some of the worst worldwide. An estimated 250,000 terminal cancer and HIV/AIDS patients suffer in pain needlessly as a result of the government's failure to provide access to inexpensive pain medications such as morphine.

Key International Actors

Because of Nigeria's role as a regional power, leading oil exporter, and major contributor of troops to United Nations peacekeeping missions, foreign governments—including the United States and the United Kingdom—have been reluctant to publicly criticize Nigeria's poor human rights record.

Although US Secretary of State Hillary Clinton spoke out forcefully against endemic government corruption during her August visit to Nigeria, she was unwilling to publicly condemn the serious abuses committed by Nigeria's security forces. The UK government continued to play a leading role in international efforts to combat money laundering by corrupt Nigerian officials. However, in fiscal year 2009 it provided £132 million in aid to Nigeria, including security sector aid, without demanding accountability for Nigerian officials and members of the security forces implicated in corrupt practices or serious human rights abuses.

Multinational oil companies operating in the Niger Delta did little to curb pollution and environmentally harmful gas flaring and oil spills caused by ageing and poorly maintained infrastructure.

In its February review under the Universal Periodic Review mechanism, the UN Human Rights Council recommended, among other things, that Nigeria improve its legal framework for the protection of human rights, declare a moratorium on the death penalty, end torture, and reform the police and criminal justice sector.

RWANDA

Rwanda in 2009 saw increasing government restrictions on political space and individual freedoms, growing intolerance of criticism of state policies, and a refusal to allow any discussion of ethnicity, leading to concerns of heightened repression among human rights groups and several international donors. Preparations for the 2010 presidential election raised fears of intimidation and violence within local communities and led to a handful of arrests of individuals supporting the formation of new political parties.

Community-based *gacaca* courts and national conventional courts continued to try individuals for crimes committed during the 1994 genocide. *Gacaca* courts were expected to close in June 2009, but the National Service of Gacaca Jurisdictions (SNJG) unexpectedly began gathering new allegations in parts of the country and extended the deadline to December. While some Rwandans feel the *gacaca* process has helped reconciliation, others point to corruption and argue that the accused receive sentences that are too lenient, or are convicted on flimsy evidence. The government increasingly but unsuccessfully called for foreign jurisdictions, including the International Criminal Tribunal for Rwanda (ICTR) in Tanzania, and several European countries, to return genocide suspects to Rwanda. It vehemently rejected calls for the ICTR to prosecute crimes committed by the Rwandan Patriotic Front in 1994.

Gacaca Jurisdictions

Corruption and undue influence by local authorities and other prominent community members marred *gacaca* proceedings, undermining trust among victims and the accused. According to the SNJG, *gacaca* courts have decided nearly 1.6 million genocide cases since their start in 2002. Recent cases increasingly related to government silencing of political dissent and private grievances, rather than events from 1994, led many Rwandans to flee the country to escape condemnation or perceived threats of renewed prosecution.

Gacaca courts spent much of the year trying thousands of sexual violence and other particularly serious cases, and imposed mandatory lifetime solitary confinement for convicted persons. In the absence of legislation setting out the implementation of this punishment, prison authorities did not isolate prisoners. Rape victims uniformly expressed disappointment at having to appear in *gacaca* rather than conventional courts, as *gacaca* proceedings—even behind closed doors—failed to protect their privacy.

Conventional Courts

With most genocide cases transferred to the *gacaca* system in 2008, conventional courts presided over only a handful of such cases in 2009, including that of Agnès Ntamabyariro, minister of justice in the post-genocide interim government, who was sentenced to lifetime solitary confinement.

Former Transport Minister Charles Ntakirutinka remained in prison, serving a 10-year sentence imposed after a flawed 2004 trial for his role in establishing a new political party, together with former President Pasteur Bizimungu, who was pardoned and released in 2007.

In January 2009 Rwanda's military captured Congolese rebel leader Laurent Nkunda, who at this writing remains in custody without charge or trial, in violation of Rwandan criminal procedure. The courts rejected all attempts to challenge the legality of his detention, and the government declined to respond to the Democratic Republic of Congo's extradition request.

Rwandan Patriotic Front Crimes

Rwanda strongly opposed renewed calls for prosecution of members of the now-governing Rwandan Patriotic Front (RPF) who committed crimes during the genocide. Despite estimates by the United Nations High Commissioner for Refugees that the RPF killed between 25,000 and 45,000 civilians in 1994, Rwanda has tried only 36 soldiers. These include four military officers charged with murdering 15 civilians (including 13 clergy) and tried perfunctorily in 2008. In February 2009 the military appeals court upheld the acquittals of the two more senior officers and reduced the junior officers' sentences from eight to five years' imprisonment.

In June the ICTR prosecutor told the UN Security Council that this RPF trial had met fair trial standards, and that he had no other RPF indictments ready to pursue. At an international conference assessing the legacy of the ICTR in July, many participants deemed the prosecutor's decision not to indict any RPF crimes to be the Tribunal's greatest failure.

International Justice

As in previous years, securing justice for genocide suspects living outside Rwanda remained elusive. Rwandan prosecutors reinforced efforts to secure suspects' extradition to Rwanda, including pairing up with US network NBC for a live television program aimed at confronting with genocide accusations a Rwandan man teaching at a Maryland university. NBC scrapped the program after it came under criticism for politicizing justice and engaging in an unethical journalism practice.

In April 2009 the UK High Court denied the extradition of four Rwandan genocide suspects, concluding they could not be fairly tried in Rwanda. Sweden consented to an extradition request in July, although an appeal lodged before the European Court of Human Rights halted the extradition and has yet to be decided. Rwanda repeated its call to the ICTR to transfer cases to Rwanda, and amended legislation seeking to secure such transfers, but no new transfer requests were filed at the ICTR.

Human Rights and Individual Liberties

Government restrictions on free speech, reproductive health, homosexuality, political association, and land use signaled increased repression and lack of freedom in Rwanda. Opposition to government policies often led the government to accuse its critics of engaging in "genocide ideology," a vaguely defined offense established in 2008 that does not require any intent to assist, facilitate, or incite violence on the basis of ethnicity. Penalties range from 10 to 25 years in prison and fines up to US$2,000, while political groups and non-profit organizations risk disbandment upon conviction. Children of any age may be sent away to rehabilitation centers for up to one year under the law—including for the teasing of classmates—and their parents and teachers face sentences of 15 to 25 years for the child's conduct.

Working groups in Parliament contemplated, and then tabled, a bill forcing couples to test for HIV before marriage or whenever a spouse requests, and requiring the forced sterilization of individuals with intellectual disabilities if three doctors so recommend. At this writing Parliament is debating a new penal code criminalizing homosexuality and providing for sentences of 5-10 years' imprisonment and significant fines. As warned by the UN Human Rights Committee in March 2009, criminalizing homosexuality would place Rwanda in violation of its obligations under the International Covenant on Civil and Political Rights (ICCPR).

Two new political parties faced difficulties in obtaining the government registration necessary to participate in the 2010 presidential election. Both groups had meetings broken up by police and party members arrested, particularly the Parti Social Imberakuri.

The government continued to roll out its land policy, directing farmers to plant only the officially designated crop for their region. Aimed at replacing subsistence farming with a fully professional agricultural industry by 2020, the policy is often enforced aggressively by local officials who uproot crops and threaten to appropriate land when a farmer fails to comply. Critics suggest that the program places farmers at risk of food insecurity and may lead to increased poverty.

The government continued expropriating land in less developed neighborhoods in Kigali and other urban areas for commercial buildings. The policy disproportionately affected poorer communities, providing landholders with inadequate compensation and little choice but to move to distant government settlements and indebt themselves to the government for any difference in value between their original property and the new land offered to them.

Media Freedom

In April 2009 the government suspended the BBC's Kinyarwanda service, alleging it provided a platform to genocide deniers. The suspension, lifted two months later, formed part of a broader pattern of government interference in the media. In assessing Rwanda's ICCPR compliance, the UN Human Rights Committee in March expressed concern over reports that the government subjected journalists critical of government policies to intimidation and harassment and charged journalists with "divisionism," a term often used interchangeably with genocide ideology.

At a presidential press conference in July, Rwanda's minister of information stated that "the days of [leading independent newspapers] *Umuseso* and *Umuvugizi* are numbered." Within days the Media High Council, which regulates the profession, recommended a three-month suspension of *Umuseso* for an article critical of President Paul Kagame, and prosecutors launched criminal defamation proceedings against the editor of *Umuvugizi* for an article exposing a sex scandal involving a high-ranking national prosecutor.

A new media law passed in August bans all Rwandan journalists without a university degree or certificate from working in the field; most independent Rwandan journalists have neither. The legislation also imposes a wide range of restrictions on gathering and reporting information, and maintains defamation as a criminal offense.

Key International Actors

Donors provide generous support to Rwanda, emphasizing its economic growth and relative stability in the region. However, the Netherlands and Sweden suspended all direct budget support in December 2008 after the release of a UN report exposing Rwanda's support of a Tutsi rebel movement in the Democratic Republic of Congo; neither has resumed assistance at this writing.

The United Kingdom remains the largest bilateral donor and successfully pushed for electoral reforms before 2010's election. Germany and Rwanda restored diplomatic relations after interrupting them in November 2008 over the arrest of Rose Kabuye under a French indictment for alleged participation in the 1994 shooting down of former president Habyarimana's plane. Rwanda also strengthened economic ties with China.

SIERRA LEONE

Throughout 2009 the government of President Ernest Bai Koroma made notable progress in addressing endemic corruption and weak rule of law, thus distancing Sierra Leone further from the issues that gave rise to its 11-year armed conflict that ended in 2002. However persistent weaknesses within the police and judiciary, and several risk factors—notably the global economic crisis, high unemployment, and growing insecurity in neighboring Guinea— illuminated the fragility of these gains.

An outbreak of politically motivated violence between supporters of the ruling All People's Congress and the Sierra Leone People's Party in early 2009 showed the weakness of the Sierra Leone police and judiciary, which failed to adequately investigate and hold accountable those responsible. However, swift reconciliation efforts by the President avoided a deepening of the crisis.

Through the efforts of the United Nations-mandated Special Court for Sierra Leone, there was significant progress in achieving accountability for war crimes committed during the country's civil war. However, there was little improvement in access to key economic rights including healthcare and primary education. Sierra Leoneans suffer the highest maternal mortality rates in the world.

Corruption

President Koroma and the Anti-Corruption Commission (ACC) continued to take meaningful steps to address the scourge of corruption that has for decades posed a major obstacle to development. During 2009 the ACC used its independent powers to investigate, prosecute, and secure 11 convictions, including that of a former ombudsman; at this writing dozens of other cases are in court. By October the equivalent of more than US$375,000 in stolen state assets had been recovered by the ACC. In November the ACC indicted the health minister for illegally awarding contracts; he was at the same time removed from his post by the president. Following Koroma's lead in 2008, nearly all senior government officials and parliamentarians had declared their assets, and in an unprecedented move, employees of the notoriously corrupt ministries of health, education, and lands were suspended and referred for investigation for corrupt practices. Concern remained, however, that the ACC had failed to take adequate action against at least one minister exposed for awarding illegal contracts.

Rule of Law

Serious deficiencies in the judicial system persist, including extortion and bribe-taking by officials; insufficient numbers of judges, magistrates, and prosecuting attorneys; absenteeism by court personnel; and inadequate remuneration for judiciary personnel. In 2009 some 90 percent of prisoners lacked any legal representation. Hundreds of people—over 40 percent of the country's detainees—were held in prolonged pretrial detention.

Local court officials frequently abuse their powers by illegally detaining persons, charging high fines for minor offenses, and adjudicating criminal cases beyond their jurisdiction. The only legal system accessible to some 70 percent of the population is one based on customary courts controlled by traditional leaders and applying customary law, which is often discriminatory, particularly against women.

A prison reform project somewhat reduced the chronic overcrowding in Sierra Leone's prisons. However, inadequate food, clothing, medicine, hygiene, and sanitation remained of serious concern. The population of the country's largest detention facility—designed for 350 detainees—stands at over 1,100. In October the government announced the reconstruction of a prison at Mafanta, planned to house several hundred inmates and help relieve the problem of overcrowding.

The completion in April of a high-profile drug trafficking case in which 15 Sierra Leoneans and Latin Americans were convicted of drug-related offences demonstrated some improvement in the capacity of the rule of law sectors.

A concerted effort by the government, UN, and United Kingdom-funded Justice Sector Development Programme (JSDP) to improve the rule of law continued to make incremental improvements in the sector, including slight improvements in healthcare and access to water for detainees, record-keeping, and pilot programs to increase the numbers of magistrates available to adjudicate cases.

Police and Army Conduct

In September police used live ammunition to break up a demonstration about crime levels and police involvement in a spate of armed robberies, leaving three demonstrators dead and some 10 injured. Other deficiencies in police professionalism included persistent allegations of crime victims being required to pay for reports to be filed or investigations conducted, and alleged police involvement in extortion and other criminal acts. However, senior police leadership demonstrated an increased willingness to investigate, discipline, and dismiss officers engaging in unprofessional or corrupt practices.

The UK-led International Military Advisory and Training Team (IMATT) has been working since 1999 to reform and advise the Republic of Sierra Leone Armed Forces (RSLAF). The restoration in 2009 of a court martial board within the RSLAF was an important step in ensuring discipline within the army. In 2009 IMATT continued to assist in downsizing the force, with the joint goal of 8,500 troops expected to be met by early 2010.

Accountability for Past Abuses

The last case to be tried at the Special Court for Sierra Leone's (SCSL) location in Freetown concluded in October after the appeals chamber decision upheld the trial chamber's February conviction of three former leaders of the rebel Revolutionary United Front, Issa Hassan Sesay, Morris Kallon, and Augustine Gbao. The three were sentenced in April to a range of between 25 and 52 years each on charges of war crimes and crimes against humanity that included (for the first time in an international court) forced marriage and attacks against UN peacekeepers, as well as rape, murder, mutilation, enslavement, and recruitment of child soldiers. To date, eight individuals associated with the three main warring factions have been tried and convicted by the SCSL. All eight were transferred in late October to Rwanda to serve out their sentences in a section of a prison that meets international standards.

The SCSL trial of former Liberian president Charles Taylor—charged with 11 counts of war crimes and crimes against humanity for his role in supporting Sierra Leonean rebel groups during the conflict—made notable progress in 2009. In February the prosecution finished its presentation of 91 witnesses. In July Taylor took the stand as the first witness in the defense's case, and testified for many weeks. Taylor is the first sitting African head of state to be indicted and face trial before an international or hybrid war crimes tribunal. For security reasons his trial is taking place in The Hague, Netherlands, instead of Freetown.

A long-awaited reparations program to war victims, as recommended by the Truth and Reconciliation Commission, registered some 28,000 war victims and initiated programs to provide medical and financial assistance to victims. The program was funded by the UN Peacebuilding Fund.

National Human Rights Commission

The National Human Rights Commission struggled to carry out its mandate to investigate and report on human rights abuses due to a persistent lack of funds. During 2009 the government ensured that basic functions were covered, while funding from the UN and other partners lapsed, leaving the commission unable to fully implement its strategic plans and make fully operational its regional offices in Bo, Kenema, and Makeni. The commission generally operated without government interference.

Key International Actors

The UN and the UK government continued to take the lead in reforming and supporting Sierra Leone's rule of law sectors. The UK remained Sierra Leone's largest donor, providing some £62 million in the last fiscal year, including support for the Anti-Corruption Commission and justice and security sector reform. The UN Peacebuilding Fund has since 2007 approved more than US$34 million for projects in Sierra Leone, which support reconciliation efforts and improving the communications, justice, and security sectors.

In September 2009 the UN Security Council extended until September 2010 the mandate of the UN Integrated Peacebuilding Office in Sierra Leone (UNIPSIL), the fourth and leanest UN mission in Sierra Leone in 10 years. With some 70 staff, the mission maintains a largely advisory role aimed at promoting human rights and strengthening democratic institutions and the rule of law, including efforts to address organized crime, drug trafficking, and youth unemployment.

While states including the UK, the US, the Netherlands, Canada, France, and Germany continue to make important contributions to the Special Court for Sierra Leone, which relies primarily on voluntary funding, the court continued to suffer from financial shortfalls.

SOMALIA

Somalia's people continue to endure one of the world's worst human rights catastrophes. Hopes of peace following the installation of a new Transitional Federal Government (TFG) under President Sheikh Sharif Ahmed in early 2009 have been dashed. The capital Mogadishu is wracked by indiscriminate warfare in which all parties are implicated in war crimes or other serious human rights abuses. Much of the rest of the country is now under the control of local administrations linked to armed opposition groups. In many of these areas the population has suffered abusive application of Sharia law and forced conscription of civilians, including children, as militia fighters.

A humanitarian crisis of enormous proportions is unfolding, fueled by years of drought and insecurity that has often prevented the effective delivery of aid. Some 3.75 million people— roughly half of Somalia's remaining population—are in urgent need of humanitarian assistance. More than a million people are displaced from their homes within Somalia and tens of thousands fled the country as refugees in 2009.

Indiscriminate Warfare in Mogadishu

In 2009 Mogadishu continued to be torn apart by indiscriminate warfare. Its dwindling civilian population continues to bear the brunt of fighting between armed opposition groups, and the TFG and African Union Mission in Somalia (AMISOM) forces. Ethiopian forces withdrew from Somalia at the end of 2008, leading thousands of people to return to the capital in hope of peace. But many were forced to flee anew when the fighting resumed with familiar patterns of deadly violence.

All parties to the conflict in Mogadishu have been implicated in war crimes in 2009. TFG and opposition forces have both recruited children into the ranks of their fighting forces, though the practice has been more widespread and coercive where practiced by opposition groups. Opposition forces including al Shabaab and Hizbul Islam have launched regular indiscriminate mortar attacks on areas of Mogadishu under TFG and AMISOM control. The use of civilians as human shields for indiscriminate attacks, often with the apparent intention of attracting reprisals that claim still more civilian lives, is a common opposition tactic. Hizbul Islam leader Sheikh Hassan Dahir Aweys has publicly acknowledged using civilians as human shields.

On the other side of the lines, the TFG's capacity to field fighting forces in Mogadishu was weak throughout 2009. It relied on notoriously abusive officials such as police chief Abdi Qeybdid, whose forces were responsible for serious human rights abuses throughout 2008.

The TFG is almost entirely reliant on the 5,000-strong AMISOM force for its protection and survival. AMISOM forces have come under sustained attack, including deadly suicide bombings, and have on some occasions responded by firing mortars indiscriminately into opposition-controlled neighborhoods, including the area around Bakara market. In February 2009, AMISOM forces were accused of firing indiscriminately into crowds of civilians after coming under attack in Mogadishu. AMISOM opened an inquiry into the incident—the only time it has apparently done so—but no final report was produced.

Abuses in Opposition-Controlled Areas

Most of south-central Somalia was under the control of local administrations linked to al Shabaab and other opposition groups throughout 2009. A level of peace and stability prevailed in some opposition-controlled areas, but many of their administrations carried out serious abuses against the populations they control.

Al Shabaab in particular has grown notorious for abusive and often arbitrary applications of Sharia law, which in at least a few cases have seen alleged crimes punished with amputations, beheadings, and, in October 2008 in Kismayo, the stoning to death of a young woman on charges of adultery. Residents of the southern town of El Wak told Human Rights Watch that in early 2009 the local al Shabaab militia forced women to stop working as tea sellers and also beat women illicitly selling the mild narcotic *qat*, which al Shabaab has sought to ban.

In some areas al Shabaab and other opposition groups have forcibly recruited men and boys into militia forces. In Jowhar, for example, al Shabaab militiamen reportedly press-ganged men into military service in 2009. Many opposition mili-

SOMALIA

"So Much to Fear"

War Crimes and the Devastation of Somalia

HUMAN
RIGHTS
WATCH

tias include children within their ranks; in at least some parts of Somalia al Shabaab has deliberately targeted children for recruitment through a mix of promises, threats, and indoctrination.

Attacks on Journalists, Human Rights Defenders, and Humanitarian Workers

Somalia's once-vibrant independent press and civil society have been decimated by violence and threats over the course of the past three years. At least six journalists were reportedly killed in 2009, some targeted for assassination and others killed by the stray gunfire that has claimed so many civilian lives. TFG and opposition forces alike have been implicated in threats directed at journalists who produce reporting they dislike.

Attacks targeting human rights defenders were much less frequent in 2009 than in 2008. But in part this reflects the fact that many of Somalia's most prominent human rights defenders have fled the country. Those who remain have seen their capacity to operate effectively dramatically diminished by the prevailing insecurity and by specific threats against them.

The delivery of humanitarian assistance to Somalia has been severely hampered by the prevailing insecurity and by threats specifically targeting humanitarian agencies. Most of the humanitarian agencies operating in Somalia have had to dramatically curtail their operations or have been driven out of south-central Somalia altogether. In opposition-controlled areas where millions of Somalis are in need of assistance, humanitarians have come under regular threat by al Shabaab and other groups who accuse them of colluding with international efforts to back the TFG in its war effort. In October 2009 leaflets circulated in Mogadishu accused hospitals of collaborating with the TFG and threatened them with violence.

Democracy under Threat in Somaliland

The self-declared republic of Somaliland has maintained a remarkable degree of peace and stability since 1991. Despite the fact that its independence has not been recognized by any country in the world, Somaliland laid the foundations for

SOMALILAND

"Hostages to Peace"

Threats to Human Rights and Democracy in Somaliland

HUMAN
RIGHTS
WATCH

democratic institutions of governance and has held its people apart from the pervasive abuses affecting Somalis further south. But Somaliland's achievements in the areas of governance and human rights are now under threat, largely due to the repeated postponement of a key presidential election originally scheduled for April 2008. Those polls should have consolidated progress toward democracy; their postponement now calls into question the Somaliland government's commitment to democracy and could threaten the territory's stability. Somaliland's government has also failed to address a range of systemic human rights problems such as the government's use of illegal security committees to imprison people, including children, without trial for a range of criminal offenses.

Key International Actors

All too often the involvement of a number of international actors in Somalia has been destructive. Western government and African Union policy has been to provide unequivocal support to Somalia's beleaguered transitional government. To this end the AU has deployed the AMISOM force of 5,000 Ugandan and Burundian troops to protect key TFG installations and officials in southern Mogadishu, with UN Security Council backing. In 2009 donors pledged over US$200 million in mostly security sector support to AMISOM and the TFG; at this writing less than one third of that assistance has materialized. The United States government has provided money and bilateral transfers of weapons to the TFG—including mortars, weapons that no side has made any effort to use in accordance with the laws of war. Many of the weapons acquired by the TFG have ended up on the open market.

The strong international backing of the TFG is driven largely by concerns over the links some of al Shabaab's leaders maintain to al Qaeda. Several hundred foreign fighters, including some Somalis with foreign passports, are estimated to be in Somalia fighting against AMISOM and the TFG alongside al Shabaab and other groups. At least one and possibly two suicide bombings have been carried out by Somali-Americans in Somalia since the end of 2008—the first time such attacks have ever been carried out by a US citizen.

Ethiopia withdrew its military forces from Somalia at the end of 2008 after a two-year intervention in the country. The Ethiopian military has continued to conduct operations inside Somalia in support of its security interests, but no longer plays a central military role in the conflict. The government of Eritrea continues to play a destructive role in Somalia, funneling arms and other assistance to armed opposition groups with the primary aim of undermining Ethiopia's interests in Somalia.

Kenya and Yemen each host large numbers of Somali refugees. Kenya's desperately overstretched Dadaab refugee camps, built for 90,000 people, are now home to some 300,000 mostly Somali refugees. Negotiations for the land required to build a badly needed new refugee camp near Dadaab stalled in 2009. Yemen's government has generally welcomed the at least 100,000 Somali refugees who reside in the country.

SOUTH AFRICA

On May 9, 2009, Jacob Zuma was inaugurated as the new president of South Africa, replacing interim president Kgalema Motlanthe, after elections that were widely viewed as free and fair. The new president faces numerous challenges in the midst of an economic recession—including widespread poverty, unemployment, high levels of violent crime, and gender inequality—which continue to undermine the country's human rights environment, especially for the most vulnerable in society.

South Africa continues to play a prominent role in international affairs, in particular on the African continent, but faces many challenges in addressing the inherent contradictions between enhancing its domestic and regional trade and investment interests, and retaining its post-apartheid reputation as a proponent of human rights and international justice. Unlike former President Thabo Mbeki, President Zuma has proved more willing to publicly criticize abuses in countries such as Sri Lanka, Burma, and Zimbabwe. This is a positive change of tone.

Refugees and Migrants

South Africa's immigration system has struggled to deal adequately with the millions of asylum seekers and migrants who have entered the country—up to an estimated 1.5 million of whom are Zimbabwean. Thousands fleeing the political and economic crisis in Zimbabwe who have applied for asylum in South Africa have faced unlawful deportation.

On April 3, 2009, then-Minister of Home Affairs Nosiviwe Mapisa-Nqakula announced a positive shift in migrant policy toward Zimbabweans, which included visa-free entry and "special dispensation permits" to legalize Zimbabweans' stay and give them work rights and access to basic healthcare and education. The Department of Home Affairs at the same time announced an immediate moratorium on the deportation of Zimbabweans from South Africa. However, the government has yet to implement the special dispensation process, which would lessen the vulnerability of Zimbabweans to violence and exploitation both in their homeland and in South Africa.

After xenophobic attacks against foreign nationals in May 2008 left 62 dead and a further 50,000 internally displaced, the government still faces significant challenges in addressing issues of reintegration, resettlement, or xenophobia in local communities. While the government has sought to quickly reintegrate the victims of that violence, some have faced further violence when returning to their communities, and others have been unable to move back for fear of repeat attacks. The government has failed to implement an independent commission of inquiry into the violence, and the pace of holding accountable those responsible for the attacks has been exceedingly slow: According to a report by the Consortium for Refugees and Migrants in South Africa in June 2009, the government had prosecuted only 469 of those responsible for the attacks out of 1,627 originally arrested, and of those prosecuted only 70 were found guilty. Convictions were mostly for the lesser crimes of assault or theft; there were no convictions for murder or rape, despite NGOs documenting many such cases during the attacks.

Health Issues and the HIV/AIDS Epidemic

The progressive realization of socioeconomic rights poses a significant challenge for Zuma's government. A report in 2009 by the South African Human Rights Commission, for example, pointed to poor service delivery in the public healthcare system throughout the country.

People with HIV/AIDS suffer from inequitable access to antiretroviral treatment and a lack of support services, despite the promulgation of a new HIV/AIDS plan adopted in 2007. The AIDS epidemic has fueled South Africa's worsening tuberculosis crisis, as well as a rise in maternal deaths, which also result from the country's inadequate public sector reproductive health services.

For migrants, high rates of HIV both in countries of origin and in South Africa, compounded by the risks related to migration make HIV prevention, diagnosis, and treatment a major public health concern. Human Rights Watch research, as well as reports from other NGOs and media outlets, has identified a striking gap between South Africa's inclusive policies and the reality of access to healthcare for refugees, asylum seekers, and especially undocumented migrants. Barriers to healthcare include lack of information, cultural and linguistic barriers, lack of documentation, user fees, and discrimination.

Women's and Girls' Rights

South Africa has in place legislation and national mechanisms to address gender inequality, including the introduction of a government ministry dedicated to women, youth, children, and disabled people. Yet the gap between the material status of women and the government's stated commitment remains huge. Levels of violence against women and girls in South Africa are shockingly high.

South Africa has the highest rates in the world of rape reported to the police. A survey released in June by the Medical Research Council of South Africa found that 28 percent of men surveyed had raped a woman or girl; one in 20 said they had raped a woman or girl in the past year. Arrest and conviction rates of rape perpetrators are extremely low, and consequently women and girls who experience these violations are denied justice, factors that contribute to the normalization of rape and violence against women and girls in South African society. Women and girls who have been raped face numerous obstacles in accessing healthcare and other forms of assistance, such as delays in the provision of medical treatment, an absence of counselling services, and lengthy waits for medico-legal examination. Despite the high rates of rape, many health facilities do not provide post-exposure prophylaxis (PEP) services. NGOs working on women's health rights continue to receive reports from healthcare workers and survivors of rape who have been unable to access timely PEP services in the public health system.

Sexual Orientation and Gender Identity

Although South Africa's constitution outlaws discrimination based on sexual orientation, and same-sex marriage has been legalized, gay and lesbian people remain vulnerable. In particular, incidents of violence against black lesbian women, and "corrective rape" in particular, continue to be reported with growing frequency. The South African Human Rights Commission and other NGOs have recommended that the criminal justice system needs to take concerted action to deal with hate crimes in the country, something that the government has yet to do.

International Role

South Africa continues to play a prominent role in international affairs, especially on the African continent. South Africa has a significant peacekeeping presence in the Democratic Republic of Congo (DRC), and is part of the African Union-United Nations Hybrid operation in Darfur (UNAMID). It has played a positive role in the Burundi peace process.

As chair of the Southern African Development Community (SADC), South Africa brokered the recent power-sharing agreement in Zimbabwe. Zimbabwe's proximity to South Africa means that it will remain a top priority for the South African government. President Zuma has been more outspoken than former President Mbeki about the political crisis in Zimbabwe. For example, during a visit to Zimbabwe in August, Zuma publicly acknowledged that progress in implementing the power-sharing agreement between President Robert Mugabe's Zimbabwe African National Union–Patriotic Front (ZANU-PF) and Prime Minister Morgan Tsvangirai's Movement for Democratic Change (MDC) had been slow and that outstanding issues needed to be addressed, implicitly due to ZANU-PF's failure to honor many of its commitments under the agreement. Zuma also played an active role in introducing the Zimbabwe situation to the agenda of the annual SADC heads of state summit in Kinshasa, DRC. Regrettably, South Africa's partners in the region have failed to ensure that the Zimbabwe power-sharing agreement is fully implemented.

The new international relations ministry under President Zuma has retained South Africa's focus on strengthening regional mechanisms and South-South cooperation. At the same time, unlike under Mbeki, recent statements and actions by the Zuma administration have indicated a shift toward respect for human rights as an important pillar of foreign policy. For example, in 2009 the South African government issued strong statements on Burma and Sri Lanka: it criticised the arrest of Aung San Suu Kyi in Burma and called for her immediate release, and expressed concerns about government actions and the humanitarian situation in Sri Lanka.

South Africa has one of the world's most progressive constitutions and has long been a proponent of international justice and ending impunity for serious international crimes. In July 2009 South Africa showed clear leadership on this issue when the director general in the International Affairs and Cooperation Ministry, Dr. Ayanda Ntsaluba, reiterated South Africa's commitment to the International Criminal Court and stated that South Africa would respect its obligation to cooperate with the ICC, including in carrying out arrest warrants for sitting Sudanese president Omar al-Bashir. As the leading African democracy, South Africa remains well placed to play a positive role in encouraging fellow African Union states that are party to the Rome Statute of the ICC to maintain their support for effective international justice. African and international civil society also looks to South Africa to challenge those African states that continue to push the continent to cease cooperation with the ICC.

SUDAN

Four years after Sudan's ruling party and the southern rebels signed the 2005 Comprehensive Peace Agreement (CPA) ending 21 years of civil war, Sudanese civilians in Darfur, northern states, and the South are still enduring human rights violations and insecurity. The Government of National Unity (GNU) has been unwilling to implement national democratic reforms as envisioned in the CPA. The failure of both Sudan's ruling National Congress Party (NCP) and the southern ruling Sudan People's Liberation Movement (SPLM) to implement other provisions of the CPA has contributed to insecurity and led to outright violence in some settings.

Accountability for human rights abuses remains practically nonexistent. On March 4, 2009, the International Criminal Court issued an arrest warrant for President Omar al-Bashir—the first for a sitting head of state by the ICC—for alleged war crimes and crimes against humanity committed in Darfur.

Darfur

The conflict in Darfur continues to involve government-backed militia forces and rebel and ex-rebel movements that have caused civilian deaths, injuries, and displacement. The government has kept its war machinery in place, with heavy military deployments throughout Darfur, including auxiliary forces such as Border Guards that have absorbed Janjaweed militia into the army. Despite international mediation and diplomatic support, the government and rebel factions have not reached a political solution to the conflict.

In early 2009 fighting between government forces and Justice and Equality Movement (JEM) rebels in Muhajeria, South Darfur, displaced more than 40,000 civilians. The government used indiscriminate force through aerial bombing, often in combination with ground forces, to attack civilian populations linked to rebel movements. In May, during government-JEM clashes in North Darfur, witnesses reported heavy aerial bombing on civilian areas with scores killed and many more injured. After a lull during the rainy season, fighting resumed in September when government forces clashed with rebel movements in North Darfur, killing more than a dozen civilians and destroying several villages.

The situation for 2.7 million displaced people and other conflict-affected people living in unprotected villages has not improved. The government's expulsion of 13 international humanitarian organizations following the ICC arrest warrant for al-Bashir has seriously undermined provision of humanitarian aid to Darfur. Stop-gap measures and one-off distributions averted an immediate catastrophe, but are not sustainable and do not cover protection and human rights programs that were closed down with the expulsions. In addition, criminal banditry and attacks on international aid workers and United Nations staff also hampered humanitarian operations. More than a dozen UN peacekeepers have died from hostilities since the mission's deployment in January 2008.

Displaced women and girls in towns, camps, and villages throughout Darfur continue to experience sexual violence by government forces, allied militia, rebels, and criminal actors. Between April and June 2009, UN human rights monitors documented 21 cases involving 54 victims, 13 of whom were under 18 and most of whom described attackers as wearing military uniforms. Human Rights Watch research on sexual violence against Darfuri women and girls suggests this number represents a small fraction of actual cases.

Beyond Darfur itself, the government continued to target suspected Darfuri rebels and human rights activists for arrest and detention, particularly after the ICC warrant. The African Union-United Nations Mission in Darfur (UNAMID) documented 16 cases of arrest and detention by government security forces of people alleged to support the ICC or to have provided information to international interlocutors. In April-May 2009 security officials arrested some 20 members of a student group affiliated with a faction of the Sudan Liberation Army (a Darfur rebel movement), which openly supported the ICC indictment by organizing events at various universities.

More suspected rebels were sentenced to death, bringing the total to 102. The trials, by special courts formed under a 2001 anti-terrorism law to try individuals accused of participating in the May 2008 JEM attack on Omdurman, fell below international standards: defendants had no access to lawyers before trial, were held incommunicado for months, and claimed their confessions were made under duress. The whereabouts of some 200 people who "disappeared" in the post-Omdurman attack crackdown remain unknown.

SUDAN

The Way Forward

Ending Human Rights Abuses and Repression across Sudan

HUMAN
RIGHTS
WATCH

Civil Society Activism and Media Freedom

The closure of three Sudanese human rights organizations after the ICC's al-Bashir arrest warrant contributed to an atmosphere of oppression in Darfur and throughout the northern states that prompted more than a dozen lawyers and activists to leave the country.

Between January and June 2009, authorities prevented publication of newspapers on at least 10 occasions through heavy censorship, harassed or arrested journalists and the author of a book on Darfur, and closed an organization that was supporting journalists. In September al-Bashir announced the end of the pre-print censorship policy, but warned journalists to abide by established "red lines," implying they should not publish articles that are seen as critical of the government.

Insecurity in Southern Sudan

The Government of National Unity's failure to implement agreements under the CPA on border demarcation and troop deployments threatens to expose civilians to further abuse and insecurity, particularly around the several disputed areas along the North-South border.

During February clashes in Malakal between the NCP-led Sudanese Armed Forces (SAF) and the southern Sudan People's Liberation Army (SPLA) soldiers, former militias whom the SAF had failed to integrate instigated violence and human rights violations. The GNU Presidency has not taken sufficient action to remove SAF ex-militias from the area and reduce the threat of further violence. Both armies have failed to downsize and fully integrate ex-militias in various locations as required by the security arrangements in the CPA.

Abyei, the oil-rich area that straddles the North-South border and is one of three transitional areas governed by separate protocol to the CPA, also remains a flashpoint. In May 2008 clashes between SAF and SPLA soldiers caused near-total destruction of the town and displaced some 60,000 civilians. The parties agreed to restore peace to the area and submitted the question of Abyei's boundaries to international arbitration. On July 22, 2009, the Hague-based Permanent Court of Arbitration awarded much of the area (excluding Meiram and Heglig) to the Dinka

SUDAN

"There is No Protection"

Insecurity and Human Rights in Southern Sudan

HUMAN
RIGHTS
WATCH

Ngok community. Leaders of the Dinka Ngok and the Misseriya (another community claiming land rights over Abyei) publicly accepted the decision, but some Misseriya leaders have made dissenting statements rejecting the demarcation. The parties to the CPA have yet to implement the terms of the Abyei Protocol and the arbitration award.

Elsewhere in the South, severe inter-ethnic fighting, usually linked to competition over resources and exacerbated by the widespread availability of weapons, is the primary and escalating threat to civilians. Intercommunal fighting occurs in many states, but has been most acute in Jonglei: in 2009 alone, attacks and counterattacks between armed members of the Murle and Lou Nuer ethnic communities killed well over 1,200 civilians. Clashes between other armed communities killed hundreds more. Southern Sudanese authorities have been unable to address the underlying causes of these conflicts or protect civilians from the inter-ethnic violence. The Southern Sudan Police Service (SSPS) and SPLA are insufficient in number or resources to repel armed attacks, and are not trained to effectively intervene to protect civilians.

Ugandan Lord's Resistance Army (LRA) rebels operating in the Democratic Republic of Congo (DRC), Central African Republic (CAR), and inside Southern Sudan attacked civilian populations, resulting in an influx of refugees to Western and Central Equatoria. An estimated 18,000 refugees from the CAR and DRC are living in camps in Southern Sudan, while 68,000 southern Sudanese are displaced by LRA violence.

Child Soldiers

Children continue to be recruited and used by armed groups in Darfur and eastern Chad, and by groups operating elsewhere in Sudan including Southern Sudan. More than 200 children were abducted by armed groups in the context of inter-ethnic fighting, and scores more were abducted by LRA rebels in attacks on civilians in Southern Sudan.

Key International Actors

International diplomatic attention shifted away from Darfur and focused more on implementation of the Comprehensive Peace Agreement and insecurity in Southern Sudan. Despite numerous high-level meetings on Sudan, key governments have not adopted a coherent common strategy. The United States strategy, released in October, broadly outlined an approach to ending conflict and human rights abuses in Darfur and promoting accountability while implementing the CPA and averting conflict. The policy did not, however, articulate clear indicators for progress, and it remains to be seen to what extent human rights and civilian protection priorities will drive US engagement.

The African Union at its July summit called on member states not to cooperate with the ICC in al-Bashir's arrest and surrender because the UN Security Council had not responded to an AU request that the council defer the case against al-Bashir. Subsequent to the AU's call for non-cooperation—which is contrary to the obligations of African states parties to the ICC—al-Bashir made moves to attend meetings in Uganda, Nigeria, and Turkey. This generated public outcries and he ultimately did not travel to any.

On October 29 the AU released the report of the High-Level Panel on Darfur offering recommendations to address accountability, impunity, peace, and reconciliation. The Sudanese government has yet to formally respond.

The two international peacekeeping missions in Sudan faced obstacles. UNAMID, now in its second year of operation, is still not fully deployed, and continues to face obstruction in its deployment and movement by the Sudanese government. This undermined its overall effectiveness, including its ability to protect civilians and monitor the humanitarian and human rights situation in Darfur. The United Nations Mission in Sudan (UNMIS), mandated to monitor the Comprehensive Peace Agreement, also faced access restrictions that undermine its ability to monitor both the ceasefire and the human rights situation, particularly in northern states. The mission has yet to adopt a clear strategy for delivering its mandate to protect civilians in the South.

UGANDA

Impunity, corruption, and the erosion of independent institutions obstruct the protection of human rights in Uganda; government efforts in 2009 to tackle these shortcomings were weak. With parliamentary and presidential elections scheduled for early 2011, the ruling party faced increased criticism from the opposition for failing to deliver electoral law reform or address the perceived partiality of the Electoral Commission, voter disenfranchisement, and incumbents' use of state resources during campaigning.

Political tensions between the central government and the Buganda kingdom exploded in violent demonstrations that rocked Kampala for two days in September, leaving at least 27 dead. Members of the opposition and media faced criminal charges for speaking before and after the events about the president's governance and the use of lethal force to quell rioters. No members of the security forces were charged. The government forced four Luganda-language radio stations off the air.

Extra-territorial military operations by Ugandan armed forces to defeat the long-running Lord's Resistance Army (LRA) insurgency led to some LRA combatants being captured. But civilians paid a heavy price in the Democratic Republic of Congo (DRC), southern Sudan, and the Central African Republic, the LRA killing over 1,000 civilians and abducting hundreds across these three countries in "revenge" attacks. Ugandan military operations have consistently failed to protect civilians adequately, leaving hundreds of thousands displaced and without reliable access to humanitarian aid.

Extrajudicial Killings, Torture, and Arbitrary Detention

During the September riots, those supporting the king of the Baganda blocked roads and burned government property. Police and military fired live ammunition at rioters, bystanders, and people hiding in their homes. The use of lethal force by government forces drew criticism, but no one was held to account for the 27 deaths. Government officials blamed the media and the rioters for inciting violence. Hundreds were arrested in police operations marked by brutality. Twenty-

three rioters who allegedly destroyed government property were charged with terrorism.

Separately, in 2009, Human Rights Watch documented unlawful arrests, illegal detention, torture, and extrajudicial killing of alleged treason and terrorism suspects by the Joint Anti Terrorism Task Force (JATT). The Ugandan armed forces and parliament publicly committed to carrying out investigations, but no action has so far been taken and reports of abuses continue.

Lawyers for five individuals "disappeared" by JATT filed habeas corpus petitions in July. Human Rights Watch research had previously established that JATT had held all five incommunicado for months without charge. The High Court ordered that JATT produce the five before the court, but in defiance of the ruling the government failed to produce the suspects and argued that they had recently reported to the Amnesty Commission. The five were ultimately granted amnesty and released, allegedly having admitted to rebel activity. The High Court questioned the voluntariness of their confessions and requests for amnesty, and ruled that the amnesty was unlawful because of their illegal detention.

In April and May government forces arrested 14 people in northern Uganda, mistreating and detaining them without charge at the JATT headquarters for several weeks. After a habeas petition was filed, the 14 were produced in court and accused of membership in a previously unknown rebel group. All remain in custody at this writing, charged with treason.

The minister of justice failed to address the legal status of 12 individuals who were under age 18 when they committed crimes that qualify for the death penalty if committed by an adult. The prisoners were convicted, but were given no sentence and should have been placed in appropriate juvenile care. Some have been held for over eight years while awaiting the minister's orders. The ministry blamed the courts for failing to turn over the appropriate reports.

Lord's Resistance Army

Efforts to negotiate an end to the war between the LRA and the government remained on hold after LRA leader Joseph Kony failed to sign an agreed peace deal in 2008. While relative calm continued to prevail in northern Uganda, the

LRA committed grave human rights abuses in the DRC, Central African Republic, and southern Sudan. Some of the worst attacks took place in December 2008 and January 2009 following the launch of Operation Lightning Thunder, a regional military assault on the LRA in the DRC led by the Ugandan military. A Human Rights Watch investigation documented how more than 865 civilians were killed and at least 160 children were abducted during these attacks. When the Ugandan military scaled back operations in March, civilian protection was largely left to the Congolese army and United Nations peacekeepers, and LRA killings and abductions of civilians continued in the DRC's Orientale province. (See also DRC chapter.)

The Ugandan government took preliminary steps to establish a special division of Uganda's High Court to prosecute serious crimes in violation of international law, as proposed during the LRA peace talks. Parliament introduced legislation to domesticate the Rome Statute of the International Criminal Court in Uganda and establish the war crimes division.

Freedom of Assembly and Expression

In August police beat and detained members of the opposition, Forum for Democratic Change, who were demonstrating in Kampala against extensions of office terms for the chairman and commissioners of the Electoral Commission, despite accusations of election malpractice. Several demonstrators were arrested and charged with organizing an illegal assembly. Throughout the year the police tried to block peaceful demonstrations and assembly in several other parts of the country.

The government's clampdown on freedom of expression intensified in 2009, especially after the September riots. Although the constitutionality of sedition has been pending before the Constitutional Court since 2005, police continue to use the charge to harass journalists and opposition leaders. Opposition members Erias Lukwago and Medard Segona were charged with inciting violence and sedition for statements made on a radio program. Unknown security operatives arrested and beat prominent journalist Robert Kalundi Sserumaga after he criticized the president's upbringing on television; Sserumaga was charged with six counts of sedition. By October at least 17 journalists had pending criminal charges against them for charges such as forgery, criminal defamation, sedition, and promoting sectarianism. All are free on bail, awaiting trial.

Government officials told television stations to stop broadcasting live pictures of the security forces' response to the riots. In some instances, security agents forcibly removed video footage from TV stations, and appropriated journalists' cameras so they could delete images of dead bodies. Police also beat some journalists who attempted to report on unfolding events, and some were detained and interrogated for their coverage of the riots. President Yoweri Museveni accused radio station CBS (part-owned by the Buganda kingdom) of running a sustained campaign against his government, and through its regulatory body, the Broadcasting Council, the government closed down CBS and three other radio stations: they were accused of inciting violence and promoting sectarianism, but had no notification or opportunity to appeal the Council's decision. The Council also banned a TV program and its host, and pressured some stations to dismiss journalists who were critical of the government's response to the riots.

Sexual Orientation and Gender Identity

At least four people were arrested for alleged homosexual activity and charged with either sodomy or "carnal knowledge against the order of nature."

The Anti-Homosexuality Bill, tabled for discussion in parliament in October, prohibits all homosexuality, making it punishable by a fine and a maximum prison sentence of 10 years, or both. The bill further prohibits the "promotion" of homosexuality through advocacy on sexual minority rights, threatening the activities of any human rights group.

HIV/AIDS

Uganda's draft HIV/AIDS Prevention and Control Bill mandates HIV testing of pregnant women, their partners, and other specified populations, and criminalizes the intentional transmission (or attempted transmission) of HIV. In addition, the bill grants health practitioners the power to notify sexual partners (and those "in close and continuous contact") of a person living with HIV of that person's serostatus, and criminalizes a wide range of conduct related to failure to follow medical orders or follow "safe procedures." Arbitrary or selective enforcement of the bill could restrict broad freedoms and undermine effective HIV prevention and treatment approaches that rely upon outreach to and empowerment of affected communities.

Key International Actors

Uganda's aid donors privately expressed concern about ongoing cases of torture and illegal detention by security forces, but did not speak out publicly to condemn abuses.

Warrants issued by the International Criminal Court for LRA leaders in 2005 remain outstanding. The United States provided material and intelligence assistance to the Uganda-led offensive in December 2008, but failed to adequately provide or plan for civilian protection. In May 2009 members of the US Congress introduced legislation requiring the Obama administration to develop a multilateral strategy to apprehend LRA leaders; the legislation is currently under review. Other actors—including the United Kingdom, the European Union, and the United Nations—failed to take effective steps toward the apprehension of LRA leaders under ICC warrant, although some expressed concern over ongoing LRA abuses.

ZIMBABWE

A power-sharing government formed in February 2009, with Robert Mugabe continuing as president and opposition leader Morgan Tsvangirai installed as prime minister, has failed to end rights abuses or to institute fundamental reforms. It has also made no attempt to repeal or substantially amend repressive legislation such as the Public Order and Security Act (POSA) and the Access to Information and Protection of Privacy Act (AIPPA), which continue to be used by Mugabe's Zimbabwe African National Union—Patriotic Front (ZANU-PF) to harass political opponents and rights activists.

ZANU-PF is supposed to be a partner with the Movement for Democratic Change (MDC) in the new government, but it has failed to implement key provisions of the power-sharing agreement. ZANU-PF continues to use its control of the security forces and the judiciary to harass, abduct, torture, and kill those it considers opponents, including senior MDC figures. Despite this, Mugabe's allies in southern Africa have repeatedly and prematurely called for the lifting of targeted travel restrictions against ZANU-PF leaders.

Political Developments

Following the controversial presidential run-off election of June 27, 2008, and the signing of a Global Political Agreement (GPA) on September 15, 2008, ZANU-PF and the MDC formed a power-sharing government on February 11, 2009. However, the deal left ZANU-PF with most of its power intact, effectively maintaining the status quo ante: It has kept control of all the senior ministries including justice, security, and defense. The MDC lacks real power and does not consistently speak out against the continued abuses, possibly seeking to save the fledgling power-sharing government.

Nevertheless, on October 16, 2009, Prime Minister Tsvangirai announced that the MDC had "disengaged" from the unity government, ostensibly over the treatment of a senior aide but mainly due to intensified ZANU-PF attacks on his supporters. On November 5-6, five heads of state from the Southern African Development Community (SADC) met Zimbabwe's leaders in Maputo, Mozambique, to address the political standoff. Presidents Zuma (South Africa), Kabila (Democratic

ZIMBABWE

False Dawn

The Zimbabwe Power-Sharing Government's Failure
to Deliver Human Rights Improvements

HUMAN
RIGHTS
WATCH

Republic of Congo, DRC), Guebuza (Mozambique), and Banda (Zambia), and King Mswati (Swaziland) gave Mugabe and Tsvangirai, plus the leader of a smaller MDC faction, 30 days to resolve all outstanding problems relating to the GPA. On the same day Tsvangirai ended his party's boycott of cabinet meetings.

Human Rights Violations in Marange Diamond Fields

At the end of June 2009 Human Rights Watch released a report detailing diamond smuggling, corruption, and widespread serious human rights abuses—including killings, torture, beatings, and child labor—in the Marange diamond fields in eastern Zimbabwe. The report highlighted the army's seizure of control of the diamond fields in October 2008 and its killing of more than 200 people in the same month.

Soon after the release of the report, the Kimberley Process Certification Scheme (KPCS), a global body that governs the diamond industry and to which Zimbabwe belongs, sent a review mission to investigate. The mission confirmed Human Rights Watch's findings and assessed that the abuses violated KPCS minimum standards. In an interim report, the mission recommended the withdrawal of the Zimbabwe Defence Forces from Marange, as well as an end to abuses and smuggling. Civil society groups active in the Kimberley Process demanded Zimbabwe's suspension until it complied with KPCS standards.

The government of Zimbabwe has so far failed to comply with the KPCS recommendations, despite initial government indications of a willingness to do so. Smuggling continues, and beatings, torture, and other abuses by the army are ongoing. The government has not withdrawn the military from Marange, but has instead rotated new units into the area.

At a plenary meeting on November 2-5 in Swakopmund, Namibia, the KPCS decided against suspension, asking instead that Zimbabwe adhere to a work plan that Zimbabwe had itself proposed. KPCS members make their decisions by consensus. The KPCS's failure to stop Zimbabwe's blood diamonds, in part due to the blocking efforts of Mugabe's allies in southern Africa, mars its credibility, and damages consumer confidence in its commitment to tackling the trade in blood diamonds.

ZIMBABWE

Diamonds in the Rough

Human Rights Abuses in the Marange Diamond Fields
of Zimbabwe

HUMAN
RIGHTS
WATCH

Humanitarian Crisis

Despite the formation of the power-sharing government and a slight improvement in the economy, serious challenges remain. Zimbabwe's longstanding authoritarian rule and associated economic crisis plunged it into a humanitarian crisis that peaked in February 2009 with a severe cholera outbreak that by June had left up to 100,000 infected and over 4,200 dead. Levels of infant and maternal mortality rose sharply, marking the collapse of Zimbabwe's health system. Over five million people faced severe food shortages and had to rely on international aid. In September United Nations agencies reported that Zimbabwe required more than 2 million metric tons of cereal but had only 1.2 million.

While the number of cholera infections has declined considerably—the World Health Organization reported that by August the cholera epidemic was under control, thanks to international aid—Zimbabwe's sanitation infrastructure will need significant investment and improvement if another cholera outbreak is to be averted. The country's hospitals, which shut down in 2008, have now reopened but face severe shortages of doctors and nurses.

Rule of Law

ZANU-PF and its supporters have continued to violently invade commercial farms in total disregard of the rule of law, and police intimidation and harassment of MDC and human rights activists persist unabated. Police, prosecuting authorities, and court officials aligned with ZANU-PF have persecuted MDC legislators and activists through politically motivated prosecutions. At least 17 MDC legislators face various trumped-up criminal charges, with at least five legislators already convicted by the courts.

On October 14, 2009, a magistrate in Mutare ordered the rearrest of senior MDC official and minister-designate Roy Bennett on charges, initiated by ZANU-PF in 2006, of sabotage, banditry, terrorism, and inciting terrorism. Although Bennett was eventually granted bail, at this writing charges against him have not been dropped, and the trial is underway.

Human Rights Defenders

Human rights defenders remain under attack from security forces, including the police and intelligence officers, as well as by members and supporters of ZANU-PF. For example, on April 21, 2009, police violently broke up a protest at Masvingo State University and arrested at least 23 students. Since then, other activists from organizations such as the Women of Zimbabwe Arise and Zimbabwe National Students' Union have been arrested for exercising their rights to peaceful protest.

On September 28 the Supreme Court of Zimbabwe dismissed a case against human rights activist Jestina Mukoko, on the grounds that state agents tortured and abducted Mukoko and thereby violated her rights during the course of her two-month detention. Mukoko, who was abducted and later arrested in November 2008, had faced charges of inciting banditry and terrorism. The charges against 30 activists who were abducted and arrested with Mukoko remain outstanding. Seven other activists who were also abducted around the same time as Mukoko remain missing.

None of the state agents and police officers who abducted and reportedly tortured Mukoko and the other activists has been brought to justice, a stark illustration of the significant challenges that the power-sharing government faces in addressing the longstanding issue of impunity for abuses in Zimbabwe.

Key International Actors

Mediation talks brokered by SADC and overseen by South Africa's former president, Thabo Mbeki, led to the signing of the Global Political Agreement and the formation of the power-sharing government in February 2009. Despite SADC and the African Union being its guarantors, the two organizations have not applied sufficient pressure on ZANU-PF to deliver rights reforms and ensure respect for human rights as stipulated in the agreement.

On August 28 President Jacob Zuma of South Africa, in his capacity as outgoing chair of SADC, visited Zimbabwe and called for full implementation of the GPA and the removal of all obstructions to it. However, at the SADC Summit in Kinshasa, DRC, on September 8, SADC leaders sided with ZANU-PF, calling for the unconditional lifting of Western sanctions against ZANU-PF supporters. Human

Rights Watch and civil society in Zimbabwe repeatedly called for long-standing and targeted travel restrictions and asset freezes on specific individuals in ZANU-PF to be maintained until there are irreversible justice and rights reforms.

After the formation of the power-sharing government, Prime Minister Tsvangirai and Finance Minister Tendai Biti embarked on separate global fundraising tours in May and June calling on international actors to reengage with Zimbabwe and to lift targeted measures against some senior ZANU-PF officials. The European Union and the United States have been cautious about reengaging until the GPA is implemented; instead, they continue to withhold direct aid to the government and keep targeted sanctions in place, citing Zimbabwe's continuing poor record of fundamental reforms, culture of impunity, and violations of rights.

Australia has bucked this trend and has provided financial assistance to the power-sharing government in the absence of meaningful progress with the GPA.

Cuba

New Castro, Same Cuba

Political Prisoners in the Post-Fidel Era

HUMAN
RIGHTS
WATCH

WORLD REPORT

2010

AMERICAS

ARGENTINA

Argentina has made significant progress in prosecuting military and police personnel responsible for "disappearances," killings, and torture during the country's "dirty war." Despite delays in judicial proceedings, 44 officials have been convicted for committing abuses since Congress annulled the amnesty laws of the 1980s.

An important challenge that Argentina faces today is modifying its laws to comply with its international obligations to protect and promote freedom of expression. In 2009 Congress approved legislative proposals submitted by President Cristina Fernandez de Kirchner to decriminalize defamation, and to regulate TV and radio. But there is no access to information law or federal-level guidelines on allocating official advertising.

Continuing human rights problems in Argentina include deplorable prison conditions, and arbitrary restrictions on women's reproductive rights.

Confronting Past Abuses

Several important cases of abuses committed during Argentina's last military dictatorship (1976-83) were reopened in 2003 after Congress annulled the 1986 "Full Stop" law, which forced a halt to the prosecution of all such cases, and the 1987 "Due Obedience" law, which granted automatic immunity in such cases to all members of the military, except those in positions of command. In June 2005 the Supreme Court declared the laws unconstitutional. In addition, since 2005 several federal judges have struck down pardons decreed by then-president Carlos Menem in 1989-90 of former officials convicted or facing trial for human rights violations.

As of July 2009, 588 people faced charges for these crimes. Since the amnesty laws were annulled, 44 people have been convicted. In March 2009, for example, a court in San Luis sentenced two former military personnel and three former policemen to life imprisonment for killing a woman, torturing a man, and two enforced disappearances in 1976. In July 2009 two former prison officers were each sentenced in Misiones to over 20 years in prison for torturing a political prisoner in 1976.

Delay in judicial processes undermines accountability, however. According to the Center for Legal and Social Studies, 193 people implicated in crimes committed during the dictatorship died before being brought to justice. An important reason for the delay was that several complex cases were on the docket to be heard by the same tribunal in the city of Buenos Aires. In March 2009 some cases were redistributed to other tribunals.

The security of witnesses in human rights trials has become a serious concern since the "disappearance" in September 2006 of a torture victim who had testified in one of the cases that concluded that year. Jorge Julio López, age 77, who vanished from his home in La Plata the day before he was due to attend one of the final days of the trial, remains missing.

Freedom of Expression and Information

In September 2009 President Kirchner presented draft legislation on TV and radio regulation that attempted to limit the ability of media corporations to own large portions of the radio frequency spectrum so as to promote diversity of comment and debate. But it also contained problematic provisions, such as the creation of an implementing body that would report directly to the executive's chief of staff. Congress approved an improved version of the bill in October. The new law, however, creates an implementing body with a diverse composition, but without complete autonomy, and contains vague definitions of what "faults" could lead to sanctions such as the expiry of broadcasting licenses. It also fails to acknowledge the need to have mechanisms available for those who currently own more licenses than allowed by law, and who might need to request compensation if they prove that the anti-trust measures in the law caused them economic damages.

In May 2008 the Inter-American Court of Human Rights ruled that Argentina had violated Eduardo Kimel's right to free expression when a court sentenced him in 1995 to one year in prison (the sentence was suspended) and ordered him to pay 20,000 pesos (US$20,000 at that time) in damages for defamation. Kimel had criticized the work of a judge investigating a massacre committed during the last military government. To comply with the Inter-American Court ruling, in September 2009 President Kirchner sent a legislative proposal to Congress to decriminalize defamation, which was approved in November.

Without clear pre-established criteria for allocating official advertising at the federal level and in some provinces, there is an increased risk of discrimination in the distribution of official advertising by rewarding local media that provide favorable coverage and punishing those with a critical editorial line. In a case against the provincial government of Neuquen, in September 2007 the Supreme Court held that although there is no right to receive official advertising, a government that grants it may not apply discriminatory criteria in granting or withdrawing it. Several bills to regulate the matter remain pending.

An executive decree allows Argentine citizens to obtain information held by the federal executive branch. However, bills giving Argentine citizens the right to information held by all federal offices have been pending before Congress for years. (Some provinces have access to information laws that allow individuals to obtain information from provincial governments.)

Criminal Justice System

In detention facilities overcrowding, abuses by guards, and inmate violence continue to be serious problems. In a landmark ruling in May 2005 the Supreme Court declared that all prisons in the country must abide by the United Nations Standard Minimum Rules for the Treatment of Prisoners.

The situation in the province of Buenos Aires remains critical. During 2006-07 there was a small reduction in the number of detainees held in police lockups, which absorb the overflow from the prison system. Yet the Center for Legal and Social Studies documented that, as of March 2009, the overpopulation in provincial prisons was at 26 percent, rising to 47 percent when taking into account prisoners held in police stations. Nearly 77 percent of prisoners are in pretrial detention, one of the main causes of overcrowding.

Children in conflict with the law who are under age 16 are subject to a procedure that lacks basic due process safeguards and provides judges broad discretion to authorize their detention. In cases where they are accused of having committed a crime, and when they are subjected to a custodial or protective measure because of their "personal or social situation," judges routinely order children to be institutionalized. In December 2008 the Supreme Court rejected a habeas corpus petition to set free dozens of detained children, but stated that the juvenile justice system violates Argentina's international obligations. At this writing a legislative proposal to modify this system in compliance with international human rights standards is pending before the Senate.

Impunity for the 1994 AMIA Bombing

To date, no one has been convicted for the 1994 bombing of the Jewish Argentine Mutual Association in Buenos Aires, in which 85 people died and over 300 were injured. In 2004 a court acquitted men accused of participating in the attack when it declared all evidence gathered during the investigation inadmissible because the judge in charge of the investigation had bribed a suspect. The judge was impeached one year later. In May 2009 the Supreme Court held that evidence gathered during the original investigation prior to October 31, 1995 (the date on which the judge bribed the suspect), was valid and could be used to investigate the suspect's participation in the bombing and other related crimes. Additionally, in October 2009 a federal judge accused former President Menem and other former high officials of a cover-up for interfering with the judicial investigation into the attack.

In October 2006 an Argentine special prosecutor accused Iran of planning the attack, and Hezbollah of carrying it out. In November 2006 a federal judge issued an international warrant for the arrest of former Iranian president Ali Akbar Hashemi-Rafsanjani and eight other Iranian former officials. A year later, the Interpol General Assembly voted to issue six arrest notices, and in September 2009 President Kirchner reiterated before the UN General Assembly the Argentine government's request that Iran collaborate with the Argentine justice system. In June 2009 a federal judge ordered the capture of a Colombian citizen accused of coordinating a Hezbollah cell that allegedly carried out the bombing.

Reproductive Rights

Women and girls in Argentina face arbitrary and discriminatory restrictions on their reproductive decisions and access to contraceptives, especially emergency contraceptive pills. Therapeutic abortions and abortions for rape victims are legal, but women continue to face obstacles even when their right to an abortion is protected by law. In May 2009 Santa Fe was the first province to adopt comprehensive guidelines to assist health professionals to conduct legal abortions. The guidelines, which follow international human rights standards and the World Health Organization's recommendations for safe abortion, were elaborated by the federal Ministry of Health in 2007.

Key International Actors

Argentina has actively promoted international resolutions to curb impunity for abuses. Its efforts led to a 2008 UN Human Rights Council resolution recognizing the importance of the right to truth, encouraging states to implement the recommendations of non-judicial bodies (such as truth and reconciliation commissions), and to establish specific mechanisms to complement the justice system to investigate gross human rights violations. The Organization of American States Permanent Council adopted a similar resolution in May 2009.

In March 2009 the UN Human Rights Council approved another resolution proposed by Argentina, which encourages states to use forensic genetics to contribute to identifying remains of abuse victims, and to restore the identity of individuals who were separated from their families, including those taken away when they were children.

BOLIVIA

Bolivia's new constitution was promulgated by President Evo Morales and came into effect on February 7, 2009, after being approved by 61 percent of the vote in a referendum on January 25. Bolivia's deep political, ethnic, and regional divisions (including over the new constitution) and the fragility of its democratic institutions contribute to a precarious human rights situation. Almost two-thirds of the population lives below the national poverty line, and over a third—mostly indigenous peoples—lives in extreme poverty.

Lack of accountability for rights abuses is a chronic problem. Both supporters and opponents of Morales, as well as the police and military, have been accused of killings during violent clashes between rival demonstrators in recent years. Investigations into these unlawful killings have almost invariably failed to establish criminal responsibility.

Although Bolivia enjoys diverse media and a vibrant public debate, political polarization has brought violent attacks on journalists and media outlets by both pro-government and opposition demonstrators.

Political Violence, Accountability, and Impunity

Violence has arisen from deep disagreements over the procedures to approve the new constitution and over demands for autonomy by five lowland departments. A tense standoff between Morales's largely indigenous supporters and the departmental prefects and their supporters in the breakaway departments led to violent clashes in 2007 and 2008 in the cities of Santa Cruz, Sucre, Tarija, and Cobija, with deaths and injuries on both sides. There were fewer incidents of political violence in 2009, after opposition legislators reached a compromise with the governing party and the new "pluri-national" constitution was approved. However, the performance of prosecutors and courts in establishing accountability for acts of violence continues to be poor.

A seriously weakened judiciary is a major problem. The chief justice is currently suspended and facing impeachment proceedings, while four other Supreme Court justices have also been suspended or have retired, leaving the court barely able to function. All the members of the Constitutional Tribunal have resigned for political reasons and will not be replaced until an election is held in 2010. In addition, there have been time-consuming conflicts over jurisdiction between regional and La Paz-based courts.

One of the most serious incidents of violence in 2009 was an attack by government supporters on the home of former vice-president Víctor Hugo Cárdenas, a prominent opponent of the new constitution. In March hundreds of indigenous peasants occupied and looted Cárdenas's home in Sankajahuira, west of La Paz. The mob beat Cárdenas's wife, children, and nephew with sticks and whips, and forced them out of the house; they were admitted to hospital for their injuries. Cárdenas was not at home at the time of the attack. By November no progress had been reported in the investigation of the incident.

In April 2009 a dynamite charge damaged the gate of the home of the Archbishop of Santa Cruz, Julio Terrazas, who has been a prominent critic of the Morales government. The following night an elite police unit stormed a hotel in the city center ostensibly in pursuit of the culprits, shot dead three hotel guests, and detained two other men. Government ministers said the five were foreign mercenaries belonging to a cell financed by right-wing separatists in Santa Cruz, and that they suspected them of planning attacks on government officials, including President Morales. Opposition leaders in Santa Cruz accused the government of staging the plot. As of November 2009 the two detainees were still being held without charge in La Paz's San Pedro prison. In August the Supreme Court ruled that a court in Santa Cruz should have jurisdiction in the case, which until then had been under investigation in La Paz. The government, which doubted the impartiality of the Santa Cruz court, threatened to impeach the justices responsible for the ruling.

The circumstances of the April shootings have still not been clarified. The police maintain that there was a 30-minute shootout during which they fired in self defense. The government has not released the findings of an inquest into the deaths, if any such investigation has been carried out. However, an Irish state pathologist who examined the body of one of the victims, Irishman Michael Dwyer, concluded that he had been shot dead with a single dumdum bullet in the heart, fired by someone standing over him, "most likely as he was sitting up in bed."

In October 2009 the prefect of Pando department, Leopoldo Fernández, was indicted on charges of homicide, terrorism, and conspiracy for the killing of at least nine pro-Morales demonstrators in Porvenir, Pando department, in

September 2008. Armed supporters of the departmental government had reportedly opened fire indiscriminately on pro-Morales demonstrators as they were running away. Some of the dozens of wounded were allegedly beaten while being taken in ambulances to hospital. Fernández had been held for more than a year without charge.

Bolivian courts still seek to establish criminal responsibility for the killing of more than 60 people in anti-government protests in September and October 2003, when the army used lethal force to quell violent protests in the highland city of El Alto. Former President Gonzalo Sánchez de Lozada resigned and left the country following the events, known in Bolivia as "Black October." In October 2007 the attorney general accused Sánchez de Lozada, 11 of his ministers, and 5 former military chiefs of genocide and torture in connection with the army's actions.

The former president, his defense minister Carlos Sánchez Berzaín, and the former energy minister Jorge Berinduague currently reside in the United States, where Sánchez Berzaín has obtained political asylum. In November 2008 Bolivia formally requested that the US extradite the three men to face trial in Bolivia. Bolivia is also seeking the extradition from Peru of three other former government ministers in connection with the same case. In May 2009 the Bolivian Supreme Court opened impeachment proceedings, and Sánchez de Lozada, Sánchez Berzaín, and Berinduague were declared to be to be fugitives from justice. The trial began in the absence of most of the 17 defendants.

Media Freedom

Bolivia enjoys a vibrant public debate, with a variety of critical and pro-government media outlets. As political polarization has deepened, many news outlets have openly taken sides. President Morales often lambasts the private media for distorting facts and seeking to discredit him. In March 2009 he sued the director of the newspaper *La Prensa* for disrespect (*desacato*) and libel following the publication in December 2008 of an article suggesting that he had given a "green light" to the smuggling of some trucks. *La Prensa*'s editor and the author of the article reportedly received anonymous death threats by telephone.

Journalists on both sides of the political divide have suffered acts of violence and intimidation. In September 2009 a police unit, led by the same official responsible for the Santa Cruz hotel raid, attacked a journalist and cameraman working for the UNITEL television network while they were reporting on an arrest in Santa Cruz. According to press reports, a police vehicle rammed their car, and three officers forced them out at gunpoint, beat them, made them lie down on the ground, shot at the vehicle, and removed their videocamera.

Human Rights Defenders

Supporters of regional autonomy in Santa Cruz have firebombed and ransacked offices of NGOs defending land rights of indigenous and peasant communities. The Center for Legal Studies and Social Research (CEJIS) has been the victim of repeated violent attacks. In February 2009 two unidentified men on a motorbike shot at a car driven by Miguel Gonzáles, CEJIS's regional director in Trinidad, capital of Beni department. A few days earlier he had shaken off vehicles that were following him. CEJIS complained that local prosecutors had failed to carry out a serious investigation into the attempted killing.

Sexual Orientation and Gender Identity

The new constitution explicitly bans discrimination on the basis of sexual orientation and gender identity. However, according to local human rights activists, by October 2009 the government had not taken effective steps to implement this protection.

Key International Actors

In 2008 the United Nations High Commissioner for Human Rights established an office in Bolivia to strengthen human rights protection. Criticizing the lack of accountability for the events in Pando, which it described as a massacre, the Bolivia office noted the judiciary's longstanding structural problems.

In July 2009 the United States deported Luis Arce Gómez to Bolivia. Arce had been minister of the interior during the dictatorship of Gen. Luis García Meza (1980-81), and had completed half a prison sentence in the USA for drug-trafficking. In 1993 the Bolivian Supreme Court convicted both Arce and García Meza in absentia for rights abuses and sentenced them to 30 years in prison. Both men are now serving time in La Paz.

BRAZIL

Brazil has in recent years consolidated its place as one of the most influential democracies in regional and global affairs but continues to face important human rights challenges. Faced with high levels of violent crime, some Brazilian police officers engage in abusive practices instead of pursuing sound policing policies. Detention conditions in the country are inhumane. Torture remains a serious problem. Forced labor persists in some states despite federal efforts to eradicate it. Indigenous and landless peoples face threats and violence, particularly in rural conflicts over land distribution.

Public Security and Police Conduct

Most of Brazil's metropolitan areas are plagued by widespread violence perpetrated by criminal gangs and abusive police. Violence especially impacts low-income communities. There were over 40,000 intentional homicides in Brazil in 2008. In Rio de Janeiro, hundreds of low-income communities are occupied and controlled by drug gangs, who routinely engage in violent crime and extortion.

Police abuse, including extrajudicial execution, is a chronic problem. According to official data, police were responsible for 561 killings in the state of Rio de Janeiro alone in the first six months of 2009. This amounts to roughly three police killings per day, or at least one police killing for every six "regular" intentional homicides. The number of killings by police in São Paulo, while less than in Rio de Janeiro, is also comparatively high: in 2008, for example, there were more fatal police shootings in alleged confrontations in São Paulo state (397) than in all of South Africa (351), a country with a higher homicide rate than São Paulo.

Police claim these "resistance" killings occur in confrontations with criminals. While many police killings undoubtedly result from legitimate use of force by police officers, many others do not, a fact documented by Human Rights Watch and other groups and recognized by Brazilian criminal justice officials. Reform efforts have fallen short because state criminal justice systems rely almost entirely on police investigators to resolve these cases, leaving police largely to police themselves.

BRAZIL

Lethal Force

Police Violence and Public Security in Rio de Janeiro and São Paulo

HUMAN
RIGHTS
WATCH

Some police officers also commit abuses while off duty. In Rio de Janeiro, police-linked militias control dozens of neighborhoods at gunpoint, extorting residents and committing murders and other violent crimes. A December 2008 report, which was unanimously approved by the Rio de Janeiro legislature, documented that 171 neighborhoods in the state were "dominated" by militias. The government has undertaken significant efforts to combat some of these groups—particularly following the release of the legislative report—but the problem remains critical.

In March 2009 civil police investigators in Itapecerica da Serra, São Paulo, uncovered a military police death squad known as the "Highlanders," a nickname derived from the group's practice of cutting off the heads and hands of their victims in an effort to cover up their crimes (a practice in the 1986 fictional film "Highlander"). The São Paulo Police Ombudsman's Office also tracked 32 killings in the first six months of 2009 by unknown assailants suspected of being police officers.

Detention Conditions, Torture, and Ill-Treatment

Brazil's prisons and jails are plagued by inhumane conditions, violence, and severe overcrowding. Delays within the justice system contribute to overcrowding; some 45 percent of all inmates in the country are pretrial detainees. The National Justice Council, the judiciary's oversight body, reported in 2009 that approximately 60,000 inmates were being held arbitrarily.

The use of torture is a chronic problem within the penitentiary system. A 2008 report by the multiparty National Parliamentary Commission of Inquiry on the Penitentiary System concluded that the national detention system is plagued by "physical and psychological torture." In one case from Goiás, the Commission received evidence that the National Security Force subjected female detainees to kicks and electric shocks, stepped on the abdomen of a pregnant woman, and forced another woman to strip naked.

The National Justice Council received reports of torture from inmates in several Brazilian prisons and jails in 2009. In August 2009 the Council confirmed that 10 inmates had suffered grave injuries, reportedly from prison personnel, in the state of Paraíba.

In October 2009 a federal delegation from the Special Secretariat for Human Rights visited eight detention centers in Espirito Santo, concluding that "inhuman conditions" are "predominant" in the state's detention centers. The delegation also noted that complaints of "torture and/or mistreatment" were made "in all of the centers visited." In October 2009, 88 women were found locked up in severely overcrowded metal containers in the state's prisons. It was reported that the containers had no ventilation, and that several of the women had skin diseases, as well as respiratory and gynecological problems. Earlier in the year several men were also found incarcerated in containers in Espírito Santo.

There were continued reports of substandard conditions at Rio de Janeiro 's juvenile detention centers run by the General Department of Socioeducational Actions (DEGASE). In September 2009 state prosecutors filed suit against the Rio de Janeiro government for failing to adhere to every single clause of a 2006 agreement with the State Prosecutor's Office that mandated improved conditions in DEGASE centers, including in the areas of health, hygiene, and education.

Forced Labor

Since 1995 the federal government has taken important steps to eradicate forced labor, including creating mobile investigation units to monitor conditions in rural areas. However, the Pastoral Land Commission collected reports of 6,997 persons in conditions of forced labor in 2008. Of these, 5,266 have since reported as having been freed. Criminal accountability for offending employers remains relatively rare.

Rural Violence and Land Conflicts

Indigenous and landless peoples face threats and violence, particularly in land disputes in rural areas. According to the Pastoral Land Commission, 28 people were killed and 168 arrested in rural conflicts throughout the country in 2008.

In August 2009, Elton Brum da Silva, a member of the Landless Rural Workers' Movement, was killed during a police operation to remove landless families from a farm in Rio Grande do Sul. Also in August 2009, rural union leader Elio Neves, was attacked and seriously wounded in his home by an unidentified gunman. He had reported receiving repeated death threats prior to the attack.

Confronting Past Abuses

Brazil has never prosecuted those responsible for atrocities committed during the period of its military dictatorship (1964-1985). A 1979 amnesty law has thus far been interpreted to bar prosecutions of state agents. At this writing, the Supreme Federal Tribunal is considering a petition by the Brazilian Bar Association arguing that the amnesty law does not cover crimes such as torture when committed by state agents.

The federal government is reportedly considering setting up a truth commission to investigate dictatorship-era abuses but at this writing no formal plan has yet been announced.

Human Rights Defenders

Some human rights defenders, particularly those working on issues of police violence and land conflicts, suffer intimidation and violence. In January 2009, Manoel Mattos, a human rights lawyer, was shot and killed in the border area between the states of Paraíba and Pernambuco. The main suspect, a police officer linked to a death squad under investigation by Mattos, has been arrested. The Brazilian attorney general has requested that federal prosecutors take over the case to ensure an independent investigation and prosecution, but the judiciary has yet to rule on his request.

Media Freedom

In July 2009 a court issued an injunction prohibiting the newspaper *O Estado de São Paulo* from publishing stories containing information from the "Operação Faktor" (formerly known as "Boi Barrica") police investigation involving Fernando Sarney, son of Senate President José Sarney. Despite strenuous criticism from national and international press freedom organizations, the ruling was confirmed by the Court of Appeals in October. At this writing the restrictions are still in force.

Key International Actors

In March 2009 the Inter-American Commission on Human Rights filed an application at the Inter-American Court against Brazil regarding the "Guerrilha do Araguaia" case. The Commission asked for the state to be held accountable for the enforced disappearance of members of the guerrilla force carried out by the Brazilian military in the 1970s, during the military dictatorship. It called on Brazilian officials to investigate the crimes, prosecute the perpetrators, and provide information and official documents on the "disappearances," including on the fate and location of the victims.

The Inter-American Court of Human Rights issued a ruling against Brazil in July 2009 in the case of *Escher et al. v. Brazil*, declaring that Brazilian authorities had violated the rights to privacy and freedom of association of members of the Landless Rural Workers' Movement. Police had illegally wiretapped the organization's phones and then broadcast nationally some of the conversations they had illegally recorded.

At the United Nations Human Rights Council, Brazil has often been reluctant to support efforts to scrutinize the human rights record of abusive governments, thereby undermining the Council's performance.

CHILE

Since the death of former dictator Gen. Augusto Pinochet in December 2006, Chilean judges have continued to prosecute and convict former military personnel accused of committing grave human rights violations under the military government. However, the Supreme Court's criminal chamber has reduced sentences in many recent cases, with the result that many convicted perpetrators eventually do not serve time in prison.

Police abuses continue to be reported in the Araucanía region, where members of some indigenous Mapuche communities asserting land claims periodically engage in violent attacks on homes and property. Overcrowding and inhumane conditions in many of Chile's prisons remain serious problems.

Confronting Past Abuses

In the pursuit of accountability for human rights abuses under military rule, as of October 2009, 559 former military personnel and civilian collaborators were facing charges for enforced disappearances, extrajudicial executions, and torture; 277 had been convicted (of whom 175 had had the verdict confirmed on final appeal), and 56 were serving prison sentences. Thirty-two of those charged or convicted had been generals in the Chilean army. Pinochet himself had been under house arrest and faced prosecution at the time of his death in 2006, but was unpunished for any crime.

In September 2009 Judge Víctor Montiglio indicted 129 former members of the DINA, Pinochet's secret police, for "disappearances" and extrajudicial executions dating from the 1970s. Half of them were facing charges for the first time. Also in September, the Supreme Court's criminal chamber confirmed a three-and-a-half year sentence against two retired air force officers for the torture of 17 people between 1973 and 1975. For the first time, the Court expressly declared torture, a systematic practice during the Pinochet years, to be a crime against humanity.

A majority of the five judges in the Supreme Court's criminal chamber now rule that an amnesty decreed by the military government in 1978 is inapplicable to war crimes or crimes against humanity, and that these crimes are not subject to a statute of limitations. However, not all of the judges agree that the amnesty is inapplicable. Given that court rulings in Chile are not binding in cases other than the one under review, and that the composition of the Supreme Court panel may change from case to case, the legal obstacles to convictions have not been entirely overcome. A bill promoted by the government to amend the criminal code so that crimes against humanity are not subject to amnesties or statutes of limitation has been deadlocked in Congress since 2005.

During 2008 and increasingly in 2009, the Supreme Court's criminal chamber has applied a "partial statute of limitations" (known in Chile as *media prescripción*) that allows those convicted for human rights violations to receive a reduced sentence in recognition of the time elapsed since the criminal act (more than 30 years in some cases). If the final sentence is less than five years, they can benefit from an alternative to prison. In fact, fewer than one-third of the 175 perpetrators whose prison sentence has been confirmed by the Supreme Court were actually serving time as of October 2009.

Criminal Justice System

Even though Chile has completely overhauled its criminal justice procedure in recent years and reinforced due process guarantees, military courts still have wide jurisdiction over civilians and over human rights abuses committed by the *Carabineros* (uniformed police), which is part of the armed forces. Following a 2005 decision by the Inter-American Court of Human Rights in the Palamara case ordering Chile to ensure that military courts no longer exercise jurisdiction over civilians, the government has been working on legislation to comprehensively reform the system of military justice. In October 2009, after long consultations, it finally presented two bills in Congress that would restrict the jurisdiction of military courts solely to military crimes committed by military personnel, and promised a third bill to ensure that military courts comply with the due process guarantees protected in the ordinary justice system.

Another issue has been the abuse of counterterrorism legislation to deal with common crimes, such as arson, committed by Mapuche activists, a practice about which several United Nations bodies have expressed concern. Under Chile's counterterrorism law, crimes against property such as burning homesteads, woods, or crops, or damaging vehicles or machinery, are considered to be terrorist crimes if judges see them as intended to spread fear in the population. Defendants under the law have restricted due process rights and face higher sentences. Unlike preceding administrations, President Michelle Bachelet's government adopted a policy of relying on the ordinary criminal law in dealing with crimes like these. However, as violence in the Araucanía region of southern Chile flared during 2009 and Mapuche activists armed with shotguns were reported to be holding up and burning trucks in nighttime attacks, the government reverted to using the counterterrorism law.

Police Abuses

In repeated incidents, carabineros have used excessive force during operations in indigenous Mapuche communities in the Araucanía region. The abuses typically occur when police intervene to control Mapuche protests and prevent land occupations, or when they enter communities in pursuit of Mapuches suspected of crimes allegedly committed during ongoing land disputes with farmers and logging companies.

Since 2002 three Mapuches have been killed by police unlawfully using lethal force. In the most recent case, in August 2009 a carabinero fatally shot Jaime Mendoza Collío, age 24, who had been participating in a land occupation near Ercilla. The police claimed that the carabinero acted in self defense, but forensic reports indicated that the bullet hit Mendoza in the back and that he had not fired a weapon. The carabinero official responsible for the zone reportedly continued to defend the officer responsible, even after the forensic results had been reported in the press. Although military prosecutors filed charges of "unnecessary violence resulting in death" against the police involved in all three cases, at this writing military courts have yet to convict anyone.

There have also been repeated incidents involving alleged ill-treatment of detainees, including children. Few cases have been clarified by judicial investigations. In October 2009 Citizen's Watch, an NGO that monitors indigenous rights, reported the case of a 14-year-old Mapuche boy who was allegedly beaten and threatened with being thrown from a police helicopter after he was captured while gathering medicinal herbs. During the same month, the government announced that a carabinero caught on film kicking a Mapuche detainee in the head would be expelled from the force. The United Nations Children's Fund (UNICEF) urged the government to improve procedures for registering and investigating complaints against the police.

Prison Conditions

Chile has more prisoners per capita than any other country in South America. The prison population has grown by almost 50 percent since 2004, in large part due to the greater efficiency of a new code of criminal procedure progressively introduced since 2000. Despite the opening of six new privately contracted prisons, 74 percent of the prison population is still held in aging facilities, and overcrowding remains a serious problem. For example, in 2009 the Southern Santiago Center for Preventive Detention, with a planned capacity of 3,170 places, had 6,690 inmates. Violence in prisons has increased in recent years. According to prison service statistics cited in a major newspaper, 46 prisoners died in fights between prisoners in the first eight months of 2009.

In June 2009 a Supreme Court official testifying before the Senate Committee on Constitution, Legislation and Justice described the conditions in which prisoners are held in punishment cells without natural light or sanitary provision as cruel and degrading. Reacting to her report, the deputy minister of justice announced the formation of a Council for Prison Reform, including NGO experts, to analyze prison policies.

Reproductive Rights

Chile is one of a handful of countries in the world that prohibits abortion for any reason, even in cases of rape or incest, or to save the life of the mother. Despite the comprehensive ban, an estimated 60,000 to 200,000 clandestine abortions are performed each year. In April 2008 the Constitutional Court ruled against a legal provision that allows free distribution of emergency contraception, including the "morning after pill." The World Health Organization recognizes that emergency contraceptive pills can prevent pregnancy and does not consider them to induce abortion. However, Chile's court ruled that such methods violate the constitutional protection of the right to life of the unborn. It thus ignored the rights of living women—particularly the poor and adolescents—to health, information, autonomy, non-discrimination, freedom of conscience, and freedom to enjoy the benefits of scientific progress.

Key International Actors

Chile has played an important advocacy role as a member of the UN Human Rights Council since 2008. Chile was one of the few governments to intervene during the 2009 Universal Periodic Review (UPR) of Cuba to raise significant human rights issues there. Chile also voted against a resolution co-sponsored by Cuba, Egypt, Saudi Arabia, and Brazil that failed to deplore the killing of civilians in Sri Lanka. It has insisted—as in the case of the Democratic Republic of Congo— that country-specific action is a key instrument of the UN to hold governments accountable, shed light on violations, and reveal the truth about the suffering of victims.

In May 2009 Chile's own human rights performance came under UPR scrutiny. Protection of the human rights of its indigenous peoples was an issue that came up frequently in questions and comments by states. Chile rejected only two recommendations, both of them concerned with extending access to abortion.

COLOMBIA

Colombia's internal armed conflict continues to result in widespread and serious abuses by irregular armed groups, including guerrillas and successor groups to paramilitaries. More than three million persons are internally displaced in Colombia, and many more become newly displaced every year due to ongoing violence. Human rights defenders, journalists, community leaders, trade union-ists, indigenous and Afro-Colombian leaders, displaced persons' leaders, and paramilitaries' victims seeking land restitution or justice are frequently the targets of threats and violence by armed actors. In 2009 there were several reports of killings of leaders of displaced persons groups, and the Awá indigenous commu-nity, in the southern border state of Nariño, was particularly targeted by various armed actors, suffering multiple massacres and killings during the year.

As President Álvaro Uribe's advisors promote a second constitutional amendment to allow him to run for a third term, his administration has been wracked by scan-dals over the national intelligence service's widespread illegal surveillance of human rights defenders, journalists, opposition politicians, and Supreme Court justices.

Guerrilla Abuses

Both the Revolutionary Armed Forces of Colombia (FARC) and the National Liberation Army (ELN) continue to engage in serious abuses against civilians. The FARC, in particular, is frequently involved in massacres, killings, threats, and recruitment of child combatants. In February the FARC massacred 17 Awá in Nariño. They were also allegedly responsible for the shooting in October of human rights defender Islena Rey in the state of Meta.

The FARC and ELN frequently use antipersonnel landmines. The President's Observatory for Human Rights reported that 109 civilians were injured and 32 were killed due to antipersonnel mines, improvised explosive devices, and unex-ploded ordnance from January through September 2009.

Paramilitaries and Their Successors

The Uribe administration claims that paramilitaries no longer exist. But while more than 30,000 individuals participated in a paramilitary demobilization process, there is substantial evidence that many were not paramilitaries. Others never demobilized, and some returned to crime after demobilizing. Law enforcement authorities never investigated most of them.

Successor groups to the paramilitaries, often led by mid-level paramilitary commanders, are rapidly growing. The Colombian National Police reported that as of July 2009 the groups had more than 4,000 members and were rapidly expanding their areas of operation. Like the paramilitaries, the groups are engaging in drug trafficking, actively recruiting, and committing widespread abuses, including massacres, killings, rape, threats, and forced displacement. In Medellín, after a steady decline in official indicators of violence, there has been a dramatic surge in homicides since 2008, apparently committed by these groups.

In recent years the Colombian Supreme Court has made unprecedented progress in investigating accusations against members of the Colombian Congress of collaborating with the paramilitaries. In what is known as the "parapolitics" scandal, more than 80 members—nearly all from President Uribe's coalition—have come under investigation. But the Uribe administration has repeatedly taken actions that could sabotage the investigations, including by issuing public and personal attacks against Supreme Court justices. Meanwhile, investigations by the Attorney General's Office into senior military officers and businesspersons who allegedly collaborated with paramilitaries have moved forward slowly.

The implementation of the Justice and Peace Law, which offers dramatically reduced sentences to demobilized paramilitaries who confess their atrocities, has been slow and uneven. Four years after the law was approved, there are still no convictions. Most paramilitaries are not even participating in the process. Prosecutors have made little progress in recovering illegal assets and land that paramilitaries took by force.

President Uribe's extradition, in May 2008, of most of the paramilitary leadership to the United States interrupted the leaders' confessions in the Justice and Peace process. It remains unclear to what extent US prosecutors are questioning the paramilitary leaders about their accomplices in Colombia, or their human rights crimes.

Military Abuses and Impunity

In recent years there has been a substantial rise in the number of extrajudicial killings of civilians attributed to the Colombian Army. Army members, under pressure to show results, kill civilians and then report them as combatants killed in action. The alleged executions have occurred throughout the country and involve multiple army brigades. Initial information indicates that the rate of killings may have dropped in 2009, possibly as a result of international attention and the opening of criminal investigations.

The Attorney General's Office is investigating cases involving more than 2,000 victims, though prosecutions are moving forward slowly. In preliminary findings after a June 2009 visit to Colombia, United Nations Special Rapporteur on Extrajudicial Executions Philip Alston noted, "The sheer number of cases, their geographic spread, and the diversity of military units implicated, indicate that these killings were carried out in a more or less systematic fashion by significant elements within the military." He said that the Colombian military justice system contributes to the problem by obstructing the transfer of human rights cases to the ordinary justice system.

President Uribe for years publicly denied the problem existed, and accused human rights groups reporting these killings of helping the guerrillas in a campaign to discredit the military. After a major media scandal in 2008 over the executions of several young men from Soacha, a low-income Bogotá neighborhood, Uribe dismissed 27 members of the military. There were several more dismissals in 2009. But President Uribe has continued to claim that the executions are only isolated cases.

Violence against Trade Unionists

For years Colombia has led the world in killings of trade unionists, with more than 2,700 reported killings since 1986, according to the National Labor School, Colombia's leading NGO monitoring labor rights. The bulk of the killings are attributed to paramilitary groups, which have deliberately targeted unions. Though the number of yearly killings has dropped from its peak in the 1990s, when the paramilitaries were in the midst of their violent expansion, more than 400 trade unionists—many of whom belonged to teachers' unions—have been killed during the Uribe government.

Impunity in these cases is widespread: in more than 95 percent of the killings there has been no conviction and the killers remain free. In recent years there has been an increase in convictions, primarily due to US pressure (see below), but even at the current rate of convictions it would take decades for Colombia to get through the backlog.

Human Rights Defenders

The Colombian Ministry of Interior has a protection program for human rights defenders, journalists, and trade union leaders. But the program does not cover all vulnerable groups.

In addition, the Early Warning System of the Ombudsman's office, which conducts on-the-ground monitoring of the human rights situation around the country with the goal of preventing abuses, regularly issues "risk reports," warning of threats to communities and individuals. But other Colombian authorities have at times ignored the risk reports, failing to take necessary measures to prevent abuses.

As noted by Margaret Sekaggya, UN special rapporteur on the situation of human rights defenders, in preliminary findings after her September 2009 visit to Colombia, "[a] prime reason for the insecurity of human rights defenders lies in the systematic stigmatization and branding of defenders by Government officials," who brand them as "terrorists" or "guerrillas."

Illegal Surveillance

In February 2009 Colombia's leading news magazine, *Semana*, reported that the Colombian intelligence service, DAS, which answers directly to President Uribe, has for years been engaging in extensive illegal phone tapping, email interception, and surveillance of a wide array of persons viewed as critics of the Uribe administration. These include trade unionists, human rights defenders, independent journalists, opposition politicians, and Supreme Court justices.

The Attorney General's Office opened an investigation into the surveillance, but *Semana* reported that prosecutors inexplicably focused almost exclusively on surveillance carried out in 2002-05 (during the tenure of former DAS chief Jorge Noguera, who is on trial for homicide and links to paramilitaries), despite evidence that the DAS has engaged in systematic surveillance for years afterwards. Two of the prosecutors conducting the investigation resigned, but the investigations have continued moving forward slowly.

Meanwhile, according to *Semana*, the illegal surveillance continued. For example, *Semana* revealed that numerous calls of Supreme Court Assistant Justice Iván Velásquez, the lead investigator of the "parapolitics" scandal, had been illegally intercepted through the end of August 2009.

Sexual Orientation and Gender Identity

In 2007 the UN Human Rights Committee found in X v. Colombia that Colombia breached its international obligations when it denied a gay man's partner pension benefits. The state has not complied with the Committee's recommendation to grant these benefits. Despite a police directive calling on state officials to protect LGBT rights defenders, in 2009 there were several reports of killings and threats against them.

Key International Actors

The United States remains the most influential foreign actor in Colombia. In 2009 it provided approximately $663 million to the Colombian government, somewhat less than in previous years. The bulk of the assistance continues to consist of military and police aid, though an increasing percentage consists of social and economic assistance. Thirty percent of US military aid is subject to human rights conditions, but the US Department of State has not consistently enforced them. In September 2009 the State Department certified, for the first time under the administration of President Barack Obama, that Colombia was meeting human rights conditions.

The US Congress has delayed ratification of the US-Colombia Free Trade Agreement until there is "concrete evidence of sustained results on the ground" with regard to impunity for violence against trade unionists and the role of paramilitaries. US pressure is probably the main factor leading to the establishment of a specialized group of prosecutors to investigate trade unionist killings.

The United Kingdom was reported to have reduced its military assistance to Colombia, apparently in response to the scandals over illegal surveillance and extrajudicial executions. The European Union provides social and economic assistance to Colombia, and has provided some aid to the government's paramilitary demobilization programs.

The Organization of American States' Mission to Support the Peace Process in Colombia, which is charged with verifying the paramilitary demobilizations, issued reports in 2009 that expressed alarm over the activities of the successor groups to the paramilitaries. It highlighted an increase in massacres, homicides, threats, and "social cleansing" by the groups.

The International Criminal Court remains engaged in analysis of the situation in Colombia. The ICC prosecutor has at times played a positive role in pressing authorities to investigate ICC crimes there.

In addition to the 2009 visits of the UN special rapporteurs on extrajudicial executions, on human rights defenders, and on the human rights and fundamental freedoms of indigenous persons, the Office of the UN High Commissioner for Human Rights is active in Colombia, with a presence in Bogotá, Medellín, and Cali.

CUBA

The change in government leadership in 2006—when Fidel Castro handed control to his brother Raul—has had little effect on Cuba's dismal human rights record. Cuba remains the one country in Latin America that represses virtually all forms of political dissent. The government continues to enforce political conformity using criminal prosecutions, long- and short-term detention, harassment, denial of employment, and travel restrictions.

Raul Castro has kept firmly in place and fully active Cuba's repressive legal and institutional structures. While Cuban law includes broad statements affirming fundamental rights, it also grants officials extraordinary authority to penalize individuals who attempt to exercise them. Article 62 of the constitution explicitly prohibits Cubans from exercising their basic rights contrary to the "ends of the socialist state."

Political Prisoners, Arbitrary Detentions, and "Dangerousness"

Cubans who dare to criticize the government are subject to draconian criminal and "pre-criminal" charges. They are exempted from due process guarantees, such as the right to a defense, and they are denied meaningful judicial protection because courts are "subordinated" to the executive and legislative branches.

The Cuban Commission for Human Rights and National Reconciliation (CCDHRN), a respected local human rights group, in August 2009 issued a list of 208 prisoners whom it said were incarcerated for political reasons. The list included 12 peaceful dissidents imprisoned in the first half of 2009, as well as 25 political prisoners sentenced in 2008. Of 75 journalists, human rights defenders, and political activists who were summarily tried and sentenced in a 2003 crackdown, 53 remained imprisoned as of November 2009.

The government continued to rely on arbitrary detention to harass and intimidate individuals exercising their fundamental rights. In all of 2007 the CCDHRN documented 325 arbitrary detentions by security forces; in roughly the first half of 2009 it reported 532 arbitrary detentions. The detentions are often used to prevent individuals from participating in meetings or events viewed as critical of the government. Security officers often offer no charge to justify the detentions—a clear violation of due process rights—but warn detainees of longer arrests if they continue to participate in activities deemed critical of the government. In March 2009 human rights defender Marta Díaz Rondon was arbitrarily detained when she attempted to visit Jorge Luís García Pérez, who was staging a hunger strike to call for an end to abuses of political prisoners.

Raul Castro's government has increasingly relied on a "dangerousness" (*estado peligroso*) provision of the criminal code that allows the state to imprison individuals before they have committed a crime, on the suspicion that they might commit an offense in the future. Scores of individuals are currently imprisoned for "dangerous" activities including handing out copies of the Universal Declaration of Human Rights, staging peaceful marches, writing critical news articles, and trying to organize independent unions.

Cuba has also applied the "dangerousness" charge to Cubans who are unemployed or self-employed without authorization. Language in the provision regards being unemployed as a form of "antisocial behavior," and thus worthy of pre-criminal arrest. In a January 2009 campaign called "Operation Victory," dozens of individuals in eastern Cuba—most of them youths—were charged with "dangerousness" for not having jobs.

Freedom of Expression

The government maintains a media monopoly on the island, ensuring that freedom of expression is virtually nonexistent. Although a small number of independent journalists manage to write articles for foreign websites or maintain independent blogs, they must publish their work through back channels—writing from home computers, saving information on memory sticks, and uploading articles and posts through illegal internet connections. The risks associated with these activities are considerable. Moreover, access to information is highly restricted, and because an hour of internet use costs one-third of Cubans' monthly wages and is available exclusively in a few government-run centers, only a tiny fraction of Cubans have the chance to read independently published articles and blogs.

According to the Committee to Protect Journalists, 22 journalists were imprisoned in Cuba as of June 2009, including Albert Santiago Du Bouchet Hernández, who was reportedly sentenced to three years in prison in a closed, summary trial in May. Cuba ranks second only to China for the number of journalists in prison.

Human Rights Defenders

Refusing to recognize human rights monitoring as a legitimate activity, the Cuban government denies legal status to local human rights groups. The government also employs harassment, beatings, and imprisonment to punish human rights defenders who attempt to document abuses. In May 2009, after authorities warned him several times that he would be imprisoned if he did not abandon his work, human rights activist Juan Luís Rodríguez Desdín was sentenced in a closed, summary trial to two years for "public disorder."

Travel Restrictions and Family Separation

The Cuban government forbids the country's citizens from leaving or returning to Cuba without first obtaining official permission, which is often denied. For example, Juan Juan Almeida García has been denied the right to leave Cuba to receive medical treatment for a rare degenerative illness (treatment is not available on the island) since 2003. Almeida has applied several times per year—including in 2009—for permission to leave, but all requests have been denied without explanation. His health has declined considerably as a result of his lack of treatment. Unauthorized travel can result in criminal prosecution.

The government frequently bars citizens engaged in authorized travel from taking their children with them overseas, essentially holding the children hostage to guarantee the parents' return. Given the widespread fear of forced family separation, these travel restrictions provide the Cuban government with a powerful tool for punishing defectors and silencing critics.

The government is also clamping down on the movement of citizens within Cuba, by more aggressively enforcing a 1997 law known as Decree 217. Designed to limit migration to Havana, the decree requires Cubans to obtain government permission before moving to the country's capital.

Prison Conditions

Conditions for prisoners are overcrowded, unhygienic, and unhealthy, leading to extensive malnutrition and illness. Political prisoners who criticize the government, refuse to participate in ideological "reeducation," or engage in hunger strikes and other forms of protest are routinely subjected to extended solitary confinement, beatings, restrictions of visits, and the denial of medical care. Prisoners have no effective complaint mechanism to seek redress, granting prison authorities total impunity. Cuba remains one of the few countries in the world to deny the International Committee of the Red Cross access to its prisons.

Death Penalty

In 2008 the government commuted the death sentences of all prisoners except three individuals charged with terrorism. Nevertheless, Cuban law continues to prescribe the death penalty for a broad range of crimes.

Key International Actors

As of November 2009 the Cuban government has yet to ratify the core international human rights treaties—the International Covenant on Civil and Political Rights (ICCPR) and the International Covenant on Economic, Social and Cultural Rights (ICESCR)—which it signed in February 2008. In May 2009 Cuba was reelected to the United Nations Human Rights Council for a three-year term.

In June the European Union reviewed its "Common Position" on Cuba, adopted in 1996, which conditions full economic cooperation with Cuba on the country's transition to a pluralist democracy and respect for human rights. In its 2009 review the EU said it remains "seriously concerned about the lack of progress in the situation of human rights in Cuba," and elected to maintain the position.

Also in June 2009 the Organization of American States lifted a 1962 resolution suspending Cuba from the group. The OAS conditioned Cuba's reintegration as a full member on Cuba's engagement in a dialogue with the group and on its conformity with the commitments, principles, and practices of the OAS. After the suspension was lifted the Cuban government publicly stated it had no interest in rejoining the OAS. In November 2008 Cuba became a full member of the Rio Group of Latin American and Caribbean countries.

The United States' economic embargo on Cuba, in effect for more than four decades, continues to impose indiscriminate hardship on the Cuban people, and has done nothing to improve the situation of human rights in Cuba. In April 2009 the US government eliminated all limits on travel and remittances by Cuban Americans to Cuba. Previously, due to legislation passed in 2004, the US government had only allowed Cuban Americans to visit the island once every three years, and had capped the support Cubans could send to relatives at $75 per month. Legislation introduced in the US Senate and House of Representatives in February 2009 would restore full travel to Cuba for all Americans without restrictions, but neither bill has yet been brought to a vote.

GUATEMALA

Guatemala's weak and corrupt law enforcement institutions have proved incapable of containing the powerful organized crime groups and criminal gangs that contribute to Guatemala having one the highest violent crime rates in the Americas. Illegal armed groups, which appear to have evolved in part from counterinsurgency forces operating during the civil war that ended in 1996, are believed to be responsible for targeted attacks on civil society actors and justice officials. More than a decade after the end of the conflict, impunity remains the norm when it comes to human rights violations. The ongoing violence and intimidation threaten to reverse the little progress that has been made toward promoting accountability.

Guatemala ranks third lowest in the United Nations Human Development Index in all of Latin America, and is also one of the most unequal countries in the region in terms of wealth distribution.

Public Security, Police Conduct, and the Criminal Justice System

Guatemala has one of the highest homicide rates in the hemisphere, reaching 48 per 100,000 inhabitants in 2008. Numbers for the start of 2009 indicate that the rate may grow even higher.

The existence of clandestine security structures and illegal armed groups or organizations is an important factor contributing to this violence. These groups employ violence and intimidation in pursuing both political objectives and illicit economic interests, including drug trafficking. Maintaining links with state officials, they consistently obstruct anti-impunity initiatives.

Powerful and well-organized youth gangs, including the "Mara Salvatrucha" and "Barrio 18," have also contributed to escalating violence in Guatemala. The gangs use lethal violence against those who defy their control, including gang rivals and former members, individuals who collaborate with police, and those who refuse to pay extortion money. The gangs are believed to be responsible for the widespread killings of public transit operators targeted for extortion: in 2008, 165 drivers were murdered, and the killings have continued throughout 2009.

Police have used repressive measures in attempting to curb gang activity, including arbitrary detentions and extrajudicial killings. Investigations by the Human Rights Ombudsman's Office and NGOs have found police involvement in "social cleansing"—killings intended to eliminate alleged gang members and criminals.

The Guatemalan justice system has so far proved largely incapable of curbing violence and containing these criminal mafias and gangs. According to official figures and data from NGOs, 98 percent of all crimes in the country go unpunished. Deficient and corrupt police, prosecutorial, and judicial systems, and the absence of a systematic witness protection program all contribute to Guatemala's alarmingly low prosecution rate. Moreover, members of the justice system are routinely subjected to attacks and acts of intimidation: Lawyers' Rights Watch Canada (LRWC), an NGO, documented the murder of 40 judges and lawyers in Guatemala between 2005 and July 2009, including four in the first seven months of 2009.

Accountability for Past Abuses

Guatemala continues to suffer the effects of the 36-year civil war. A UN-sponsored Commission on Historical Clarification (CEH) estimated that as many as 200,000 people were killed. The CEH attributed 93 percent of the human rights abuses it documented to state security forces and concluded that the military had carried out "acts of genocide." Very few of those responsible for grave human rights violations during the civil war have been held accountable. Of the 626 massacres documented by the commission, only three cases have been successfully prosecuted in the Guatemalan courts. Guatemala's first conviction for the crime of enforced disappearance occurred in August 2009, when an ex-paramilitary leader was sentenced to 150 years in prison for his role in "disappearing" individuals between 1982 and 1984. The verdict was made possible by a landmark ruling by the country's Constitutional Court in July 2009, which established the permanent character of the crime of enforced disappearance.

Guatemalans seeking accountability for past abuses face daunting obstacles. Prosecutors and investigators receive grossly inadequate training and resources. The courts routinely fail to resolve judicial appeals and motions in a timely manner, allowing defense attorneys to engage in dilatory legal maneuvering. The army and other state institutions resist cooperating with investigations into abuses committed by current or former members. And the police regularly fail to provide adequate protection to judges, prosecutors, and witnesses involved in politically sensitive cases.

The July 2005 discovery of approximately 80 million documents of the disbanded National Police, including files on Guatemalans who were killed or "disappeared" during the conflict, could play a key role in the prosecution of past human rights abuses. Documents in the archive led to the March 2009 arrest of two ex-agents of the National Police for their alleged participation in the 1984 "disappearance" of student leader and activist Edgar Fernando Garcia. President Álvaro Colom has ordered the archives transferred to the institutional authority of the Ministry of Culture, and the process of opening the files to the public is underway.

In February 2008 President Colom announced that he would open the military archives spanning the civil war. Following a Constitutional Court ruling in favor of releasing military archives, in September 2008 Congress passed the Law of Access to Public Information, which orders that "in no circumstances can information related to investigations of violations of fundamental human rights or crimes against humanity" be classified as confidential or reserved. The Guatemalan military, however, has only released a small portion of its archives.

Human Rights Defenders and Journalists

Attacks and threats against human rights defenders are commonplace, significantly hampering human rights work throughout the country. The Protection Unit of Human Rights Defenders (UDEFEGUA), an NGO, reported 220 attacks on human rights defenders in 2008, and 171 attacks in the first six months of 2009. According to the UN special rapporteur on extrajudicial, summary, or arbitrary executions, there were 12 reported killings of human rights defenders in 2008.

Journalists, especially those covering corruption, drug trafficking, and accountability for abuses committed during the civil war, face threats and attacks for their work. The Center for Informative Reports on Guatemala (CERIGUA) reports that in 2008 three journalists were killed, 13 were assaulted, and 10 others received death threats. In April 2009 gunmen killed Rolando Santis, a reporter investigating the murder of a suburban bus driver.

Labor Rights and Child Labor

Freedom of association and the right to organize and bargain collectively are endangered by an increase in anti-union violence, including attacks on union offices, threats, harassment, and killings of trade unionists. The International Trade Union Confederation reports that nine trade unionists were killed in 2008, the second highest total in the Americas. According to UDEFEGUA, there were 49 attacks on trade unionists between January and June 2009, including five killings.

Workers pressing for their rights in labor cases must rely on labor courts, whose work is stymied by dilatory legal measures, lengthy backlogs, and an inability to enforce rulings. Employers routinely ignore court orders for the reinstatement of illegally fired workers. The lack of enforcement paves the way for employers to circumvent labor code provisions, especially in the export processing zones (EPZs) where "maquilas" (export-processing factories) are located. According to a 2008 United States Department of State report, only two out of the 216 companies operating in the EPZs had recognized labor unions, and none had a collective bargaining agreement. Abuses and sex discrimination against women working in the maquila sector are commonplace.

Guatemala has one of the highest rates of child labor in the Americas. The International Labour Organization reported in 2008 that 16.1 percent of children ages five to fourteen are obliged to work, many in unsafe conditions.

Sexual and Gender-Based Violence

Violence against women is a chronic problem in Guatemala, and the vast majority of perpetrators are never brought to trial. An estimated 722 women were murdered in Guatemala in 2008. The Human Rights Ombudsman's Office reports that approximately 14 percent of victims show signs of torture, and about 13 percent show signs of sexual abuse. According to the UN special rapporteur on extrajudicial, arbitrary, and summary executions, investigations into crimes against women, including transgender women, are often inadequate and obstructed by investigating police who act with a gender bias.

Key International Actors

In September 2007 the UN secretary-general appointed a Spanish former prosecutor and judge to lead the newly-founded Commission Against Impunity in Guatemala (CICIG). The commission's unique mandate allows it to work with the Guatemalan Attorney General's Office, the police, and other government agencies to investigate, prosecute, and dismantle the criminal organizations operating in Guatemala. The CICIG can partake in criminal proceedings as a complementary prosecutor, provide technical assistance, and promote legislative reforms. As of September 2009 the commission has undertaken 39 investigations and is participating in eight prosecutions. In July the Guatemalan Congress ratified the extension of the CICIG's mandate until September 2011.

The UN High Commissioner for Human Rights has maintained an office in Guatemala since 2005 that provides observation and technical assistance on human rights practices in the country.

In a landmark ruling, Spain's Constitutional Court held in September 2005 that, in accordance with the principal of "universal jurisdiction," cases of alleged genocide committed during Guatemala's civil war could be prosecuted in the Spanish courts. In July 2006 a Spanish judge issued international arrest warrants for former military dictator Gen. Efraín Ríos Montt and seven other Guatemalan officials on charges of terrorism, genocide, and torture. In December 2007 the Guatemalan Constitutional Court held that the arrest and extradition requests issued by Spain were invalid. The Spanish court has pushed ahead with the case by collecting evidence and testimony in Spain. However, in November 2009 the Spanish government enacted legislation to limit the application of universal jurisdiction by Spanish courts. At this writing it is unclear what the impact of this legislation would be on the Guatemala case.

HAITI

Despite continued progress toward a stabilized government, Haiti suffers from high crime rates and chronic human rights problems, including inhumane prison conditions, police violence, threats against human rights defenders, and impunity for past abuses. Lasting effects of food riots and four devastating hurricanes in 2008, compounded by corruption, drug trafficking, and the global economic crisis undermine the state's ability to safeguard fundamental rights.

Public Security, Police Conduct, and the Criminal Justice System

Haiti is plagued by very high levels of violent crime, though reported kidnapping cases decreased from 157 in the first half of 2008 to 48 in the first half of 2009. There were seven reported child abductions between March and September 2009. Sexual violence is a serious problem, targeting women and girls almost exclusively. An estimated 50 percent of rapes are committed against girl children; the United Nations reported 84 rapes of girls and boys between March and September 2009.

Police ineffectiveness and abuse contribute to overall insecurity. Although some police units have gained capacity and received training on human rights and arrest procedures, the police continue to experience severe shortages of personnel, equipment, and training. Since January 2007, UN police and the Haitian National Police (HNP) have opened investigation files to verify the professionalism and integrity of 6,557 of the 9,715 HNP officers.

HNP officers reportedly use excessive and indiscriminate force, commit torture, make arbitrary arrests, and are involved in criminal activity, including kidnappings. For example, in January 2009 three people reported that police officers in Cap-Haitien beat them with baseball bats and batons, with UN officials attesting to fresh wounds on the victims and blood on their clothes. The following month, several people reported police brutality during Carnival festivities in Jérémie, and a man in Cap-Haitien reported a police beating to UN officials, who verified he had suffered head injuries.

In the absence of effective law enforcement, public lynching is a chronic problem. The United Nations reported 60 lynching cases in the first eight months of 2009, as compared to 47 reported for the entire year in 2008.

Judicial accountability for past abuses is rarely achieved. For example, in February 2004 in La Scierie, Saint Marc, armed anti-government gangs assaulted a police station, and government-linked forces responded with excessive force. Several killings, including of civilians, resulted from clashes between the groups, but no one has been held responsible for the deaths. In March 2009 justice was further delayed for the April 2000 murder of journalist Jean Dominique, as the sixth investigative judge appointed to the case, Fritzner Fils-Aimé, was removed on suspicion of corruption. Only one suspect was ever arrested; he has been in custody since August 2007.

Haiti's justice system is plagued by politicization, corruption, lack of resources, and lack of transparency. In 2008 Haiti was ranked 177 out of 180 on Transparency International's Corruption Perceptions Index, which serves as a recognized standard for international corruption comparisons.

Detention Conditions and Torture

Haiti's prison system suffers from severe overcrowding. As of December 2008, Haiti's 8,204 prisoners were held in facilities with a capacity of 2,448. More than 76 percent of all inmates in Haiti are pretrial detainees. The cities of Gonaïves and Petit Goâve lack penitentiaries and instead use the police station as a detention center—the 274 people detained at the Gonaïves police station exceeded the capacity of 75 by more than 350 percent. Conditions in detention facilities are dire, with prisoners held in dirty, crammed cells often lacking sanitary facilities. Detainees in some facilities take turns sleeping and standing due to lack of space and beds, and many rely on their families to deliver food in order to eat. Reports of untreated tuberculosis, malaria, scabies, and malnutrition are common in Haitian detention facilities.

According to the Institute for Justice and Democracy in Haiti, a local NGO, as of May 2009, 40 percent of prisoners in three prisons reported in a prison census that government agents subjected them to torture or other abuses, such as beating with pistols, nightsticks, and bottles.

Child Labor and Access to Education

Only about half of primary-school-age children in Haiti attend school and less than 2 percent of children finish secondary school, according to the United Nations Children's Fund. Although enrollment in public schools is supposed to be free, the costs of uniforms, books, and other school supplies are often too high for many parents to meet.

The UN special rapporteur on contemporary forms of slavery estimates there are from 150,000 to 500,000 child domestic workers in Haiti, 80 percent of whom are girls. Known in Haitian Creole as *restavèks*—from the French "rester avec" (to stay with)—they form part of a longstanding system by which parents from mostly low-income rural areas send their children to live with other families, typically in urban areas, in the hope that the receiving families will care for their children in exchange for the children performing light chores. These children are often unpaid for their work, denied an education, and physically and sexually abused.

Human Rights Defenders

Human rights defenders remain the targets of threats and attacks. In 2009, members of the human rights organization Action Citoyenne pour le Respect des Droits Humains (ACREDH) reported being pursued and detained by police after a family reported to ACREDH that a police officer had intimidated a 17-year-old girl into having sex with him in exchange for the release of her father in October 2008. In December 2008 the father was released, but was abducted and killed in March 2009. In April 2009 the Inter-American Court of Human Rights ordered the state to take measures to protect the life and integrity of the family and ACREDH members, yet they continued to receive threats during the court-ordered period of state protection.

Lovinsky Pierre-Antoine, a well-known human rights advocate and former coordinator of Fondasyon Trant Septanm—an organization that worked on behalf of victims of the 1991 and 2004 coup d'états—was abducted in August 2007, while serving as an adviser to a delegation of human rights advocates from Canada and the United States who were traveling in Haiti. His whereabouts remain unknown at this writing. Wilson Mesilien, a Fondasyon Trant Septanm co-founder who was serving as interim coordinator following Pierre-Antoine's disappearance, reported receiving threats and has gone into hiding with his wife and four children.

Key International Actors

Since 2004 the UN stabilization mission in Haiti (known by its French acronym MINUSTAH) has played a prominent role in efforts to shore up the country's democratic institutions and strengthen the rule of law and protection of human rights. The UN Security Council voted in October 2009 to extend MINUSTAH's mandate to October 15, 2010. The UN force, present in Haiti since 2004 and currently under Brazilian command, contains 7,057 troops and 2,066 police. Reports of MINUSTAH abuses have decreased since the 2007 reports of sexual misconduct against children.

On May 19, 2009, UN Secretary-General Ban Ki-Moon appointed former US President Bill Clinton as UN special envoy for Haiti. On August 11 Clinton appointed prominent doctor, professor, and founder of Partners in Health, Paul Farmer, as UN deputy special envoy.

The UN special rapporteur on contemporary forms of slavery, Gulnara Shahinian, visited Haiti in June and issued a report on abuses against *restavèk* children.

HONDURAS

Political upheaval in Honduras in 2009, which culminated with the military's removal of the democratically elected Honduran President Manuel Zelaya in June, led to widespread human rights abuses by security forces during the demonstrations that followed the coup. The de facto government led by Roberto Micheletti sought to consolidate control of the country through repressive measures.

Facing international pressure to step down, the de facto government responded by continuing to abuse protestors and issuing decrees suspending basic liberties. It also applied the law selectively in what looked like a campaign to persecute opponents, doing serious damage to human rights and the rule of law. In addition, the government turned a blind eye to other human rights problems, including the ongoing abuse of transgender people by police forces.

Excessive Force and Arbitrary Detentions

Following the military coup the de facto government imposed an immediate curfew and issued a decree suspending key civil liberties, including freedoms of the press and assembly. It also gave the military broad authority to quell protests. In the ensuing days the military occupied opposition media outlets, temporarily shutting down their transmissions, as well as government institutions and government-run companies such as the telecommunications company, Hondutel.

Protests soon followed. The vast majority of demonstrations were peaceful, and there were no reports of protestors carrying or using lethal weapons, although there were scattered reports of protestors throwing rocks and other debris at security forces, and several businesses were looted. Police and military personnel responded with excessive force in cases where marchers posed little or no threat to others.

The excessive use of force resulted in at least four deaths. Isis Obed Murillo Mencías died after being shot in the head while participating in a demonstration outside Tegucigalpa's Toncontin Airport on July 5. The body of Pedro Magdiel Muñoz, which bore signs of torture, was found on July 25 in the department of El Paraíso. Witnesses told the Inter-American Commission on Human Rights that

Muñoz had participated in a rally in front of military roadblocks that day and had been arrested by the military. Roger Vallejos Soriano, a teacher, was shot in the head during a protest in Comayagüela on July 30. Pedro Pablo Hernández was shot in the head by a soldier at a military roadblock in the valley of Jamastran on August 2, according to testimony collected by the Commission. Local rights advocates identified several more homicides that they believe may have also been the result of excessive force by Honduran security forces.

Security forces also repeatedly used wooden batons, metal tubes, and chains to beat protestors who had been taken into custody or subdued. There were numerous reports from local human rights organizations of continued physical and verbal abuse in police posts and detention centers. According to human rights organizations who visited the detention centers, police posts, and jails, the security forces did not always register detainees or accuse them of any criminal activity.

While many detained protesters were charged with destruction of public property and theft, prosecutors also filed charges against approximately 70 persons for "sedition." In one case, the judge sought to keep the accused, a teacher and sister of a prominent Zelaya supporter, in jail, even while the judge released a man accused of the same crime on the same day in the same place. The accused woman was later released on bond, but the "sedition" charges remained.

Obstruction of Human Rights Investigations

Following the coup, the small human rights unit in the Attorney General's Office began investigations into some killings, illegal and arbitrary detentions, and cases of alleged excessive use of force by security officials. The unit also filed a motion objecting to the decree limiting freedoms of the press and assembly, which the de facto government had used to bar two media outlets from broadcasting. But the unit met with resistance from their superiors in the Attorney General's Office, delays by the Supreme Court in ruling on motions, and acts of obstruction, including direct threats from members of the armed forces.

During one investigation an army officer threatened one member of the unit, telling him, "I wish I were in the Cold War, the days of Pinochet, the days when you could just disappear [someone]." The prosecutor interpreted this as a direct threat. Two other members of the unit were barred from entering an army battalion to work on a case. The attorney general also began a new practice of vetting the unit's motions before the Supreme Court.

Media Freedom

On September 27, six days after Zelaya secretly returned to Honduras and sought refuge in the Brazilian embassy, de facto President Micheletti publicly declared that two opposition media outlets, Canal 36 television and Radio Globo, would face charges of "media terrorism." In the early morning of September 28 the military took control of both stations, as well as a radio affiliate owned by Canal 36. Soldiers also confiscated the media outlets' equipment. The government's communications' commission, CONATEL, justified these government interventions by saying that both stations were inciting violence and injurious acts by calling on Zelaya supporters to protest the coup.

On October 5, on the verge of a visit from the Organization of American States to facilitate dialogue between the sides, the de facto government announced it would withdraw the decree suspending constitutional freedoms, including freedom of the press. But it did not publish an official withdrawal of the decree, and the media that had been shut down on September 28 remained closed. On the same day, the government announced a second decree further limiting freedom of the press. On October 19, Radio Globo and Canal 36 returned to the air hours after the government officially published its decision to rescind the first decree.

However, the second decree specifically limiting the press was not revoked, and the threat of closure continued to hang over the media. Journalists working for mainstream publications in Honduras told Human Rights Watch that they were engaging in self-censorship due to fear they would lose their programs or jobs, or be otherwise harassed. A number of journalists and photographers reported suffering injuries or attacks while covering protests.

HONDURAS

"Not Worth a Penny"

Human Rights Abuses against Transgender People in Honduras

HUMAN
RIGHTS
WATCH

Violence against Transgender Persons

In May 2009 Human Rights Watch issued a report detailing a surge in rape, beatings, extortion, and arbitrary detention of transgender persons in Honduras by law enforcement officials. At least 17 *travestis* (as many transgender people are called) were killed in public places in Honduras between 2004 and early 2009, including leading transgender rights activist Cynthia Nicole on January 9, 2009. None of these killings were subject to an effective investigation which would have resulted in prosecution or conviction of the perpetrators.

The situation only worsened after the coup with non-governmental organizations in Honduras reporting that six transgender people were killed between July and mid-November. They also reported having discovered a clandestine prison used by municipal police to "disappear" individuals, detainees and transgender persons among them, were held, beaten, and released without any official record of them ever having been arrested or detained.

Key International Actors

The United States government exerts the most influence on the key political, military, and economic actors in Honduras. The US is Honduras' principal trading partner. The US military has a long-established relationship with the Honduran armed forces, part of which includes use of the Soto Cano air force base where the US has 500 troops stationed.

Following the overthrow of Zelaya, the US condemned the coup and called for Zelaya to be restored to power. However, the US waited several weeks before imposing key sanctions (including freezing the visas of military, economic, and political actors) to pressure the de facto government to restore Zelaya to office. At this writing, US efforts to broker a resolution to the political crisis appeared to have stalled.

The Organization of American States (OAS) also denounced the coup and sanctioned the de facto government by suspending its OAS membership. It also sought unsuccessfully to broker a resolution to the political crisis. The Inter-American Commission of Human Rights of the OAS was critically important during this crisis. It sent a fact-finding delegation that shed light on human rights abuses—including deaths, mass detentions, and excessive force by security forces in Honduras—following the coup.

The United Nations also increased its attention to the country. On October 1 the UN Security Council authorized the Office of the High Commissioner for Human Rights to produce a report on human rights abuses since the coup.

MEXICO

President Felipe Calderon has relied heavily on the armed forces to fight drug-related violence and organized crime. While engaging in law enforcement activities, Mexico's armed forces have committed serious human rights violations, including killings, torture, rapes, and arbitrary detentions. Mexico routinely allows the military to investigate itself through a military justice system that leads to impunity for army abuses.

Mexico's criminal justice system is plagued by human rights problems, such as torture and ill-treatment by law enforcement authorities, and routinely fails to adequately prosecute crimes. Increasing violence against journalists who report on organized crime and government corruption has generated a climate of self-censorship in parts of the country.

Impunity for Military Abuses

Mexican soldiers continue to commit egregious abuses while engaged in law enforcement activities. The number of alleged army abuses presented before Mexico's National Human Rights Commission increased six-fold between 2006 and 2008, and reached 559 in the first six months of 2009.

In February 2009, for example, soldiers arbitrarily detained an indigenous man in Oaxaca for six hours, beat him, and subjected him to waterboarding. In March soldiers detained 25 Tijuana municipal police officers at a military base where they repeatedly beat them, administered electric shocks including to their genitals, and asphyxiated them with plastic bags. In August soldiers detained two men in Morelos, threatened them to death, blindfolded, and beat them.

Military authorities routinely assert jurisdiction to investigate and prosecute army abuses. As a result, the vast majority of army abuse cases are never successfully prosecuted. The military justice system lacks the independence necessary to carry out reliable investigations, and its operations suffer from a general absence of transparency. The ability of military prosecutors to investigate army abuses is further undermined by a fear of the army, which inhibits civilian victims and witnesses from providing information to military authorities.

Criminal Justice System

The criminal justice system routinely fails to provide justice to victims of violent crime and human rights violations. The causes of this failure are varied and include corruption, inadequate training and resources, and abusive policing practices without accountability.

Torture remains a widespread problem. One perpetuating factor is the acceptance by some judges of evidence obtained through torture and other mistreatment. Another is the failure to investigate and prosecute most cases of torture.

Over 40 percent of prisoners in Mexico have never been convicted of a crime. Rather, they are held in pretrial detention, often waiting years for trial. The excessive use of pretrial detention contributes to prison overcrowding. Prison inmates are also subject to abuses by guards. Children are often detained in poor conditions in police stations and other institutions, and many juvenile detainees do not have access to educational programs.

In June 2008 Mexico passed a constitutional reform that creates the basis for an adversarial criminal justice system with oral trials, and contains measures that are critical for promoting greater respect for fundamental rights, such as including presumption of innocence in the constitution. Two provisions, however, violate Mexico's obligations under international law. The first allows prosecutors, with judicial authorization, to detain individuals suspected of participating in organized crime for up to 80 days before they are charged with a crime. The second denies judges the power to decide, in cases involving offenses on a prescribed list, whether a defendant should be provisionally released pending and during trial. The government has eight years to implement the reform.

Impunity for "Dirty War" Crimes

During its five-year existence, the Special Prosecutor's Office established in 2001 to investigate and prosecute abuses committed during the country's "dirty war" in the 1960s-1980s made very limited progress. It did not obtain a single criminal conviction. Of the more than 600 "disappearance" cases, it filed charges in 16 and obtained indictments in nine. The office determined the whereabouts of only

MEXICO

Uniform Impunity

Mexico's Misuse of Military Justice to Prosecute Abuses
in Counternarcotics and Public Security Operations

HUMAN
RIGHTS
WATCH

six "disappeared" individuals (four had been sent to psychiatric institutions and two had been killed in detention).

After Calderon officially closed the office in 2007, the cases were transferred to another, non-specialized unit within the Attorney General's Office, which has not made significant advances in the investigations.

Freedom of Expression and Information

Journalists, particularly those who have investigated drug trafficking or have been critical of state governments, have faced harassment and attack. In July 2009, for example, the badly beaten body of a journalist was found buried near Acapulco, with his hands and feet tied and his head wrapped in tape. Seven Mexican journalists have gone missing since 2005, including five who had investigated links between local officials and organized crime. Such cases have generated a climate of self-censorship in parts of the country.

Since 2007, defamation, libel, and slander are no longer federal criminal offenses. However, criminal defamation laws in the states continue to be excessively restrictive and tend to undermine freedom of expression.

A 2002 federal law on transparency and access to information and a 2007 constitutional reform increased avenues for public scrutiny of the Mexican government. However, progress made in promoting transparency within the federal executive branch has not yet been entirely matched in other branches of government, in autonomous institutions, or at the state level.

Human Rights Defenders

The United Nations has documented 128 instances of violence or intimidation against Mexican human rights defenders since 2006, including 27 in the first half of 2009. The most common method of intimidation has been threats to the life or physical integrity of defenders issued through email, phone calls, or anonymous notes left at workplaces. The list also includes 10 killings. For example, the bodies of two defenders who allegedly had been kidnapped by police in Guerrero in February 2009 were found several days later with visible signs of torture.

Reproductive Rights, Domestic Violence, and Sexual Abuse

Mexican laws do not adequately protect women and girls against domestic violence and sexual abuse. Some provisions contradict international standards, including provisions that define sanctions for some sexual offenses with reference to the "chastity" of the victim, or penalize domestic violence only when the victim has been battered repeatedly. Existing legal protections are often not enforced vigorously. Girls and women who report rape or violence to the authorities are generally met with suspicion, apathy, and disrespect. Victims are thus often reluctant to report crimes and such underreporting undercuts pressure for necessary legal reforms. This leads to impunity for rampant sexual and domestic violence against women and girls.

In August 2008 the Supreme Court affirmed the constitutionality of a Mexico City law that legalized abortion in the first 12 weeks of pregnancy. However, abortion continues to be criminalized in the rest of Mexico and during 2009 several states attempted to incorporate the right to life of the unborn in their constitutions. Every state allows abortion in certain specific circumstances, including after rape, but authorities often thwart pregnant rape victims' attempt to terminate their imposed pregnancy by treating them dismissively and with hostility.

Labor Rights

Legitimate labor-organizing activity continues to be obstructed by collective bargaining agreements negotiated between management and pro-management unions. These agreements often fail to provide worker benefits beyond the minimums mandated by Mexican legislation. Workers who seek to form independent unions risk losing their jobs, as inadequate laws and poor enforcement generally fail to protect them from retaliatory dismissals.

National Human Rights Commission

Mexico's official human rights institution has provided detailed and authoritative information on specific human rights cases and usefully documented some systemic obstacles to human rights progress. But, despite its broad mandate and immense resources, it has routinely failed to follow up by pressing government institutions to remedy the abuses it has documented and to promote reforms needed to prevent them. In November 2009 the Senate appointed a new president to the Commission for a five-year term.

Key International Actors

The Merida Initiative is a multi-year aid package agreed upon in 2007 through which the United States would provide Mexico US$1.12 billion to address the increasing violence and corruption of heavily armed drug cartels. When authorizing the funds, the US Congress decided that most of the aid for Mexican security forces could be made available immediately, but that 15 percent of most funds would only be available after the US secretary of state reports to Congress that the Mexican government has met four human rights requirements: ensuring that civilian prosecutors and judicial authorities investigate and prosecute federal police and military officials who violate basic rights; consulting regularly with Mexican civil society organizations regarding the implementation of the Merida Initiative; enforcing the prohibition on the use of testimony obtained through torture or other ill-treatment; and improving the transparency and accountability of police forces.

Unfortunately, the effectiveness of setting these conditions was undermined when in August 2009 the US State Department issued its first report on the Merida human rights requirements, which does not assess whether Mexico met the requirements and does not show that Mexico is ensuring that civilian authorities are investigating army abuses. Congress authorized the release of a portion of the withheld funds but requested additional information that should be included in the next State Department report.

During 2009 the Inter-American Commission on Human Rights sent four cases concerning military abuses in Guerrero to the Inter-American Court, which will issue decisions that are binding on Mexico. The cases involve an enforced disappearance during the "dirty war," the arbitrary detention and torture of two environmentalists in 1999, and the rape of two indigenous women in 2002.

In 2009 the United Nations Human Rights Council conducted Universal Periodic Review of Mexico. The Mexican government supported most recommendations to improve its human rights practices, but did not accept those questioning its use of military courts to prosecute army abuses.

The United Nations High Commissioner for Human Rights maintains an in-country office that provides valuable documentation of human rights problems and recommendations for addressing them, such as its 2009 report on the situation of human rights defenders in Mexico.

PERU

Peru made history in 2009 by convicting a former elected president for grave human rights violations. Yet efforts to prosecute others responsible for abuses committed during Peru's internal armed conflict (1980–2000) have had mixed results and most perpetrators continue to evade justice. Investigations of massacres and enforced disappearances by government forces have been obstructed by lack of cooperation from the military.

Torture and ill-treatment of criminal suspects are chronic problems. Police sometimes overstep international norms on the use of lethal force in controlling protests and demonstrations.

Confronting Past Abuses

According to Peru's Truth and Reconciliation Commission, almost 70,000 people died or "disappeared" during the country's internal armed conflict. Many were victims of atrocities committed by the Shining Path and the Túpac Amaru Revolutionary Movement (MRTA), and others of human rights violations by state agents.

On April 7, 2009, in a unanimous verdict, a three-judge panel of the Peruvian Supreme Court convicted and sentenced former president Alberto Fujimori to 25 years' imprisonment for crimes against humanity. He was the first democratically elected Latin American leader to be convicted for grave human rights violations in his own country. The court found him responsible for the extrajudicial execution of 15 people in the Barrios Altos district of Lima in November 1991, the enforced disappearance and murder of nine students and a teacher from La Cantuta University in July 1992, and two abductions. Fujimori's lawyers appealed the sentence and a final verdict is still pending at this writing. The trial was respectful of due process guarantees and consistent with international standards of fair trial. By October 2009 Fujimori had been convicted and sentenced in each of the other cases for which he was extradited from Chile in 2007, involving charges of corruption, bribery, and phone-tapping.

In a separate trial, in April 2008 Gen. Julio Salazar Monroe, former head of the National Intelligence Service during the Fujimori government, was sentenced to 35 years in prison for ordering the Cantuta killings. By the end of September 2009, 13 members of the Colina group, the government death squad directly responsible for the La Cantuta and Barrios Altos killings, had been convicted.

Efforts to investigate and prosecute former officials and military officers implicated in scores of other killings and "disappearances" dating from the beginning of the armed conflict have had meager results. Lack of cooperation by the military has consistently hampered the investigation of human rights cases. Moreover, President Alan García's government has repeatedly questioned the legitimacy of human rights trials. In 2009 top government and military officials suggested that efforts by Peru's human rights organizations to combat impunity undermined military morale. The defense minister, Rafael Rey, claimed at a War Marines ceremony in October that the military and police did not commit crimes against humanity because they did not kill for religious, racial, political, or ideological reasons.

According to information published by the human rights Ombudsman in December 2008, of 218 cases monitored by the institution—which include abuses committed by insurgent groups—only eight had led to convictions, while 122 were still under investigation by prosecutors several years since the investigations were opened. In October 2009 the National Human Rights Coordinator, an NGO that monitors accountability, reported that the National Criminal Court, created in 2004 to deal with human rights violations and terrorism, had acquitted 52 military and police agents and convicted 12. The ratio of acquittals to convictions increased significantly in 2008-09: the court acquitted 29 agents and convicted only two. In September 2009 the Supreme Court overturned one of the two convictions.

In this case, the court annulled the 20-year prison sentence of a naval officer for the murder of Indalecio Pomatanta, a 17-year-old who was captured in 1995 by a military patrol, tortured, and burned alive. The court based its decision on inconsistencies between the accused officer's testimony and his earlier statements to a military tribunal, which in 2004 the Supreme Court had ruled not competent to hear the case. In October the National Criminal Court acquitted five former top-ranking army officers responsible for counterinsurgency operations in the

Huallaga region of enforced disappearances in 1990, discounting evidence that "disappearance" was a systematic practice at the time.

Political Violence

During the current decade there have been several violent clashes between protesters and police, with deaths on both sides. The circumstances of these incidents are usually disputed. Prosecutorial investigations rarely clarify the circumstances of incidents in which police were accused of unlawfully using lethal force.

In June 2009, 33 people were killed (23 police and 10 civilians) in violent clashes between police and indigenous protesters in the provinces of Utcubamba and Bagua in the Peruvian Amazon. Eighty-two were treated in hospital for gunshot wounds, according to a report by the Ombudsman's Office. The police were clearing a stretch of road blocked by indigenous groups who were demanding that the government abandon a series of legislative decrees intended to facilitate economic activities in the Amazon region. Three indigenous witnesses who participated in the protest and were interviewed by a journalist in hospital where they were recovering from gunshot wounds said that the police fired live ammunition directly at them. Other witnesses claimed that several police were shot by demonstrators who had seized police weapons. Indigenous demonstrators also killed 10 policemen taken captive while guarding an oil pipeline.

According to the Ombudsman's Office, 84 civilians were later facing court proceedings for the violence, 18 of whom were in detention. The Attorney General's Office also opened an investigation into possible police responsibility for unlawful killings. In August a prosecutor started proceedings against 16 police officers alleged responsible for deaths and injuries. However, the attorney general accused the prosecutor of acting without a mandate by opening the case after being notified that she had been replaced. The case was dropped, and another prosecutor is still collecting evidence at this writing.

Torture and Ill-Treatment

Torture and ill-treatment of criminal suspects continue to be problems in Peru. A poor record of prosecuting state agents for abuses hinders eradication of these practices. The Ombudsman received 503 complaints of torture and ill-treatment between January 2003 and October 2008.

The crime of torture was incorporated into the criminal code in 1998, but some judicial authorities have failed to grasp the seriousness of the crime. In 2008 a Supreme Court panel annulled a conviction for torture on the erroneous grounds that torture—which comes under the heading of crimes against humanity in the criminal code—exists only at times of political conflict. The court ordered a new trial, and in August 2009 a new panel found the perpetrator guilty only of causing injury and reduced the penalty to a suspended prison sentence of four years. In another case, a prosecutor used the same argument to drop charges of torture against a military officer accused of beating a recruit in 2001. He declared the lesser charge of causing injury to be subject to a statute of limitations, depriving the victim of any redress.

Media Freedom

Journalists in Peru's provinces are vulnerable to intimidation and threats. Individuals acting in support of, or working for, municipal authorities have assaulted, and even murdered, journalists who publicize abuses by local government officials.

In June 2009 the government revoked the broadcasting license of a local radio station in the Peruvian Amazon, La Voz de Bagua, after the minister of the interior and members of the president's American Revolutionary People's Alliance (APRA) party accused it of "inciting violence" during its coverage of the civil unrest in Bagua. Although the broadcasting authorities claimed the station was operating illegally, the timing and circumstances of the revocation suggested that it was an act of censorship or punishment in response to coverage of the anti-government protests.

Human Rights Defenders

Former president Fujimori's supporters in Congress, as well as some top government officials, have aggressively sought to discredit NGOs that advocate for human rights accountability. Such NGOs have been falsely accused of sympathy with terrorist groups or of undermining the armed forces.

Rights advocates face anonymous threats. In September 2009 Salomón Lerner, former president of the National Truth and Reconciliation Commission, reported that the dogs at his property had died from poisoning. Two weeks later he received anonymous phone calls both at his house and at the Institute for Democracy and Human Rights at the Catholic University of Peru, of which he is president. The caller left a message warning, "What we did to your dogs we will do to you."

Reproductive Rights

Peru's restrictive abortion laws and policies, which criminalize abortion generally and provide only vague guidance on when an abortion may be procured lawfully, contribute to maternal death and disability. Approximately 16 percent of maternal deaths in Peru are attributable to unsafe abortions. In October 2009 a special congressional committee set up to review the country's penal code proposed decriminalizing abortion in cases of rape, incest, and fetal abnormalities.

Key International Actors

In June 2009 the United Nations special rapporteur on indigenous people, James Anaya, visited Peru on a mission to investigate the events in the Peruvian Amazon. In August, in its final observations on Peru's report to the UN Committee on the Elimination of Racial Discrimination, the committee urged Peru to implement Anaya's recommendation that an independent commission with indigenous representation be formed to impartially investigate the events.

VENEZUELA

President Hugo Chávez and his supporters have effectively neutralized the independence of Venezuela's judiciary. In the absence of a judicial check on its actions, the Chávez government has systematically undermined journalists' freedom of expression, workers' freedom of association, and the ability of civil society groups to promote human rights.

Police abuses remain a widespread problem. Prison conditions are among the worst on the continent, with a high rate of fatalities from inmate violence.

Independence of the Judiciary

In 2004 Chávez and his supporters in the National Assembly launched a political takeover of the Supreme Court, filling it with government supporters and creating new measures that make it possible to purge justices from the Court. Since then, the Court has largely abdicated its role as a check on executive power. It has failed to uphold fundamental rights enshrined in the Venezuelan constitution in key cases involving government efforts to limit freedom of expression and association.

Prosecution of Political Opponents

In 2009 several prominent opposition figures were targeted for criminal prosecution, raising concerns that without independent courts they have little chance of a fair trial. The targeted leaders included the former governor of Zulia state and opposition candidate in the 2006 presidential election, Manuel Rosales, whose arrest on corruption charges was ordered in March 2009. In an October 2008 speech, Chávez had publicly appealed to the attorney general and the Supreme Court to take this action against Rosales: "[A] type like that should be in prison.... I'll put myself in charge of the operation, and the operation will be called 'Manuel Rosales, you go to jail.'" To avoid arrest, Rosales left Venezuela and was granted political asylum in Peru in April 2009. Raúl Baduel, an army general who commanded the military operation that returned Chávez to power during the April 2002 coup attempt, is currently in Ramo Verde military prison, facing trial by a military court on corruption charges. Baduel was an outspoken critic of constitutional reforms proposed by Chávez and his supporters in the National Assembly.

Media Freedom

Venezuela enjoys vibrant public debate in which anti-government and pro-government media are equally vocal in their criticism and defense of Chávez. However, in its efforts to influence the control and content of the media, the government has engaged in discriminatory actions against media that air opposition viewpoints, strengthened the state's capacity to limit free speech, and created powerful incentives for government critics to engage in self-censorship.

Laws introduced since Chávez took office that have contributed to a climate of self-censorship include amendments to the criminal code extending the scope of *desacato* (disrespect) laws, and a broadcasting statute that encourages self-censorship by allowing the arbitrary suspension of channels for the vaguely defined offense of "incitement."

The government has used the broadcasting law to target Globovisión, the only remaining outspokenly critical television outlet on public airwaves. As of November 2009 the channel was facing six investigations by CONATEL, the state telecommunications commission, for alleged infractions of the law's vague public order provisions. In May 2009, for example, CONATEL opened an investigation against Globovisión on the grounds that its coverage of an earthquake, which called for calm but also criticized the government for slowness in providing information, "could generate alarm, fear, anxiety, or panic in the population."

The government has abused its control of broadcasting frequencies to punish radio stations with overtly critical programming. In July 2009, 32 stations were summarily taken off the air after CONATEL found that their licenses were not in order. The stations were given no opportunity to present arguments or evidence so that their claims could be assessed in a transparent manner. Moreover, many argued that over the years CONATEL had failed to respond to their requests to regularize their legal status. CONATEL's director announced in September that another group of 29 radio stations would shortly be closed, and that the status of a further 177 was under review. By early November, however, no action had been taken.

President Chávez has repeatedly responded to critical coverage by threatening television stations that they would lose their broadcasting rights as soon as their concessions expired. Radio Caracas Television (RCTV) lost its concession in 2007, after Chávez announced at a nationally broadcast military ceremony that RCTV would not have its concession renewed because of its support for the 2002 coup attempt. Neither this accusation nor an alleged breach of broadcasting standards was ever proved in a proceeding in which RCTV had an opportunity to present a defense.

The government has taken, or proposed, other measures to extend government control over broadcasting content. Under a decree issued in September 2009, private radio stations will have to broadcast for three-and-a-half hours every day programs selected by the government and produced by government-certified independent producers. In July CONATEL's director proposed imposing limits on the ability of private radio stations to share their own programming on a voluntary basis. No more than three private radio stations would be allowed to group together to transmit programming of their own, and for no longer than half an hour a day.

In July 2009 the attorney general proposed legislation on "media crimes" that would establish prison sentences of up to four years for anyone who, through media outlets, provides "false" information that "harm[s] the interests of the state." After strenuous objections to the proposal both within Venezuela and by international organizations, the president of the National Assembly announced that it would not be debated.

Labor Rights

The Chávez government has engaged in systematic violations of workers' rights aimed at undercutting established labor unions while favoring new, parallel unions that support its political agenda.

The government requires that all union elections be organized and certified by the National Electoral Council (CNE), a public authority. This mandatory oversight of union elections violates international standards, which guarantee workers the right to elect their representatives in full freedom and according to the conditions they determine. Established unions whose elections have not been certified by the CNE are barred from participating in collective bargaining.

The government has promised for several years to reform the relevant labor and electoral laws to restrict state interference in union elections. Yet new regulations introduced by the CNE in May 2009 set out detailed rules governing union elections, and fail to state clearly that elections not organized and certified by the CNE are legally valid. At this writing, a long-awaited reform of labor legislation is still under consultation and no bill has yet been presented in the legislature.

In the crucial state oil industry, government officials have themselves interfered in union elections. In 2009 the CNE repeatedly postponed an election in the oil workers' federation, FUTPV, due to challenges to the electoral register lodged by union factions backed by the government, thereby delaying negotiation of a collective contract for the industry. The president of the state oil company, PDVSA, who is also the minister of energy and oil, announced at a televised political rally that he would "discuss the collective contract only when the revolution gains control of the FUTPV," and would not "sit down to discuss a collective contract with any enemy of Chávez." He said he was backing one of the factions in the elections and accused its opponents—most of whom also supported the government, but were critical of the company management—of being "disguised enemies" of the revolution. The union elections, finally held on October 1, resulted in the victory of the faction backed by PDVSA.

Police Abuses

Violent crime is rampant in Venezuela and extrajudicial killings by security agents remain a recurring problem. Thousands of extrajudicial executions have been recorded in the past decade. Impunity for these crimes remains the norm. The attorney general reported in 2009 that investigations had been opened into 6,422 cases of human rights abuses by police by September 2008, resulting in the prosecution of 463 officers.

In April 2008 the Chávez government issued by decree an Organic Law of Police Service and National Police, which includes measures aimed at improving police accountability. It created a new office within the Ministry of Interior and Justice, called the Police Rector, to evaluate the performance of all police departments, including their compliance with human rights standards. Implementation of the law, however, has been slow.

Prison Conditions

Venezuelan prisons are among the most violent in Latin America. Weak security, insufficient guards, and corruption allow armed gangs to effectively control prisons. Overcrowding, deteriorating infrastructure, and the poor training of guards contribute to the brutal conditions. In May 2009 the director of the prison service claimed that levels of violence had fallen by 52 percent as a result of government efforts to "humanize" the penitentiary system. Venezuelan prison reform advocates deny that violence has declined.

Human Rights Defenders

The Chávez government has aggressively sought to discredit local and international human rights organizations. In September 2009, for example, a senior official of the ruling United Socialist Party of Venezuela, who has his own show on state television, accused Liliana Ortega, director of COFAVIC, an NGO that works for the victims of police violence, of pocketing part of their compensation money. Officials, including the president, have repeatedly made unsubstantiated allegations that human rights advocates were engaged in efforts to destabilize the country. The government often tries to have local rights advocates barred from international human rights gatherings, typically on grounds that their work is political or that they receive US or other foreign funding. Rights advocates have also faced prosecutorial harassment.

Key International Actors

The Venezuelan government has increasingly rejected international monitoring of its human rights record. In May 2009, reacting to the Venezuela chapter of the

Inter-American Commission on Human Rights annual report, President Chávez threatened to take Venezuela out of the Organization of American States and create an alternative organization of "free peoples." The government has referred to the commission's "biased position" as its reason for not inviting it to visit the country since 2002.

In a December 2008 ruling, the Supreme Court called on the government to revoke Venezuela's ratification of the American Convention on Human Rights.

"We Have the Promises of the World"

Women's Rights in Afghanistan

HUMAN
RIGHTS
WATCH

WORLD REPORT

2010

ASIA

AFGHANISTAN

2009 was another year marked by growing violence and insecurity, with the armed conflict continuing to spread. Insurgent attacks increased, killing greater numbers of civilians.

The second half of the year was dominated by presidential and provincial council elections in August 2009, which saw high levels of violence and intimidation, primarily by the Taliban and other insurgent groups. The elections were marred by widespread fraud and low turnout in conflict areas. A runoff was ordered between President Hamid Karzai and his main challenger, Adbullah Abdullah, but following the refusal by the Karzai-appointed electoral commission to accept anti-fraud measures for the second round his opponent withdrew, and Karzai was declared the winner.

The vulnerability of women's basic rights was demonstrated by the passing of the discriminatory Shia Personal Status Law by the Parliament, followed by President Karzai's signing of it into law.

Armed Conflict and Related Human Rights Abuses

The United Nations reported that approximately 2,021 civilians were killed by coalition, government, and insurgent forces in the first 10 months of 2009, an increase on 1,838 killed during the same period in 2008. Of these, 69 percent were attributed to "anti government elements," and 23 percent to international-led military forces. In 2008 the international-led military forces were responsible for more than one-third of civilian deaths. Reforms in United States and NATO operational guidelines appear to have resulted in a reduction in casualties of around 30 percent in the first 10 months of 2009, compared to the same period in 2008.

Civilian casualties caused by the Taliban and other insurgent groups continued to rise. Improvised explosive devices caused most deaths, with targeted killings and summary executions, including beheadings, adding to the death toll and levels of fear in communities. The Taliban continued to be involved in the forcible and voluntary recruitment of children to take part in fighting.

Civilian casualties from United States and NATO airstrikes continued, although the US and NATO belatedly took steps to decrease the number of deaths. Perceived excessive use of force and cultural insensitivity during "night raids" by international military forces into Afghan homes continued to be a significant concern. The US continued its extralegal detention practices at Bagram airbase, though changes in policy should bring modest improvements, such as regular review hearings for detainees.

Governance and Impunity

The absence of due process of law remains a fundamental failing of the Afghan legal system, as Afghans continue to face arbitrary detention, are frequently denied access to a lawyer, and are often denied the right to challenge the grounds of their detention before an impartial judge. Court proceedings are often marred by corruption and the abuse of power. There are persistent reports of torture and abuse against detainees being held by the National Directorate of Security, with human rights officials receiving only erratic access to detention facilities where abuses are believed to be taking place.

Kidnapping of Afghans for ransom is common, including NGO workers, and businessmen and their children. The most active areas are in the south, east, and central regions, where kidnappings significantly contribute to levels of insecurity, sharply curtailing movement for women and children in particular. Kidnappings are carried out by criminal gangs, and are also used by insurgent groups for money and leverage over prisoner releases. The police seem largely incapable or unwilling to tackle kidnappings or other abuses by powerful interests.

In many areas of the country local strongmen and former warlords continue to exert significant power over communities, using intimidation and violence to maintain their control. The Afghan government has continued to lose public legitimacy because of these abuses, widespread corruption, failure to improve living standards, and lack of progress in establishing the rule of law even in areas under its control. Afghans frequently cite police corruption as a problem, with internationally-funded police reform efforts showing limited impact. New measures for tackling corruption were announced in the post-election period, with the government under unprecedented levels of pressure to reform from international partners.

Human rights abusers continued to enjoy almost complete impunity. President Karzai attempted to secure his reelection in 2009 through a series of deals with former warlords from all the main ethnic factions. The choice of Mohammad Qasim Fahim as Karzai's vice presidential running mate was emblematic of this trend; Fahim has long been implicated in possible war crimes from the 1990s and is widely perceived by many Afghans to be connected to criminal gangs.

The government did little to implement the Action Plan for Peace, Reconciliation and Justice, a plan launched in 2005 for transitional justice in Afghanistan. Human rights groups continued to document war crimes, with growing numbers of civil society groups working with victims of war crimes.

Women's and Girls' Rights

The vulnerability of women's and girls' rights was demonstrated in February-March 2009 when the Parliament passed and the president signed the Shia Personal Status Law, which contained many articles offensive and dangerous to women. After a national and international outcry, and an unprecedented campaign by Afghan women's rights activists, the law was amended, but many articles remained that conflict with the Afghan constitution and international human rights standards. One provision grants child custody rights exclusively to fathers and grandfathers. Another forbids a wife from leaving her house without her husband's permission unless she has "reasonable legal reasons," which are unspecified.

A more positive legislative development was the success of Afghan women's rights activists in getting a law on the Elimination of Violence Against Women passed. Although there are serious flaws in the legislation, it creates the crime of rape in Afghan law for the first time. Violence against women and girls remains endemic, with prevention or justice for victims obstructed by cultural barriers as well as bias and misogyny among many security officials and judges.

Many of the women who campaigned against the Shia law came under threats and pressure.

Attacks on Education

As part of their campaign of terrorizing the civilian population, the Taliban and other insurgent groups continued to target schools, in particular girls' schools. According to the Ministry of Education, in the first five months of the Afghan year 1387 (April-August 2009), 102 schools were attacked using explosives or arson, and 105 students and teachers were killed by insurgent attacks. Three girls' schools in the central region were attacked with chemicals (thought to be pesticide or insecticide) in April and May 2009, which the Ministry of Education says injured 196 girls.

Human Rights Defenders and Independent Journalists

Freedom of expression for those who criticize government officials or powerful local figures remains limited. Threats, violence, and intimidation are regularly used to silence opposition politicians, critical journalists, and civil society activists. Women all over the country mourned the murder in April 2009 of Sitara Achakzai, an outspoken human rights defender and local councilor in Kandahar. No one was charged with her murder. The killing of a high-profile figure like Achakzai created widespread fear among women and human rights defenders in the southern region.

In September, 23-year-old student Sayed Parviz Kambakhsh was released early after spending 20 months in prison on blasphemy charges (he was accused of downloading, doctoring, and distributing an article among friends), after a trial and appeal process that did not respect Afghan law or meet international standards. He had originally been sentenced to death, commuted to 20 years' imprisonment.

The Afghan Independent Human Rights Commission continued to be an active and outspoken human rights organization. It came under increasing pressure from the government in 2009 to curtail its activities, including the threat of legal action against one of the commissioners by the Attorney General's Office. The move was strongly resisted by the commission.

The blossoming of an independent media sector was once seen as a rare success of the post-Taliban government. But the increasingly authoritarian government has repressed critical journalism, leading to widespread self-censorship. In the days before the elections of 2009, the government attempted to overtly censor the media by issuing a ban on the reporting of election-related violence. Dozens of journalists were beaten or detained in 2009 by security officials, and some were held without charge for days, weeks, or months.

Insurgent groups used murder, arson, kidnapping, and intimidation to try to stop reporting they see as unsympathetic. In September 2009 the Taliban in Kunduz province kidnapped an Afghan and a British journalist, leading to a rescue operation in which the Afghan, Sultan Munadi, was killed.

Key International Actors

The United States continued to be the key external actor and donor. It maintained enormous influence over the government of President Karzai through its financial and military support, including the deployment of as many as 68,000 troops, with additional US troops expected in 2010. The United States announced an international "civilian uplift" to implement its strategy in Afghanistan. President Obama repeatedly stressed the importance of a stable Afghanistan to the security of the United States, but rarely discussed the importance of human rights protections for Afghans.

The US military continued to operate in Afghanistan without an adequate legal framework, such as a status-of-forces agreement, and continued to detain hundreds of Afghans without adequate legal process. Evolving plans to reform US detention practices in Afghanistan were welcome but fell short of international standards.

By many estimates, Afghanistan continued to receive significantly less per capita donor assistance than other post-conflict countries (estimated to be less than US$80 per person per year for reconstruction over the past six years, as compared to approximately US$250 for the people of Bosnia and Timor-Leste).

The credibility of the United Nations in Afghanistan was tarnished in the post-electoral fallout by the very public discord between the deputy head of mission, Peter Galbraith, and the special representative for Afghanistan, Kai Eide, over how to respond to the fraud allegations. Galbraith was sacked after accusing Eide of downplaying levels of fraud. In general the UN mission remains understaffed, with the human rights and rule of law offices well below capacity. On October 28, 2009, an attack on a guesthouse where many UN election staff were staying killed five UN staff and three Afghans, and resulted in 600 international UN staff being relocated or removed from Afghanistan.

Bangladesh

Bangladesh returned to democratic rule in 2009. Constitutionally guaranteed rights, suspended during most of 2007 and 2008, were in place and the elected government under Prime Minister Sheikh Hasina made strong commitments to address a number of serious human rights problems. Yet extrajudicial executions, custodial torture, and impunity for members of the security forces continue. Following a bloody rebellion within the Bangladesh Rifles (BDR), thousands of guards were arrested, many tortured, and some killed in detention.

Political Developments

In January 2009 the military-backed interim government that ruled Bangladesh under a state of emergency during 2007-08 stepped down following parliamentary elections. An Awami League-led alliance won 263 of the 300 contested seats in parliament. Domestic and international election observers generally considered the elections to be more free and fair than previous elections.

The new government has recommended the withdrawal of many of the corruption cases initiated against Awami League supporters charged in connection with the interim government's anti-corruption drive on the grounds that the cases were politically motivated. The similar legal processes initiated against members of the political opposition are, with few exceptions, continuing.

The government moved toward implementing the Chittagong Hill Tracts (CHT) Peace Accord signed between the government and the United People's Party of the Chittagong Hill Tracts in 1997. As part of this process the government removed some of its army troops in the area in 2009.

In July parliament adopted a new Human Rights Commission Act, under which an independent commission is mandated to investigate violations. At this writing the commission has yet to be constituted.

Elements in the Bangladesh Rifles, the country's border guard unit, staged a rebellion at BDR headquarters in Dhaka, the capital, on February 25-26, 2009. In the rebellion 74 people, including 57 commanding officers seconded from the

army, were killed. Despite pressure from the armed forces to place those suspected of involvement in the rebellion before a court martial, the government decided
in accordance with a recommendation of the Supreme Court to try them in civilian
courts and under the BDR ordinance. As of September 2009 about 3,700 border
guards were detained as a result of the indiscriminate arrests that followed the
rebellion.

Extrajudicial Killings

On several occasions during 2009 the government promised that it would end the
grave problem of extrajudicial executions by members of the security forces. Yet
the Rapid Action Battalion (RAB)—an elite paramilitary law enforcement agency—
and the police continued to kill people in what the authorities refer to as "crossfire" killings, "encounters," and "shootouts" but in fact constitute thinly disguised extrajudicial executions. According to the human rights group Odhikar,
109 such killings were reported in the press between January 1 and October 31,
2009. The killings increased significantly during the second half of the year, suggesting a lack of commitment to confront the security forces once the government
settled into office. Alleged members of outlawed left-wing political parties are
particularly targeted. In echoes of previous governments' statements that had
been heavily criticized by the Awami League while in opposition, the government
claimed that law enforcement agencies were only exercising their right to self
defense.

On May 27, RAB killed two Dhaka polytechnic students, Mohammad Ali Jinnah
and Mohsin Sheikh, in what RAB referred to as a "shootout." However, witnesses
stated that the two men were arrested at night at their campus. Jinnah's family
has filed a murder case against 10 RAB officers questioning how the victims,
while allegedly running to escape, were shot in the chest, abdomen, and throat.

Torture

Torture continues to be used by law enforcement officials to force confessions in
criminal investigations and to extort money. The bodies of those who are killed by
RAB and the police regularly have physical marks and injuries indicating that they
were subjected to torture.

Several persons taken into custody following the BDR rebellion in February 2009 died under suspicious circumstances. Many detainees were subjected to physical torture, including beatings and electric shocks. Relatives of Mobarak Hossain, one of the BDR members who died after being detained, allege that he was tortured to death. Sources at the Dhaka Medical College morgue told the media and human rights workers that Hossain's wrists, arms, knees, and shoulders were swollen and badly bruised. In May the government announced that a commission had been established to investigate the deaths of BDR members in custody. The findings of the commission, which was to have submitted its report within 15 days, have not been made public at this writing.

On October 22, F.M. Masum, a journalist at the *New Age* newspaper, was detained by RAB officers and tortured. Masum has written several reports about the paramilitary unit for *New Age*, including on its involvement in extrajudicial killings.

Laws that facilitate torture by removing or undermining fundamental safeguards against arbitrary arrests and detention remain in effect, including the Special Powers Act and the newly adopted Anti-Terrorism Act.

Impunity

In 2009 Human Rights Watch could identify no cases of members of the security forces being convicted and imprisoned for killings, acts of torture, or illegal detentions. The government removed from their positions a few individuals responsible for human rights abuses committed by the Directorate General of Forces Intelligence (Bangladesh's most important military intelligence agency) during the former interim government's anti-corruption campaign.

Legal provisions that have traditionally shielded members of the security forces and other public officials from prosecution, by requiring government approval for criminal actions to be initiated, remain in effect.

The government is moving toward bringing to trial those responsible for international crimes in connection with the war of 1971. Parliament in 2009 passed amendments to the International Crimes (Tribunals) Act of 1973, but the law still falls short of international standards.

Ignoring Executions and Torture

Impunity for Bangladesh's Security Forces

HUMAN
RIGHTS
WATCH

Freedom of Expression and Information

Despite the election of a new government, few journalists feel that they are able to write freely about the involvement of members of the armed forces in human rights abuses, corruption, and other illegal practices. There is no indication that the government is working to implement the Awami League's election promise of bringing to justice those responsible for past killings of journalists.

Several reporters scrutinizing the affairs of politicians and alleged criminals were physically attacked. On April 11, 2009, journalist Abdullah Al-Amin Biplob of the *Samakal* newspaper was severely beaten by a group of men identifying themselves as supporters of an Awami League member of parliament. Earlier the same day the parliamentarian had, according to Biplob, threatened to give him "a lesson" if he continued to write articles criticizing him.

A right to information ordinance adopted under the former interim government was turned into law in 2009, providing the right for people to access most kinds of government-held information.

Women's and Girls' Rights

While women occupy several key positions in the government, discrimination against women is common in both the public and private spheres. Bangladesh's reservations against the requirement in the Convention on the Elimination of All Forms of Discrimination against Women to ensure equal rights for women and men remain in effect.

Domestic violence is a daily reality for many women, and long-awaited laws on domestic violence and sexual harassment were still pending in 2009. The Acid Survivors Foundation reported 90 acid attacks, primarily against women, between January and September, but only eight convictions. There were reports of village elders and clerics issuing fatwas that resulted in women being caned for adultery or for talking to non-Muslim men.

Sexual Orientation and Gender Identity

Section 377 of Bangladesh's criminal code, an inheritance of British colonial rule, punishes consensual homosexual conduct with up to life imprisonment.

Human Rights Defenders

The NGO Affairs Bureau, which approves projects and funding of NGOs, created obstacles for some organizations trying to obtain permission to receive foreign donor funding. In August 2009 the Bureau cancelled an ongoing anti-torture project implemented by Odhikar on the grounds that the Ministry of Home Affairs objected to it.

Staff members of several human rights organizations were subjected to harassment by members of the security forces. Advocate Shahanur Islam Saikot of the Bangladesh Institute of Human Rights, who filed several cases against members of the army, RAB, and police for torture, received several death threats from individuals identifying themselves as belonging to these agencies.

Key International Actors

Foreign governments including the United States and the European Union raised concerns about extrajudicial executions and other abuses, and continued to stress the importance of addressing the impunity problem. They also provided financial support to a range of human rights groups in Bangladesh.

In the hope of future cooperation with RAB on organized crime, Islamic militancy, and terrorism, the United Kingdom and United States continued to conduct human rights training for selected RAB members.

In 2009 Bangladesh was reelected to the United Nations Human Rights Council. However, the government has issued no standing invitation to the Council's special procedures to visit Bangladesh. In spite of their poor human rights record, Bangladesh's armed forces and police continue to be major contributors to UN peacekeeping operations.

BURMA

Burma's human rights record continued to deteriorate in 2009 ahead of announced elections in 2010. The ruling State Peace and Development Council (SPDC) systematically denies citizens basic freedoms including freedom of expression, association, and assembly. More than 2,100 political prisoners remain behind bars. This, and the politically-motivated arrest and trial of Aung San Suu Kyi only to send her back to house arrest for another 18 months, confirmed that Burma's military rulers are unwilling to allow genuine political participation in the electoral process. The Burmese military continues to perpetrate violations against civilians in ethnic conflict areas, including extrajudicial killings, forced labor, and sexual violence.

Trial of Aung San Suu Kyi

Aung San Suu Kyi, one of the leaders of the opposition National League for Democracy (NLD), has been under house arrest since 2003. On May 14, 2009, authorities arrested her (along with her two housemaids, who are NLD members) on charges that she breached terms of her house arrest order by permitting the intrusion of an American man, John Yettaw. Suu Kyi and her two staff were transferred to Insein prison, and went on trial on May 18 for allegedly violating the 1975 State Protection Act, the draconian law used to justify her house arrest extension orders.

The trial dragged on for three months, with frequent delays and with international fair trial standards lacking. Suu Kyi was allowed legal representation, but the court did not meet her counsel's request to present a number of witnesses (there were 14 prosecution but only two defense witnesses). The court was closed to the public, with foreign diplomats and the press permitted to observe the trial only on a few occasions. On August 11 Suu Kyi was found guilty, and sentenced to three years' hard labor, but almost immediately Home Affairs Minister Gen. Maung Oo read out a letter from President Than Shwe declaring the sentences of Suu Kyi and her staff would be commuted to 18 months' house arrest. The court sentenced Yettaw to seven years' hard labor for breaching Suu Kyi's house arrest conditions and for immigration violations, but he was released a week later on

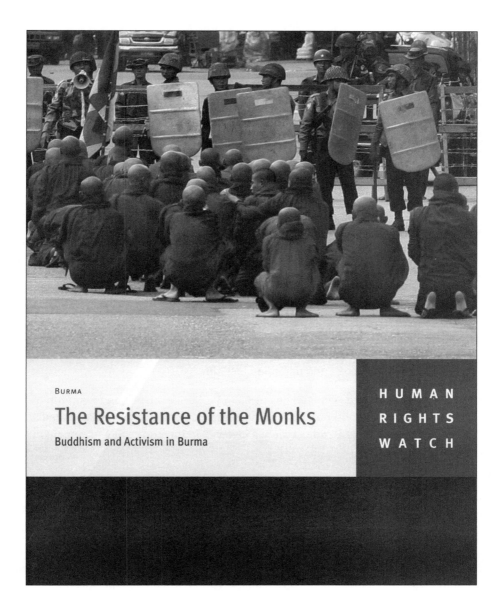

BURMA

The Resistance of the Monks

Buddhism and Activism in Burma

HUMAN
RIGHTS
WATCH

humanitarian grounds during a visit by US Senator Jim Webb. Suu Kyi appealed her sentence, but the Rangoon Division Court dismissed the appeal on October 1.

Political Prisoners and Human Rights Defenders

Activists arrested in 2007 and 2008, especially those involved in the 2007 mass protests, were sentenced by unfair trials in closed courts. In 2009 the SPDC conducted two prisoner amnesties, releasing 6,313 prisoners in February and 7,114 in September, but only 31 of those released in February and an estimated 130 released in September were political prisoners. They included journalist Eine Khine Oo, arrested in 2008 for helping victims of Cyclone Nargis, and magazine editor Thet Zin. An estimated 2,100 political prisoners remain incarcerated for their peaceful activities in Burma. Many prominent prisoners, such as student leader Min Ko Naing and famed comedian and social activist Zargana, have been transferred to isolated prisons with poor health and sanitation facilities.

Meanwhile, arrests of human rights defenders, activists, and NLD members continued throughout 2009. On September 3, authorities arrested US citizen Kyaw Zaw Lwin when he arrived in Rangoon. Zaw Lwin, who had been active in international campaigns on the rights of political prisoners, has reportedly been tortured in prison. The International Committee of the Red Cross (ICRC) is still denied access to Burmese prisons and detention facilities.

Buddhist monks and key monasteries throughout Burma suspected of anti-junta activity are closely monitored by the authorities to deter any renewed monk-led protests. More than 230 Buddhist monks involved in the 2007 protests remain in prison.

Ethnic Conflict Areas, Internal Displacement, and Refugees

The Burmese military continues to attack civilians in ethnic conflict areas, particularly in eastern and northern Burma. In May 2009, attacks by the army and its proxy force, the Democratic Karen Buddhist Army (DKBA), displaced thousands of civilians and forced an estimated 5,000 refugees into Thailand. In late July attacks by Burmese army troops against 39 villages in central Shan state displaced an estimated 10,000 civilians in the area.

Tensions between the military government and an estimated two dozen armed militias with longstanding, semi-official ceasefire agreements increased during 2009 as the government instructed them to disarm and transform into smaller "Border Security Guard" forces ahead of the 2010 elections. In August 2009, government attacks against an official ceasefire militia, the Myanmar National Democratic Alliance Army in northern Shan state, drove some 37,000 ethnic Kokang and Chinese civilians into southern China. Some of the refugees have returned, but thousands have remained in China due to fears of further fighting.

Abuses such as sexual violence against women and girls, extrajudicial killings, forced labor, torture, beatings, and confiscation of land and property are widespread. In clear violation of international humanitarian law, the Burmese army and non-state armed groups continue to routinely use antipersonnel landmines, and target food production and means of civilian livelihood.

There are an estimated half-million internally displaced persons in eastern Burma, and 140,000 refugees remain in nine camps along the Thailand-Burma border, despite a large-scale resettlement program by international agencies. More than 50,000 refugees from Chin state remain in eastern India, and 28,000 ethnic Rohingya Muslims live in squalid camps in Bangladesh.

Millions of Burmese migrants, refugees, and asylum seekers live in Thailand, India, Bangladesh, and Malaysia and are sometimes subject to trafficking. Thousands of ethnic Rohingya from western Burma and Bangladesh made perilous journeys by sea to Thailand, Malaysia, and Indonesia in late 2008 and early 2009. In January Thailand pushed back a number of boats into open waters, despite an international outcry (see also Thailand chapter).

Child Soldiers

Burma continues widespread and systematic forced recruitment of child soldiers. In June the United Nations Security Council working group on children and armed conflict released its report on Burma, calling on the SPDC to increase its efforts to end the culture of impunity for the forcible recruitment of child soldiers. The SPDC has instituted cosmetic and largely ineffectual policies to end the recruitment of child soldiers, with a low number of prosecutions of perpetrators that has not

BURMA

"We Are Like Forgotten People"

The Chin People of Burma: Unsafe in Burma,
Unprotected in India

HUMAN
RIGHTS
WATCH

addressed the full extent of the problem. The junta limits its engagement with the UN Burma country team efforts through the International Labour Organization (ILO), which has been effective in releasing a small number of child soldiers. Non-state armed groups such as the DKBA increased their forcible recruitment and use of child soldiers in 2009.

Humanitarian Concerns

Humanitarian engagement in areas of the Irrawaddy Delta affected by May 2008's Cyclone Nargis has given international and private Burmese relief agencies greater freedom to operate. However, basic freedoms of expression and information, assembly, and movement are still denied or curtailed. Private Burmese relief agencies have markedly proliferated, but must still navigate government controls, and most operate clandestinely. The SPDC delayed or denied work visas to some foreign aid workers posted to Burma. An increase in international humanitarian assistance has not been matched by junta programs—although the SPDC accrues billions of dollars annually in natural gas sales, little of it is disbursed to urgently needed health and livelihood programs.

Parts of Burma remain either off-limits to humanitarian relief organizations, or with tight controls imposed on movement and monitoring of projects, such as western Arakan state and conflict zones in eastern Burma. Conditions in these areas, particularly in Rohingya communities, continue to present a serious human rights challenge to international agencies working in Burma.

Key International Actors

Key international actors on Burma including the United States, European Union, Australia, and the Association of Southeast Asian Nations (ASEAN) sharply criticized the trial of Suu Kyi and called for her immediate release. On June 16 five special rapporteurs of the United Nations Human Rights Council issued a joint statement that the trial violated substantive and procedural rights. In August the EU imposed a new set of targeted measures including extending its assets freeze to enterprises owned and controlled by junta members, and to members of the judiciary; the latter were also added to the list of persons under travel ban.

UN Secretary-General Ban Ki-moon visited Burma in July and met with senior junta leaders. Despite repeated requests he was denied permission to visit Aung San Suu Kyi. Ban stated his three calls to the SPDC to be the immediate release of political prisoners, an all-inclusive dialogue between the junta and Suu Kyi, and for the planned elections in 2010 to be "implemented in an inclusive, participatory, and transparent manner." Ban gave a speech in Rangoon at the end of his visit in which he deplored the human rights situation in Burma and called on the military government to work with the UN and the international community on seeking real political change and humanitarian development.

The UN secretary-general's special advisor on Burma, Ibrahim Gambari, visited Burma three times in 2009 to meet with senior junta officials. In September the "Group of Friends of Burma" met during UN General Assembly proceedings in New York and reiterated its call for the SPDC to work with the UN on substantive change. China blocked formal discussion of Burma in the Security Council in October.

The UN special rapporteur on human rights in Burma, Tomás Ojea Quintana, visited Burma in February for a five-day tour. He was allowed to meet with government-screened political prisoners in Rangoon and Hpa-an (Karen state), and with government officials, representatives of pro-SPDC civil society organizations, and members of legally registered political parties. Two requested further visits in 2009 were postponed. Quintana's August report to the UN General Assembly called for the SPDC "to take prompt measures to establish accountability and responsibility with regard to the widespread and systematic human rights violations reported in [Burma]."

In February US Secretary of State Hillary Clinton announced an official review of US policy toward Burma. The review was released in October, with the US retaining existing trade, investment, and targeted financial sanctions but announcing new high-level diplomatic engagement with the SPDC (Senator Webb's visit in August, ostensibly for private mediation efforts, had included meetings with senior military leaders, and afterward Webb had called on international actors to reconsider sanctions and engage with the SPDC). In November US Under-Secretary of State Kurt Campbell and other US officials paid the highest-level official visit to Burma in 15 years, meeting senior military leaders and Aung San Suu

Kyi. President Barack Obama met Burmese Prime Minister Thein Sein at a November US-ASEAN summit meeting with all 10 ASEAN leaders, marking the first meeting between Burmese and US leaders in decades.

ASEAN in 2009 made several criticisms of the SPDC and called for Suu Kyi's release, particularly in a strongly-worded statement issued by Thailand as the ASEAN chair in late May. ASEAN Secretary-General Surin Pitsuwan renewed the Tripartite Core Group to assist with post-cyclone aid, and repeated calls to engage with the SPDC on political reform. But ASEAN members Singapore, Vietnam, and Laos continued to support Burma internationally. China and Russia also continue to provide diplomatic support for the SPDC.

China, Thailand, and India are major trade and investment partners. In March Chinese officials secured an agreement with Burma to construct a pipeline to transport natural gas from western Burma to China. Sales of natural gas continue to account for the largest share of the SPDC's revenue, and this project, scheduled for completion in 2013, will generate considerable additional profits for the junta. The Kokang fighting on China's border prompted a rare public rebuke from China, however, which said the SPDC had "harmed the rights and interests of Chinese citizens living there."

In 2009 international calls increased for an investigation into war crimes and crimes against humanity in Burma, and for a UN arms embargo to be imposed. No government has yet taken the lead in either initiative at the UN, despite calls for imposing tougher measures on the SPDC for its use of child soldiers. China, Russia, and North Korea still sell arms to the SPDC.

CAMBODIA

Cambodia's respect for human rights continued its downward spiral during 2009, with dramatic setbacks in press freedom, misuse of the judiciary to silence government critics, and imposition of strict new restrictions on peaceful protests.

The ruling Cambodian People's Party of Prime Minister Hun Sen continued to use an array of repressive tactics, including harassment, threats, violence, and arbitrary arrest, to suppress political rivals, opposition journalists, land rights activists, and trade unionists. In late 2009 the government pushed new laws through the National Assembly with little input from civil society, including a new penal code.

Known rights abusers gained increasing power, with the promotion of several military officials implicated in torture, extrajudicial killings, and political violence, including two military commanders linked to the deadly 1997 grenade attack on an opposition rally.

Cambodia's epidemic of forced evictions of the urban poor and confiscation of farmers' land in the countryside reached crisis proportions in 2009. Military units were often deployed to carry out forced and violent evictions of villagers whose ownership claims to the land had never been properly or fairly dealt with by a court.

Freedom of Expression, Association, and Assembly

The government controls all television and most radio stations. It regularly suspends, threatens, or takes legal action against journalists or news outlets that criticize the government. Controversial publications are frequently banned or confiscated. Reporters covering sensitive issues risk dismissal, imprisonment, physical attack, or even death. Politically motivated murders of opposition journalists, such as Khim Sambo, who was killed in July 2008, and many others in the past 15 years remain unresolved.

The new penal code approved in October 2009 retains defamation and disinformation as criminal offenses. Government critics can now be criminally prosecuted for peaceful expression of their views not only about individuals, but government institutions. Media defamation cases are no longer covered by the penal code but by Cambodia's 1995 press law, which does not carry criminal liability or imprisonment as a penalty.

During 2009 at least 10 government critics were prosecuted for criminal defamation and disinformation based on complaints by government and military officials. Among those convicted were four journalists, two of whom were jailed on disinformation charges: opposition editor Hang Chakra, sentenced to one year's imprisonment in June, and journalist Ros Sokhet, sentenced to two years' imprisonment in November. In July editor Dam Sith closed *Moneaksekar Khmer*, one of Cambodia's oldest opposition papers, as the only way to prevent government lawsuits that could have landed him in prison.

Criminal defamation, disinformation, and incitement lawsuits were also filed against opposition Sam Rainsy Party (SRP) members, including party leader Sam Rainsy, SRP parliamentarians Mu Sochua and Ho Vann, and SRP youth activist Soung Sophorn. Prime Minister Hun Sen pressed defamation charges against the lawyer defending SRP cases, spurring the lawyer's withdrawal from the cases in July. As a result, Mu Sochua lacked legal counsel during her July 24 trial, in which she was found guilty of defaming the prime minister and ordered to pay US$4,100 in fines and compensation.

In a major step backwards, a new law on demonstrations passed in October bans public protests of more than 200 people, citing the need to safeguard "public order and security." It also requires protest organizers to seek advance permission and bans protests in front of or inside government buildings and factories. Authorities continued to forcibly disperse demonstrations during 2009, for example in October, when riot police blocked a march on World Teachers' Day by teachers calling for pay hikes.

Freedom of association remains under pressure. Workers who organize or strike for better wages and working conditions are subject to harassment, physical attacks, and unfair dismissal. Authorities failed to investigate or prosecute perpetrators of violence against union activists, including three union leaders murdered since 2004.

Arbitrary Detention, Torture, and Detention Conditions

Police arbitrarily rounded up sex workers, homeless children and families, beggars, and people who use drugs, and detained them in government-run social affairs centers where they were subject to physical mistreatment, sexual abuse, and insufficient food and medical care. During 2009 hundreds of people were unlawfully arrested in Phnom Penh during such sweeps, which spiked in advance of large public events.

Violence against women goes largely unpunished. Trafficking of women and girls for sexual exploitation, as well as arbitrary arrest and abuse of sex workers, is rampant. Regular police crackdowns on sex workers are fueled in part by a 2008 anti-trafficking law that criminalizes prostitution, spurring authorities to focus on closing brothels and arbitrarily detaining sex workers, rather than prosecuting traffickers. In 2009 Phnom Penh police arrested more than 60 sex workers during July alone, beating some of them in custody before sending them to NGO shelters, where those with HIV/AIDS were unable to access their medication.

Over 2,000 people who use drugs were arbitrarily detained in 11 government-run drug detention centers, where arduous physical exercises and forced labor are the mainstays of their "treatment," and torture is common. The centers hold people regardless of assessments that they are not dependent on drugs.

Police and military police routinely used torture to extract confessions from detainees in police stations, jails, and prisons. The bodies of several detainees who died in policy custody during 2009 showed marks of torture, such as Neak Neam, who died on May 27 while in the custody of the Pailin district police.

Cambodia's prisons continued to be overcrowded and failed to provide sufficient food, water, healthcare, and sanitation.

Land Confiscation and Forced Evictions

Land disputes escalated during 2009. Soaring real estate prices, development projects, and illegal land concessions spurred the forced eviction of thousands of urban poor and the illegal confiscation of farmers' land. With the vast majority of urban and rural poor lacking land title, more than 150,000 people nationwide were estimated to be at risk of losing their land and their homes. Despite this, in September the government terminated a US$24 million World Bank-funded land titling program.

Authorities rarely provided adequate housing, land, services, and compensation to people displaced or made landless and jobless by evictions and land grabbing. In one particularly egregious example, in June 2009 authorities relocated 40 families with HIV/AIDS to cramped, metal sheds in a remote resettlement site outside Phnom Penh, far from medical services and jobs.

Police and soldiers frequently used excessive force in evictions. In January police used teargas and water cannons to forcibly evict 400 families from Dey Krahom community in Phnom Penh. In March police opened fire on unarmed farmers protesting confiscation of their land in Siem Reap, seriously wounding four villagers. Authorities continued to arrest community activists protesting forced evictions and land grabbing, often on spurious charges, with more than 60 people imprisoned or awaiting trial during 2009 for their involvement in land conflicts.

Khmer Rouge Tribunal

Ongoing political interference by the Cambodian government in the work of the United Nations-backed Khmer Rouge tribunal (the Extraordinary Chambers in the Courts of Cambodia, ECCC) seriously undermined the court's integrity, independence, and credibility. Hun Sen, who maintained his grip on the country's judiciary, repeatedly demanded that the court not prosecute suspects other than five currently in custody. Credible reports of widespread corruption at the US$100 million hybrid tribunal, presided over by both Cambodian and international judges, were not sufficiently addressed.

Refugees and Asylum Seekers

Montagnard and ethnic Vietnamese asylum seekers face the threat of forced repatriation to Vietnam, where they are at risk of torture, persecution, and imprisonment, in violation of Cambodia's obligations under the 1951 Refugee Convention, to which it is a state party.

While the Cambodian government stated that it considers Khmer Krom (ethnic Khmers from southern Vietnam) who move to Cambodia from Vietnam to be Cambodian citizens, authorities routinely failed to provide protection in the form of political asylum, let alone full citizen's rights, to many Khmer Krom living in Cambodia. During 2009 Cambodia's Refugee Office continued to rule out consideration of all Khmer Krom asylum seekers from Vietnam, including Tim Sakhorn and five other Khmer Krom Buddhist monks who fled to Cambodia after having been imprisoned in Vietnam for peaceful expression.

Key International Actors

In July 2009 Cambodia's development partners, including the World Bank, Asian Development Bank, United Nations, European Commission, and several embassies, issued a rare public appeal for the government to stop forced evictions until it implements fair and transparent mechanisms to address land disputes and resettlement issues. In August the European Union and several embassies raised concerns with the government about the crackdown on peaceful expression.

Overall, Cambodia's donors remained ineffective in persuading the government to keep its annual promises to protect human rights and establish the rule of law. Years of funding for judicial reform have had virtually no effect. Japan, Cambodia's largest donor and the single largest funder of the ECCC, maintained its policy of not confronting the government about rights violations. China, another major investor and donor to Cambodia, continued not to link aid to reforms.

In addition to support for rule of law and human rights projects, United States aid to Cambodia included training and material assistance to the Cambodian military, police, and counterterrorism units with track records of serious human rights abuses. In September eight US lawmakers queried the US Defense Department about US support to Cambodian military units alleged to have committed rights violations. In 2009 the US retained Cambodia's anti-trafficking ranking at Tier 2, citing the failure to protect trafficking victims and abuses committed against "prostituted women" in police custody and state-run centers.

283

In September 2009 the UN Human Rights Council renewed the mandate of the UN special rapporteur on Cambodia, who made one visit to Cambodia during the year.

CHINA

In 2009 the Chinese government continued to impose restrictions put in place for the 2008 Olympics, fearing unrest around a series of "sensitive" anniversaries including the 20th anniversary of the Tiananmen massacre and the 60th anniversary of the founding of the People's Republic of China. Officials obstructed civil society organizations, including groups and individuals working with victims of the May 2008 Sichuan earthquake, broadened controls on Uighurs and Tibetans, and tightened restrictions on lawyers and human rights defenders.

The Chinese Communist Party continues its monopoly on political power and, despite legal system reforms, requires judicial institutions to toe the party line. Citizens face significant limits on freedom of expression, association, and religion; government surveillance and censoring of internet communications is far reaching. While China's international profile and economic clout continue to grow, it is also drawing increasing international scrutiny for a foreign policy that fails to prioritize civil and political rights.

Freedom of Expression

China's journalists, bloggers, and estimated 338 million Internet users are subject to the arbitrary dictates of state censors.

Proponents of freedom of expression in China scored a rare victory on June 30, 2009, when the Chinese government indefinitely delayed a plan to compel computer manufacturers to pre-install the Internet filtering software Green Dam Youth Escort on all personal computers sold in China. That decision followed weeks of scathing criticism from some of China's more than 300 million netizens, unprecedented opposition by foreign computer manufacturers and international business associations, and a threat from both the United States trade representative and secretary of commerce that Green Dam might prompt a World Trade Organization challenge.

At this writing at least 28 Chinese journalists are in prison on ambiguous charges including "inciting subversion" and "revealing state secrets." In May 2009 authorities in Guangdong province demanded that state media outlets reduce "negative" coverage of government officials and public protests, among other issues. On August 31, two private security guards employed by the Dongguan municipal government in southern Guangdong province attacked *Guangzhou Daily* reporter Liu Manyuan when he attempted to take photos at a crime scene. The guards beat him, prompting his temporary hospitalization.

On February 13, 2009, the Chinese government issued a new "code of conduct," which threatens Chinese news assistants working for foreign correspondents with dismissal and loss of accreditation for engaging in "independent reporting." Foreign correspondents also noted an increase in reprisals against sources in 2009, particularly in the run-up to the one-year anniversary of the massive May 12, 2008, Sichuan earthquake. On April 6, 2009, for example, security forces in the Sichuan town of Shifang temporarily detained a father whose child died in a collapsed school to prevent him from speaking to a German TV crew.

Foreign correspondents in China also continue to face restrictions and are barred from visiting Tibet freely. The Chinese government allowed significantly greater foreign media access to Urumqi following deadly rioting there on July 5-7, 2009, than it did to Tibet during the unrest that began there in March 2008, but access to areas outside Urumqi, particularly the city of Kashgar, was more restricted. On July 10, 2009, government authorities in Kashgar forced Elizabeth Dalziel, an Associated Press photographer, and Mark Mackinnon, correspondent for the *Globe & Mail*, to leave the city due to an unspecified "security" threat. Paramilitary police punched and kicked three Hong Kong television journalists covering a peaceful public protest in Urumqi on September 4. On September 18 a group of unidentified individuals attacked three reporters from Japan's Kyodo News Agency who were covering a rehearsal in Beijing for the October 1 National Day parade.

Activists also face persecution for working on behalf of victims of the 2008 Sichuan earthquake. Huang Qi, a veteran activist and founder of www.64tianwang.com, a website dedicated to publicizing human rights abuses across China, faced a one-day trial on August 5, 2009, on charges of "revealing state secrets" and "subversion" for his investigation of allegations that shoddy construction contributed to the collapse of schools in the earthquake zone. On August 12 Tan Zuoren faced trial on charges of "incitement to subvert state

power" for compiling a list of children killed in the earthquake. Tan had also allegedly tried to organize a public commemoration of the 20th anniversary of the 1989 Tiananmen massacre. Authorities blocked the blog of renowned Chinese architect Ai Weiwei after he began posting names of student victims of the quake. On August 12, 2009, police broke into Ai's hotel room in Chengdu, the capital of Sichuan province, in the middle of the night. A policeman punched Ai in the face and then detained him for 11 hours, preventing him from giving evidence at Tan's trial.

Legal Reform

There has been slow progress in rights awareness and judicial professionalization in China, but the government continues to dominate the legal system. The new president of the People's Supreme Court (SPC), Wang Shengjun, continued the 2008 "Three Supremes" campaign, which emphasizes the centrality of the Communist Party to judicial work. Judicial personnel are asked to subordinate the demands of the law to maintenance of social stability and elimination of challenges to the party.

Reflecting growing concern over the rising number of public protests across of the country— 100,000 in 2008, up from 8,000 in 1994, according to official estimates—the SPC announced a program in September 2009 to train judges. This program aims to teach judges how to handle cases related to rising protests and so-called "mass cases," claiming that "hostile forces are gaining strength both at home and abroad" and menacing "national security and social stability."

The government also announced long-awaited revisions to the law on the protection of state secrets, a law that obstructs transparency and media freedom and is often used against human rights activists, journalists, and dissidents. The proposed revisions, expected to be adopted in 2010, do little to narrow scope of "state secrets," allow for retrospective classification of material as "secret," and extend the definition to cover internet and electronic information.

The criminal justice system remains plagued by forced confessions and torture of suspects by police, lack of due process, and sharp limits on legal representation. Officials have indicated that China will not reform its deeply flawed criminal procedure law before 2011. Government commitments to permit lawyers to meet clients in detention without prior police approval also remain unfulfilled.

In a case that generated a storm of internet debate, officials from a detention facility in Yunnan tried to explain the death of a 24-year-old prisoner, Li Qiaoming, telling his family that he died while "playing hide-and-seek." After it emerged that Li had died as a result of sustained beatings, the officials were fired.

In August 2009, however, press reports announced the drafting of measures that would make evidence obtained under torture inadmissible in court, a longstanding demand by human rights organizations and Chinese legal experts.

China continues to lead the world in the number of executions of prisoners, which different estimates put at between 3,000 and 10,000 annually, despite an official policy of reducing the number. Officials claim that the People's Supreme Court has rejected the death penalty about 15 percent of the time since it regained the authority to vet such cases in 2007.

On April 13, 2009, the government issued its first National Human Rights Action Plan (NHRAP). Described as proof that the government "unswervingly pushes forward the cause of human rights in China," the plan does not discuss serious and ongoing human rights abuses in China and does not provide a roadmap to end the violations, punish perpetrators, and assist victims.

Human Rights Defenders

China's growing number of right activists paid a high price in 2009 for their willingness to continue to push for greater civil and human rights. Police surveillance and monitoring of NGOs, critical intellectuals, dissidents, and civil rights lawyers, often coupled with threats, warnings, or periods of house arrest, continued unabated. The government took unprecedented measures against several high profile activists whose activities they had previously treated less harshly.

In late May, Beijing judicial authorities, without giving any reason, refused to renew the professional licenses of about a dozen of China's most prominent civil rights lawyers, leaving them unable to practice law. Control over the yearly renewal of professional licenses remains one of the main obstacles to the independence of China's legal profession, but Beijing officials had until then been seen as relatively tolerant in granting renewals. One particular law firm, Yitong, was apparently targeted; some of its partners had challenged the government-controlled Beijing Lawyers Association over its mode of election and were subsequently suspended for six months in June.

On June 23, Liu Xiaobo, one of China's most well-known dissidents, was formally arrested after six months of arbitrary detention. Liu had helped draft Charter 08, a document calling for the gradual development of rule of law and democracy. Police arrested Liu on December 8, 2008, in an apparent effort to prevent publication of the charter on December 10, International Human Rights Day. Several Nobel laureates wrote a letter to President Hu Jintao asking for his release, but in June the Xinhua News Agency announced that Liu was being charged with "incitement to subvert state power," a charge regularly leveled against government critics.

In mid-July the government shut down the Open Constitution Initiative (OCI), a ground-breaking legal aid and research NGO, detaining its founder, Xu Zhiyong, and another staff member for three weeks on suspicion of "tax evasion." Beijing authorities accused Xu and OCI of not having paid taxes on a grant received from Yale University, and deregistered the group. A domestic and international outcry probably helped secure Xu's release, but China's leading public interest law NGO remains shuttered.

Other prominent activists arrested by the authorities include Xie Changfa, sentenced to 13 years in prison for attempting to set up a branch of the China Democracy Party in Hunan province, and Gao Zhisheng, whose whereabouts remain unknown since he was taken by state security personnel in February 2009. Officials continue to deny that he is in custody.

Migrant and Labor Rights

Independent trade unions are prohibited in China, leaving the All-China Federation of Trade Unions as the sole legal representative of workers.

An estimated 23 million workers, mostly internal migrants, have lost their jobs as a result of the global financial crisis since 2008. In several cases in 2009, officials helped defuse possible unrest by dispatching mediators and making severance payments. In late January 2009, for example, Shenzhen municipal government officials used a government fund to pay back wages to 2,100 laid-off furniture factory workers whose management had absconded without paying 10 million yuan (US$68 million).

The household registration, or *hukou*, system, which is based on a person's place of birth, continues to effectively render large numbers of internal migrants unable to access public benefits including medical care and children's education. In March 2009 the Guangzhou municipal government announced that it would grant migrant workers rights to social insurance, vocational training, and legal aid previously reserved only for *hukou*-bearing residents. In June 2009 the Shanghai municipal government unveiled a plan to extend permanent residency status to migrants who meet rigorous educational, family planning, and tax payment history criteria, though this will only apply to a small fraction of Shanghai's estimated total of six million migrants.

Sexual Orientation and Gender Identity

Shanghai saw the country's first gay pride festival in June 2009, followed by a seven-day LGBT-themed film festival. Though homosexual conduct is no longer criminalized in China, the police shut down two film screenings and a play.

After a series of police raids on gay men's meeting places in public parks, about 100 gay men held a protest in People's Park in Guangzhou on August 25, 2009. Police questioned protest leaders for several hours in the park's public security house. This protest in defense of gay rights has been hailed as a milestone in LGBT rights organizing in China.

Women's and Girls' Rights

Chinese women continue to be victims of entrenched gender-based discrimination and violence. Women in rural areas are particularly vulnerable to abuses including gender-based discrimination, unequal access to services and employment, sexual trafficking, and violence. The case of Deng Yujiao, a 21-year-old pedicurist who on May 10, 2009, stabbed to death a local official in Hubei's

Baodong town after he allegedly tried to rape her, prompted widespread public attention to and concern about sexual violence in China.

HIV/AIDS

Chinese security forces continue to pressure HIV/AIDS activist organizations to maintain low public profiles. Chinese police forced prominent HIV/AIDS activist Wan Yanhai to leave Beijing and travel to the northern city of Changchun in the days leading up to the June 4 Tiananmen anniversary to avoid what they described as "possible conflict."

A new anti-drug law went into effect in June 2008 but fails to address ongoing abuses against injecting drug users (IDUs) that contribute to HIV/AIDS transmission. The law prohibits the use of China's notorious "re-education through labor" (RTL) system to confine IDUs but replaces it with ill-defined "community rehabilitation," prompting fears that abuses will continue under a new name.

Freedom of Religion

China's constitution guarantees freedom of religion, but the government restricts religious expression to government-registered temples, monasteries, mosques, and churches. The government vets religious personnel, seminary applications, and religious publications, and periodically audits religious institutions' activities, financial records, membership, and employees. The Chinese government considers all unregistered religious organizations, including Protestant "house churches," illegal; members risk fines and criminal prosecution. It also continues to designate certain groups as "evil cults," including the Falun Gong, and regularly cracks down on followers. There are no publicly available data about how many people are serving prison or reeducation-through-labor sentences for practicing their religion outside of state-sanctioned channels.

Tibet

The Tibet Autonomous Region and the adjacent Tibetan autonomous areas in Qinghai, Sichuan, Gansu, and Yunnan provinces remain tense, closely monitored, and saturated with troops long after the eruption of protests in the region in

March 2008. Two Tibetans were executed in 2009 for their involvement in the 2008 protests. At this writing, foreigners' access to Tibet remains tightly constrained.

The whereabouts of several hundred Tibetans accused of participating in the protests remain unknown. While several trials have been held, they have been highly politicized affairs. The trials of Phurbu Tsering, a Tibetan religious leader in Sichuan, and Dhondup Wangcheng, arrested in connection with the filming of an unauthorized documentary in 2008, were indefinitely postponed by authorities in 2009 after reports of torture and serious procedural irregularities made their way to international media.

In Lhasa the authorities increased police operations aimed at identifying and detaining people suspected of hindering the government's anti-separatism campaign or planning to join protests in the run-up to the 50th anniversary of the Dalai Lama's escape to India in March 2009. These included former political prisoners and their families, minor offenders, and temporary visitors.

The government continues to arrest, detain, and sentence protesters and people suspected of having irredentist sympathies across all Tibetan areas. Authorities compel thousands of monks and nuns to follow political indoctrination programs, at times through coercive means such as collective detention in unmarked facilities.

In October 2009 Chinese officials suggested the government would resume talks with representatives of the Dalai Lama, but only if he stopped meeting with world leaders.

Xinjiang

In July 2009 Xinjiang was rocked by one of the worst episodes of ethnic violence in China in decades, followed by a massive deployment of troops and a harsh crackdown. The unrest began on July 5, when Uighurs in Urumqi protesting the killing of Uighur workers in a Guangdong toy factory turned violent after riot police tried to disperse them and arrested up to 70 of them. By that evening, large groups of Uighur youths launched brutal attacks against Han Chinese residents in southern parts of Urumqi, leaving scores dead or injured and setting dozens of buildings and cars on fire. Han Chinese mobs retaliated by attacking Uighurs. Security forces did not reestablish control until the morning of July 6. On July 7 they attempted to prevent retaliatory assaults by Han Chinese residents of Urumqi, although at least some Uighurs fell victim to these attacks. Official figures put the death toll from the protests at 197 people, the majority of them Han. More than 1,600 were injured. Uighur groups continue to question the official death toll, saying it vastly underestimates the number of Uighur victims.

In the aftermath of the riots, Chinese police, People's Armed Police, and the military conducted numerous large-scale sweep operations in two predominantly Uighur areas of Urumqi—Erdaoqiao and Saimachang. According to witnesses, the security forces sealed off entire neighborhoods, searching for young Uighur men and boys. In addition to large-scale sweeps, the security forces also detained an unknown number of people in the course of targeted raids, usually involving smaller groups of police officers or soldiers who took Uighur men from their homes, places of work, hospitals, or the street. In some cases, the security forces seemed to act on leads received from previously detained individuals. These raids continued at least through mid-August. The victims of disappearances documented by Human Rights Watch were young Uighur men—most in their 20s, although the youngest victim was 14 years old.

Chinese authorities were quick to accuse a variety of external forces of masterminding and sponsoring the unrest. They specifically blamed Rebiya Kadeer, an activist and former political prisoner from Xinjiang living in exile in the United States, for planning and organizing the protests. No evidence, however, has been provided to support those claims, and many analysts believe the protests were largely a reaction to China's longstanding discriminatory policies toward the Uighur minority.

Chinese authorities also blocked channels of uncensored information, including the internet, international phone lines, and text messaging for all but accredited foreign reporters. At the same time, the Chinese government used both the official media and other means of mass propaganda to promote its version of events domestically and internationally.

On November 9 state media reported that eight Uighur men and one Han man had been put to death for their role in the rioting. All the trials took place without prior public notice, were conducted in less than a day, and did not meet minimum international standards.

Hong Kong Special Administrative Region

Hong Kong authorities still have not provided a clear roadmap for moving to fully democratic elections of the chief executive and all members of the Legislative Council, prompting fears that they will water down the "universal suffrage" requirement of Hong Kong's Basic Law.

Decisions by immigration authorities to deny entry to several visitors critical of China's human rights record raised concerns that the territory's autonomy was being eroded. On September 30, 2008, Hong Kong authorities handed over to mainland authorities an ex-dissident who had tried to enter the territory from Macao on a borrowed passport.

Key International Actors

The Chinese government continues to provide diplomatic and financial assistance to abusive regimes, including Burma, Sudan, and Zimbabwe, though it uncharacteristically agreed in July 2009 to United Nations Security Council sanctions against 15 North Korean officials. Chinese authorities contend that China is prioritizing economic development in its aid programs and foreign relations, but its foreign policy has come under scrutiny for ignoring human rights. The issue drew attention again in October 2009 with the announcement of a multi-billion dollar Chinese investment in Guinea just weeks after Guinea's military gunned down unarmed pro-democracy protesters.

In July 2009 Chinese prosecutors took the unusually aggressive step of arresting an Australian executive of mining giant Rio Tinto on charges of violating state secrets, causing concern in the international business community. The government also harshly criticized the Australian government for allowing the Melbourne Film Festival to show a documentary about Uighur activist Rebiya Kadeer, and the

Germany government for allowing the Frankfurt Book Festival to invite Chinese writers critical of the Chinese government.

A number of governments appeared to take a softer position on China's human rights record. The EU gave in to Chinese pressure and limited NGO participation in two rounds of the "EU-China Human Rights Seminar" in 2009, including the session in Europe. En route to Beijing in February 2009, US Secretary of State Hillary Clinton stated that human rights "shouldn't interfere" in the US-China relationship, and President Barack Obama decided not to meet the Dalai Lama prior to his November visit to Beijing. While in China, Obama raised human rights broadly in his public statements but did not directly engage pressing issues of freedom of expression, religious minorities, the disbarment of civil rights lawyers, or ongoing crackdowns in Xinjiang and Tibet.

In February 2009 the Chinese government made its debut appearance before the United Nations' Human Rights Council as part of the UN's Universal Periodic Review (UPR), but it opted to brush aside rather than seriously consider the recommendations made during the process. In the UPR "Outcome Report," the government rejected every single recommendation, including those pertaining to freedom of expression and association, lawyers and rights defenders, the death penalty, "re-education through labor," and torture. Instead, the government asserted that, "There is no censorship in the country," "No individual or press has been penalized for voicing their opinions or views," and "There is no such thing as law enforcement organs using state secrets [prosecutions] to suppress human rights defenders."

INDIA

The ruling alliance led by the Congress Party returned to power after elections in 2009. In its first term in office the Congress-led coalition made only modest progress on rights. It has not yet addressed some of India's most pressing needs, including better training and reform of its police force; providing health, education, and food security to millions still struggling for subsistence despite the country's economic growth; ending discrimination against Dalits, tribal groups, and religious minorities; and protecting the rights of women and children.

A spate of indiscriminate bombings in various Indian cities, culminating in the seaborne-based attack in Mumbai in November 2008, which killed at least 171, and injured over 300 people, led to continued tensions with Pakistan. While the Mumbai attack was attributed to the Pakistan-based Lashkar-e-Taiba, earlier deadly bombings were blamed on Muslim and Hindu extremist groups. Under intense public pressure, the government amended the Unlawful Activities (Prevention) Act, reinstating harsh provisions from previous counterterrorism laws that had either been allowed to lapse or been repealed.

Maoist insurgents known as Naxalites broadened their attacks in 2009, resulting in increased deployment of paramilitary and police forces. Although government officials announced a "zero tolerance" policy for human rights violations during security operations against the Maoists, separatist militants, and other armed groups in various parts of the country, cases of custodial killings, torture, and arbitrary arrests continued.

These abuses occur in part because of failure by the government to properly train or modernize its police force. Police officers face dismal working conditions and recruitment lags far behind increasing duties, creating an overstretched force that is likely to take short-cuts to gain convictions. Embittered and overworked, the police regard themselves as enforcers of the law—but not beholden to it.

The government's failure to protect minorities and other vulnerable groups engenders justified grievances and contributes to militant activity around the country. At senior levels of government there is growing acceptance that Maoists are attracting supporters in part because of the state's long failure to address basic socioeconomic needs; the continued arbitrary displacement of families to make way for government-backed infrastructure, mining, and factory projects; and discrimination based on caste or ethnicity.

Justice and Accountability

India points to its independent judiciary, vibrant media, and active civil society as evidence that it is a thriving, rights-respecting democracy. Yet fundamental, structural problems remain including, most glaringly, widespread impunity for human rights violations. The government routinely fails to hold security forces accountable for abuses.

2009 marked the 25th anniversary of mass killings of Sikhs to avenge the assassination of Prime Minister Indira Gandhi by her Sikh bodyguards in 1984. A10-year security operation against Sikh militants, who were responsible for numerous human rights abuses, resulted in the arbitrary detention, enforced disappearance, and extra-judicial killing of thousands of young Sikh men for suspected affiliation with separatist groups. Many victims, witnesses, and alleged perpetrators have died in the long, fruitless wait for accountability.

In Jammu and Kashmir and in the state of Manipur and elsewhere in the northeast, many citizens have lost confidence in the state's willingness to hold perpetrators of human rights violations accountable. Kashmiris protested on the streets after the death of two women in Shopian in May, refusing to believe a police investigation would be fair. An ongoing inquiry by the Central Bureau of Investigation has calmed tempers, but the protests were symptomatic of the government's failure to address impunity. In July an unarmed 27-year-old in Manipur was shot and killed by police in a crowded market place, a killing captured by a photo-journalist. Despite widespread outrage, the Manipur chief minister initially praised the police for shooting a "militant." Only after weeks of protests did the state government order a judicial inquiry.

Laws such as article 197 of the Criminal Procedure Code and the Armed Forces Special Powers Act provide legal protection for members of the security forces who violate human rights. The problem of *de jure* impunity is likely to be exacerbated by December 2008 amendments to the Unlawful Activities (Prevention) Act, which expand the already vague definition of terrorism, authorize search and seizure with few safeguards, and double periods of pre-charge detention to 180 days, 30 of which may be in police custody. The use of draconian laws such as the Maharashtra Control of Organised Crime Act, which allows confessions to police to be used as evidence despite it being evident that they are coerced, is a cause for serious concern, as are efforts by other states such as Gujarat to enact similar legislation.

While India claims that its National Human Rights Commission ensures the protection of rights, the commission often defends government behavior, lacks sufficient resources to conduct its own investigations, and is not empowered to investigate violations by the army. State human rights commissions are even more poorly equipped and vulnerable to political pressure.

Conduct of Security Forces

Militants in many parts of the country have been responsible for large numbers of killings. Nearly 2,000 people, including over 500 civilians and 350 security personnel, were killed by militants in 2009, while over 1,000 civilians and nearly 400 security personnel were killed in 2008. At the same time nearly 2,000 alleged terrorists have been killed since January 2008.

The Indian government and militants in various parts of the country are locked in a vicious cycle of violence. Cases of arbitrary arrest, torture and forced confessions by Indian security forces are common. The use of "fake encounters"—in which people are taken into custody and shot, with officials falsely claiming that the deaths occurred during an armed exchange—are a continuing cause of serious concern. Police torture is also common, including in counterterror operations. Some Indian Mujahidin suspects, blamed for a series of indiscriminate bombings in Bangalore, Ahmedabad, Jaipur, and Delhi in 2008, have claimed that they were tortured and forced to make false confessions, as have Hindu militants arrested for bombings in Malegaon, Maharashtra.

Broken System

Dysfunction, Abuse, and Impunity in the Indian Police

HUMAN
RIGHTS
WATCH

Violence against Minorities

Following attacks on Christians in Orissa in 2008, mob attacks on churches and other Christian institutions, apparently instigated by Hindu extremist groups, occurred in several states. While some of the alleged perpetrators of the Orissa attacks have been arrested, there has been little success in containing Hindu extremists.

Women's and Girls' Rights

The rights of women are often neglected. A 2005 UN study estimated that two-thirds of married women in India suffer domestic violence. Female infanticide and sex-selective abortions are the primary causes of skewed sex ratios and reflect the unequal share of resources made available to women and girls in areas such as access to education, food, and medical aid.

In part because of healthcare system failures, tens of thousands of Indian women and girls die each year in childbirth and pregnancy. More suffer preventable injuries, serious infections, and disabilities. Recent data show that more than a fourth of maternal deaths worldwide take place in India. The country's maternal mortality ratio is many times that of Russia, China, and Brazil, and a girl who reaches reproductive age in India is 100 times more likely to die from such causes than a girl in the developed world.

Access to Education, and Child Soldiers

Millions of children in India have abysmal educational opportunities. While the constitution provides for free and compulsory primary education, actual delivery remains patchy. High numbers of students are out of school for reasons that include poverty (with millions of children still employed in hazardous and other "worst forms" of labor), gender discrimination, early marriage, poor quality of teachers and curriculum, and lack of basic facilities. Many are further affected by internal conflicts. For instance, the education of tens of thousands of children has been disrupted by the Maoist conflict, with the Maoists bombing remote government schools and government security forces occupying and using schools as long-term outposts.

The Maoists admit that it is standard practice to recruit 16 and 17-year-old children in their forces; they have used children as young as 12 in some armed operations.

Sexual Orientation and Gender Identity

In a positive development, the Delhi High Court in July ruled that section 377 of the Indian Penal Code can no longer be used to treat consensual homosexual conduct between adults as a criminal offense. While the ruling was challenged in the Supreme Court by a few groups and individuals, the Indian government decided not to oppose the verdict.

International Role

India has failed to adequately use its considerable influence to address human rights problems in other countries or to be a human rights promoter at the United Nations. India has played a negative role at the UN Human Rights Council, siding with a bloc that opposes strong action to address violations. As India's regional and global influence grows, it needs to modernize its foreign policy to reflect its status as the world's largest democracy.

In the past India was a strong opponent of apartheid in South Africa, supported the democratic opposition in Burma, and backed groups demanding democracy in Nepal and Bangladesh. But officials now often use the language of "non-interference in the internal affairs" of other countries to defend their inaction. In part, this reflects India's growing strategic concerns about China's role in the region, which has strongly invested in Burma and Pakistan and is expanding its influence in Nepal, Bangladesh, and Sri Lanka.

India claims that it needs good relations with its neighbors to counter threats to national security by groups operating across borders. It wants Bangladesh, Burma, and Pakistan to arrest and prosecute separatists. In particular, it wants the international community to pressure Pakistan to end tacit protection of groups blamed for attacks like the one in Mumbai in November 2008.

Key International Actors

India's rapidly growing economy and increasing importance as a trading partner has meant that its domestic human rights record rarely elicits serious international scrutiny, including from the US, the country with the greatest external influence.

After a visit to India in March 2009, UN High Commissioner for Human Rights Navanethem Pillay called upon the government to bridge the gap in implementing "national laws and policies that promote and protect human rights and seek to support the most vulnerable." She also sought repeal of laws such as the Armed Forces Special Powers Act "that breach contemporary international human rights standards" and encouraged India to welcome the visits of UN special rapporteurs. India is yet to act on those recommendations. India has also not responded to international recommendations that it more effectively combat caste- and religion-based discrimination.

India has been repeatedly urged to play a greater role in advancing human rights and protecting civilians in Burma and Sri Lanka. While India claims that it privately raises such subjects with the governments concerned, Indian officials say little publicly and do not play a leadership role in protecting rights.

INDONESIA

Despite its growing reputation as an emerging Muslim-majority democracy, Indonesia saw little human rights progress in 2009. In July President Susilo Bambang Yudhoyono was reelected by a wide margin, providing him the opportunity to take more decisive action against impunity, religious intolerance, and other continuing threats to human rights. At this writing, there is little indication the government has the political will to do so.

Indonesia has a diverse and vibrant media sector, but freedom of expression continues to be undermined by powerful officials and business figures using criminal and civil defamation laws to silence criticism, and by repressive measures on expression in Papua.

Impunity

Impunity remains the rule for members of the security forces responsible for abuses. Indonesian military officers and militia leaders have yet to be brought to justice for past atrocities committed in Timor-Leste, Papua, Aceh, the Moluccas, Kalimantan, and elsewhere.

The elite Kopassus military special forces continue to engage in abuses. In Merauke, Papua, Kopassus soldiers arrested Papuans without legal authority and subjected them to beatings and mistreatment at the Kopassus barracks. Commanders made no serious effort to uphold military discipline or to hold soldiers accountable for abuses.

In December 2008 a Jakarta court acquitted Maj. Gen. Muchdi Purwopranjono, former Kopassus commander and deputy in the State Intelligence Agency, of the murder of human rights advocate Munir bin Thalib, in a trial marred by witness coercion and intimidation. In June 2009 the Supreme Court rejected the prosecutor's appeal. In 2005 President Yudhoyono had said that Indonesia's response to the killing would be a "test case" of how much the country has changed.

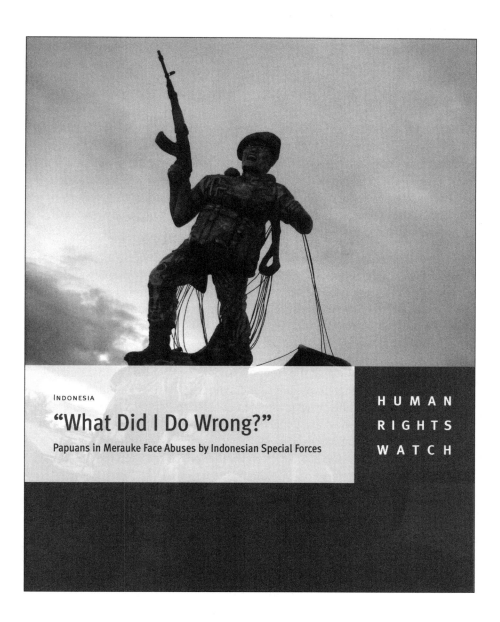

In March the Ministry of Foreign Affairs ordered the International Committee of the Red Cross (ICRC) to close its field offices in Jayapura (Papua) and Banda Aceh (Aceh).

Papua and West Papua

Indonesian authorities have responded to a longstanding, low-level armed separatist insurgency in the provinces of Papua and West Papua with a strong troop presence and often harsh and disproportionate responses to non-violent dissent or criticism. Human Rights Watch has long expressed concerns over anti-separatist sweeps by the police, which often result in individuals who peacefully express support for independence being arrested and detained on charges of treason or rebellion (*makar*).

The government continues to restrict access by foreign human rights monitors and journalists to Papua, exacerbating the existing climate of impunity and making investigations extremely difficult. Prior to being ordered to close its Jayapura office, the ICRC had been visiting detainees in Papua's Abepura prison, where prison guards continued to torture inmates, including political prisoners Buchtar Tabuni and Yusak Pakage.

In July a series of shootings at the Freeport goldmine in Timika left three people dead, including one Australian. Police, declaring that the Free Papua Movement (OPM) was involved in the attacks, arrested at least 20 Papuans in relation to the killings and declared seven as suspects. The OPM denied any involvement, and those targeted by the police insisted that they were neither affiliated with the OPM nor participants in the attacks. In November police released the final seven Papuans detained in connection with the incident.

In November a Manokwari district court convicted three men of *makar* (rebellion), for raising a pro-independence flag.

Aceh

Aceh continued to face violence, particularly during the months preceding April legislative elections, Aceh's first since a 2005 agreement between the government and the Free Aceh Movement brought an end to three decades of armed conflict. Between January and April 2009, unidentified attackers killed five politicians from the Aceh Party, the political party of the Free Aceh Movement, including the party head in Langsa, in a string of shootings and grenade attacks that killed at least 16 people. Indonesian police detained several individuals but no one was charged.

In September the outgoing Provincial House of Representatives approved a local bylaw that calls for married adulterers to be stoned to death and prescribes flogging as a punishment for a range of sexual offenses including consensual homosexual conduct. Despite resistance from the provincial governor, the bylaw automatically entered into force in October.

The central government has made no serious efforts to establish a truth and reconciliation tribunal to investigate crimes committed before the signing of the 2005 peace agreement, despite the fact that under the 2006 Law on the Governing of Aceh, such a tribunal was to be operational by August 2007.

Military Reform

Just prior to the expiry of a five-year deadline in October 2009, President Yudhoyono issued a decree transferring control of certain business interests of the Indonesian armed forces (TNI). The decree fails to end the TNI's involvement in all business activity, as mandated by a 2004 law, and gives control of the businesses that are transferred to the Ministry of Defense—led by a civilian, but largely staffed by military officers. The disappointing result was emblematic of extremely slow and modest progress on military reform in recent years.

Corruption

While the government of President Yudhoyono has taken steps to combat corruption, serious obstacles remain. Increasing tensions between the Anti-Corruption Commission (KPK) and police and prosecutors in 2009 seem to have played a role in the suspension and arrest of three KPK officials, one in May and two in October. In November the Constitutional Court aired five hours of telephone conversations, wiretapped by the KPK, that appeared to show efforts on the part of certain prosecutors and police to undermine the KPK following its investigation of a police bribery case. Subsequently, a fact-finding team appointed by Yudhoyono announced that it had found insufficient evidence for the arrest of two of the commissioners and urged that the police and prosecutors implicated in wrongdoing be disciplined.

In September 2009 President Yudhoyono issued a decree renewing the KPK's authority. However, under the decree, trial panels are no longer required to be staffed by a majority of ad hoc judges, a change that threatens to erode the commission's effectiveness and independence.

Anti-corruption measures have been underutilized to address the rampant theft and corruption in the country's forestry sector. Those responsible for losses due to illegal logging, corruption, and mismanagement are rarely held accountable.

Freedom of Expression and the Media

Powerful government and business figures continue to use criminal and civil defamation laws to intimidate journalists, human rights defenders, and other critics. Following his acquittal of the murder of Munir, Muchdi filed a criminal defamation complaint with the police against prominent human rights activist Usman Hamid for statements Hamid made on the courthouse steps. In September 2009 police called Hamid in for questioning on defamation charges.

In October police summoned two employees of Indonesia Corruption Watch for questioning on possible criminal defamation charges filed by the Attorney General's Office, after they suggested in a newspaper article that it had mismanaged 7 trillion rupiah (approximately US$738 million) in funds recovered from corruption investigations.

In a positive development for media freedom, in April the Supreme Court overturned a US$110 million civil defamation award against *Time* magazine stemming from a 1999 story on the wealth amassed by the late Indonesian president Suharto and his children.

In January 2009 the Jayapura State Court in Papua acquitted human rights lawyer Sabar Olif Iwanggin of charges of inciting violence against public authorities;

Iwanggin had forwarded a text message to friends critical of President Yudhoyono. At the time of his acquittal, Iwanggin had been detained by the authorities for over 15 months.

Freedom of Religion

Despite Indonesia's constitutional guarantees of freedom of religion, the government continues to impose legal restrictions on religious activities considered to deviate from the tenets of the six religions officially recognized under Indonesian law. For example, in June 2008 a joint ministerial decree ordered Ahmadiyah members to cease public religious activities or face up to five years' imprisonment. Over 100 Ahmadiyah members who were evicted from their homes by a violent mob in 2005 still reside in an internally displaced persons shelter in Lombok.

Muslim clerics and Islamist militants continued to invoke a 2006 decree requiring anyone building a "house of worship" to obtain "community approval" as a justification for forcibly blocking the building and operation of Christian churches.

More than 200 local laws based on Sharia (Islamic law) are on the books throughout regencies in Indonesia. Some mandate dress restrictions for women or permit civil servants to refuse government services to women not wearing headscarves. Others mandate the ability to recite the Quran as a prerequisite for promotion in the civil service.

Migrant Domestic Workers

Approximately 4.5 million Indonesians, mostly women, work abroad. Many migrate as domestic workers and are subject to exploitative labor conditions, abuse, and poor legal protections. In 2009 Indonesia suspended women's migration for domestic work to Malaysia and Kuwait due to concerns about continuing abuses (see chapters on Malaysia and Kuwait). Indonesia and Malaysia began renegotiating a 2006 Memorandum of Understanding to address issues like a minimum wage and the right to keep one's passport.

Indonesia failed to make significant progress in preventing local labor recruiters deceiving prospective migrants about their jobs abroad or imposing excessive fees.

Child Domestic Workers

Hundreds of thousands of girls in Indonesia, some as young as 11, are employed as domestic workers. Many work long hours, with no days off, and are forbidden to leave the house where they work. In the worst cases, girls are physically, psychologically, and sexually abused. Indonesia's labor law excludes all domestic workers from the basic labor rights afforded most workers.

Health and Human Rights

Tens of thousands of cancer patients and people living with HIV/AIDS suffer from severe pain without access to adequate treatment. The government has not taken effective action to ensure that opioid pain medications are adequately available outside of specialist centers and that medical staff are trained in their use. Unreasonably limiting access can lead to violations of the right to the highest attainable standard of health and amount to cruel, inhuman, or degrading treatment.

In September the House of Representatives passed an anti-narcotics bill classifying any "personal use" of a controlled substance as a criminal offense, and prescribing fines and up to six months' imprisonment for parents who fail to report a child's drug addiction to the authorities. The bill authorizes the death penalty for a wide range of offenses including buying, selling, and delivering controlled substances.

Key International Actors

Indonesia's relations with several strategic partners grew closer during 2009, particularly in the area of security cooperation. Indonesia continued to play a positive role within the Association of Southeast Asian Nations (ASEAN) in pressing Burma on its lack of progress on democratic reform. Indonesia also urged ASEAN member states to strengthen their recently inaugurated human rights body.

INDONESIA

Workers in the Shadows

Abuse and Exploitation of Child Domestic Workers
in Indonesia

**H U M A N
R I G H T S
W A T C H**

In February United States Secretary of State Hillary Clinton visited Indonesia and announced discussions on developing a comprehensive partnership. A week earlier, over 100 TNI personnel joined US, Thai, Japanese, and Singapore forces in multilateral military exercises.

The US maintains a ban on assistance to Kopassus special forces, and in October the US declined to issue visas to Defense Ministry secretary-general Syafrie Syamsuddin and Kopassus commander Promono Edhie Wibowo. Also in October the United Kingdom's Joint Counter Terrorist Training and Advisory Team conducted training for members of Kopassus, despite its extensive record of abuses.

In January the chief of the Australian Defence Force signed a Joint Statement on Defense Cooperation with TNI Commander in Chief Gen. Djoko Santoso. In September the Australian federal police reopened a war crimes investigation into the 1975 killing of five Australia-based journalists by Indonesian forces in Timor-Leste. The Indonesian Ministry of Foreign Affairs responded that it considered the case closed and that the investigation could have implications for bilateral relations.

MALAYSIA

In April Malaysia's new prime minister, Seri Najib Tun Razak, articulated his view of a multicultural, nondiscriminatory Malaysia and pledged to "uphold civil liberties" and exhibit "regard for the fundamental rights of the people." He demonstrated a new direction for the government by lifting a ban on two opposition party newspapers, releasing 13 Internal Security Act (ISA) detainees, and promising a review of internal security and other repressive laws. But to date, the record has been, at best, mixed.

Freedom of expression and freedom of assembly are still restricted for government critics. Najib and his ministers defend preventive detention and outdated repressive laws in the name of public security and a fragile multi-ethnic society.

Detention without Charge or Trial

The Internal Security Act permits indefinite detention, without charge or trial, of anyone officials regard as a threat to national security, such as suspected terrorists, individuals allegedly promoting ethnic or religious divisiveness, and government critics.

From April 3, 2009, his first day in office, Prime Minister Najib signaled his intent to amend the law. Within a month the government agreed to form a Law Reform Committee headed by a deputy minister in the Prime Minister's Department, and released all but nine ISA detainees. It has itself refrained from using the ISA to detain political opponents, but has rejected calls by the Human Rights Commission of Malaysia (Suhakam), the Bar Association, and civil society organizations to repeal the law.

Migrant Workers, Refugees, Asylum Seekers, and Trafficking

As of March 2009 there were more than two million documented migrants in Malaysia and an estimated one million without valid residency status. The United Nations High Commissioner for Refugees says that, of these, 49,000 are registered refugees and asylum seekers. Refugee communities estimate that an additional 45,000 are not registered.

The Malaysian Immigration Act 1959/1963 does not distinguish refugees and asylum seekers from other undocumented migrants: all those without proper documentation are subject to arrest, detention, and deportation. Members of the half-million-strong People's Volunteer Corps (RELA), who do not need warrants to search premises and arrest suspected undocumented migrants, often join with immigration officers and police to conduct raids on worksites and living quarters. Previously, undocumented Burmese caught in raids usually were deported to the Thai border where they risked being trafficked by organized criminal groups. In April 2009 US Senator Richard Lugar delivered a report to the US Senate Committee on Foreign Relations outlining the collusion between Malaysian immigration officials and human traffickers and smugglers at the border. After the report, the deportations stopped.

Stepped-up arrests, combined with fewer deportations, have increased overcrowding in immigration detention facilities and produced a deterioration of already abysmal living conditions, including contaminated water supplies, inadequate access to medical care, and poor and insufficient food. In May two Burmese migrants detained at the Juru Detention Center in Penang died and 24 others were treated for leptospirosis, a bacterial infection usually caused by contact with water contaminated by urine from infected animals. In August another six Burmese died from leptospirosis probably contracted at the Semenyih Detention Center.

In 2009 Malaysia met a long-sought goal by guaranteeing a day off a week for its estimated 300,000 domestic workers, primarily Indonesian migrants. However, the government still fails to ensure prompt payment of an adequate minimum wage, reasonable limits to work hours, and protection from physical abuse and sexual harassment.

Indonesia suspended the migration of domestic workers to Malaysia in June in response to the continuing high number of abuses, including the highly-publicized case of Siti Hajar, who was owed 17,000 ringgits (US$5,000) in back wages and was badly scarred from years of violence including repeated scaldings. In another much publicized case, in October Mantik Hani's employer was charged with murder after Mantik died from a savage beating. As of November 2009 Indonesia and Malaysia were still negotiating a revised bilateral agreement including a special Malaysian task force to deal with employer abuse and a higher minimum wage.

Freedom of Assembly and Police Abuse

Article 10 of Malaysia's constitution guarantees freedom of assembly, but the Police Act 1967 severely restricts its application. Police are empowered to break up unlicensed demonstrations, arrest participants, and use force if orders to disperse are not promptly obeyed. Public rallies organized by government critics are routinely denied permits, while those supportive of government positions may proceed unencumbered even without the requisite permit. On August 20, 2009, Home Minister Hishamuddin Hussein announced a review of the Police Act to allow for assembly in stadiums and "certain corners of town." The announcement followed police use of indiscriminate and excessive force to break up an August 1 march supporting repeal of the Internal Security Act, when security forces arrested nearly 600 people (including 44 children), many of them some 10 hours before the demonstration even began, and used teargas and chemically-laced water shot from water cannon trucks to turn back the crowds.

Freedom of Expression and the Media

In April Prime Minister Najib proclaimed, "We need a media ... that is empowered to responsibly report what they see, without fear of consequence." But Malaysia continues to systematically restrict free expression through a series of laws specifically limiting press freedom, as well as the broadly-worded Sedition Act, the Police Act which limits peaceful assembly, and a mainstream media ownership structure favoring the government. Despite its earlier pledge not to censor the internet, the government has found new ways to limit the cyberspace challenge to information controls.

The 1984 Printing Presses and Publications Act acts as a censor by requiring annual renewal of publishing licenses and by controlling production and distribution of foreign publications. In August 2009 the government confiscated copies of the inaugural issue of *Gedung Kartun*, a political satire magazine, on the questionable grounds that it had not yet received a permit. The issue's cover satirized Najib's alleged indiscretions.

Also in August opposition parliamentarian Karpal Singh went on trial for sedition for commenting to journalists that the legality of a decision to return control of Perak state's government to Malaysia's ruling coalition could be questioned in court.

In September the leading online news portal *Malaysiakini* refused to comply with a Communication and Multimedia Commission order to remove two videos from its website on the grounds that it had posted "content which is indecent, obscene, false, menacing or offensive in character." After investigation, the matter was referred to the Attorney General's Chambers.

Freedom of Religion

Although Islam is Malaysia's official state religion, the constitution affirms that Malaysia is a secular state protective of religious freedom for all. However, Malaysia's dual-track legal system permits Sharia courts to rule on religious and moral offenses involving Muslims and on issues involving marriage, inheritance, divorce and custody battles, and burial rites, many involving inter-religious disputed claims.

In July 2009 the Sharia High Court in Pahang state sentenced Kartika Sari Dewi Shukarno to six strokes of a cane for drinking beer in a nightclub. In September the Kuantan Sharia High Court Appeals Panel upheld the sentence. Should it be imposed, Kartika will be the first woman caned in Malaysia.

Human Rights Defenders

Malaysian authorities continue to harass and arrest human rights defenders including lawyers, journalists, NGO activists, opposition politicians, and even outspoken members of Suhakam, Malaysia's official human rights watchdog.

In May police arrested five lawyers seeking to meet with their clients, many of them elected representatives who had been arrested for taking part in one of a series of peaceful vigils supporting activist Wong Chin Huat. Police used the Sedition Act to arrest Wong earlier that month for holding a press conference on behalf of Bersih (Coalition for Clean and Fair Elections) asking supporters to wear black to "mourn the death of democracy " in Perak, where the national ruling coalition had engineered sufficient defections in the state assembly to retake control.

Although NGOs criticize Suhakam for its lack of action, several commissioners have reminded critics that it lacks enforcement powers. The commission was established by law as an advisory committee and falls under the Prime Minister's Department, with the prime minister exercising exclusive control over commissioner appointments. As a result, the executive can prevent investigations from going forward and can dismiss investigative reports without explanation. The International Coordinating Committee of National Institutions for the Promotion and Protection of Human Rights, a body that assesses the extent to which national human rights commissions comply with the Principles relating to the Status of National Institutions (Paris Principles), has warned it may recommend downgrading Suhakam's status.

Key International Actors

During a joint press conference on May 14, 2009, US Secretary of State Hillary Clinton and Malaysia's Foreign Minister Y.B. Datuk Anifah bin Aman agreed to work together on Burma policy, counterterrorism, refugee policy, and human trafficking. To those ends, the United States acceded to the Treaty of Amity and Cooperation in Southeast Asia on July 22. What may prove contentious is signatories' pledge of non-interference in other states' domestic affairs.

The US Trafficking in Persons 2009 report downgraded Malaysia to Tier 2 for its failure to adequately combat human trafficking. After Senator Lugar's report the head of the US Office to Monitor and Combat Trafficking in Persons welcomed the arrests of immigration officials, but said the US wants to see "sustainability" and court cases.

In February the UN Human Rights Council examined Malaysia under its Universal Periodic Review mechanism. However, Malaysia refused to accept numerous recommendations by member states, including ratification of core human rights treaties and the Refugee Convention, and issue of an open standing invitation to UN special procedures.

NEPAL

The Comprehensive Peace Agreement (CPA), hammered out to end the 10-year fighting between the Maoists and government forces that claimed more than 13,000 lives, was thrown into jeopardy in May 2009 when the Maoists withdrew from the government. The precipitating event was the president's refusal to back the Maoists' demand to sack the army chief, Gen. Rookmangud Katawal. Maoist Prime Minister Pushpa Kumar Dahal (alias Prachanda) and the Maoists went into opposition, leading to the formation of a 22-party governing coalition led by the United Marxist Leninist party (CPN-UML). The Maoists then boycotted the Constituent Assembly, voted in to draft a new constitution.

The result was political instability, a weak government, and failure to make progress on crucial issues of economic development and the framing of a new constitution. The Maoists demanded a parliamentary debate to censure the president. With the ruling parties reluctant, at this writing the Maoists are preventing the Constituent Assembly from meeting.

Meanwhile, no member of the security forces or the Maoists has ever been held criminally responsible for grave human rights abuses committed during the conflict. Addressing impunity to ensure that abusive officers and soldiers are removed from the ranks of the army and Maoists is crucial, particularly due to fears that the peace process may break down. Laws to forbid enforced disappearances and create a Truth and Reconciliation Commission were also delayed.

Accountability for Past Abuses

Accountability for human rights abuses continued to be promised by political parties but was again not a priority in 2009. The army continued to make unsupported claims that it dealt with abusers in its ranks, yet promoted officers identified as alleged perpetrators of human rights violations, including enforced disappearances and extrajudicial executions. Particularly controversial was the appointment of Maj. Gen. Toran Bahadur Singh as acting army chief. As head of the 10th Division, Singh was accused of involvement in cases of enforced disappearances in Maharajgunj in 2003. At this writing the prime minister is blocking his promotion to lieutenant general, but the army is insisting that it go ahead.

NEPAL

Still Waiting for Justice

No End to Impunity in Nepal

HUMAN
RIGHTS
WATCH

ADVOCACY
FORUM

The police report that the army continues to refuse to cooperate in investigations into army abuses: the army refuses to allow the police onto army bases, and the police have come under pressure and threats not to open investigations or recommend prosecutions against the army. The government claimed that it was too weak to initiate prosecutions against the army.

The Maoists have also refused to hold their own personnel accountable for human rights abuses. Among the members of the Maoists elected to the Constituent Assembly were known perpetrators of human rights abuses. In October 2008 the Maoist-led government decided to withdraw 349 cases against Maoists pending in court, claiming that they were "political" in nature and had been filed simply because the accused were Maoists.

After the Maoist-led government in August 2008 announced that it would compensate "victims of conflict," families of victims have in some cases suspended their pursuit of criminal investigations, fearing they may negatively influence their applications for compensation.

Ongoing Abuses and Impunity

The failure to hold people accountable for serious human rights abuses has provided an impetus to ongoing abuses and impunity by political groups. Groups like the Young Communist League (YCL, the Maoists' youth wing), the Youth Force (the youth wing of the CPN-UML), and the youth wing of the Nepali Congress, committed serious abuses in 2009. The YCL was particularly abusive, though attacks by all the youth groups decreased in the second half of the year.

The police remained largely above the law, with torture and mistreatment in custody widespread. The perpetrators continue to escape justice. Instead, cases against them are withdrawn, and the victims are offered token amounts of compensation.

Integration of Maoist Combatants

At the crux of the political stalemate is the question of the integration and rehabilitation of 19,602 Maoist combatants verified by the United Nations Mission in

Nepal (UNMIN), who have been held in cantonment sites around the country for nearly three years. The army and many politicians from the older mainstream parties maintain that former Maoist combatants should be integrated into society. The Maoists insist on the integration of Maoist combatants into the security forces. The 2006 Comprehensive Peace Agreement states that the interim cabinet "shall form a special committee to carry out monitoring, integration and rehabilitation of the Maoist combatants."

On May 5, 2009, local media leaked a video recording of a speech that Prachanda had made in January 2008 at a cantonment site in Chitwan, during which he said that the Maoists had inflated the number of their combatants presented for registration and verification. He also said that some money allocated for the cantonments would be used to "prepare for a revolt." Despite later attempts by Prachanda to explain the context of the statement, it drew wide public condemnation and raised serious doubts about the Maoists' commitment to the peace process and accountability for human rights abuses.

In mid-2009 there was some progress with the discharge and rehabilitation process for 4,008 Maoist combatants, including 2,973 former child combatants. A special committee was established as recommended under the CPA. However, the political stalemate has stalled the committee's work and the rehabilitation and integration process.

Dalits

In a positive development, in September 2009 Nepal announced its support for the draft United Nations principles and guidelines to eliminate caste discrimination, which were contained in the final report on discrimination based on work and descent (the UN terminology for caste discrimination) published by the Human Rights Council in May 2009. This is an important step, particularly because it sets a precedent for other countries, particularly India, that have resisted UN intervention in addressing rampant caste-based discrimination.

Sexual Orientation and Gender Identity

Despite the 2007 Supreme Court directive to the government to repeal laws that discriminate against lesbian, gay, bisexual, and transgender people, and to institute protections, there has been at least one instance of arbitrary detention of gay men. Police raided a private party in Kathmandu in early June 2009, and detained the participants for 12 hours before releasing them without charge.

In September 2009 the government authorized and provided a budget for a seven-member committee tasked with studying same-sex marriage laws in other countries and making recommendations for passing the same in Nepal.

Terai

Ethnic tensions persist over the rights of Madheshi communities in the southern Terai region (the southern plains bordering India), who want greater autonomy and proportionate representation in government jobs. In February 2008 an eight-point agreement was signed conceding the demand for an autonomous Terai region in a federal system, but was subject to approval by the then-proposed Constituent Assembly; that approval is still lacking.

Some Madheshi groups contested elections and are now members of the Assembly. After Prachanda's resignation, some of these Madheshi representatives entered the intense negotiations over the allocation of portfolios in the new government, and the main Madheshi party, the Madheshi People's Rights Forum, split as a result. Other Madheshi groups have continued their armed resistance to press their demands.

Tibetan Refugees

The Maoists demonstrated their friendship with China by increasing pressure and engaging in a harsh crackdown on Tibetan refugees. In an effort to appease China, since 2008 Nepali authorities have effectively sealed the border to prevent the arrival of Tibetan refugees.

Key International Actors

While Nepal, as an aid-dependent country, was susceptible to external pressure to ensure protection of rights during the conflict, international attention has now shifted to other countries in the region, leaving the Nepali authorities and political parties relatively free to ignore the urgent need for accountability and to address current human rights problems.

Traditional donors such as Japan, the United States, the United Kingdom, and the European Union have the ability, however, to have significant influence in Nepal, including on human rights.

Nepal has to maintain a balance of relations between its two powerful neighbors India and China. While traditionally Nepal has closer ties to India because of social, cultural, and economic ties (including its dependence on India for access to sea trade), the Maoist-led government attempted to strengthen ties with China, which invested substantial sums in reconstruction after the conflict, and played an increasingly important role in Nepal.

Another key international actor is the United Nations peacekeeping department, as the Nepal army continues to be a key troop contributor and depends on funds and prestige from participation in peacekeeping operations globally. Army assurances that personnel responsible for human rights violations would be excluded from United Nations peacekeeping duties appeared hollow given the absence of investigations, and neither the UN nor foreign embassies committed the resources to undertake proper vetting, relying on anecdotal reports instead.

The UN Office of the High Commissioner for Human Rights (OHCHR) in Nepal continued to play a key role in promoting and protecting rights and, in particular, working for accountability and establishing institutions that can provide better protections in the future. The National Human Rights Commission still faced enormous challenges, including limited resources and an unresponsive government that failed to implement most of its recommendations. The OHCHR's mandate to provide assistance and training to create a stronger national human rights institution with a strengthened capacity in monitoring, investigating, promoting, and reporting on the human rights situation remained highly relevant in 2009.

NORTH KOREA

In April 2009 the parliament of the Democratic People's Republic of Korea (North Korea) revised the country's constitution to include, among others, a provision that North Korea "respects and protects human rights." North Korea seems to be trying to improve its international image in response to continuing criticism over its poor human rights record.

The revised constitution defines the chairman of the National Defense Commission (currently Kim Jong Il) as "supreme leader" of the country overseeing all "national business." As Kim has been undisputed leader since the 1994 death of his father Kim Il Sung, the change appears to be an attempt to quell rumors of his weakened leadership after a reported stroke in September 2008.

Despite lip-service to human rights in the constitution, human rights conditions in North Korea remain dire. There is no organized political opposition, free media, functioning civil society, or religious freedom. Arbitrary arrest, detention, and torture and ill-treatment of detainees, and lack of due process remain serious issues. North Korea operates detention facilities including those popularly known as "political prison camps" where hundreds of thousands of its citizens—including children—are enslaved in deplorable conditions for various anti-state offenses. Collective punishment is the norm for such crimes. Periodically, the government publicly executes citizens for stealing state property, hoarding food, and other "anti-socialist" crimes.

Food Shortages

Although the country recovered from the 1990s famine that killed millions, North Korea's lack of high-quality seeds, fuel, fertilizer, advanced agricultural technologies, and even decent storage facilities have repeatedly resulted in domestic production being far too inadequate to feed its entire population. In September 2009 the World Food Programme reported that a third of North Korean women and children are malnourished and the country will run short by almost 1.8 million metric tons of food, which North Korea would need to import or obtain as aid.

Since the famine, markets have replaced the practically defunct ration system as the main source of food for most North Koreans. Very few (mostly high-ranking members of the military or security forces) still receive full rations. Reports of crackdowns and restrictions on market activities raise concerns about their effect on the livelihood of the North Koreans who depend on such activities to survive.

Refugees and Asylum Seekers

North Korea criminalizes leaving the country without state permission. Border-crossers face grave punishments upon repatriation such as torture, lengthy terms in horrendous detention facilities, and even execution, depending on what they did and who they met while abroad.

In early October 2009, 11 North Koreans aboard a fishing boat drifted into South Korean waters. South Korean authorities interrogated the arrivals and announced that all 11 sought asylum, rejecting North Korea's repeated demand that they be repatriated. Some 17,000 North Korean refugees live in South Korea.

Most North Koreans escape through the country's northern border with China. Hundreds of thousands have fled since the 1990s, and some have settled in China's Yanbian Korean Autonomous Prefecture. Despite its obligation to offer protection to refugees, Beijing categorically labels North Koreans in China "illegal" economic migrants and routinely repatriates them. Many North Korean women in China live with Chinese men in de facto marriages. Even if they have lived there for years, they are not entitled to legal residence and remain vulnerable to arrest and repatriation. Some North Korean women and girls are trafficked into forced marriage or forced prostitution in China.

Other than South Korea, a relatively small number of North Korean refugees have settled in other countries. At this writing, Japan has accepted about 200, and the United States has accepted close to 100, North Koreans in total. Germany, the United Kingdom, and a few other European countries together have accepted more than 500 North Koreans in recent years. Some were given humanitarian status, rather than refugee status.

Children's Rights

In a December 2008 report, Citizens' Alliance for North Korean Human Rights, a Seoul-based NGO, said children in North Korea face discrimination in access to education, humanitarian aid, and health protection, depending on which political class their families belong to. Their status also affects whether they must perform military service, including before age 18.

Thousands of children in China born to North Korean mothers and Chinese fathers are forced to live without a legal identity or legal access to elementary education, to avoid their mothers being identified and repatriated. North Korean children who migrate to China have no legal right to obtain household registration papers. By law, North Korean and half-North Korean children should be admitted to schools without being required to submit household registration papers, but in reality, most schools require such documentation. Some parents and guardians of North Korean children resort to bribery or trickery to ensure children can go to school.

Labor Rights

About 40,000 North Korean workers are employed in North Korea's Kaesong Industrial Complex (KIC) where they produce mostly consumer goods for South Korean businesses. The law governing working conditions in the complex falls far short of international standards on freedom of association, the right to collective bargaining, gender discrimination and sexual harassment, and hazardous child labor.

North Koreans are also reportedly employed in Bulgaria, China, Iraq, Kuwait, Mongolia, and Russia. In some countries, activists have expressed concern about Pyongyang's attempt to restrict the workers' freedom of movement and association, the constant presence of "minders" accompanying workers, and that large portions of their salaries are reportedly taken by agencies or the North Korean government.

In an August 2009 documentary, the BBC reported that about 1,500 North Korean workers are employed in Russian logging camps. A local official with a timber firm told the BBC the North Koreans have only two rest days per year and face punishments when they fail to meet their production target. Some of those who escaped such camps have been living in hiding in Russia.

Key International Actors

In 2009 North Korea's missile and nuclear weapons program grabbed headlines across the world and dominated diplomatic efforts by foreign governments.

North Korea launched a long-range ballistic missile in April. The United Nations Security Council issued a statement condemning the move, and in protest North Korea quit multilateral efforts at ending its nuclear weapons program—the so-called Six-Party talks involving the two Koreas, the US, China, Japan, and Russia.

North Korea then conducted a nuclear test in May, sparking widespread condemnation. In response, the UN Security Council adopted a resolution in June that called for an expansion of an arms embargo and for UN member states to inspect cargo vessels and airplanes suspected of carrying military materiel in or out of North Korea.

The start of 2009 saw deteriorating relations between the two Koreas. Since President Lee Myung-bak took office in early 2008, South Korea (North Korea's main donor for a decade) suspended aid and openly criticized North Korea's nuclear ambitions, in a new policy that emphasizes reciprocity. In March North Korea arrested Yoo Seong-jin, a technician for South Korea's Hyundai Group working at the KIC, for allegedly criticizing the North Korean political system. In July North Korea detained four South Korean fishermen who accidentally strayed into its waters. By August, however, North Korea began sending conciliatory signals to South Korea by releasing Yoo and the fishermen, and sending a high-level delegation to the funeral of former President Kim Dae-jung. In September it allowed family reunion meetings, after a two-year suspension. North Korean officials hinted that they expect food aid from South Korea in return.

The longstanding issue of some 500 South Koreans allegedly abducted by the North Korean government for propaganda or to train spies remains unresolved. South Korea also believes hundreds of South Korean prisoners of war from the 1950-53 Korean War remain in North Korea against their will.

North Korea's relations with the United States remained largely unchanged, but the two countries held a couple of high-level meetings. In March North Korea arrested two US journalists, Euna Lee and Laura Ling from California-based Current TV, on charges including illegal entry. They were sentenced to 12 years of labor, but reportedly remained in detention at a government guesthouse. In August, upon the visit of former US president Bill Clinton, Kim Jong Il pardoned the two and sent them home.

In September the US government appointed a new envoy on human rights in North Korea. In late October, Ri Gun, director general of North American Affairs at North Korea's Foreign Ministry, visited the US to meet with Sung Kim, US special envoy for the Six-Party talks.

In October, upon his return from a three-day visit to Pyongyang, Chinese Prime Minister Wen Jiabao called for the US and North Korea to engage in a dialogue to revive multilateral talks aimed at ending North Korea's nuclear weapons program.

North Korea's relations with Japan remained frosty, largely due to a dispute over abductees. North Korea admitted in 2002 that its agents had abducted 13 Japanese, and returned five to Japan, but claimed the other eight had died. Japan insists that the number of its abducted citizens is higher.

In a September 2009 report for the UN General Assembly, Vitit Muntarbhorn, UN special rapporteur on human rights in North Korea, criticized North Korea for its "abysmal" human rights record, citing food shortages, public executions, and torture, and called on North Korea to stop punishing people seeking asylum elsewhere, and institute democratic processes. In November the General Assembly adopted a new resolution criticizing serious human rights violations in North Korea.

PAKISTAN

2009 was another tumultuous year in Pakistan. The security situation significantly worsened, with bombings and targeted killings becoming a daily fact of life even in the country's biggest cities. Over two million people were displaced during major fighting between government forces and the Taliban. The economy suffered severe setbacks, food prices skyrocketed, and there were chronic shortages of energy and food. A re-assertive military publicly undermined the civilian government in the areas of national security, foreign policy, and human rights. President Asif Ali Zardari's government, initially keen to promote human rights, made some headway but then lost momentum as it tried and largely failed to deal with these issues.

Ongoing rights concerns include the breakdown of law enforcement in the face of acts of terrorism across the country, the failure of the judiciary to transform its newfound independence into non-partisan dispensation of justice, continuing torture and mistreatment of terrorism and other criminal suspects, unresolved enforced disappearances of terrorism suspects and opponents of the previous military government, military abuses in operations in the tribal areas and Swat, and discriminatory laws against and mistreatment of religious minorities and women.

Militant Attacks, Counterterrorism, and Enforced Disappearances

Pakistan was rocked by a spate of suicide bombings, armed attacks, and killings in 2009 by Taliban and al Qaeda militants and their affiliates that targeted civilians, the political elite of the country, educational institutions, hospitals, marketplaces, and even the visiting Sri Lankan cricket team. The capital, Islamabad, its twin city Rawalpindi, and the provincial capitals of Lahore and Peshawar were repeatedly sites of attacks. Armed groups also continued to recruit and use children, including for suicide attacks.

The government's response to militant attacks routinely violated basic rights. Suspects were frequently detained without charge or, if charged, were often convicted without a fair trial. Hundreds were detained in a country-wide crackdown on militant groups, particularly in the conflict zones in Swat and the tribal areas, but only a handful of the most prominent were charged. Many suspects were detained in two different military facilities in Swat, one in the Khyber agency of the tribal areas, and at least one more in Northwest Frontier Province. At this writing, the military had not allowed independent monitors access to most of these detainees.

Pakistan's Interior Ministry has estimated that 1,100 people were "disappeared" under the military regime of Gen. Pervez Musharraf. It is impossible to ascertain the precise number because of the secrecy surrounding counterterrorism operations, but this number is almost certainly an underestimate. The Zardari administration promised to resolve these cases, but it has made negligible progress. Pakistan has yet to sign the international treaty banning enforced disappearances.

In October 2009 the government amended the country's anti-terrorism laws through presidential ordinance to further curtail the legal rights of terrorism suspects. Under the ordinance, suspects can be placed in "preventive detention" for a period of 90 days without benefit of judicial review or the right to bail. Confessions made before the police or military are now deemed admissible as evidence despite the fact that torture by Pakistan's police and the military's intelligence services continues to be routine. That same month the leak of a video showing the military torturing terrorism suspects in the presence of police officials in Swat sparked widespread revulsion.

Security Operations and Displaced Persons

The Taliban and other militant groups conducted numerous attacks on the Pakistani military, including targeted killings of military personnel. In October Taliban militants attacked the General Headquarters of the Pakistan Army and took senior military officers hostage.

Since September 2008 the United States' aerial drones are believed to have carried out dozens of missile attacks on suspected militant hideouts in Pakistan's tribal areas, killing hundreds of civilians in addition to alleged militants, and prompting allegations that US attacks have violated the laws of war. The areas of the attacks are generally inaccessible to independent monitors, making it difficult to assess the allegations. In October 2009 United Nations Special Rapporteur on Extrajudicial Executions Philip Alston reported to the UN General Assembly that the US government's failure to respond to specific questions about the drone attacks fanned perceptions that the US was "carrying out indiscriminate killings in violation of international law."

On April 13, 2009, President Zardari signed an ordinance imposing Sharia (Islamic law) in the Swat Valley and adjoining areas as part of a deal with the Pakistani Taliban. This effectively empowered the Taliban to impose its authority in the areas, which it did through summary executions, including beheadings, of state officials and political opponents, public whippings, and large-scale intimidation of the population. Responding to domestic and international outrage, on May 7 the government reversed course and declared an end to the deal, vowing to "eliminate" the Taliban. The ensuing military operation triggered a massive displacement crisis as some two million civilians fled the fighting to adjoining districts.

While Pakistan forces succeeded in driving Taliban fighters from Swat's towns, civilians said that the Pakistani army often gave no, or insufficient, advance warning of attacks, forcing residents to flee their homes under crossfire. After the end of the active phase of the military operation, Swat remained largely closed to independent monitors and journalists, with sporadic access limited to Mingora, the valley's largest town. Reports surfaced of extrajudicial executions in Swat by the army, tribal militias acting in support of the state, and the Taliban.

In October Pakistan's military began a fresh offensive in the South Waziristan agency of the tribal areas, considered a hotbed of Taliban and al Qaeda militancy. At this writing, well over 200,000 civilians had fled South Waziristan, some alleging discrimination, house demolitions, and arbitrary detentions by the military. The area was closed to journalists and human rights monitors, so it was not possible to verify this information.

Independence of the Judiciary

After initially resisting, the government in March 2009 restored to office ousted Supreme Court Chief Justice Iftikhar Chaudhry. Many other justices and judges dismissed by Musharraf were also restored in 2009. Subsequently, the Supreme Court declared illegal all appointments made by Musharraf to the judiciary and overturned earlier rulings declaring opposition party leader Nawaz Sharif ineligible to hold public office.

In 2009 Pakistan's senior judiciary became fully independent of the legislature and the executive, a major victory for the "lawyers' movement" which had formed in opposition to Musharraf's sacking of the chief justice and other judges and imposition of constitutional amendments. In November, under severe pressure from human rights groups and the families of the "disappeared," the Supreme Court resumed hearings into the arbitrary detention and enforced disappearance of terrorism suspects and others by Pakistan's military and its intelligence services.

Balochistan

The Zardari government took a major step forward by acknowledging that human rights violations against the Baloch, including the "disappearance" of hundreds of people, took place during Musharraf's military government. However, the military has blocked attempts by the government to locate the victims and continues to exercise sway over the province through its intelligence agencies. Targeted killings by Baloch nationalists of non-Baloch settlers in the province spiked sharply in 2009, while reports of torture and arbitrary detention of Baloch nationalists at the hands of the military's intelligence agencies continued. In October, Shafiq Ahmed Khan, the provincial education minister, was shot dead. Baloch nationalists claimed responsibility.

Women's and Girls' Rights

Violence and mistreatment of women and girls, including rape, domestic violence, and forced marriage, remain serious problems.

In an important step forward, Pakistan's parliament unanimously passed legislation in November to amend Section 509 of the Pakistan Penal Code (PPC) in order to penalize sexual harassment of women at any public or private workplace, or in public spaces. The changes to the PPC are already in effect and are expected to become part of a more comprehensive anti-sexual harassment bill pending in parliament at this writing. In another significant move, the National Assembly passed the Domestic Violence (Prevention and Protection) Bill in August 2009. The law seeks to prevent violence against women and children through quick criminal trials and a chain of protection committees and protection officers.

Attacks on Education

The Taliban destroyed hundreds of schools in Swat and parts of the tribal areas under their control. Schools in Pakistani cities received threats from militants throughout the year and had to frequently shut down. In October twin suicide attacks at the International Islamic University in Islamabad resulted in the deaths of nine students, mostly women targeted in the women's cafeteria on campus.

Treatment of Minorities

Discriminatory laws and violence against religious minorities also continued to be a serious concern. Pakistan's infamous "Blasphemy Law" remained in place and religious minorities continued to be targeted under it.

Attacks on religious and social minorities continued. In August, seven Christians were burnt alive and 18 others injured and at least 50 houses set on fire by a mob accusing the victims of blasphemy in the town of Gojra in Punjab province. Though federal authorities reacted promptly and an inquiry recommended the suspension of police officials accused of negligence, the incident sparked renewed controversy about Pakistan's blasphemy laws. The Ahmadi religious community also continued to be targeted under blasphemy laws and was threatened by extremist militant groups that regard Ahmadis as heretics to Islam.

In a positive development, Pakistan's Supreme Court ruled in July that *hijras* (male-to-female transgender individuals) must receive equal protection of the law and directed federal and provincial government welfare programs to provide financial support to the *hijra* community.

In a significant move, Pakistan's government allocated US$425 million to launch the Benazir Income Support Program—the country's first social protection program that aims to provide income support to the poorest 15 percent of the population.

Media Freedom

Nationally, there has been a marked decrease in government-sponsored attacks on and intimidation of journalists since the Zardari government assumed office. However, journalists continue to face pressure and threats from elements of Pakistan's intelligence apparatus and non-state actors, including the Taliban, who repeatedly have threatened journalists and television stations in the country. Taliban intimidation was particularly high in 2009 in the tribal areas and the Malakand division. In September Afghan journalist Janullah Hashimzada was murdered in Pakistan, allegedly by Afghan Taliban. In July the homes of two journalists, Behroz Khan and Rehman Buneri, from the Buner Valley in Malakand division, were destroyed by the Taliban in response to their reporting.

In Balochistan the Pakistani military continued to intimidate and muzzle the press. It forced the closure of Urdu-language daily *Asaap* in August. In February, Jan Muhammad Dashti, owner and editor-in-chief of *Asaap*, was shot and seriously wounded. In April a correspondent on the English-language daily *Baluchistan Express* was killed. In August the staff of the *Baluchistan Express* and the Urdu-language daily *Azadi,* were threatened, and their staff intimidated and questioned by paramilitary forces. Balochistan provincial officials said that they are unable to prevent the military, which was implicated in the above incidents, from committing such abuses.

Death Penalty

Pakistan's prime minister announced in June 2008 that more than 7,000 inmates on death row in Pakistan would have their sentences commuted. To date, there has been no movement on the commutations. However, while at least 15 executions took place in Pakistan in 2008, none have been reported in the country in 2009.

Key International Actors

The United States remained the key external actor in Pakistan. Anti-US sentiment deepened markedly in Pakistan in 2009 due to perceived US violations of Pakistani sovereignty through aerial drone strikes in the tribal areas that killed hundreds of civilians and persistent rumors, denied by Pakistani authorities, that personnel from the private military company Xe Services (Blackwater) are conducting covert operations in Pakistan. Substantial sections of Pakistani society, particularly opinion makers and the media, blamed US behavior for the surge in militant attacks in the country, even as they expressed broad support for the government's fight against the Taliban and affiliated groups.

However, a significant shift from past US practice of focusing only on counterterrorism and supporting Pakistan's military at the cost of democracy and constitutional rule was also in clear evidence. The US became the largest bilateral assistance provider to Pakistan in the aftermath of the massive displacement caused by the Swat operation in May. In September, the Friends of Democratic Pakistan forum, co-chaired by Presidents Obama and Zardari and the United Kingdom Prime Minister Gordon Brown, held its first summit in New York. The meeting pledged to provide concrete economic and political support to strengthen democratic governance and the rule of law.

In October President Obama signed into law the Enhanced Partnership with Pakistan Act, promising US$7.5 billion in non-military aid over five years. However, in a public attempt to destabilize the elected government, the Pakistani military led a nationalist backlash, publicly rebuking the government for not opposing conditions relating to military conduct that it said compromised Pakistan's national security.

A three-member United Nations Inquiry Commission began its investigation into the 2007 assassination of former prime minister Benazir Bhutto.

THE PHILIPPINES

The Philippines is a multiparty democracy with an elected president and legislature, a thriving civil society sector, and a vibrant media. Several key institutions, including the judiciary and law enforcement agencies, however, remain weak, meaning the military and police still commit human rights violations with impunity. Politically motivated extrajudicial killings and targeted killings of alleged petty criminals continue, with the government failing to acknowledge and address involvement by the security forces and local officials.

Extrajudicial Killings and Enforced Disappearances

Hundreds of leftist politicians, political activists, journalists, and outspoken clergy have been killed or abducted since 2001. So far only 11 people have been convicted for these extrajudicial killings, two in 2009. No member of the military active at the time of the killing has been brought to justice for such crimes. In an April 2009 follow-up report to the United Nations Human Rights Council, UN Special Rapporteur on Extrajudicial, Summary or Arbitrary Executions Philip Alston observed that while the government has taken some steps to address extrajudicial killings, it fails to implement needed reforms such as institutionalizing the principle of command responsibility. He also noted that the military has not changed its counterinsurgency methods to eliminate the likelihood of unlawful killings.

On November 23, 2009, in the worst apparent politically motivated violence in recent history, about a hundred armed men abducted and executed at least 47 people, including a dozen members of a candidate's family and accompanying journalists in Maguindanao province. The victims were en route to file Buluan Vice Mayor Ishmael Mangudadatu's certificate of candidacy for governor in the May 2010 elections. Local officials, police, and paramilitary forces were implicated in the killings. President Gloria Macapagal Arroyo ordered an investigation.

In March 2009 former Police Superintendent Rafael Cardeno, one of the men who ordered the December 31, 2001 murder of Young Officers' Union spokesperson Baron Cervantes, was convicted of murder. On April 29, 2009, Joy Anticamara was convicted of homicide and sentenced to 17 years' imprisonment for the July 2006 killing of radio broadcaster Armando Pace.

In August 2009 a Manila court acquitted Aniano Flores, a military agent, of the 2002 killing of activist Edilberto Napoles, an organizer of the leftist political party Bayan Muna. The judge noted that prosecutors should have included Gen. Jovito Palparan on the charge sheet, on the basis of command responsibility. In 2002 prosecutors had recommended the court dismiss the complaint against Palparan and Sgt. Rizal Hilario, finding there was no probable cause to indict them for conspiracy to murder. Palparan, a retired military commander and now party-list representative in Congress, was considered a "prime suspect behind the extrajudicial killings" by the government's 2006 Melo Commission.

Meanwhile, optimism over Supreme Court writs to compel military and other government officials to release information on people in their custody was dampened by difficulty in enforcing the writs of amparo and habeas data. In September 2008 the Court of Appeals granted writs for the release of Karen Empeno and Sherlyn Cadapan, abducted allegedly by military personnel in mid-2006. In March 2009, however, the court failed to enforce the writs.

Targeted Killings of Petty Criminals and Street Youths

So-called death squads operating in Davao City, General Santos City, Digos City, Tagum City, and Cebu City continue to target alleged petty criminals, drug dealers, gang members, and street children. Police officers and local government officials have been implicated in the decade-old killing spree that has plagued Davao City: according to human rights groups, more than 89 Davao residents were murdered in death squad killings from January to early September 2009, bringing the total to more than 926 victims since 1998. In May 2009 President Arroyo ordered the Department of Interior and Local Government and the police to "get to the bottom" of the killings.

The national Commission on Human Rights (CHR) has spearheaded efforts to investigate the death squads, holding three public hearings in Davao City since March 2009, and in June setting up a multi-agency taskforce involving police, military, and other government agencies to conduct investigations. The taskforce has uncovered human remains, guns, and ammunition on land belonging to a former police officer, but in the courts it has faced obstructions and unnecessary bureaucratic delays.

Conflict in Mindanao

The armed conflict between the Philippine government and the Moro Islamic Liberation Front intensified in the first half of 2009, but a ceasefire has been in place since July. At this writing the number of internally displaced persons (IDPs) due to the conflict stands at 250,000. In addition to poor humanitarian conditions in IDP camps, civil society groups alleged violations of the laws of war and human rights abuses by both sides, including forced disappearances, extrajudicial killings, torture, and wanton destruction of houses. On June 30, the 6th Infantry Division spokesman Col. Jonathan Ponce referred to IDPs as "enemy reserve forces."

The military failed to take all feasible precautions to minimize civilian harm during military operations. In mid-July a military raid in Maguindanao province resulted in the death of Halima Bansil, age 11, while asleep in her family home, and the wounding of her father and brother, who were taken into custody.

The army continued to fight Abu Sayyaf, an armed group implicated in numerous attacks and abductions against civilians, particularly in Sulu and Basilan. Abu Sayyaf kidnapped three staff of the International Committee of the Red Cross in January, releasing two in April and the third in July.

Conflict with the New People's Army

Military operations between government forces and the communist New People's Army continue especially in Central and Northern Luzon, Southern Tagalog, Bicol, Eastern Visayas, Negros, and Southern and Northern Mindanao. Around 1,700 people in Surigao del Sur, Mindanao, were displaced for over two months having fled their homes in June due to fears of being abused by government forces or caught in the fighting after government forces moved into their area.

Women's Rights and Filipino Workers Abroad

On August 14, 2009, President Arroyo signed into law the "Magna Carta for Women," which sets out the state's responsibility to ensure women's equal access to resources and development outcomes. The law includes recognizing all women's rights protected in international treaties ratified by the Philippines, repealing all laws discriminatory to women within three years, achieving 50-50 representation in the third-tier level of government, and increasing the proportion of women in sectors that respond to gender-based violence, such as the police and medico-legal services. It establishes a gender ombudsperson under the CHR.

Approximately two million Filipinos work abroad, including hundreds of thousands of women who work in other parts of Asia and the Middle East as domestic workers. While the Philippine government has made some efforts to support and protect migrant domestic workers, many women continue to experience abuses abroad including unpaid wages, food deprivation, forced confinement in the workplace, and physical and sexual abuse (see also Saudi Arabia and UAE chapters).

Pain Treatment

Tens of thousands of cancer patients and people living with HIV/AIDS in the Philippines suffer from severe pain without access to treatment, due to unnecessarily burdensome narcotics regulations and a poor supply and distribution system for controlled medications. As the government controls the import and supply of all strong pain medications, unreasonably limiting access can lead to violations of the right to the highest attainable standard of health, and can amount to cruel, inhuman, or degrading treatment. Government action to remedy this situation has been insufficient to date.

Key International Actors

The United States is the most influential ally and, together with Australia and Japan, one of the three largest bilateral donors to the Philippines. In July President Arroyo met US President Barack Obama to discuss closer military and counterterrorism cooperation. In November US Secretary of State Hillary Clinton visited the Philippines, but neither she nor Obama pressed Arroyo to address continuing impunity for extrajudicial killings. The US military has access to Philippine lands and seas under a Visiting Forces Agreement, and the two militaries hold annual joint exercises. In fiscal year 2008-09 the US government authorized US$30 million to be provided to the Philippines under Foreign Military Financing for procurement of military equipment and US$1.7 million in the International Military Exchange Training program, under which military officers are trained in the United States. Of this, US$2 million is contingent on the Philippine government showing progress in addressing human rights violations, including extrajudicial killings.

Australia is similarly developing closer military-military ties, having signed a Status of Visiting Forces Agreement on May 31, 2007; this agreement remains before the Philippine Congress awaiting passage.

In October 2009 the European Union announced a €3.9 million program to address extrajudicial killings and strengthen the criminal justice system by providing training and technical assistance in 2009-11.

In its May 14, 2009 concluding comments, the UN Committee against Torture expressed deep concerns about allegations of routine and widespread torture of suspects in police custody, failures to investigate and prosecute such allegations, and a "climate of impunity." On October 2 the Committee on the Rights of the Child urged the Philippines to take "all necessary measures to prevent extrajudicial killings of children and to thoroughly investigate all alleged cases of killings and bring the perpetrators to justice," following its September review of the Philippines' compliance with the Convention on the Rights of the Child. Within a month of the April release of the report by UN Special Rapporteur on Extrajudicial Executions Philip Alston, President Arroyo abolished the Inter-Agency Legal Action Group by Executive Order 808, implementing one of Alston's recommendations: Alston had said that the Group used prosecutions to dismantle civil society organizations and political groups that the government believes to be communist fronts.

In September the International Labour Organization conducted a high-level mission to the Philippines in response to a complaint by the trade union Kilusang Mayo Uno, alleging killings, grave threats, harassment, and other forms of violence against members of workers' organizations.

Singapore

Singapore's legal framework continues to perpetuate an authoritarian state tightly controlled by the ruling People's Action Party (PAP). Although the party has won all elections since 1959 and is currently represented by 82 of the 84 parliamentarians with full voting rights, it is concerned that the next election, slated for no later than 2011, may demonstrate significant erosion of its popular support. To bolster its standing, the PAP has touted a relaxation of curbs on free expression, assembly, and association, and has expressed intent to introduce amendments to the constitution and the Parliamentary Elections Act to guarantee a minimum of nine opposition members of parliament.

Appearances, however, are deceiving. In the interests of security, public order, morality, national harmony, or friendly foreign relations, Singapore law authorizes censorship of content and distribution of print material and films, severe limits on public processions and assemblies, and prolonged detention of suspects without trial. Mindful of the disruptions by civil society organizations at the 2006 World Bank–International Monetary Fund meetings in Singapore, parliament passed the draconian Public Order Law 2009 to preempt any such disruption at the Singapore-hosted November 2009 Asia-Pacific Economic Cooperation (APEC) summit.

Freedom of Assembly, Expression, and Association

In April 2009, seven months after the government rescinded the need for a police permit if more than four people wished to gather or stage a rally at Singapore's Speakers' Corner, parliament passed the Public Order Act 2009, effectively negating the earlier move. The new Act requires permits for any "cause-related activity"—such as a procession or assembly—no matter how many people are involved (a "cause related activity" is defined as a show of support for or against a position, person, group, or government). For "major" events, the Act permits police to issue "move-on" orders and to prohibit filming of their own activities.

Despite the October acquittal of three leaders and two supporters of the opposition Singapore Democratic Party, space has not opened up for political opponents. The five were tried for conducting a procession without a permit on

September 17, 2007, while wearing T-shirts reading "Democracy Now" and "Freedom Now." The judge first noted that although the home minister could make bylaws regulating assemblies and processions, nothing in the act defined what constituted either, and then ruled that the "natural and ordinary" meaning of procession was not applicable to the five walking casually on pedestrian pathways, taking breaks and impeding no one. However, the judge refused to rule the act unconstitutional, leaving in place a de facto police ban on outdoor political activities by opposition political parties. On October 12, 2009, the Attorney General's Chambers filed an appeal.

Some of those involved in that "procession" are defendants, along with other Singapore Democratic Party members and supporters, in four other trials for "assembly without a permit," "attempted procession without a permit," or "speaking in public without a permit." Fines imposed after earlier trials have bankrupted the party's secretary-general, Dr. Chee Soon Juan, and his sister, Chee Siok Chin.

In March a judge found *Wall Street Journal* senior editor Melanie Kirkpatrick in contempt of court for allegedly impugning the independence of Singapore's judiciary. In October the *Far Eastern Economic Review* and its editor-in-chief Hugo Restall lost an appeal in a defamation suit brought by Singapore founder Lee Kuan Yew and his son Prime Minister Hsien Loong Lee for a 2006 article they said implicitly suggested they may have abused the public's trust. Damages and legal fees filed on November 13 totaled Singapore $405,000 (US$292,438).

The Newspaper and Printing Presses Act requires yearly renewal of licenses and empowers authorities to limit circulation of foreign newspapers alleged to "engage in the domestic politics of Singapore." Internet content is less tightly controlled. Some political films and videos such as *Singapore Rebel*, a film biography of Chee Soon Juan, are approved, in part because their circulation cannot be controlled. But films containing "partisan or biased references to or comments on any political matter" are prohibited.

State law and political repression, including the threat of defamation suits and attendant bankruptcy, prevent the establishment of human rights NGOs and limit individual willingness to challenge the government. The Societies Act requires that most organizations of more than 10 people register with the government but limits engagement in "political activities" to registered political parties. Trade unions may not contribute to political parties, and the National Trade Union Congress, with which most unions affiliate, does not permit members supportive of opposition policies to hold office.

Criminal Justice System

Singapore's Internal Security Act (ISA), Criminal Law (Temporary Provisions) Act (CLA), Misuse of Drugs Act (MDA), and Undesirable Publications Act permit arrest and detention without warrant or judicial review. The ISA and CLA also authorize preventive detention. The MDA permits the Central Narcotics Bureau chief to detain suspected drug users for three years in "rehabilitation centers" without recourse to trial; those who relapse face extended prison terms and caning (even though relapse is a common milepost on the road to recovery from drug dependence).

Singapore's penal code mandates caning along with imprisonment for some 30 offenses, including drug and security offenses. Its use is optional for other crimes involving force. From January to September 2008, courts reportedly sentenced 4,078 males between ages 16 and 50 to caning. Women may not be caned.

Singapore is believed to have one of the world's highest per capita execution rates, although statistics are not made public. Most sentences involve some 20 drug-related offenses for which execution is mandatory and which, according to the MDA, require the alleged perpetrator to prove his innocence to escape conviction. Singapore remains vocal in its defense of the death penalty. In March 2009 Singapore defended the death penalty for drug offenses at the United Nations Human Rights Council, notwithstanding conclusions by UN human rights mechanisms and UN drug and human rights agencies that the death penalty for drug offenses violates international law.

Sexual Orientation and Gender Identity

Although Singapore law bans private and consensual sexual relations between men, movement toward acceptance is noticeable. A May 2009 rally at Speakers' Corner, which drew some 2,500 gay rights supporters, proceeded without government interference despite the deputy prime minister cautioning against stridency. In July Singapore's law minister, referencing the state's conservative leanings and affirming that Singapore would not follow India's example and decriminalize its own law, nevertheless stated that the courts were free to interpret it as they saw fit.

Migrant Domestic Workers and Trafficking

Although progress has been made on successfully prosecuting abusive employers and on recovery of back wages for foreign domestic workers, Singapore has failed to regulate recruitment fees. Out of a two-year contract, repayment costs workers 8-11 months' wages.

The US Trafficking in Persons 2009 report listed Singapore on Tier 2: countries that are not doing enough to address trafficking. Women are trafficked to Singapore for domestic work and commercial sexual exploitation. Singaporean authorities misrepresent the number of trafficking victims by eliminating those who were deceived into migrating by false promises.

Key International Actors

Singapore is a key member of the Southeast Asia Regional Centre for Counter-Terrorism along with the United States, Malaysia, and others, and is an active participant in regional and sub-regional security issues including maritime and aviation security and combating of money laundering.

At a March 2009 meeting of the Association of Southeast Asian Nations (ASEAN), Singapore's prime minister raised the issue of the region's inability to solve the problem of a safe haven for stateless Rohingyas fleeing persecution in Burma (see also Burma and Thailand chapters). However, a senior minister of state for foreign affairs later clarified that Singapore would not accept refugees or asylum seekers but could only offer humanitarian aid "so they could depart for a third country."

As an important financial center for Southeast Asia, Singapore faced criticism for reportedly hosting bank accounts containing ill-gotten gains of corrupt leaders and their associates. Two banks named as holding the proceeds of Burma's sales of natural gas, which are not duly reflected in official Burmese budgets, denied the allegations.

SRI LANKA

The endgame and aftermath of the armed conflict between the Sri Lankan government and the separatist Liberation Tigers of Tamil Eelam (LTTE) dominated events in Sri Lanka throughout 2009. During the last months of the war, both sides committed serious violations of international humanitarian law, in what a senior United Nations official described as a "bloodbath," while the overall human rights situation in the country continued to deteriorate as the government adopted increasingly repressive policies.

During the final months of the conflict that ended in May, the LTTE continued to forcibly recruit civilians, including children, into its forces, used civilians as human shields, and physically prevented and at times shot at Tamil civilians under their control trying to flee the fighting. Government forces indiscriminately shelled densely populated areas, including hospitals. Both parties prevented vital humanitarian assistance from reaching the civilian population.

Since March 2008 the government has confined displaced Tamils fleeing the fighting. The population of the detention camps skyrocketed to over a quarter million people after the LTTE's defeat in May. Security forces also detained, in many cases in violation of domestic and international law, more than 10,000 people suspected of LTTE involvement or sympathies. Threats, physical attacks, and arbitrary arrests against journalists, human rights defenders, and humanitarian workers continued unabated, causing significant numbers to leave the country. As in the past, rights violators enjoyed near-complete impunity.

Violations of Laws of War

On May 19, 2009, the Sri Lankan government declared victory over the LTTE, marking an end to a 26-year-long armed conflict that had caused between 80,000 and 100,000 deaths. During the last months of the war both the Sri Lankan armed forces and the LTTE repeatedly violated the laws of war, causing unnecessary civilian suffering and casualties.

Forced to retreat by government offensive operations, the LTTE drove civilians into a narrow strip of land on Sri Lanka's northeastern coast, effectively using several hundred thousand people as human shields. The LTTE shot at and injured or killed many of those trying to flee from the war zone to government-held territory. LTTE forces also deployed near densely populated areas, placing civilians in increased danger of attack. As the fighting intensified, the LTTE stepped up its practice of forcibly recruiting civilians, including children, into its ranks and, to hazardous forced labor on the battlefield.

Government forces repeatedly and indiscriminately shelled densely populated areas, sometimes using heavy artillery and other area weapons incapable of distinguishing between civilians and combatants. As the LTTE-controlled area shrank, the government unilaterally declared "no-fire zones" or "safe zones" on three different occasions, calling upon civilians to seek shelter there; nevertheless, government forces continued attacking these areas. In disregard of the laws of war, government forces also fired artillery at or near hospitals on at least 30 occasions.

High-level government officials tried to justify attacks on civilians by arguing that people remaining in the war zone were LTTE sympathizers and therefore legitimate targets, indicating possible intent to commit war crimes.

Civilians in the war zone also suffered from lack of food, water, shelter, and medicines. The government's decision in September 2008 to order humanitarian agencies out of the LTTE-controlled area greatly exacerbated their plight. Ongoing fighting, lack of oversight, and the manipulation of aid delivery by government and LTTE forces contributed to the deepening humanitarian crisis.

Exact information on the extent of humanitarian law violations by both sides as well as casualty figures remains limited, largely because the government barred all independent observers, including the media and human rights organizations, from operating near the war zone. The UN estimated that at least 7,000 people were killed and 13,000 injured during the last five months of the war.

Detention Camps for Internally Displaced Persons

Since March 2008 the government has confined virtually all civilians displaced by the war in military-controlled detention camps, euphemistically called "welfare centers." In violation of international law, the government denied more than

SRI LANKA

War on the Displaced

Sri Lankan Army and LTTE Abuses against
Civilians in the Vanni

HUMAN
RIGHTS
WATCH

280,000 displaced their rights to liberty and freedom of movement. As of November 18, 2009, six months after the end of hostilities, the government continued to hold more than 129,000 people (more than half of them women and girls) in the camps. Over 80,000 of these were children.

The government's refusal to release displaced persons from the camps contributed to severe overcrowding, with many of the camps holding twice the number recommended by the UN. As a result, access to basic requirements such as food, water, shelter, toilets, and bathing, has been inadequate. These conditions imposed particular hardships on the elderly, children, and pregnant women.

The authorities failed to provide camp residents with sufficient information about the reason for their continued detention, the whereabouts of relatives, or the criteria and procedure for their return home. Families in the detention camps had no access to mechanisms for finding missing relatives who might be in other camps or in unofficial detention centers. The military camp administration prevented humanitarian organizations, including the UN and the International Committee of the Red Cross (ICRC), from undertaking effective monitoring and protection in the camps.

Arbitrary Detention and Enforced Disappearances

The government detained more than 10,000 displaced persons at checkpoints and from the camps on suspicion of LTTE involvement, in many cases citing vague and overbroad emergency laws still in force after the end of the war. Many arrests were carried out in violation of domestic and international law. The authorities failed to inform families of their relatives' fate and whereabouts, raising fears that some detainees were forcibly disappeared.

The authorities also specifically targeted key witnesses to the final stages of the war. They arrested and held for several months several government doctors who had been working in areas under LTTE control and had reported on government shelling and resulting civilian casualties. While in detention the doctors retracted wartime statements, raising suspicion of undue pressure and ill-treatment.

Enforced disappearances and abductions, a longstanding and widespread problem in Sri Lanka, continued, especially in the north and east. From January to June 2009, 16 enforced disappearances were reported in Trincomalee district alone.

Attacks on Civil Society Actors

Threats and attacks against outspoken and critical civil society actors continued in 2009, including after the end of the war, further shrinking the already limited space for public debate.

On numerous occasions unidentified perpetrators attacked journalists and media outlets critical of the government. In one of the most brazen attacks, unidentified armed men in January assassinated *Sunday Leader* newspaper editor Lasantha Wickremetunga, a senior journalist acclaimed for his investigative reporting. On June 1, unidentified men abducted and severely beat Poddala Jayantha, general secretary of the Sri Lanka Working Journalists Association, who was later released.

The government continued to use anti-terror laws and emergency regulations against peaceful critics. On August 31 the Colombo High Court, in a deeply flawed trial, sentenced J.S. Tissainayagam, a journalist who had written critically of the government's military campaign, to 20 years' hard labor under the Prevention of Terrorism Act. He and his publishers had been arrested and detained in March 2008, but he was not formally charged for nearly six months. The hostile, sometimes deadly, media environment drove at least 11 Sri Lankan journalists into exile in the 12 months to June 2009, according to the Committee to Project Journalists.

Human rights activists were also targeted. On May 7, armed men in uniform abducted Stephen Suntharaj, a staff member of the Centre for Human Rights and Development who had just been released by a Supreme Court order after having spent two months in police detention. Suntharaj is still missing. On August 20, Paikiasothy Saravanamuttu, the executive director of the Centre for Policy Alternatives, a leading Sri Lankan NGO, received a death threat in an anonymous letter blaming him for Sri Lanka's possible loss of European Union trade privileges. Two weeks later police detained him briefly at the airport as he was reentering the country.

Government officials continued to publicly accuse international agencies, including the UN and the ICRC, of being LTTE supporters or sympathizers. In September the government expelled a UNICEF spokesperson who had drawn attention to the plight of children during and in the aftermath of the war. In July the government asked the ICRC to close its offices in eastern Sri Lanka, and barred it from accessing most displaced persons in the north.

Justice and Accountability

Despite government promises, including in a May 23, 2009 joint statement by President Mahinda Rajapaksa and UN Secretary-General Ban Ki-moon, no serious steps have been taken to investigate allegations of human rights and laws-of-war violations during the war's final months. On the contrary, high-ranking government officials, including the president, repeatedly dismissed such allegations, claiming that there had been no violations by the armed forces. A committee of experts established by Rajapaksa in October to look at United States government allegations of war crimes in Sri Lanka does not have the mandate, resources, or independence to conduct an adequate investigation.

The government's refusal to address accountability for serious abuses continues a longstanding pattern of impunity for rights violations by state security forces. Past efforts to address shortcomings through the establishment of ad hoc mechanisms in Sri Lanka have produced few results. In June a presidential commission of inquiry into human rights abuses disbanded after having investigated only 7 of the 16 mandated cases. In the most prominent case, the commission, without sufficient basis, exonerated the armed forces in the execution-style slaying of 17 aid workers in 2006. An International Independent Group of Eminent Persons withdrew from its observer role to the commission in 2008 because of flaws in the commission's working methods. To date the president has yet to release the commission's report on any of the cases.

Reflecting the continuing impunity for even the most egregious human rights violators, the government in April 2009 appointed as minister of national integration

V. Muralitharan, who as LTTE-leader Colonel Karuna was implicated in the execution of hundreds of police officers in the early 1990s and the recruitment of thousands of children into LTTE ranks and, later, his splinter group.

Key International Actors

While many governments and diplomats worked hard to persuade the Sri Lankan
government to respect rights and to avoid civilian casualties in the conflict, it
largely ignored such entreaties. The United States and some European Union governments publicly condemned violations by both sides and called for a humanitarian corridor for civilians trapped in the war zone. Collectively, however, international actors signally failed to address the humanitarian crisis. The UN Security
Council did not even discuss the unfolding crisis as part of its official agenda.
During a special session on Sri Lanka at the UN Human Rights Council in May,
governments including Brazil, Cuba, India, and Pakistan led efforts to prevent the
passage of a strong resolution, ensuring the adoption of a deeply flawed resolution that largely commended the Sri Lankan government for its current policies.

While some UN actors, such as the Office of the High Commissioner for Human
Rights and the special rapporteur on extrajudicial executions, were outspoken
during the crisis, others, such as the senior UN official in Sri Lanka and Secretary-
General Ban Ki-moon, failed to adequately denounce laws-of-war violations
against civilians trapped in the conflict zone and rights violations against displaced persons. In contrast to other conflicts, for instance, the UN refused to publish its estimates of the number of civilian casualties. And Ban failed to hold the
Rajapaksa government to commitments made in their May 23 joint communiqué.

In September the European Commission completed an investigation into Sri
Lanka's compliance with 27 international conventions on human rights, labor
rights, and environmental standards to determine whether Sri Lanka qualified for
an extension of a preferential trading scheme called GSP+. Sri Lanka's refusal to
cooperate with the investigation and grave concerns about its human rights
record put into question whether the privilege would be extended in December
2009. The US State Department War Crimes Unit issued a report on the final
months of the war in October that detailed laws of war violations by both sides.

The International Monetary Fund granted Sri Lanka a US$2.6 billion loan in July. The vote was delayed for weeks because of concerns about the human rights situation in the country. At the vote, five countries—the United States, United Kingdom, France, Germany, and Argentina—made the highly unusual move of abstaining from the vote in a show of disapproval of Sri Lanka's human rights violations.

THAILAND

Political instability and polarization continued in 2009 and occasionally resulted in violence when anti-government groups, affiliated with Thaksin Shinawatra, clashed with Thai security forces. Public pledges of the army-backed government of Prime Minister Abhisit Vejjajiva (who succeeded Somchai Wongsawat in December 2008) to give priority to human rights and the restoration of democracy have largely been unfulfilled.

Political Violence

Episodes of political violence involving supporters of former prime minister Thaksin broke out throughout the year. On April 7, anti-government protests turned violent when protesters from the Thaksin-backed United Front for Democracy against Dictatorship (UDD) attacked Prime Minister Abhisit's motorcade in Pattaya. The red-shirted protesters then clashed with pro-government groups in Pattaya on April 10 and 11. After UDD protesters broke into the meeting site of the summit of the Association of Southeast Asian Nations (ASEAN), the summit was cancelled. In response, the government declared a state of emergency in Pattaya on April 11 and in Bangkok and surrounding provinces on April 12. UDD protesters on April 12 forced their way into the Interior Ministry in Bangkok, where Abhisit was meeting with senior government officials, and again attacked the prime minister's motorcade, dragging people from cars and beating them.

Street battles erupted in Bangkok on April 13 when UDD protesters, who had been blocking main intersections in Din Daeng district with buses and taxis, attacked approaching soldiers with guns, petrol bombs, and other improvised weapons. UDD protesters also threatened to blow up trucks with liquefied petroleum gas near residential areas and hospitals. Soldiers used teargas and live ammunition to disperse the protesters and clear the blockades; while most gunfire was into the air, some soldiers fired assault rifles directly at the protesters. Clashes spilled across Bangkok through the next day, when two members of neighborhood watch groups were shot dead in a clash with UDD protesters. At least 123 people were injured, including four soldiers wounded by gunshots.

Leaders and members of the UDD were arrested and briefly detained after the dispersal of their protests. At this writing, the UDD continues periodically to mobilize anti-government protests across the country.

On September 7 the National Counter Corruption Commission (NCCC) ruled that National Police Chief Patcharawat Wongsuwan and six other high-ranking police officers should be charged with criminal offenses and subject to disciplinary action, and criminal charges should be brought against former prime minister Somchai and then deputy prime minister Chavalit Yongchaiyut, in connection with the crackdown on protesters from the anti-Thaksin People's Alliance for Democracy (PAD) on October 7, 2008, when police violently dispersed about 2,000 protesters in front of parliament. Two PAD supporters died and 443 were injured; about 20 police officers were wounded.

There has been no independent and impartial investigation into politically motivated violence and human rights abuses committed by the yellow-shirted PAD during its protests in 2008, which included occupying Bangkok's Suvarnabhumi airport. Prosecutions of PAD leaders and members have been delayed amid growing public perception that the PAD is immune to legal accountability. Ultra-nationalist protesters in the network of the PAD violently clashed with villagers, who were mobilized by the Interior Ministry and local politicians, during a rally in Srisaket on September 19, 2009.

Freedom of Expression and the Media

In 2009 Thai authorities have closed down more than 18,000 websites after accusing them of promoting anti-monarchy sentiments and posing threats to national security. The charge of *lese majeste* (insulting the monarchy, penal code article 112) has been used against Thai citizens and foreigners, journalists and academics, bloggers and web board discussants; government critics such as Giles Ji Ungpakorn, Jakrapob Penkair, and Suchart Nakbangsai have fled or been unable to return to the country after being so charged.

Those accused have reason to fear the consequences. On January 14, 2009, Suwicha Thakor was arrested for allegedly posting *lese majeste* comments on the internet, and on April 3 was sentenced to 10 years in prison under article 112 and the Computer Crimes Act. On January 18 Australian author Harry Nicolaides was sentenced to three years in prison for defaming the crown prince in his 2005 novel "Verisimilitude"; he was pardoned and freed on February 19 after an international outcry. On August 28 government critic Daranee Charnchoengsilpakul (also known as Da Torpedo) was sentenced to 18 years in prison for insulting the monarchy in her speeches at a UDD rally. She was reportedly put in solitary confinement in Lard Yao prison. On March 6 Chiranuch Premchaiyaporn of online news forum *Prachatai* was arrested and her office raided by police. She was accused of violating the Computer Crimes Act and disseminating *lese majeste* content on the website in October-November 2008. She has been released on bail while the Attorney General's Office processes the case.

On November 1 Katha Pajariyapong and Theeranan Vipuchan were arrested by police for posting on the internet their comments and Thai translations of international media reports about King Bhumibol Adulyadej's poor health. They have been charged under the Computer Crimes Act with feeding false information causing harm to national security and the public. Both received bail, on condition that they must not leave Thailand while police undertake further investigation.

Abusive Anti-Narcotics Policy

Abhisit supported the reopening of investigations into the 2,819 extrajudicial killings that allegedly accompanied Thaksin's "war on drugs" in 2003. Facing strong resistance from the Royal Thai Police, which was implicated in many of these killings, slow progress has been made to bring perpetrators to justice and end systematic police brutality and abuse of power in drug suppression operations. In a positive development, in September 2009 nine police officers from Kalasin and Bangkok were charged with murder and other serious offenses related to two separate "war on drugs" cases.

The government responded to a surge in drug sales and use by resuming executions of convicted traffickers, after a six-year hiatus. Bundit Jaroenwanit and Jirawat Poompreuk, convicted in March 2001, were executed by lethal injection on August 24, 2009. TV news reported their execution minute-by-minute in reality show style.

After arrest, many drug users are subject to compulsory treatment at centers run by the military and the Interior Ministry. Each year 10,000-15,000 people are sent to such centers, where drug treatment is based on military-style physical exercise. Most people experience withdrawal from drugs while detained in prison for assessment, with little or no medical supervision or medication provided.

Violence and Abuses in the Southern Border Provinces

There were fewer reports in 2009 of abuses committed by security forces in the southern border provinces of Pattani, Yala, Narathiwat, and Songkhla, as the government appeared to take seriously the human toll and the cycle of violence that such abuses contribute to. However, gunmen from a local Aor Ror Bor militia unit were suspected of responsibility for the massacre of 10 ethnic Malay Muslims inside Al-Furquan mosque in Narathiwat's Joh Ai Rong district on June 8, 2009. Despite public commitments from the government to bring the perpetrators to justice, at this writing no arrests have been made.

Separatist groups continue to target civilians, including roadside ambushes and beheading victims or burning them to death. Some attacks were aimed at spreading terror among Buddhist Thais, or justified by insurgents as reprisal for abuses committed by Thai security forces against ethnic Malay Muslims. Insurgents burned down government schools and continued to engage in killings of teachers; many government schools were closed temporarily in response to security threats. The insurgents recruit children from private Islamic schools to participate in the armed hostilities and to serve other secondary roles, such as spying or carrying out arson attacks. In response, government security forces have at times raided private Islamic schools, and detained teachers and students for questioning.

The Attorney General's Office decided in February not to press charges against soldiers and police officers responsible for the Krue Se mosque killings on April 28, 2004, while the provincial court of Songkhla ruled on May 29 that Thai security forces were not responsible for the death of 78 ethnic Malay Muslims in the Tak Bai incident of October 25, 2004. Both decisions fly in the face of the facts and led to outrage in the Muslim community in the south. No progress was made in 2009 in the criminal prosecution of soldiers from the army's 39th Taskforce who

tortured and murdered Imam Yapa Kaseng in Narathiwat's Rue Soh district on
March 21, 2008.

Refugees and Migrant Workers

Thai authorities continue to violate the international principle of nonrefoulement
by returning refugees and asylum seekers to countries or origin where they were
likely to face persecution. Throughout 2009, Lao Hmong seeking asylum in
Petchabun continued to be repatriated to Laos. Staff of the United Nations High
Commissioner for Refugees were barred from access to Lao Hmong detention
camps in Petchabun or from taking part in the refugee status determination
process. There were also reports that exiled Chinese dissidents, many of them
linked with Falungong, were arrested and deported to China. Ongoing raids of
undocumented migrants have forced Burmese human rights and democracy
activists in northern Thailand to close down their offices.

Thai authorities adopted a hard-line stance toward Rohingya boatpeople from
Burma and Bangladesh. In January 2009 the National Security Council (chaired by
Abhisit) ordered authorities to intercept incoming Rohingya boats and detain pas-
sengers in off-shore holding centers. After being exposed by human rights groups
and the international media, the government admitted that its navy had pushed
some boats laden with Rohingyas back to international waters (see also Burma
chapter). Despite many public promises, Thai authorities did not conduct independent investigations into this and related allegations of abuses.

Migrant workers remain largely unprotected by Thai labor laws, making them vulnerable to arrest, extortion, and other abuse.

Human Rights Defenders

There has been little progress in official investigations into the cases of 20
human rights defenders killed during the Thaksin administration. These include
the 2004 "disappearance" and presumed murder of well-known Muslim lawyer
Somchai Neelapaijit, whose case was accepted by the UN Working Group on
Enforced or Involuntary Disappearances in June 2005. The Justice Ministry's
Department of Special Investigation has since 2006 taken over investigation of

Somchai's case from the Royal Thai Police, which was implicated in his "disappearance," but still failed to determine what happened to Somchai and who was responsible.

Key International Actors

The United States, United Kingdom, Australia, and the European Union worked to promote the restoration of democracy in Thailand, and expressed strong opposition to attempts by conflicting political factions to incite a military coup and violence.

Thailand, as the chair of ASEAN for 2009, has been active in promoting a regional human rights mechanism. But these efforts have been limited by the ASEAN principles of non-interference and consensus decision making. Human rights groups have little expectation that the ASEAN Intergovernmental Commission on Human Rights could take any meaningful steps in promoting and protecting human rights.

Vietnam

Vietnam intensified its suppression of dissent in 2009 in an effort to bolster the authority of the Communist Party. Authorities arrested dozens of peaceful democracy advocates, independent religious activists, human rights defenders, and online critics, using vaguely-worded national security laws such as spreading "anti-government propaganda" or "abusing democratic freedoms." The courts convicted at least 20 political or religious prisoners in 2009, including five people sentenced in October whom the previous month the United Nations Working Group on Arbitrary Detention had determined to be arbitrarily detained. People imprisoned in Vietnam for the exercise of fundamental rights number more than 400.

The government tightened its controls on internet use, blogging, and independent research, and banned dissemination and publication of content critical of the government. Religious freedom continued to deteriorate, with the government targeting religious leaders—and their followers—who advocated for civil rights, religious freedom, and equitable resolution of land disputes.

Repression of Political Opposition

In an effort to eliminate challenges to the Communist Party and curb social unrest in advance of a key June 2009 party plenum, in May the government launched a wave of arrests, detaining 27 people for alleged links to the banned Democratic Party of Vietnam (DPV). At least five were prosecuted on national security charges, including prominent lawyer Le Cong Dinh; their trial is pending at this writing. The arrests of at least eight other dissidents, bloggers, and political activists followed.

Freedom of Association and Assembly

The government bans independent trade unions and human rights organizations, as well as opposition political parties. Workers are prohibited from conducting strikes not authorized by the party-controlled labor confederation. Activists who promote workers' rights and independent unions are harassed, arrested, or jailed.

While government officials often tolerate farmers gathering in Hanoi and Ho Chi Minh City to file complaints about land confiscation or local corruption, political protests are generally banned. Police crackdowns on protests—especially those in the countryside—often take place away from the public spotlight. In May, for example, police dispersed demonstrations in the Mekong delta by ethnic Khmer farmers protesting land grabbing, and arrested Huynh Ba on charges of organizing the protests. Since his arrest, he has been held incommunicado in Soc Trang prison.

Freedom of Religion

Vietnamese law requires that religious groups register with the government and operate under government-controlled management boards. Adherents of some unregistered religious groups, as well as religious activists campaigning for inter-nationally-guaranteed rights, are harassed, arrested, or placed under house arrest.

In the Central Highlands, authorities in 2009 arrested dozens of Montagnard Christians accused of belonging to unregistered house churches considered sub-versive by the government, planning land rights protests, or conveying informa-tion about rights abuses to activists abroad. A focus of the crackdown was Gia Lai province, where more than 50 Montagnards were arrested and at least nine sen-tenced to prison during the year. On several occasions police beat and shocked Montagnards with electric batons when they refused to sign pledges to join the government sanctioned church.

Authorities continued to persecute members of the banned Unified Buddhist Church of Vietnam, whose supreme patriarch remained under pagoda arrest for his public criticism of government policies. Other religious activists imprisoned in Vietnam include Roman Catholic priest Nguyen Van Ly, a Mennonite pastor, and several Hoa Hao Buddhists.

In July as many as 200,000 Catholics peacefully protested in Quang Binh after police destroyed a temporary church structure erected near the ruins of an his-toric church. Police used teargas and electric batons to beat parishioners, arrest-ing 19, of whom seven were charged with disturbing public order.

In September authorities forcefully expelled more than 300 Buddhist monks and nuns from a meditation center in Lam Dong established in 2005 with government

On the Margins

Rights Abuses of Ethnic Khmer in Vietnam's Mekong Delta

HUMAN
RIGHTS
WATCH

approval. At least two monks were placed under house arrest after authorities forced them to return to their home provinces. Authorities took steps to close the center after its founder, peace activist Thich Nhat Hanh, proposed in 2007 that the government ease religious freedom restrictions.

Freedom of Expression and Information

The government strictly controls the media. Criminal penalties apply to authors, publications, websites, and internet users who disseminate information or writings that oppose the government, threaten national security, reveal state secrets, or promote "reactionary" ideas.

In 2009 the prime minister issued Decision 97, which prohibits publication of research that critiques or opposes the government or party, and limits research by private organizations to 317 government-approved topics. The Institute of Development Studies, one of Vietnam's only independent think-tanks, closed in September, one day before Decision 97 went into effect.

The government controls internet use by monitoring online activity, arresting cyber-dissidents, and blocking websites of certain human rights and political groups. Internet cafe owners are required to obtain photo identification from internet users, and to monitor and store information about their online activities. A 2008 circular regulating blogs calls for bloggers to limit their postings to personal content, and bans posting of articles about politics or issues the government considers state secrets, subversive, or threats to national security and social order.

Journalists covering controversial topics have been fined, fired, and arrested. In January 2009 the editors of two leading Vietnamese newspapers that had exposed a major corruption scandal in 2005 were dismissed from their jobs.

While the government tolerated some public debate about its sensitive relations with China in 2009, it selectively took punitive measures against commentators who characterized Vietnam's China policies as conciliatory, especially regarding China's controversial claims to disputed offshore islands and its investment in Central Highlands bauxite mines. In April authorities suspended publication of *Du Lich* newspaper for its critical coverage of China's territorial disputes with Vietnam, and in May the paper's deputy editor was dismissed. In August and

September police arrested and briefly detained two bloggers and an internet journalist on national security charges for articles criticizing China. Also in September the government fined the editor of the Communist Party's website for publishing "unauthorized" information about China training its military in order to defend its maritime borders with Vietnam.

Criminal Justice System

Police torture is prevalent, particularly during interrogation of political and religious prisoners, who are typically held incommunicado prior to trial and denied family visits and access to lawyers. Vietnamese courts lack independence and impartiality. Political and religious dissidents are often tried without the assistance of legal counsel in proceedings that fail to meet international fair trial standards.

Lawyers representing political or religious activists face intense harassment and even arrest, such as Le Cong Dinh. In February 2009 police raided the office of Le Tran Luat, a lawyer defending Catholics arrested during 2008 prayer vigils in Hanoi. Authorities confiscated his computer and documents, blocked him from meeting his clients, and detained and interrogated him to pressure him to drop the case.

Vietnamese law authorizes arbitrary "administrative detention" without trial. Under Ordinance 44, dissidents and others deemed national security threats can be involuntarily committed to mental institutions or detained in state-run "rehabilitation" centers.

Sex workers, trafficking victims, street children, people who use drugs, and street peddlers are routinely rounded up and detained without warrants in state rehabilitation centers. They are subject to beatings, sexual abuse, insufficient food, and little, if any, access to healthcare, including drug dependency treatment for an estimated 50,000 people who use drugs who are held in such centers.

Prison conditions are harsh and even life threatening. During pretrial detention—which can last more than a year—prisoners are often placed in solitary confinement in dark, cramped, unsanitary cells, with no bedding or mosquito nets. Convicted prisoners must perform hard labor, sometimes under hazardous conditions.

VIETNAM

Not Yet a Workers' Paradise

Vietnam's Suppression of the Independent Workers' Movement

HUMAN
RIGHTS
WATCH

Key International Actors

Vietnam, which served as president of the UN Security Council in October, made few efforts to improve its poor rights record or cooperate with UN human rights mechanisms in 2009, despite significant diplomatic pressure from donors and UN member states.

During the UN Human Rights Council's Universal Periodic Review of Vietnam's rights record in 2009, Vietnam rejected 45 key recommendations from a broad range of member states, such as lifting its restrictions on the internet, authorizing independent media, taking steps to end the practices of torture, arbitrary detention, and capital punishment, and recognizing the rights of individuals to promote human rights, conduct peaceful public protests, and express their opinions.

A September report by the UN Working Group on Arbitrary Detention determined that the government had unlawfully detained 10 dissidents. It criticized penal code provisions for violating human rights treaties and called for the immediate release of journalist Truong Minh Duc, currently serving a five-year sentence for "abusing democratic freedoms."

Donors pledged more than US$5 million in aid to Vietnam during their annual meeting in December 2008. During 2009 they raised a wide range of rights concerns with the government, including arrests of dissidents, censorship of media and blogs, religious freedom, treatment of ethnic minorities, children's rights, administrative detention, and environmental and social impacts of the bauxite mines.

As Vietnam's largest export market, the United States focused on developing its trade, investment, and security relations with Vietnam while exhorting Vietnam to improve its rights record, particularly in regard to media freedom, criminalization of peaceful dissent, and restrictions on blogs and independent research. Issues discussed during a political-military dialogue in 2009 included possible joint operations against drugs and terrorism.

Japan continued its policy of not overtly criticizing Vietnam's rights record, despite its considerable leverage as Vietnam's largest donor and third-largest investor. In March Japan resumed aid and loans to Vietnam after suspending assistance in 2008 over a corruption scandal in one of its projects.

GEORGIA/RUSSIA

Up In Flames

Humanitarian Law Violations and Civilian Victims
in the Conflict over South Ossetia

WORLD REPORT

2010

EUROPE
AND CENTRAL ASIA

ARMENIA

The Armenian authorities have yet to ensure meaningful investigations into excessive use of police force during March 2008 clashes with opposition supporters protesting alleged fraud in the previous month's presidential election, and address related allegations of abuse in police custody. A number of opposition supporters reportedly remain imprisoned in connection with the March 2008 events. During May 2009 municipal elections in the capital, Yerevan, international observers reported intimidation and attacks on domestic observers and journalists.

Broadcasting law amendments bring greater transparency to the licensing process, but an independent television station that has been off air for over seven years remains without a new license despite a European Court of Human Rights ruling in its favor. Authorities have failed to conclusively investigate physical attacks on journalists.

Lack of Accountability for Excessive Use of Force

The authorities have yet to ensure a meaningful investigation into and full accountability for excessive use of force by security forces during clashes with protestors on March 1-2, 2008, following the disputed February presidential election. The clashes resulted in at least 10 deaths, including two security officials and eight protestors. Soon after the March events the police dismissed several top officials, although none was charged in relation to the violence. Officials claimed to have opened 200 internal inquiries into police conduct, but only four police officers have been charged in two separate cases for excessive use of force. The trials continue at this writing.

In September 2009 a parliamentary commission investigating the March 2008 events and dominated by the ruling Republican Party concluded that despite isolated incidents of excessive force, law enforcement actions had been "largely legitimate and proportionate." A separate fact-finding working group, with opposition participation, had been dismissed by President Serj Sargsyan in June.

ARMENIA

Democracy on Rocky Ground

Armenia's Disputed 2008 Presidential Election, Post-Election
Violence, and the One-Sided Pursuit of Accountability

HUMAN
RIGHTS
WATCH

More than 50 civilians were prosecuted in relation to the March violence, with some sentenced to lengthy prison terms. Although a June 19, 2009 presidential pardon released many, local human rights groups maintain that 17 opposition supporters remain imprisoned on politically motivated charges.

Torture and Ill-Treatment

Over 100 opposition supporters were detained following the March 2008 events, and many alleged physical abuse during apprehension, transfer to police station, and in detention. The Armenian Helsinki Association reported at least four cases of torture of opposition supporters in custody in 2009 related to investigation into the March 1 events.

Helsinki Citizens' Assembly (HCA)'s Vanadzor office reported five cases of torture and ill-treatment in police custody in 2009. Despite HCA's appeal to the relevant prosecutorial and judicial authorities, there have been no efforts to ensure accountability for these abuses.

Despite a June 2008 court order to reopen the investigation into the May 2007 death in custody of Levon Gulyan, prosecutors closed the case again in April 2009. Gulyan was found dead after police arrested and interrogated him. The authorities allege that while being held for questioning, Gulyan jumped from a second-story window of a police station while trying to escape, a claim denied by Gulyan's relatives who believe he was tortured.

Municipal Elections

Although election observers from the Council of Europe's Congress of Local and Regional Authorities (CLRAE) stated that the May 31, 2009 Yerevan City Council elections were broadly in compliance with European standards, they also documented cases of intimidation of party proxies and domestic observers by unidentified persons. Unidentified assailants attacked opposition newspaper journalists Gohar Veziryan (*IV Estate*), Tatev Mesropyan (*Hayq*), and Marine Kharatyan (*Zhamanak*), and prevented them from accessing polling stations. The journalists complained to police, and the investigation is still ongoing.

Media Freedom

On May 6, 2009, two unknown assailants attacked Nver Mnatsakanyan, anchor for the private television station Shant, near his home after work. A week earlier, Argishti Kvirikyan, editor for the Armenia Today online news agency, was attacked in similar circumstances and hospitalized with severe injuries. On November 17, 2008, an unknown assailant attacked Edik Baghdasaryan, the editor of the online news magazine *Hetq* and chairman of the Investigative Journalists' Association. He was hospitalized with a concussion. No conclusive investigations followed any of these incidents. In April 2009 the Organization for Security and Co-operation in Europe (OSCE) representative on freedom of the media, Miklos Haraszti, urged the authorities to swiftly investigate the attacks.

Despite the June 2008 decision of the European Court of Human Rights finding Armenia in violation of article 10 (freedom of expression) of the European Convention on Human Rights (ECHR) in relation to A1+, an independent television station, A1+ has not been able to resume broadcasting due to a suspension in all new licensing until digitalization of frequencies, due in 2010.

Parliament amended broadcasting laws in April 2009. The OSCE positively assessed some of the amendments, including those that ensure greater trans-parency regarding approval for broadcast licenses. However, it also criticized the amendments for failing to ensure political and ideological pluralism of the licens-ing body, the Council for Public Television and Radio, whose members are appointed by the president.

In August the authorities released Arman Babajanyan, editor of the independent newspaper *Zhamanak Yerevan*, from prison for health reasons. Babajanyan was convicted in 2006 of forging documents in order to evade compulsory military service and served most of a three-and-a-half-year sentence.

Freedom of Assembly

The authorities continue to restrict freedom of assembly by frequently denying requests to hold rallies, usually on technical grounds. Out of 84 opposition requests for demonstrations and rallies, only 28 were granted. Opposition parties and some NGOs allege particular difficulties in securing meeting venues for indoor events.

In July three youth opposition activists, Tigran Arakelyan, Sahak Muradyan, and Herbert Gevorgyan, were hospitalized after plainclothes security officials attacked them in downtown Yerevan. The activists were publicizing a rally for the opposition Armenian National Congress. Arakelyan was later charged with hooliganism and grave abuse against law enforcement personnel, and remanded to two months pretrial custody, but was released in October pending trial. In September Gevorgyan was convicted of causing minor bodily injury and sentenced to one year in prison and fined, but amnestied. Muradyan is under investigation for hooliganism.

Human Rights Defenders

While monitoring the May Yerevan City Council elections, Arshaluys Hakobyan of the Armenian Helsinki Association was expelled from a polling station. A few days after filing a complaint about this incident with the authorities, police appeared at his home to summon him for questioning. After an argument over his signature on the summons, police arrested Hakobyan for allegedly resisting authority. Hakobyan alleges he was then beaten and ill-treated in custody. Although he filed a complaint and testified to his ill-treatment during his September trial on the charge of resisting authority, the police have failed to comprehensively investigate the claim. Hakobyan remains in custody.

Mariam Sukhudyan, whose activism primarily relates to environmental concerns, in November 2008 publicized on a national television program the case of two girls who alleged sexual harassment at their Yerevan school. Police charged Sukhudyan with falsely reporting a crime. Human rights activists believe the charges are designed to intimidate Sukhidyan in retaliation for her environmental work.

The investigation into the May 2008 attack on Armenian Helsinki Association Chairman Mikael Danielyan was halted allegedly for lack of criminal intent. Danielyan was wounded when an assailant shot him from a pneumatic gun, following an argument. Danielyan's appeal against the decision to close the investigation is pending at this writing.

Key International Actors

In May 2009 Armenia and the European Union signed a Joint Declaration on Eastern Partnership. Armenia is already part of the European Neighbourhood Policy (ENP), which pledges significant financial and other assistance. The April ENP Action Plan progress report commended Armenia for certain progress, but expressed concerns about repercussions of the February 2008 presidential election.

In June the Millennium Challenge Corporation (a United States government program for reducing rural poverty) decided to take US$64 million out of an original US$235.6 million budget for road reconstruction, citing the Armenian government's failure to meet the program's "eligibility criteria" on civil rights. The fund was originally suspended following the March 2008 events.

The Parliamentary Assembly of the Council of Europe (PACE) has adopted four resolutions on Armenia since the March 2008 events, setting concrete benchmarks for addressing human rights concerns. In its June 2009 session PACE welcomed incremental progress in meeting the benchmarks, but decided to remain seized of developments.

The Council of Europe also issued a report in September 2009 on the situation of minority languages in Armenia, in which it called upon the authorities to "develop a structured policy to make available sufficient teacher training and updated teaching materials in Assyrian, Yezidi and Kurdish at all education levels."

In December 2008 the European Court of Human Rights found Armenia in violation of article 3 (the prohibition against inhuman or degrading treatment), article 6 (the right to a fair trial), and article 2 of protocol 7 (the right to appeal) of the ECHR in relation to three participants of opposition protests following the February-March 2003 presidential election. The men were detained in cramped and unsanitary detention cells without bedding and with restricted access to toilet facilities. During their trial, the judge heard their cases only very briefly.

In its January 2009 concluding observations, the United Nations Committee on the Elimination of Discrimination against Women urged the government, among other things, to enact a gender equality bill, which would establish a national machinery for the advancement of women.

Azerbaijan

Azerbaijan's human rights record further deteriorated. A February 2009 referendum on constitutional amendments abolished presidential term limits, which many local and international observers believed will make it possible for President Ilham Aliyev to remain in office indefinitely. The government continued to use defamation and other criminal charges to intimidate and punish journalists and bloggers expressing dissenting opinions; at least nine are serving prison sentences at this writing.

New amendments to the religion law restrict freedom of conscience. Other serious problems persist, including torture and ill-treatment in police custody, political prisoners, and harassment of human rights defenders.

Media Freedom and Civil Society Activism

Since November 2008 at least nine independent or pro-opposition journalists and editors were convicted on criminal libel or defamation charges. They were: Ali Hasanov, the editor of *Ideal* newspaper, who was sentenced in November 2008 to six months in prison, and pardoned in April 2009 after serving all but one month of his sentence; Asif Merzili, chief editor of the newspaper *Tezadlar*, and Zumrud Mammadova, a journalist there, who in April were sentenced to one year in prison and six months of corrective labor respectively (a higher court annulled the convictions two days later); Nazim Guliyev, the founder of *Ideal*, convicted in May and sentenced to six months in prison; Sardar Alibeili and Faramaz Allahverdiev, editor-in-chief and a correspondent of *Nota* newspaper, who in October received four- and three-month prison terms respectively, and staffer Ramiz Tagiyev, who received a six-month suspended sentence; and Zahir Azamat, chief editor of sports website, Fanat.az, and a staff member, Natig Mukhtarli, who were sentenced in October to six months and one year of corrective labor respectively.

In July youth activists and bloggers Emin Milli and Adnan Hajizade were physically attacked, apparently unprovoked, in a Baku restaurant. They were detained, interrogated, and put in custody when they went to the police to complain about the attack; their attackers were released. Milli and Hajizade were convicted in

November of hooliganism and deliberately causing bodily harm and sentenced to two-and-a-half and two years in custody, respectively.

Other imprisoned journalists include Eynulla Fatullayev, an outspoken government critic and editor-in-chief of two newspapers, who was convicted of fomenting terrorism and other criminal charges in 2007 and sentenced to eight-and-a-half years for his writings; Ganimed Zahidov, editor-in-chief of the opposition daily *Azadlig*, who was convicted in March 2008 on questionable hooliganism charges and sentenced to four years in prison; and Mushfig Huseynov, opposition daily *Bizim Yol* correspondent, who is serving a five-year term handed down in January 2008 (to be followed by a two-year publishing ban), on questionable extortion charges.

The government failed to meaningfully investigate several incidents of violence and threats against journalists. In February 2009, Idrak Abbasov, of the media monitoring organization Institute for Reporter Freedom and Safety (IRFS), visited Nakhichevan autonomous region, where he was called to the local ministry of security and allegedly blindfolded and beaten. IRFS Nakhichevan regional correspondent Elman Abbasov received telephone death threats throughout the year, and no official investigation followed his numerous complaints. In October the Baku Appeals Court upheld a district court decision not to investigate the illegal detention and ill-treatment by police of IRFS chairman Emin Huseynov, who had been detained in June 2008, beaten in custody, and hospitalized for more than 20 days for his injuries. In April ANS TV employees Nijat Suleymanov, Elmin Muradov, and Azer Balayev were allegedly beaten up by about 30 policemen as they were trying to document the destruction of a mosque in Baku. Police temporarily confiscated the filming equipment, which they also broke; they did not return the confiscated videotape. In May Elchin Hassanov, a correspondent for two newspapers, sustained multiple bodily injuries from an alleged assaulted by police at the Sabail district police department as he inquired about a group of detained youths.

In December 2008 the National Television and Radio Council banned the transmission of foreign radio stations via FM frequencies, making them accessible only through satellite receiver or the internet. The February 2009 constitutional amendments ban the audio recording, filming, or photographing of a person without his or her consent, seriously hampering investigative journalism in Azerbaijan. March amendments to the mass media law allow the government to request a court to suspend a media outlet for up to two months for several reasons, including failure to send free obligatory copies to "relevant government bodies."

The minister of interior filed a libel suit in December 2008 against human rights activist Leyla Yunus based on statements she made in a media interview that simply repeated courtroom testimony by a defendant during an open trial. The lawsuit accused her of "insulting" the ministry and causing "moral damage" to the reputation of the police. The case was dropped in February 2009.

In June the government introduced, but then withdrew, a draft law on NGOs that would have imposed extensive restrictions on the founding and operation of civil society groups.

Freedom of Religion

In May a new religion law and amendments to both the criminal and administrative codes came into force, requiring all registered religious organizations to reregister by January 2010—the third time since the country's independence. The amendments ban a religious organization from conducting religious activity beyond the legal address where it is registered, and also restricts producing, importing, circulating, or selling religious literature without specific permission from the State Committee for Work with Religious Organizations.

In June another set of restrictive amendments were adopted by parliament, requiring all religious rituals of the Islamic faith to be led only by citizens of Azerbaijan who were educated in the country.

Torture and Ill-Treatment

Torture and ill-treatment in custody continue to be a widespread problem and occur with impunity. The Azerbaijan Committee against Torture, an independent group that monitors penitentiary institutions, received over 90 complaints alleging torture and ill-treatment in custody. In each case where law enforcement agencies responded to the complaint, they denied that torture or ill-treatment had taken place. At least three prisoners are reported to have died in custody in 2009 after allegedly being ill-treated.

In August Novruzali Mammadov, editor-in-chief of *Talyshi Sado* newspaper, died in custody apparently after the government failed to provide him with adequate treatment for health problems. In February he was kept in solitary confinement for 15 days and deprived of bedding and warm clothes, which is believed to have aggravated his illness. At this writing a court is hearing a wrongful death complaint filed by Mammadov's family.

In April the European Court of Human Rights found Azerbaijan in violation of article 3 (the prohibition against inhuman or degrading treatment) of the European Convention on Human Rights in relation to Mahira Muradova, a participant in opposition protests following the October 2003 presidential election. Muradova alleged that she had been subjected to an act of police brutality and that the authorities failed to carry out an adequate investigation into the incident.

Political Prisoners

The government continues to hold a number of political prisoners, prompting the Parliamentary Assembly of the Council of Europe in March 2009 to appoint a rapporteur on the issue of political prisoners in Azerbaijan. Government officials, businessmen, and opposition politicians arrested prior to the November 2005 parliamentary elections on allegations of attempting to overthrow the government remain in custody. Parts of their trials were completely closed and lawyers said there were procedural violations, raising concerns about the trials' fairness. Three political prisoners arrested in connection with the 2003 presidential election, Elchin Amiraslanov, Safa Poladov, and Arif Kazimov, also remain incarcerated.

Key International Actors

A large number of international and regional institutions and bilateral partners criticized Azerbaijan's human rights record, especially regarding media freedoms and the imprisonment of the bloggers Milli and Hajizade. In February 2009 the Council of Europe secretary general expressed concern about the number of imprisoned journalists in Azerbaijan and urged the authorities to examine each case. These concerns were echoed by the Organization for Security and Co-operation in Europe (OSCE) representative on freedom of the media, Miklos Haraszti, in his April and July reports to the OSCE Permanent Council.

In March 2009 the Council of Europe's Venice Commission, the advisory body on constitutional matters, criticized the constitutional amendments, stating that they distort the balance of power and contradict European practice.

Azerbaijani civil society, together with international human rights groups, successfully campaigned against Azerbaijan's reelection to the United Nations Human Rights Council in May. A number of UN treaty bodies reviewed Azerbaijan's treaty compliance, including the Human Rights Committee, the Committee on the Elimination of Racial Discrimination, and the Committee on the Elimination of Discrimination against Women. The resulting concluding observations of these bodies urged Azerbaijan to take immediate steps to bring the country's human rights record into full compliance with the relevant conventions.

In May Azerbaijan and the European Union signed a Joint Declaration on Eastern Partnership. Azerbaijan is already part of the European Neighbourhood Policy (ENP). The April ENP Action Plan progress report was critical of the government for making no or limited progress in implementing the Action Plan, particularly in the areas of political dialogue and reform, including protection of human rights and fundamental freedoms.

BELARUS

Belarusian authorities continue to restrict civil society activism and the media through the criminal justice system and burdensome administrative requirements. Authorities have made some positive steps, including restarting state distribution of three independent publications, registering one radio station and one nongovernmental organization, and releasing all political prisoners in 2008. However, despite the appearance of liberalization, 2009 saw progress reversed; authorities placed four more political prisoners behind bars, violently dispersed several demonstrations, and refused to register at least two NGOs and three newspapers for unfounded reasons.

Freedom of Association

Independent civil society groups in Belarus remain active despite authorities' attempts to control them. The government requires groups to register, a lengthy and costly process, and authorities often deny registration for missing application materials or other easily resolved minor, technical problems. Authorities prohibit residences to be used as legal addresses, which are required for registration. NGOs enjoyed discounted rent until an April 2008 Presidential Edict changed the pricing structure of state-owned property; now independent groups pay as much as commercial organizations, while organizations whose activities the government deems to be "humanitarian" in nature continue to receive discounted office rent.

Authorities registered the first independent NGO since 2000, "For Freedom," in late 2008, but in 2009 continued a policy of denying registration to other outspoken organizations. The government several times refused to register Nasha Viasna, most recently in August, for alleged problems with the list of founders and the legal address. Nasha Viasna is the successor to Viasna, a well-known human rights organization that worked to develop civil society in Belarus. Viasna was forcibly disbanded in 2003 for submitting allegedly invalid documents for registration, and because of its leaders' monitoring of the 2001 presidential election. In August 2007 the United Nations Human Rights Committee found that Viasna's closure violates article 22 of the International Covenant on Civil and

Political Rights. In 2009 authorities twice denied registration to the Belarusian Assembly of Pro-democratic Nongovernmental Organizations, an unofficial umbrella organization for Belarusian NGOs that provides legal guidance and conducts advocacy on their behalf. Authorities allege the organization's name does not describe its activities, and procedural violations in its creation. The group's appeal of the denial was rejected.

Due to frequent registration denials, many activists are forced to continue their activities without official registration. Under article 193.1 of the criminal code, acting on behalf of an unregistered organization is a criminal activity punishable by up to two years in jail. Since 2006 more than 15 activists have been fined or imprisoned under this article, and at this writing LGBT activist Svyataslau Semyantsou is charged with violating article 193.1 for participating in the unregistered NGO TEMA Information Center. Belarusian and international human rights organizations and foreign governments have called on the Belarusian government to abolish this article.

In March 2009 Belarusian Helsinki Committee activist Leonid Svetik was convicted of violating two articles of the criminal code: article 130.1 (fomenting national and religious enmity) and article 367 (insulting the honor of the president) and fined 31 million rubles (US$10,890). His case had been reopened in March after being suspended in September 2008 for unknown reasons. In May 2008, after breaking into Svetik's home where they seized equipment and printed materials, the KGB (Belarus's state security agency) had interrogated him for nine hours about a case he was allegedly witness to, warned him against commenting on the case to certain people, and imposed travel restrictions. He was told at that time that he was suspected of violating article 130.1.

Authorities also prevented international monitors from entering Belarus in 2009: Souhayr Belhassen, president of the International Federation for Human Rights, who was planning to attend Nasha Viasna's court hearings, was denied a visa, and Nikolay Zboroshenko from the Moscow Helsinki Group was told by a border guard on a train entering Belarus that he was on a list of foreigners barred from the country.

Freedom of Assembly

Activists are required to apply for demonstration permits, but the onerous application process serves to restrict the right to hold peaceful assemblies. Civil society activists are frequently subjected to arrests, fines, and detention for participating in unsanctioned assemblies.

Authorities used force to disburse three demonstrations in September and October, including on September 9 against Russian-Belarusian joint military exercises, and on September 16 and October 16 to commemorate the 10th anniversary of the "disappearance" of former parliamentary deputy speaker Viktor Gonchar and businessperson Anatoly Krasovskii. During the September 9 demonstration police detained 20 demonstrators; 17 received fines. Police detained 22 demonstrators during the October 16 demonstration. They forcibly tried to prevent journalists from filming each of these demonstrations.

Media Freedom

The government restricts press freedom and authorities monitor the internet. Journalists are frequently harassed and detained for covering opposition rallies and other events authorities try to suppress. Twelve officially registered independent newspapers and one journal remain unavailable at newsstands. In positive moves, however, three independent papers were allowed to be officially distributed in 2009, *Nasha Niva, Narodnaia Volia*, and *Uzgorak,* and European Radio for Belarus received permission to officially register an office.

In February 2009 President Alexander Lukashenka signed a law requiring all media outlets to register, including already registered outlets. This gives authorities the option to deny a license to any outlet they deem undesirable, and allows them greater control of online media by subjecting them to the same restrictions as print and broadcast media. The restrictions also prohibit foreign funding. However, the new law no longer requires media outlets to obtain special permits for distribution from local authorities, removing a major obstacle to registering new media outlets.

Two new independent newspapers, *Novaia Gazeta Babruiska* and *Nasha Pravincia*, were denied registration in September because the publishers' offices were not registered to the home addresses of the owners of the publications. A third, *Mahiliouski Chas*, was denied registration because its editor-in-chief has not received a higher education degree. These reasons for denial are not listed in Belarus's media law.

Political Prisoners

Authorities released all remaining political prisoners in 2008. However, at least four activists were arrested and imprisoned on politically motivated charges in 2009.

Mikalaj Autukhovich, Uladzimir Asipienka, and Yury Lyavonau were detained in February and charged under article 218 of the criminal code (intentional damage to or destruction of citizens' property) for alleged arson against local officials' property. Autukhovich and Asipienka remain in prison; Lyavonau was released in August. Autukhovich is also charged with illegal weapons possession and preparing a terrorist act. Authorities claim he attempted to murder a local official in Hrodna. The three activists' imprisonment is more likely in connection with their civil society activism: Asipienka and Lyavonau have previously been imprisoned for their involvement in the entrepreneurs' movement, while Autukhovich attempted to unite veterans in an opposition organization and ran in parliamentary elections as an independent candidate.

In July Artsiom Dubski was sentenced to one year in prison for violating the terms of a sentence of "limitation of freedom without transfer to an open correctional institute" (a version of house arrest that restricts a person to home and work) handed down in 2008 for taking part in a January 2008 demonstration against new policies affecting small businesses.

Death Penalty

Belarus is the only country in Europe that continues to use the death penalty. At least two people were sentenced to death in 2009. Families of those executed are not provided with information on the date of the execution or where the body is buried.

Key International Actors

In March the European Union agreed to allow Belarus to join the so-called Eastern Partnership, a newly established framework that offers preferential economic treatment, enhanced political contact, and the potential for visa-free travel with EU member states. Following the Belarus authorities' release of political prisoners in 2008, EU foreign ministers in October 2008 suspended the travel ban imposed on President Lukashenka and most of his inner circle; in March 2009 the suspension was extended for another nine months. The EU also launched an annual human rights dialogue with Belarus, the first round taking place in Prague, Czech Republic, in June. The European Commission has committed to giving Belarus €300,000 for projects aimed at strengthening the role of civil society.

The Parliamentary Assembly of the Council of Europe in June indicated its readiness to restore special guest status to Belarus, pending "substantive and irreversible progress towards Council of Europe standards," particularly in regard to the electoral process, respect for political freedom and media pluralism, and the death penalty. The Council of Europe stripped Belarus of its special guest status in 1997 over human rights concerns.

United States Assistant Secretary of State Philip Gordon and a delegation of US congressmen visited Belarus on separate occasions. Gordon outlined requirements for improved relations with the US, including the release of political prisoners, freedom of the media, and free and fair presidential elections. The six-member congressional delegation pressed for the release of imprisoned US lawyer Emanuel Zeltser; he was released and pardoned on June 30. President Obama renewed the Democracy Act of 2004, which authorizes assistance to organizations that promote democracy and civil society in Belarus.

BOSNIA AND HERZEGOVINA

An escalating political crisis about Bosnia's constitution and the status of its Serb entity Republika Srpska further weakened the central state and polarized the country along ethnic lines, leaving human rights overshadowed. National security policy impacted negatively on human rights. War crimes accountability remained an area of progress.

War Crimes Accountability

The trial of Bosnian Serb wartime president Radovan Karadzic at the International Criminal Tribunal for the former Yugoslavia (ICTY) for genocide, including at Srebrenica, crimes against humanity, and war crimes, began on October 27, 2009. Karadzic initially boycotted proceedings, and is representing himself. Earlier the same month, the court rejected Karadzic's petition for a lengthy delay in the start of the trial and his claim that it lacked jurisdiction because of an alleged post-war immunity agreement. On November 9 the court decided to maintain Karadzic's right of self-representation but assigned standby counsel to him to take over the case should he demonstrate further obstructionist behavior when the trial resumes on March 1, 2010.

Ratko Mladic, fellow indicted architect of the Srebrenica massacre, remains at large at this writing.

In September Momcilo Krajisnik, a Bosnian Serb wartime leader, began a 20-year sentence in the United Kingdom following the March ruling by the ICTY Appeals Chamber affirming his convictions for deportation, forcible transfer, and persecution (convictions for extermination and murder were quashed).

In July the ICTY convicted and sentenced Milan and Sredoje Lukic to life and 30 years' imprisonment respectively for crimes against humanity and war crimes against Bosniak (Bosnian Muslim) civilians in Visegrad.

The trial of Mico Stanisic and Stojan Zupljanin, former high-ranking Bosnian Serb officials, on war crimes charges, began at the ICTY in September.

The War Crimes Chamber in Sarajevo completed 20 cases in the first nine months of 2009, prioritizing the most serious cases according to the criteria developed in its war crimes strategy adopted in December 2008. The Bosnian parliament in October 2009 rejected extending the mandate of foreign judges and prosecutors in the chamber, which ends in December. In July the Bosnian Council of Ministers, reversing an earlier decision following international criticism, had approved extending the mandate.

Local courts completed nine war crimes cases during the first nine months of 2009, according to the Organization for Security and Co-operation in Europe, with 34 further cases pending. There was little progress toward remedying the obstacles faced by local courts prosecuting war crimes, which include nonexistent witness protection and support in most courts, insufficient staffing, inadequate cooperation among prosecutors and with police, and insufficient public outreach.

Return of Refugees and Displaced Persons

The return of refugees and internally displaced persons (IDPs) to their areas of origin continues to decline. During the first six months of 2009 the United Nations High Commissioner for Refugees registered only 191 returns by Bosnian refugees and 110 by IDPs. As of June 2009, more than 117,451 Bosnians were registered as internally displaced (including 7,500 in collective centers): 66,215 in Republika Srpska (almost all ethnic Serbs), 50,468 in the Federation (90 percent Bosniaks and 10 percent Croats) and 768 in the Brcko district. There are no reliable estimates of the number of refugees outside Bosnia.

The few displaced persons who return largely do so to areas where their ethnic group constitutes a majority. Most are elderly persons moving back to rural areas. Lack of economic opportunities and inadequate housing remain the main impediments to returns, but the political crisis and related ethnic division makes the climate for returns even less favorable. Roma refugees in Bosnia, mostly from Kosovo, remain vulnerable and dependent on periodic extensions of their temporary status.

Debate in June on a revised national returns strategy stalled in the House of Peoples (the upper house of parliament) over whether greater resources should be allocated to return to place of origin (favored by Bosniak parties) or divided between return and reintegration (as Serb parties advocate).

Citizenship and National Security

The controversial Bosnian state commission established to review wartime naturalization decisions was dormant throughout 2009. But five of those whom it stripped of Bosnian nationality remain in detention without charge on national security grounds based on secret evidence to which they and their lawyers have no access. Imad Al Husin remains detained despite a January 2008 intervention by the European Court of Human Rights blocking his deportation to Syria. Local and international NGOs raised concerns in May about the risk of refoulement in the case of Awad Aiman, whom Bosnia also wishes to deport to Syria. The other detainees are Omar Frendi (Algerian), Ammar Al Hanchi (Tunisian), and Abdullah Baura (Iraqi). On October 6 the detainees went on hunger strike to protest their continuing detention. On November 12 a sixth man, Benkhira Aissa from Algeria (who had also been on hunger strike), was released from indefinite detention in Lukavica after his Bosnian citizenship was restored on appeal.

Sexual Orientation and Gender Identity

In a positive step, parliament approved in June a non-discrimination law, including reference to lesbian, gay, bisexual, and transgender people. Bosnia's Inter-Religious Council, representing the country's main religious communities (Muslim, Orthodox, Roman Catholic, and Jewish) protested the law, which it believes could legalize gay marriage.

In July Emir Kadric, the director of the state-run Sarajevo Student Center, stated that "gay students do not belong in student dormitories in Sarajevo." A similar declaration was made around the same time by Dragan Mikulic, director of the state-run student dormitory of the University of Mostar. While civil society representatives and the media protested what they described as unacceptable hate speech, government authorities remained silent on the issue.

Ethnic and Religious Discrimination in the Political System

Bosnia continues to prohibit members of communities other than Bosniaks, Serbs, and Croats from standing for election to the federal Presidency, or becoming members of the House of Peoples, in violation of international human rights law. In June the Grand Chamber of the European Court of Human Rights heard a challenge to the prohibition by two Bosnian citizens, a Roma and a Jew, who were barred from standing for public office because of their ethnicity. A ruling was expected by the end of 2009.

Media Freedom

According to the Bosnian Ministry of Security, there was a 40 percent increase in attacks against journalists during the first nine months of 2009, with 24 cases reported to the police, mostly verbal, but including physical abuse. At this writing the perpetrators have not been held to account. The Office of the High Representative (OHR), the European Commission, and some European embassies expressed concern about deteriorating conditions for journalists.

In March, Slobodan Vaskovic, an investigative journalist with a news program broadcast in the Federation, was pushed and insulted by two men in Trebinje, Republika Srpska, while filming a program exploring links between the local Orthodox Church and politicians in Republika Srpska. The two men also attempted to destroy the camera operators' equipment. Vaskovic and his colleagues subsequently filed a report to the police before being escorted by the police out of town to protect them against an angry mob. The US embassy condemned the attack.

Key International Actors

The key international actors in Bosnia and Herzegovina—the combined Office of the High Representative/European Union Special Representative and the United States—backed by the Peace Implementation Council (PIC) focused their efforts on responding to Bosnia's political crisis, including secessionist threats from Milorad Dodik, the prime minister of Republika Srpska, and angry rhetoric from mainstream parties across ethnic lines. The OHR, the EU, and the US organized high-level negotiations in October to forge compromise on constitutional reform to strengthen the central institutions necessary for a functioning state, an end to international supervision, and future EU membership.

On March 11 Austrian diplomat Valentin Inzko replaced Miroslav Lajcak as high representative and EU special representative. The decision to appoint a new high representative underscored the PIC's assessment that Bosnia has yet to meet the criteria for full self-governance.

A political confrontation between the OHR and Republika Srpska authorities escalated after the high representative used his executive "Bonn powers" in September to impose laws to reestablish a national power company, including in the Brcko district (linked to an effort to end Brcko's international supervision in 2009). Bosnian Serb authorities seek to establish their own company. Milorad Dodik rejected the new laws, threatening to pull Republika Srpska officials from central government. The PIC qualified this move as a "direct challenge to the Dayton Peace Accords."

The European Commission's annual report on Bosnia and Herzegovina published in November 2009 linked identity politics to slow returns, threats to journalists, and intimidation against NGOs, while praising ongoing progress on war crimes accountability.

CROATIA

A halt until October in Croatia's negotiations to join the European Union, arising from a border dispute with Slovenia, and the unexpected resignation of Prime Minister Ivo Sanader in July, left the country in political limbo for much of 2009. Meanwhile, human rights reform took a back seat.

Croatia continues to prosecute suspected war criminals, but its inconsistent cooperation with the International Criminal Tribunal for the former Yugoslavia (ICTY) and the disproportionate number of Serb defendants (many of them in absentia) remain of concern.

Persons with mental disabilities in Croatia are vulnerable to the denial of their rights, and disability law has been used to restrict liberties. Despite improvements, crucial safeguards are still lacking for asylum seekers and detained migrants. Threats to media freedom came increasingly from political interference in state media and pressure on journalists, rather than violent attacks.

War Crimes Accountability

The prosecution of Croatian generals Ante Gotovina, Ivan Cermak, and Mladen Markac at the ICTY continued during 2009. The three are charged with war crimes and crimes against humanity arising from a 1995 military offensive against rebel Serbs. Croatian authorities continued to deny possessing key documents requested by the ICTY prosecutor. The European Commission called on Zagreb in October to take "all necessary steps" to resolve the issue.

The Supreme Court was scheduled to hear in November the prosecutor's appeal against the length of the seven-year sentence given in 2008 to Gen. Mirko Norac and the acquittal of Gen. Rahim Ademi on charges of war crimes against ethnic Serb civilians. The case is the first transferred to Croatia by the ICTY.

Serbs remain the majority of defendants in domestic war crimes prosecutions. In the first eight months of 2009, Croatian authorities issued eight new war crimes indictments against 16 individuals, 14 of whom were Serbs.

The first eight months of 2009 saw the completion of 20 war crimes trials in Croatia; of the 61 defendants involved in these trials, 37 were Serbs. Little over half of the defendants were present at trial, including 20 Serbs, many of them defendants in two cases before the Vukovar County Court. One of the Vukovar trials, running for more than four years, concluded in February 2009 with most defendants being convicted.

In May Croatian MP Branimir Glavas and five codefendants were found guilty of war crimes against Serb civilians and given sentences of five to ten years' imprisonment. On the day of the verdict Glavas, who has dual Croatian-Bosnian citizenship, fled to Bosnia. Croatia's extradition request was denied because Bosnia (like Croatia and Serbia) does not permit the extradition of its citizens. During 2009 there was no movement toward Croatia's facilitating the extradition of its citizens to neighboring states, despite Croatia having given a positive signal of this in 2008.

Serb Return and Integration

Internally displaced and refugee Serbs continue to face obstacles to sustainable return. In the first half of 2009, 456 refugees, all ethnic Serbs, returned to Croatia, and according to the United Nations High Commissioner for Refugees (UNHCR) 95 internally displaced persons (IDPs) returned to their homes in the same period, mostly ethnic Croats. Among the remaining 2,402 IDPs in Croatia, 1,638 are Serbs.

While government-sponsored programs continued to enable those who return to apply for and receive social housing, thousands of cases remained pending or had been refused as of September, and more than 2,000 persons approved had yet to receive homes. There was no progress toward compensating Serbs stripped during the war of the property right to occupy socially-owned housing.

There was positive movement in restoring occupied agricultural land to Serb owners. In April the government, former occupants, and current owners reached an out-of-court settlement restoring possession of 28 parcels of agricultural land to their Serb owners.

There was some progress in recognizing for pension eligibility wartime periods of work by Serbs in formerly rebel-held areas. As of August 2009, 55 percent of the 17,586 requests made had been processed, although barely half were resolved positively, in part because of disputes about admissible evidence.

Rights Abuses Related to Mental Disability

In December 2008 the European Court of Human Rights ruled in *X v. Croatia* that the country had violated the right to family life of a mentally disabled woman when its courts had her daughter adopted without the mother's involvement or consent.

Excessive and unnecessary forced institutionalization of people on the grounds of mental illness remains a paramount concern. The case of Ana Dragicevic, made public in 2009, is illustrative. Dragicevic was placed in a psychiatric hospital by her parents at age 16 in 2004, after they learned of her romantic relationship with another girl. She was released from the institution in May 2008 after an intervention by the State Attorney's Office, following a long campaign by the local media and a civil society organization. At this writing her civil claim for wrongful institutionalization is pending.

The treatment of people in mental health institutions is also of significant concern, with frequent reports of abuse and neglect. One such incident occurred in May 2009, when a young man at the Center for Autism in Zagreb received life-threatening burns from hot water while a member of the staff showered him. The staff member responsible was fired, and a criminal complaint filed in June by the victim's mother is pending at this writing.

Croatian NGOs working on disability issues continue to press the government to amend the official Croatian translation of article 19 of the Convention on the Rights of Persons with Disabilities, which erroneously allows confinement in a residential institution to be categorized as a "community living option."

Treatment of Asylum Seekers and Migrants

Croatia's treatment of asylum seekers and migrants continues to fall short of international and European standards. More asylum seekers were detained in 2009, according to UNHCR, despite fewer being charged with illegal entry. Asylum seekers and migrants held at the Jezevo Detention Center are unable to challenge their detention in a timely manner. Asylum seekers now are able to communicate through an interpreter at all stages of the procedure, but new arrivals at the border have inadequate access to an interpreter.

The refugee recognition rate remains extremely low: only one of 93 applicants in the first seven months of 2009 was granted.

Media Freedom

Concerns about political interference in the state media were highlighted in December 2008 when the host of a popular news program on state television, Denis Latin, lost his contract and was prohibited from appearing on other state shows, after he protested a decision by management to bar an investigative journalist from appearing on his program. Media freedom was under sustained pressure during 2009: Journalists investigating corruption and sensitive subjects were subject to threats, removal from their posts, or court action.

In February the interior minister, Tomislav Karamarko, brought a criminal case against journalist Zeljko Peratovic for "disseminating information likely to upset the population," after Peratovic accused him of obstructing an investigation into the death of a witness in a war crimes case. The charge carries a maximum sentence of one year in prison as well as a fine. The case is pending at this writing.

Physical attacks against journalists decreased in 2009, but limited progress was made in investigating murders and attacks on journalists from 2008. In separate investigations, Croatian prosecutors indicted six and Serbian prosecutors two individuals for the October 2008 killings of Ivo Pukanic, the editor of *Nacional*, and his marketing director, Niko Franjic. The police in Croatia have yet to identify any suspects in the June 2008 attack on the investigative journalist Dusan Miljus.

Human Rights Defenders

Personal attacks on human rights defenders in the state and commercially-owned media made the environment for human rights work in Croatia increasingly hostile, but groups remain free to operate.

Key International Actors

With final accession negotiations for membership scheduled to occur in 2010, the European Union remains the most influential international actor. For much of 2009 negotiations were stalled due to a border dispute with neighboring Slovenia, but this was near resolution in October when Slovenia removed its veto on Croatian membership.

The European Commission progress report released in October identified accountability for war crimes against Serbs, access to justice, and freedom of expression as areas where further progress is required. It concluded that since the last report there had been "no progress" on deinstitutionalization and community integration of people with mental health issues.

Croatia became a NATO member in April.

EUROPEAN UNION

The European Union moved closer to stronger safeguards for rights during 2009 after the last member state, the Czech Republic, signed the Lisbon Treaty in November. The treaty makes significant changes to EU decision making and its Charter of Fundamental Rights binding EU law, and commits the EU to becoming a party to the European Convention on Human Rights.

EU institutions frequently showed a lack of will to hold member states to account for breaches of European standards on human rights. European Commission proposals for a new five-year EU justice and home affairs agenda in June lacked specificity and emphasized the rights of citizens, raising concerns over adequate attention to the human rights of immigrants; the European Council was due to adopt the agenda, known as the Stockholm Program, in December 2009. The European Parliament adopted a report in January 2009 deploring the refusal of member states to accept robust scrutiny of their human rights records and the consequent undermining of the credibility of EU foreign policy on human rights.

The Parliament gave its backing in April to a proposed anti-discrimination directive aimed at reducing discrimination in access to goods and services based on religion, belief, age, disability, or sexual orientation. At this writing the Council has yet to approve the directive.

Many EU countries continue to pursue counterterrorism measures that violate human rights, including national security removals despite the risk of ill-treatment upon return, inadequate safeguards in detention, use of administrative measures to bypass due process standards for criminal suspects, and interference with the rights to freedom of expression and to privacy.

Migration and asylum policies remain focused on controlling borders, rather than on human rights, with several member states adopting measures to criminalize irregular immigration, lengthen administrative detention, and restrict access to asylum.

The growing popularity of far-right political parties, evidenced by results in the European Parliament elections in June, heightened concerns about racism and xenophobia, particularly targeting Roma and Sinti, migrants, Muslims, and Jews.

Counterterrorism Measures and Human Rights

Rulings by the European Court of Justice in December 2008, June 2009, and September 2009 highlighted concerns about the fairness of procedures for determining inclusion on the EU's terrorism blacklist, and led the European Council to remove the People's Mujahideen Organization of Iran from the list in January. In April the European Commission proposed reforms to the procedures.

Information continued to surface during 2009 about now-closed CIA secret detention centers on EU territory, including new allegations in August that the CIA held and questioned suspects in the Lithuanian capital Vilnius through 2005. In November the Lithuanian parliament launched a parliamentary investigation into the allegations. Romania repeated its denials of having hosted a secret CIA prison, despite credible reports in August that the facility was located on one of Bucharest's busiest streets. The Polish government failed to fully cooperate with a national prosecutor's investigation into an alleged secret prison near Szymany airport.

EU countries were slow to act on pledges to resettle detainees held by the United States at Guantanamo Bay who cannot be returned safely to their countries of origin. At this writing only Belgium, France, Portugal, and Ireland have accepted detainees (a total of six former prisoners), while Italy, Hungary, and Spain have indicated they might do so.

Common EU Asylum and Migration Policy

The failure of the European Commission to hold Italy and Greece fully to account for treatment of asylum seekers and migrants in breach of European standards undermined efforts toward the development of a genuine common asylum system. Commissioner for Justice, Freedom and Security Jacques Barrot offered only conditional criticism of Greece's dysfunctional asylum system during his June visit. Barrot was tardy in criticizing Italy's policy, enacted in May, of pushing back to Libya migrants intercepted at sea, his initial response being instead to propose reviving a deeply flawed idea to externalize EU refugee processing to countries like Libya. In September, however, Barrot used stronger language in calling the situation of migrants and asylum seekers in Libya unacceptable and reminding Italy of its nonrefoulement obligations.

There was limited progress toward the consolidation and improvement of a common asylum policy and standardized procedures throughout the Union. Following Commission proposals, in May the European Parliament adopted an "asylum package" proposing amendments to the Reception Conditions Directive, the Dublin II Regulation, and the European fingerprint database for asylum seekers and irregular migrants, as well as endorsing the creation of a European Asylum Support Office. Negotiations to arrive at common positions are ongoing. Justice and Home Affairs Council meetings in June and September confirmed the lack of consensus on reform of the Dublin II Regulation, focusing instead on burden-sharing through voluntary resettlement and coordinated resettlement from third countries.

A significant drop in arrivals by sea was attributed to the global economic downturn, push-backs at sea, and joint patrols under the auspices of Frontex, the EU's external border agency. In at least one case Frontex assisted Italy's interdiction of boat migrants, whom Italy then pushed back to Libya.

Human Rights Concerns in Select EU Member States

France

A government-appointed committee in September released recommendations for reforming French criminal procedure. The committee recommended significant changes, notably elimination of the function of investigating judge, but failed to remedy insufficient safeguards against ill-treatment and impediments to an effective defense for terrorism suspects in police custody (with suspects held for up to six days with severely limited access to a lawyer). The French government is expected to use the committee's recommendations as a basis for legislation in 2010.

Tensions over Muslim veiling were heightened following President Nicolas Sarkozy's declaration that what he referred to as the burqa was not welcome on French territory and parliament's appointment of an ad hoc fact-finding commit-

FRANCE

Lost in Transit

Insufficient Protection for Unaccompanied Migrant Children
at Roissy Charles de Gaulle Airport

HUMAN
RIGHTS
WATCH

tee in June to consider a possible public ban on face-covering veils. In June the European Court of Human Rights rejected as inadmissible complaints filed by four Muslim girls and two Sikh boys expelled from public schools in 2004 under a ban on religious headgear in school, once again failing to give proper weight to the religious freedom of non-Christian minorities.

The Paris Appeals Court overturned in February the 2007 terrorism convictions of five former Guantanamo Bay detainees after throwing out all evidence emanating from interrogations conducted at the US detention facility by French intelligence officers, citing a failure to disclose the evidence to the defense and other procedural irregularities.

French police dismantled a makeshift migrant camp in Calais in September, arresting nearly 300 people, including scores of unaccompanied children. All of those arrested were later released. In October France deported three Afghan men to Kabul on a joint charter flight with the UK.

Following its June review of France, the United Nations Committee on the Rights of the Child said it was "deeply concerned" about the situation of unaccompanied children held in airport waiting zones. Those arriving at Paris Charles de Gaulle airport were routinely detained with adults and deported, including to countries they had merely transited. Children were unable to challenge effectively decisions that put them at risk. Those seeking protection as refugees faced obstacles to filing a claim and appealing negative decisions based on fast-track evaluations.

Germany

Angela Merkel was reelected chancellor in September elections that gave her center-right Christian Democratic Union and its new coalition partner the Free Democrats a majority in parliament.

A special parliamentary inquiry concluded in June that German authorities and intelligence agencies had no responsibility for the renditions by the United States and subsequent ill-treatment of Khaled el Masri, Murat Kurnaz, and Mohammad Zammar. A dissenting minority argued the federal government obstructed the investigation. The Constitutional Court ruled in July that the government, in having

GERMANY

Discrimination in the Name of Neutrality

Headscarf Bans for Teachers and Civil Servants in Germany

HUMAN
RIGHTS
WATCH

restricted the evidence it provided to the inquiry committee without giving sufficient justifications, had breached the constitution.

The federal government adopted new administrative regulations in September
governing the Residence Act, endorsing the use of diplomatic assurances to
deport individuals to countries where they face the risk of torture or ill-treatment.
German courts have nonetheless struck down the use of such assurances, including in two cases in January and March.

The UN Human Rights Council under the Universal Periodic Review in March and
the UN special rapporteur on racism in July drew attention to continuing problems
of racism, xenophobia, and discrimination in Germany. Discrimination against
migrants in housing and employment were identified as key concerns, with the
special rapporteur on racism expressing his concern about overrepresentation of
children with a migrant background in the lowest stratum of Germany's three-
tiered education system.

A pregnant woman was stabbed to death and her husband seriously injured in a
Dresden courtroom in July by the man she had successfully sued for calling her a
"terrorist" and an "Islamist." The deceased, Marwa el-Sherbini, a German resident of Egyptian nationality, wore a headscarf. Her killer was sentenced in
November to life in prison for murder, attempted murder, and grievous bodily
harm; the prosecutor's office had cited hatred of non-Europeans and Muslims as
the motive. The German Office for the Protection of the Constitution reported in
May that right-wing extremist crimes rose significantly in 2008.

The UN special rapporteur on racism noted that bans on the wearing of religious
symbols by public school teachers in some German states had a disproportionate
impact on Muslim women who wear the headscarf. In August the Federal Labor
Court ruled against a North Rhine-Westphalia educational social worker who had
substituted her headscarf with a pink beret. The Court ruled the beret demonstrated the social worker's religious faith in contravention of North Rhine-Westphalia's
2006 law prohibiting teachers from wearing religious clothes and symbols in public schools.

Greece

The socialist party Pasok returned to power after winning a parliamentary majority in October elections, defeating the New Democracy party in power since 2004.

Demonstrations and riots broke out around the country in December 2008 and January 2009 after a police officer shot and killed a 15-year-old boy in Athens. Human rights groups complained that police used excessive force during crowd control, including during otherwise peaceful demonstrations. In June the European Committee for the Prevention of Torture noted persistent allegations of police abuse of criminal suspects during arrests and interrogations.

In February Council of Europe Commissioner for Human Rights Thomas Hammarberg criticized "grave and systematic deficiencies" in Greece's asylum procedure. Fewer than 1 percent of asylum claims are granted at first instance, and in June the government abolished the right to lodge an appeal against rejection except in very narrow circumstances, leading the United Nations High Commissioner for Refugees to discontinue cooperation with the process. The government also increased immigration detention time limits to as long as 18 months.

Migrants are kept in deplorable detention conditions. The European Court of Human Rights condemned Greece in June for the unlawful detention of a Turkish asylum seeker in 2007, finding also that the conditions of his detention amounted to degrading treatment. The newly elected government closed the notorious detention center on Lesvos Island in November.

The authorities failed to protect unaccompanied children, who were routinely detained for prolonged periods, often with adults, and subjected to mistreatment. Authorities offered little or no assistance to migrant children who are vulnerable to exploitation and trafficking.

Greece launched a crackdown on migrants between June and August, systematically apprehending asylum seekers and other migrants, and summarily expelling many of them to Turkey where they are at serious risk of ill-treatment and refoulement.

GREECE

Left to Survive

Systematic Failure to Protect Unaccompanied
Migrant Children in Greece

HUMAN
RIGHTS
WATCH

Italy

In May Italy began intercepting boat migrants at sea and returning them to Libya, prompting widespread international criticism. No screening was conducted to identify refugees or vulnerable people in need of protection, in violation of Italy's international obligations. There were credible reports that Italian officials used undue force during the interdiction operations, and confiscated property and documents. All the migrants were detained upon arrival in Libya. Italy and Libya announced the beginning of joint naval patrols in Libyan territorial waters, under the terms of a "Treaty of Friendship" that entered into force in March 2009.

A Sicilian court acquitted in October three members of the German humanitarian organization Cap Anamur of abetting illegal immigration for rescuing boat migrants in 2004. In November seven Tunisian fishermen were acquitted of similar charges arising from a 2007 rescue. Two of the seven were convicted of resisting a public official and of violence against a military vessel.

Italy continued to deport terrorism suspects to Tunisia despite the risk of ill-treatment and 10 rulings in 2009 by the European Court of Human Rights that such returns put individuals at risk. In February the Court condemned Italy for the June 2008 expulsion of Essid Sami Ben Khemais in breach of interim measures issued by the Court requesting a suspension of the expulsion pending its examination of the case. In August Italy expelled Ali Ben Sassi Toumi also in breach of interim measures, prompting criticism from the Council of Europe.

Racism and xenophobia, characterized by violence as well as hostile political discourse, continued to be a serious problem. Attacks included the beating and setting on fire of an Indian immigrant, and assault by a large group of club-wielding men on four Romanians, leaving two in hospital. Emergency measures adopted since 2008 were made permanent in July 2009 when parliament passed the so-called Security Package: Irregular entry and stay in Italy were made crimes punishable by a fine of up to €10,000, and a national framework for officially-approved "citizens' groups" was created, arousing fears of violence by state-sponsored vigilantes (some existing groups have close ties to the far-right). Elected officials have used inflammatory rhetoric, prompting President Giorgio Napolitano in May and the Roman Catholic Church to express concern about growing xenophobic discourse in Italy. Racism and xenophobia, discrimination

and unacceptable housing conditions for Roma and Sinti, and anti-immigrant legislation were highlighted in a damning report by Council of Europe Human Rights
Commissioner Thomas Hammarberg in April.

In October a Milan court convicted 23 US citizens, including the former Milan CIA
station chief, and two Italian military intelligence officers for the 2003 abduction
and rendition to Egypt of Hassan Mustafa Ossan Nasr (known as Abu Omar).
Three of the 26 US citizens tried in absentia, including the Rome CIA station chief,
were determined to enjoy diplomatic immunity. The judge said he could not pro-
nounce a verdict against the other five Italian defendants because the evidence
against them was covered by state secrecy, following a March Constitutional Court
ruling.

Malta

The Maltese government continued to detain asylum seekers and irregular
migrants, including unaccompanied children, pregnant women, and people in
poor health, for prolonged periods. Delays in processing asylum claims and lack
of access to legal aid persisted. Following its January 2009 visit to Malta, the UN
Working Group on Arbitrary Detention concluded that Malta's detention policy is
not in line with international law and described as appalling conditions in two
detention centers. A protest in March by over 500 migrants detained at Safi barracks ended in violence.

Nine NGOs called on Maltese authorities to address racist violence in Malta after
two Somali migrants were attacked in July, leaving one hospitalized.

Italy and Malta continued to dispute who is responsible for rescuing boat
migrants in distress. The death of over 70 African migrants trying to reach Italy in
August sparked widespread criticism of Malta for its failure to rescue migrants
stranded at sea. The United Nations High Commissioner for Human Rights
accused the Maltese government of falling short on its international human rights
obligations.

Pushed Back, Pushed Around

Italy's Forced Return of Boat Migrants and Asylum Seekers,
Libya's Mistreatment of Migrants and Asylum Seekers

**HUMAN
RIGHTS
WATCH**

The Netherlands

Reviews during 2009 by Council of Europe Human Rights Commissioner Thomas Hammarberg and the UN Human Rights Committee identified a range of human rights concerns in the Netherlands, including problematic counterterrorism measures, and the lack of safeguards in and excessive length of asylum procedures.

The government in July ordered a comprehensive evaluation of counterterrorism measures, following the conclusions of a temporary commission that efforts to combat terrorism were poorly coordinated and arbitrary. Pending the outcome of the review, parliament suspended consideration of draft legislation that would restrict the movement of terrorism suspects and impose reporting restrictions on them.

The government in April announced measures to dissuade immigration deportees from filing last-minute applications, including ending the right to remain in the country during review of a repeat asylum request in the absence of new facts or circumstances. Also, all asylum seekers without identity papers will have to convince authorities they did not destroy them or their asylum request will be rejected. Separate draft reforms to the asylum law, laid before parliament in July, would extend the timeframe for evaluation of applications under the accelerated procedure from five to eight days in order to expand the number of fast-tracked claims. Hammarberg and the Human Rights Committee expressed concerns that the current procedure and the proposed changes did not give asylum seekers the opportunity to adequately support their claims.

In April the government announced it would no longer automatically grant temporary asylum to Somalis. The Dutch Council of State denied an Iraqi couple's request for temporary residency in May on the grounds that the situation in Iraq did not pose risks of random acts of violence. The decision followed a February judgment by the European Court of Justice on a referral of the same case, indicating that the EU directive on refugee recognition (Qualification Directive) does not require an applicant to prove he or she is specifically targeted when the level of indiscriminate violence in a country is sufficiently severe.

The government announced in October its intention to impose stricter language and integration tests for prospective spouses of Dutch residents from non-

Western countries. The requirements have been criticized as discriminatory against Moroccan and Turkish migrants.

Poland

The European Commission referred Poland to the European Court of Justice in May for missing the deadline for implementation of three EU directives on gender discrimination. The latest draft of a comprehensive domestic anti-discrimination law raised concerns with respect to protection from multiple discrimination or discrimination based on sexual orientation. The government-controlled Office of the Plenipotentiary for Equal Treatment, created in 2008, lacks autonomy, and does not have a mandate to take complaints or assist individual victims, but the government resisted calls to establish an independent anti-discrimination body.

In a landmark decision in August, a regional court fined a woman for hate speech against her gay neighbor that had triggered harassment by others. Discrimination based on sexual orientation remains a serious problem, however, with hate speech apparently on the rise.

Poland continues to have one of the most restrictive abortion laws in Europe, and access to contraception and prenatal testing is limited. During a visit in May the UN special rapporteur on the right to health observed that women in Poland face significant barriers to accessing legal abortions and other reproductive health services. In September a court ordered a Roman Catholic magazine to compensate a woman it had publicly vilified for seeking an abortion on medical advice.

Spain

Counterterrorism measures in Spain continued to attract international criticism. The UN special rapporteur on human rights while countering terrorism and the Human Rights Committee, in December 2008 and January 2009 respectively, both expressed concerns over broad definitions of terrorism-related offenses and the continued use of incommunicado detention.

Spain extradited ethnic Chechen Murat Gasaev in late December 2008 to Russia on the basis of diplomatic assurances of humane treatment and a fair trial.

Gasaev, whose extradition had been sought in connection with an attack on government buildings in Ingushetia in 2004, was released without charge in August, after 10 months in pretrial detention.

In July the European Court of Human Rights upheld, as a legitimate and proportionate interference with freedom of association, a 2003 ban on Basque political parties Batasuna and Herri Batasuna on the grounds they were linked to the ETA. On the same day, the Court ruled against the applicants in two related cases, finding that their inability to stand for election due to links to the banned political parties did not violate their right to freedom of expression.

Cooperation with France led to more ETA members being arrested in 2009, including Jurdan Martitegi Lizaso in April, the fourth military leader to be arrested since May 2008. ETA claimed responsibility for three separate car bomb attacks over the summer that claimed the lives of a police officer and two civil guards, and destroyed a Civil Guard barracks.

In April the Audiencia Nacional acquitted 10 out of 14 men accused of helping some of the alleged perpetrators of the March 11, 2004 Madrid train bombings to flee Spain, finding the case against them insufficient after excluding email correspondence that was intercepted without proper authorization. The other four were convicted and sentenced to prison terms ranging from two to nine years.

Police unions denounced pressure to arrest irregular immigrants on the basis of quotas, and the use of racial and ethnic profiling in identity checks. In a landmark decision in July the Human Rights Committee held Spain responsible for race discrimination in the 1992 identity check of Rosalind Williams, an African-American who became a Spanish citizen in 1969. The decision is the first international ruling that racial or ethnic profiling violates the right to non-discrimination.

Arrivals by sea were down in the first half of 2009, in part due to increased surveillance and interceptions. Unaccompanied migrant children in the Canary Islands were still housed long-term in substandard accommodation designed as temporary shelter. Spain suspended deportations of unaccompanied children to Morocco in 2008 following numerous court decisions blocking such returns. In September 2009 a court ruled that Spain had to allow back a Moroccan national illegally expelled as a child in 2006.

United Kingdom

Allegations of complicity by UK intelligence services in extraordinary renditions and the torture of terrorism suspects, including UK nationals, dogged the government throughout the year. The Parliamentary Joint Committee on Human Rights and the House of Commons Foreign Affairs Committee issued critical reports in August. The Joint Committee and human rights groups called for an independent inquiry into all allegations, calls the government has rejected.

In March the attorney general ordered a criminal investigation into alleged collusion by Security Service (MI5) agents in the torture and ill-treatment of Binyam Mohamed, an Ethiopian UK resident released from Guantanamo Bay and returned to the UK in February. Police are also investigating a separate case involving alleged complicity by Secret Intelligence Service (MI6) personnel in the abuse of an unnamed foreign national. The UK High Court ruled in February that it could not publish summaries of classified intelligence documents from the United States that support Mohamed's allegations of torture while in Pakistan, due to concerns about disrupting UK-US intelligence cooperation.

In June the Law Lords ruled that reliance by the government on secret evidence to impose control orders on terrorism suspects restricting their liberty violated the right to a fair hearing. The ruling followed a February judgment from the European Court of Human Rights against the UK for its now-defunct policy of indefinite detention, in which the Court stressed that denying terrorism suspects the right to know the case against them violates their rights.

Since June the High Court has quashed three control orders—including two in November where it rejected government arguments that less restrictive orders did not require disclosure of the evidence on which they were based—and obliged the government to modify another, while the government lifted another order rather than reveal all the evidence. In September the government asked the independent reviewer of terrorism legislation to conduct an assessment of the control order regime.

Three men were sentenced to life imprisonment in September for conspiring to kill thousands of people in 2006 by using home-made liquid bombs to explode airplanes flying from London to the United States. A fourth man was sentenced to a minimum of 22 years.

Efforts to deport terrorism suspects on the basis of unreliable diplomatic assurances of humane treatment continued. In February the Law Lords ruled the government could deport two Algerians and Jordanian Omar Othman (known as Abu Qatada) under the terms of assurances provided by the governments of their respective countries of origin. Abu Qatada appealed the ruling to the European Court of Human Rights, which at this writing has yet to hear the case. The UK government signed a Memorandum of Understanding with Ethiopia containing similar diplomatic assurances in December 2008.

The government announced in April 2009 it would increase the number of detention facilities for failed asylum seekers and those being processed under the "detained fast-track" procedure. Particularly vulnerable asylum seekers with complex claims, including women who survived sexual violence, were routed through this accelerated procedure and faced detention and removal without adequate consideration of their claims. The UK continued to detain migrant children with their parents, with demonstrable negative impact on their mental and physical health.

UNITED KINGDOM

Cruel Britannia

British Complicity in the Torture and Ill-treatment
of Terror Suspects in Pakistan

HUMAN
RIGHTS
WATCH

GEORGIA

President Mikheil Saakashvili faced a political crisis as thousands of opposition supporters took to the streets in the capital, Tbilisi, in early April 2009 demanding his resignation and early presidential elections. Protests lasted for two months, before opposition unity faded. During the protests, human rights groups documented a suspicious pattern of attacks on opposition activists by unidentified assailants, and police used excessive force against and detained protestors, and attacked journalists.

More than a year after the August 2008 Georgian-Russian conflict over South Ossetia, the government has not investigated comprehensively international human rights and humanitarian law violations committed by the Georgian military. Russia continued to exercise effective control over South Ossetia and another breakaway region, Abkhazia, preventing international observers' access and vetoing international missions working there. A European Union-funded international inquiry into the 2008 conflict highlighted the dramatic lack of accountability.

Freedom of Assembly and Police Violence

Thousands of opposition supporters demanding Saakashvili's resignation blocked Tbilisi streets from April to early June. Although the government tolerated protracted protests, police used excessive force against demonstrators and journalists, and dozens of activists were arrested, some later claiming ill-treatment in custody. Moreover, in a spate of attacks in April and early May, unidentified men in civilian clothes, often armed with rubber truncheons and wearing masks, beat and threatened a number of individual demonstrators leaving protests at night; civil society groups and the ombudsman reported dozens of similar incidents. The authorities opened over 50 individual cases, but failed to meaningfully investigate—suggesting acquiescence or support for such attacks.

On May 6 three young activists, including one minor, were taken into custody on alleged hooliganism charges. All three claimed they were beaten and threatened before being released a day later on bail. Following these activists' detention, an opposition leader illegally entered the Tbilisi police headquarters compound by climbing over a fence. A confrontation between police and opposition supporters ensued. Although some protestors wielded sticks at police, police failed to exhaust less violent crowd control means before firing rubber bullets without warning into the crowd at close range, resulting in serious head injuries for several demonstrators.

On June 15, police attacked about 50 opposition supporters again gathered outside the police headquarters protesting the detention of youth activists the day before. Without warning, police chased and beat demonstrators with rubber truncheons, resulting in at least 17 demonstrators being injured. Police claimed that opposition supporters blocked the main entrance and road. They detained 38 demonstrators, releasing 33 after imposing fines and sentencing 5 to 30 days' administrative detention. Many of those released reported abuse in police custody. Police also assaulted several journalists and confiscated their cameras; although police later released the equipment, several journalists claimed that video and photo images had been deleted.

Police apologized for impeding the work of the media during the June 15 incident, yet conducted no independent investigation. Several officers (whose identities were not disclosed) received reprimands following an internal inquiry only. No meaningful investigation was conducted into the police use of excessive force.

Apparently in response to the protests, in July parliament adopted regressive amendments to the Administrative Code, increasing administrative detention, including for minor hooliganism and defying police orders, from 30 to 90 days. The measure appears excessive given that pretrial detention for criminal charges is only 60 days. July amendments to the Law on Assemblies and Manifestations banned full or partial blocking of roads during rallies unless the rally cannot be held elsewhere due to the number of participants.

Despite repeated calls from key international actors, the government has refused to launch a comprehensive investigation into events of November 7, 2007, when police used excessive force against largely peaceful political demonstrations in Tbilisi, resulting in at least 500 injured.

Lack of Accountability for Laws of War Violations

Well over a year since the Georgian-Russian conflict over South Ossetia, Georgian authorities have yet to ensure a comprehensive investigation into and accountability for international human rights and humanitarian law violations by their forces (see also Russia chapter).

During the war the Georgian military used indiscriminate force, including firing multiple rocket launchers—an indiscriminate weapon that should not be used in civilian areas. The military also used tanks and machine-guns to fire at buildings in Tskhinvali, the capital of South Ossetia, including at apartment buildings where civilians sheltered; South Ossetian forces had fired on Georgian forces from at least some of these buildings. The military also used cluster munitions against Russian military, including in civilian-populated Georgian territories adjacent to the administrative border with South Ossetia.

Some 20,000 ethnic Georgians from South Ossetia still remain displaced.

Criminal Justice System

Prison overcrowding leading to poor conditions remains a problem, despite construction of new prisons and several presidential pardons and amnesties. Although official statistics showed a decrease in the use of pretrial detention, the total number of prisoners increased to 19,504 by June 2009, a more than 50 percent increase since 2006. The frequent use of consecutive custodial sentencing is largely responsible for this increase. Allegations of deliberate ill-treatment of prisoners continue, including at the newly-built prison near Tbilisi.

In two judgments, the European Court of Human Rights found a violation of the prohibition on torture and inhuman or degrading treatment for the government's failure to provide adequate conditions or medical care in prisons. In *Ghavtadze v. Georgia*, the European Court also concluded that despite logistical and financial problems, Georgia is obliged to ensure dignified conditions in prisons.

The government has failed to conduct a thorough investigation into the March 2006 operation to quell a riot in Tbilisi Prison No. 5, which left seven prisoners dead and dozens injured.

The government maintains the minimum age of criminal responsibility at 12, in defiance of a June 2008 United Nations Committee on the Rights of the Child recommendation to reinstate it at 14. However, the government continued a moratorium on criminal charges against those under 14 until the creation of a separate juvenile justice system, which was planned for mid-2008 but has not been completed.

Media Freedom

The media environment remains mixed, with diverse print media, but nationwide television broadcasting limited to the state-owned public broadcaster and pro-government Rustavi 2 and Imedi stations. Transparency of media ownership remains a concern. On June 15, 2009, two Tbilisi-based pro-opposition television stations, Maestro and Kavkasia, briefly suspended broadcasting after their journalists were attacked and their equipment confiscated during the clash at the police headquarters. On May 30 the local cable network in Rustavi, near Tbilisi, removed Maestro from its lineup, allegedly under pressure from local authorities. In October a local court ordered Channel 25, the only independent regional television station in the Ajara Autonomous Republic, to pay a US$166,000 tax debt. The station's owners dispute the fine, alleging that it is intended to close the station ahead of upcoming local elections.

Print media outlets, although vibrant, depend on newsstand sales and advertising for revenue. Claims by Tbilisi municipal leaders in September that newsstands tarnish the city's image raised concerns about newsstands' potential removal, a move that would threaten many print outlets' existence.

Several journalists alleged pressure and attacks. Nato Gegelia, a journalist for the regional newspaper *Guria News*, was assaulted in a police station on June 10 in Chokhatauri, in western Georgia, as she investigated an opposition activist's detention.

Key International Actors

The United States and the European Union deepened their engagement and financial backing of Georgia, but failed to make full use of their leverage to ensure

417

meaningful human rights improvements. Meanwhile, Russia continued to occupy Georgia's breakaway regions South Ossetia and Abkhazia, and barred access to international observers. In December 2008 Russia blocked an extension of the mandate of the Organization for Security and Co-operation in Europe mission in Georgia, and in June 2009 vetoed the UN Observer Mission working in Abkhazia.

A 1,129-page report released in September by the EU-funded international inquiry into the August 2008 conflict found that international human rights and humanitarian law violations were committed by all sides, and highlighted a dramatic lack of accountability. The International Criminal Court—to which Georgia is a party—continued to keep under analysis crimes committed by all parties to the conflict.

In May 2009 Georgia signed a Declaration on New Eastern Partnership with the European Union, providing for additional assistance and cooperation. Georgia is already part of the European Neighbourhood Policy (ENP), which pledged over €120 million through 2010 plus an additional €500 million following the August 2008 war. The April 2009 ENP Action Plan progress report commended Georgia for progress in certain areas, but raised concerns about media freedom. The first round of a structured human rights dialogue between the EU and Georgia was held the same month. The EU extended the mandate of 200 unarmed EU observers in Georgia; Russia continued to block their access to the breakaway regions.

The US and Georgia signed a Charter on Strategic Partnership in January 2009, envisaging increased cooperation, including on strengthening human rights. As part of a US$1 billion pledge to support Georgia's recovery following the 2008 war, in May the US released US$53.3 million, including US$20 million for good governance, civic participation, and election and media reform. In a show of political support, US Vice President Joe Biden visited Tbilisi in July.

The Parliamentary Assembly of the Council of Europe adopted several resolutions on the Humanitarian Consequences of the War between Georgia and Russia, calling on all sides to conduct meaningful investigations into the violations during the conflict. The Council of Europe Human Rights Commissioner issued a report in May on human rights following the conflict, also emphasizing the need for meaningful accountability.

KAZAKHSTAN

After adopting several welcome, albeit modest reforms in early 2009, the government of Kazakhstan dealt a series of blows to human rights that undermine Kazakhstan's role as the chair of the Organization for Security and Co-operation in Europe (OSCE) in 2010. It failed to implement more meaningful reforms it had promised. Authorities sentenced the country's leading human rights defender to four years' imprisonment following an unfair trial, adopted restrictive amendments to media and internet laws, did not allow peaceful demonstrations and protests, and used national security interests to justify incommunicado detention and denial of access to legal counsel. Throughout much of 2009 international criticism of the country's human rights record grew.

Trial of Evgeniy Zhovtis

On September 3, 2009, Evgeniy Zhovtis, founding director of the Kazakhstan International Bureau for Human Rights and the Rule of Law, was found guilty of manslaughter following a motor vehicle accident in which a young man was killed. The investigation and trial leading to his conviction were marred by serious procedural flaws that denied him the right to present a defense and gave rise to concern that this tragedy may have been politically exploited.

On July 27, the day after the accident, the authorities opened a criminal case, a normal procedure after a car accident with a casualty. The investigation initially designated Zhovtis as a witness, changing that status to suspect the next day but informing Zhovtis and his lawyer about this only two weeks later, a serious violation of Kazakh law. At trial the judge either rejected or postponed all defense petitions without ruling on them. These actions served to deny Zhovtis the opportunity to challenge the evidence against him, violating his right to defend himself. Zhovtis was sentenced to four years in a settlement colony.

On October 20 the Almaty Province Court upheld the verdict. Zhovtis was not allowed to attend the hearing, and again his defense team was not allowed to present evidence or to challenge prosecution expert evidence.

On September 19 an official with the OSCE Office for Democratic Institutions and Human Rights (ODIHR) expressed concern about reports "of numerous violations of Zhovtis' right to a fair trial." Other international actors, including the European Union, the French government, and the United States government, issued similar statements.

Freedom of Expression and Information

On February 6, 2009, President Nursultan Nazarbaev signed into law a set of amendments affecting the media. These simplify the registration process for the electronic media by dropping the requirement that they register (which had duplicated some of the requirements for the licensing process) and eliminating the requirement that all media outlets reregister in the event of a change in editor-in-chief or legal address. The amendments also made it possible for media outlets to appeal to court against denials of governmental information, and allowed media workers to use audio recorders and cameras to collect information without permission of an interviewee.

The amendments do not address broader problems with media freedoms, such as the domination by government loyalists of broadcast media outlets, threats and harassment against independent journalists for criticizing the president or government policies and practices, prohibitive penalties for civil defamation with no cap on defamation awards, and the existence of criminal penalties for libel. Moreover, on July 10 Nazarbaev signed another package of amendments to laws dealing with the media and the internet, under which all forms of internet content—including websites worldwide, blogs, and chatrooms—could potentially be considered "internet resources" and therefore subject to existing restrictive laws on expression. The law also expands the grounds for banning media content relating to elections, strikes, and public assemblies, using broad wording that could give rise to arbitrary interpretation. Taken together, these conditions maintain a chilling environment in which media outlets and journalists are faced with the constant threat of lawsuits and crippling defamation penalties.

Among examples where that threat was realized, Ramazan Yesergepov, editor of the newspaper *Alma-Ata Info*, received a three-year prison sentence on August 8, 2009, for disclosing state secrets, after the newspaper published an article making corruption allegations against local authorities based on classified documents. Yesergepov's trial was closed, and he did not have access to legal counsel of his own choosing. In June the independent Almaty weekly *Taszhargan* had to cease publishing after an appellate court upheld a prior decision awarding Romin Madinov, a member of parliament, 3 million tenge (about US$20,000) in "moral damages" for an article alleging that Madinov's business interests benefited from his legislative work. In September an Almaty court ordered the weekly *Respublika* to pay 60 million tenge (about US$400,000) in "moral damages" to the BTA Bank, which had sued the newspaper after a March article discussing the bank's possible bankruptcy allegedly cost the bank the equivalent of US$45 million in deposits. The appeal is still pending, but the newspaper is not able to pay the fine, and will cease publishing if the decision is upheld.

Freedom of Assembly

The government made no effort to liberalize legislation on freedom of assembly. A public meeting of a political nature that is not organized directly or indirectly by the government, or that is not in support of government policies, is likely to be denied a permit, and broken up by police if it goes ahead. Kazakhstan's law on public assemblies requires demonstrations as small as a one-person picket to be registered with the authorities at least 10 days in advance. It allows local authorities to "additionally regulate" public assemblies "with regard to local conditions," which amounts to a virtual carte blanche to limit freedom of assembly.

The law prevented at least several public gatherings in 2009. For example, on February 13 several citizens' groups and political parties made coordinated applications to the mayors' offices in 12 cities to hold protests on February 25, but not a single group received permission. In another example, on April 21, 12 activists with the youth human rights organization Ar.Rukh.Khak were detained by police for three hours when they tried to meet with journalists at the main square in Almaty to discuss concerns regarding a proposal for introducing mandatory drug testing of students.

On September 11 Viktor Kovtunovsky, an independent journalist, was fined the equivalent of US$210 for standing alone on Almaty's central square with a banner that said "Today Zhovtis, tomorrow you." Six days later, Andrei Sviridov, another journalist, was fined for staging a similar picket.

Access to Legal Counsel

In several high-profile cases in 2009 Kazakhstan's Committee for National Security (KNB) deprived defendants of their right to legal counsel of their own choosing on grounds that lawyers must have special clearance to be engaged in cases involving state secrets. For example, Daniyar Kanafin is defense lawyer for Mukhtar Dzhakishev, president of KazAtomProm (a state-owned nuclear company), who stands accused of expropriation and embezzlement. After Kanafin publicly complained that the KNB violated national and international law by preventing him from meeting his client, on July 7 the KNB sent a request to the Almaty Bar Association and the Almaty Department of Justice to disbar Kanafin on the grounds that he "created a negative perception" of the authorities. The Almaty Bar Association rejected the request, but Kanafin remains unable to access his client.

At this writing Dmitry Parfenov and Malkhaz Tsotsoria, vice presidents of KazAtomProm, have been in KNB "safe houses" since June, allegedly in the framework of a witness protection program; both men are state witnesses against Dzhakishev. The men have no access to legal counsel of their own choosing and instead have only state defense lawyers provided by the KNB who have special security clearance. Both the KNB and the state defense lawyers pressured the men's wives not to complain to international organizations and diplomats about their husbands' treatment "if they do not want to worsen the situation."

Freedom of Religion

In one positive development, on February 11, 2009, Kazakhstan's Constitutional Council ruled that a proposed religion law violated the constitution. One of the key elements of the ruling was its finding that certain provisions in the proposed law "do not ensure equality between religious communities" and that many of its provisions were vague and thus might create problems for implementation.

Key International Actors

The OSCE remained engaged with Kazakhstan throughout 2009 on issues relating to the upcoming chairmanship. In early 2009 Miklos Haraszti, the OSCE's representative on freedom of the media, welcomed amendments to the media law but said the law "still fails to meet several international standards." He urged the government to carry out reforms aimed at "de-monopolizing the media market" and "decriminalizing libel and insult." Later in 2009 Haraszti urged President Nazarbaev to veto the new internet law.

Germany assisted the Kazakh government in preparing for the chairmanship, but made no discernible effort to challenge the Kazakh government on human rights setbacks and promote change. This was disappointing, given that Germany had been Kazakhstan's strongest supporter in its bid for the 2010 OSCE chairmanship. In February 2009 the European Union and the United States issued public statements welcoming the February 2009 reforms and underlining the need for further progress in the lead-up to Kazakhstan's OSCE chairmanship. In September both the EU and US expressed their concern regarding the adoption of the internet law, the sentencing of journalist Ramazan Yesergepov, and the fair trial violations in Evgeniy Zhovtis's case. In particular the EU stated it "regrets" that it had to "to express its concern with regard to freedom of the media in Kazakhstan on a number of occasions."

KYRGYZSTAN

Respect for human rights deteriorated in Kyrgyzstan during 2009, especially in the run-up to a presidential election on July 23 that was won by the incumbent, Kurmanbek Bakiev. The government violated fundamental rights, including freedom of association, assembly, and expression, and civil society activists and journalists were a particular target of pressure. Furthermore, the government has failed effectively to address longstanding problems of torture and ill-treatment of detainees, as well as gender-based violence.

The Organization for Security and Co-operation in Europe (OSCE) Office for Democratic Institutions and Human Rights concluded that the elections "failed to meet key OSCE commitments" and noted many problems with the conduct of the vote, including fraud.

Civil Society and Freedom of Association

In early 2009 Kyrgyzstan's civil society was shaken by draft amendments to the 2000 law "On noncommercial organizations" and the 1996 law "On state registration of legal entities." The proposed amendments outlined new, arbitrary bases for rejecting the registration applications of NGOs, imposed onerous reporting requirements and administrative and financial obstacles on local and foreign NGOs, forbade NGOs from engaging in "political" activities, and set out a new regime of government inspections and warnings. When viewed in the context of a worsening climate for human rights, the amendments appeared intended to stifle Kyrgyzstan's vibrant civil society.

After an outcry from local civil society groups and the international community, the presidential administration recommended that parliament postpone consideration of the amendments. To date, no new draft has been introduced. However, civil society groups remain concerned that some iteration of the draft might still be put forward.

Media Freedom

Violence and harassment of journalists increased significantly during the run-up to the July presidential election. It was not always clear whether specific journalists were targeted because of their work or were victims of common crime. Yet the attacks functioned to intimidate other journalists. In a number of these cases the perpetrators have not been identified or held accountable.

At least seven journalists were physically attacked in Kyrgyzstan in 2009. On March 3, Syrgak Abdyldaev of the independent weekly *Reporter Bishkek* was severely beaten near his apartment and stabbed more than 20 times, and within months he fled the country because of ongoing harassment. On March 7, Bahadyr Kenzhebaev, a television cameraman, was severely beaten on his way home from work in the southern city of Osh. On March 26, Ulugbek Babakulov, the editor-in-chief of the weekly *Moskovskiy Komsomolets-Kyrgyzstan* and his colleague Yelena Ageeva were severely beaten and robbed by two unknown attackers in Bishkek; Babakulov was hospitalized. On June 5, Abduvakhab Moniev, a journalist with the opposition weekly *Achyg Sayasat*, was beaten by an unknown assailant in Bishkek. In early April the prosecutor's office had summoned several *Achyg Sayasat* journalists and warned them "not to insult or offend the president" after a number of articles criticizing government officials. On July 10, Almaz Tashiev, a freelance journalist from Osh, died following injuries received in a beating by a police officer on July 4; the circumstances surrounding the beating are not clear. On November 2, Kubanychbek Joldoshev, an Osh-based journalist with *Osh Shamy*, was attacked by three unknown assailants on his way home, sustaining head injuries.

In July the OSCE representative on freedom of the media called on the Kyrgyz authorities "to do everything in their power to halt the wave of violent attacks against journalists, which is threatening media pluralism ahead of the presidential elections." The European Union called on Kyrgyzstan to "regain its reputation of a country where freedom of expression is enjoyed."

Freedom of Religion

In January 2009 President Bakiev signed a controversial new law "On freedom of conscience and religious organizations." The OSCE's Office for Democratic Institutions and Human Rights and the Council of Europe's Venice Commission had criticized the law in October 2008 for, among other things, its "vagueness," "discriminatory registration requirements," and "interference with religious autonomy." Nevertheless, the law signed by the president retained these problematic provisions. The new law increases from 10 to 200 the number of people required to officially register a religious organization, and restricts freedom of expression by prohibiting proselytizing and the dissemination of religious material in public places or by going house to house. Watchdog organizations such as Forum 18, an independent, international religious freedom group, reported arbitrary implementation of the law, and harassment of smaller religious communities throughout the year.

Criminal Justice, Torture, and Ill-Treatment

Although Kyrgyzstan ratified the Optional Protocol to the Convention against Torture in 2008, torture and ill-treatment remain rampant. The events in Nookat (a town in southern Kyrgyzstan) are a stark illustration of the problem.

In autumn 2008 Nookat residents applied to the mayor's office for permission to organize a celebration on the main square to mark the end of Ramadan. The mayor's office denied the application, but authorized the celebration to be held at a stadium outside town. When residents arrived for the celebration on October 1, the stadium was closed. The crowd then proceeded to the mayor's office to protest.

Accounts vary as to the number of protesters and the conduct of the protest. The authorities claim that the protest was violent and organized by a thousand followers of Hizb ut-Tahrir, an international Islamic organization that is banned in Kyrgyzstan and several other countries in the region. In contrast, Nookat residents claim that several hundred local protesters gathered peacefully at the mayor's office, but some teenagers in the crowd threw stones when the police began arresting protestors to clear the entrance to the building.

On October 13 the State Committee for National Security announced that it had detained 32 people. Although these individuals had initially been charged with organizing or participating in mass unrest, other charges were added during the investigation, including the charge that all defendants were members of Hizb ut-Tahrir. On November 27 the Osh Province Court found the defendants guilty of a number of offenses, including "incitement to cause or participate in mass unrest," "separatism," "attempted overthrow of the constitutional order," and "spreading ethnic or religious strife." The defendants were sentenced to prison terms ranging from nine to 20 years.

At their trial, the defendants testified that they had been tortured and ill-treated, but the judge neither urged the prosecutor's office to investigate the allegations nor dismissed the evidence allegedly obtained under torture.

A commission established by the Kyrgyz ombudsman concluded in February 2009 that most of the defendants had been ill-treated and tortured during their arrest and in pretrial detention. The ombudsman's report, which was based on interviews with the defendants, their lawyers, and court documents, described how law enforcement officials had poured hot and cold water on detainees, beat them on the soles of their feet, and almost suffocated them using plastic bags or gas masks. Detainees also had to stand in their underwear in a cold room with their feet in water for up to three days, were not allowed to use sanitary facilities, and did not receive needed medical treatment.

A January 2009 report by the Russian human rights organization Memorial documented similar violations. After the report's publication, its author was deported from Kyrgyzstan and barred from reentering.

In May 2009 Kyrgyzstan's Supreme Court reviewed the case and upheld the verdicts. It slightly reduced the sentences for two women and three minors, but did not investigate the defendants' torture allegations.

Sexual and Gender-Based Violence

In November 2008 the United Nations Committee on the Elimination of Discrimination against Women (CEDAW) raised serious concern about widespread domestic violence in Kyrgyzstan. It requested that the government submit information within one year on measures taken to eliminate violence against women and bride abduction. At this writing the government has not submitted such information, and has taken no new steps to prevent such violence or punish perpetrators.

The UN special rapporteur on violence against women visited Kyrgyzstan on November 9-16, 2009. She concluded that "formal commitments [to protect women's rights] have to a large extent not been translated into concrete actions and improvements on the ground and in the lives of ordinary women," and that "women and girls' vulnerability to violence, exploitation and destitution has increased."

Lesbians, bisexual women, and transgender men in Kyrgyzstan experience discrimination as a result of their sexual orientation or gender identity, and often face violence, rape, psychological abuse, and confinement. These groups also experience police harassment and abuse, and there are reports of police harassing organizations that defend the rights of LGBT persons.

Key International Actors

In March the European Union expressed concern about restrictive legislative trends in Kyrgyzstan reflecting "a tendency which threatens to distance the country from the implementation of its OSCE commitments." It urged the government to "thoroughly investigate" recent attacks on journalists and opposition politicians. The second round of the EU's annual human rights dialogue was held in mid-October.

The United States prioritized the struggle to retain its airbase at Bishkek's Manas airport over human rights, and did not speak out about the deteriorating situation in the first half of the year. In February President Bakiev announced he would close the airbase, but after the United States agreed to pay higher rent in late June he allowed the base to stay. On June 11 President Obama sent a letter to President Bakiev acknowledging Kyrgyzstan's important role in stabilizing the situation in Afghanistan and in the campaign against terrorism.

RUSSIA

The brazen murders of at least five civic rights activists and violence and harassment toward several others marked a severe deterioration in the human rights climate in Russia. These shocking developments contrasted sharply with some positive rhetoric by President Dmitry Medvedev recognizing the importance of civil society.

Civil Society

2009 saw an increase in violence and threats against human rights defenders, civic activists, and independent journalists in Russia, particularly those working on the North Caucasus. These attacks—along with restrictive laws, harassment of independent groups, and hostile official attitudes—worsened the already negative environment for civil society.

On January 19, 2009, Stanislav Markelov, a prominent human rights lawyer who had defended victims of rights violations in Chechnya, was shot dead on a central Moscow street in broad daylight. Anastasia Baburova, a journalist with him, was also killed. Two people were charged with the killings. In March, Lev Ponamaryev, head of the Za Prava Cheloveka movement, was severely beaten in Moscow. In July unknown attackers shot Albert Pchelintsev, an anti-corruption activist in Khimki near Moscow, in the mouth with a stun gun, telling him it was to shut him up.

In summer 2009 three local civic activists were abducted and killed in Chechnya. On July 15, Natalia Estemirova, a leading human rights defender who documented abuses by Chechen law enforcement and security agencies for the Memorial Human Rights Center, was abducted in Grozny, the Chechen capital; her body was found later the same day. Estemirova's shocking murder was followed by harassment and intimidation of several Memorial staff in Chechnya; one had to be evacuated due to threats to his security. On August 10, Zarema Sadulayeva and her husband Alik Dzhabrailov, who worked for Save the Generation, a humanitarian organization, were abducted from their Grozny office and were found murdered the next day. Local law enforcement and security personnel are implicated in the abduction and murder of Sadulayeva and Dzhabrailov, and their involvement in Estemirova's murder cannot be excluded.

In October, Maksharip Aushev, a prominent opposition and civic activist in Ingushetia, was murdered when unknown shooters sprayed his car with bullets.

Following Estemirova's murder, Oleg Orlov, chairman of the Memorial Human Rights Center, made a statement implicating Ramzan Kadyrov, the president of Chechnya, in the crime. Kadyrov sued Orlov for defamation and lodged a criminal complaint against him. In October a Moscow civil court ordered Orlov to pay a fine and issue a public retraction, and police launched an investigation against Orlov for criminal libel, which carries a maximum sentence of three years' imprisonment.

In 2009 President Medvedev made several statements underscoring the importance of democracy and human rights in Russia and acknowledging areas where change is needed. Notably, Medvedev appointed a working group to propose reforms to the restrictive 2006 law on NGOs. As a result, in June parliament adopted modifications to the registration and accounting procedures for noncommercial organizations.

Most restrictive aspects of the 2006 law and its implementing regulations remain, however, which subject Russian and foreign NGOs to excessive, unwarranted government scrutiny and interference. The authorities also use tax inspections, inspections for fire code or labor code compliance, police raids, and politically motivated criminal charges to harass and intimidate in particular organizations that receive foreign funding or work on controversial issues. For example, in July the Kazan Human Rights Center, which assists victims of police abuse, and Agora, a consortium of human rights organizations, endured a series of harassing inspections and legal action against their leaders that appeared to be aimed at stopping their work.

Many NGOs are vulnerable to being targeted under the 2002 Law on Countering Extremist Activity, which designates certain forms of defamation of public officials as extremist and allows any politically or ideologically motivated crime to be designated as extremist.

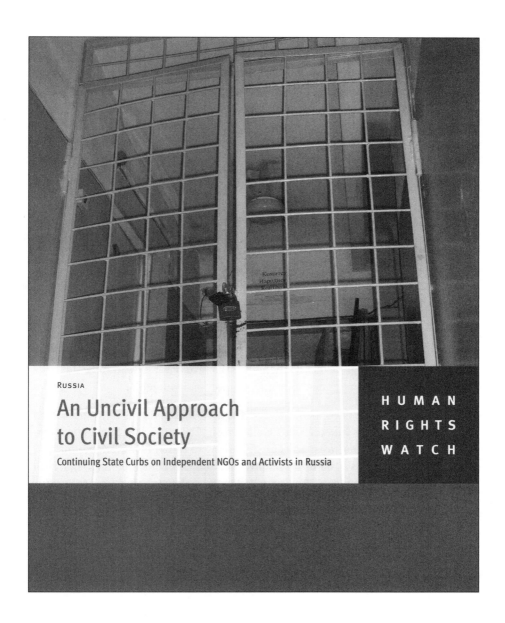

RUSSIA

An Uncivil Approach
to Civil Society

Continuing State Curbs on Independent NGOs and Activists in Russia

HUMAN
RIGHTS
WATCH

The North Caucasus

The Islamist insurgency in the North Caucasus republics of Chechnya, Dagestan, and Ingushetia appeared to intensify in 2009. Casualties among civilians and law enforcement and security forces increased. Counterterrorism operations continue to involve grave human rights violations such as torture, enforced disappearances, and extrajudicial executions. Impunity for these abuses is rampant.

On April 16, federal authorities announced that they had ended the counterterrorism operation in Chechnya, marking a formal end to the armed conflict. The announcement had no bearing on the authorities' use of torture and illegal detention in counterterrorism efforts. Collective punishment against people with suspected rebel ties became a pronounced trend beginning in June 2008 and continuing into 2009: Memorial and Human Rights Watch documented at least 30 cases in which such individuals' homes were deliberately burned, apparently by Chechen law enforcement personnel. No one has been held responsible for the house burnings. High-level Chechen officials, including President Kadyrov, made public statements stressing that insurgents' families should expect to be punished unless they convince their relatives among the insurgents to surrender.

The July murder of Natalia Estemirova (see above) highlights the danger to those who expose abuse. High-level Chechen officials have made threatening statements accusing human rights activists of supporting insurgents.

In 119 rulings by November, the European Court of Human Rights has held Russia responsible for serious human rights violations in Chechnya. In almost all cases the court also found Russia responsible for failing to properly investigate these crimes. In most cases Russia has promptly paid the compensation and legal fees as required by the judgments. But it has failed to implement measures to rectify violations in individual cases, including ensuring effective investigations and holding perpetrators accountable. It has also failed to adopt so-called general measures to implement the rulings, which entail policy and legal changes to prevent similar violations recurring. This failure serves to perpetuate the violations described above.

In Dagestan, according to local groups, at least 18 persons were abducted in 2009. The bodies of 11 were found shortly after their abduction, bearing gunshot

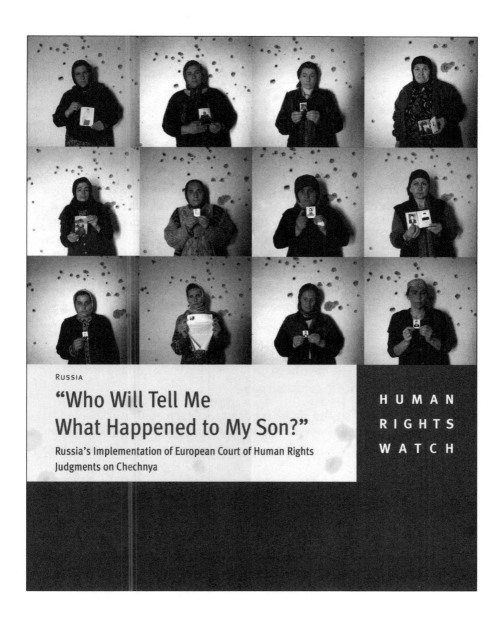

RUSSIA

"Who Will Tell Me
What Happened to My Son?"

Russia's Implementation of European Court of Human Rights
Judgments on Chechnya

HUMAN
RIGHTS
WATCH

or other wounds indicating a violent death. One of them was Nariman Mamedyarov, who had told Human Rights Watch that in September 2008 he was abducted and held by authorities in incommunicado detention and tortured. Mamedyarov was abducted again in September 2009 and was found shot dead; the authorities claimed he died during an armed clash with law enforcement officials. Of the other abductees, three were released or escaped their captors, and four remain missing. In some cases, the individuals' Islamic practices made them vulnerable to being branded "extremists" by the authorities, and in others the authorities suspected them of some connection with the insurgency.

Human rights activists and independent journalists in Dagestan have been subjected to violence and intimidation. On August 20 an arson attack burned the office of the Mothers of Dagestan for Human Rights (MDHR), an independent organization that documents abusive counterterrorism practices. The fire followed the shooting death on August 11 of Abdumalik Akhmedilov, a newspaper editor who had criticized law enforcement officials for suppressing political and religious dissent in their campaign against religious extremism. In September several local activists, journalists, and lawyers received leaflets with explicit death threats.

Insurgent attacks on public officials, security and law-enforcement personnel, and civilians in Ingushetia have been on the rise since 2007, with a marked increase in such violence in summer 2009.

The Ingush leadership stands out for making at least a rhetorical acknowledgment of human rights obligations. In April 2009 Yunus-Bek Yevkurov, president of Ingushetia, committed to ensuring that counterinsurgency operations are carried out in line with Russia's legal obligations. In 2009 he held numerous meetings with local human rights defenders and relatives of the "disappeared." He also created a human rights council to advise him. In June Yevkurov suffered severe injuries from an assassination attempt.

Despite this rhetorical commitment, local organizations continue to report that government forces commit extrajudicial executions, unlawful, abduction-style detentions, and torture and cruel or degrading treatment during the course of counterinsurgency operations.

RUSSIA

"Are You Happy to Cheat Us?"

Exploitation of Migrant Construction Workers in Russia

HUMAN
RIGHTS
WATCH

The Armed Conflict over South Ossetia

More than a year after the August 2008 conflict between Russia and Georgia over South Ossetia, impunity for violations of international humanitarian law by all sides of the conflict still prevails. More than 20,000 individuals displaced from deliberately destroyed ethnic Georgian villages in South Ossetia remain unable to return to their homes.

In September 2009 a European Union-funded independent fact-finding mission published its report, concluding that Georgian, Russian, and South Ossetian forces committed international human rights and humanitarian law violations during the conflict. The violations included indiscriminate attacks by the Georgian and Russian militaries, and a widespread campaign of looting and burning of ethnic Georgian villages, along with ill-treatment, beatings, hostage-taking, and arbitrary arrests, by South Ossetian forces. The report also found that the Russian military failed to prevent or stop violations by Ossetian militia.

Migrant Worker Rights

Russia has between 4 and 9 million migrant workers, over 80 percent of whom come from other countries of the former Soviet Union. Forty percent of migrant workers are employed in construction, where they face abuses that include confiscation of passports, denial of contracts, non-payment or delayed payment of wages, and unsafe working conditions. Migrant workers have few effective options for redress for these abuses. Government agencies continue to consider and implement measures that reverse progressive reforms of laws affecting migrant workers enacted in 2007.

Police frequently use document inspections to extort money from visible minorities, including migrant workers.

Health Issues and the HIV/AIDS Epidemic

Hundreds of thousands of people in Russia are dependent on opioids. The government's decision to shift funding away from harm reduction programs, which have saved thousands from becoming infected, is a devastating blow to HIV prevention efforts in the country. Paired with its stubborn refusal—despite over-whelming evidence of its effectiveness—to allow drug treatment with methadone, the Russian government's new position is putting injection drug users at grave risk of HIV infection.

Poor availability of morphine due to unnecessarily strict drug laws continues to cause tremendous suffering for hundreds of thousands of patients with pain due to cancer, HIV/AIDS, and other conditions.

Key International Actors

The European Bank for Reconstruction and Development (EBRD) adopted a new Russia Strategy in 2009. The strategy did not adequately reflect serious problems with Russia's commitment to pluralism and the rule of law, and did not reflect EBRD policies requiring measures to ensure that recipients of the bank's funding do not benefit from the exploitation of workers, including migrant workers.

The European Union held two rounds of human rights consultations with Russia, meetings ultimately undermined by the lack of high-level Russian participation and adequate follow-up mechanisms. Apart from ad hoc statements and bilateral interventions by select European leaders, notably Germany's chancellor Angela Merkel, human rights concerns overall appeared to remain largely absent from higher-level talks between the EU member states and the EU institutionally and Russia. The EU continued negotiations on its Partnership and Cooperation Agreement with Russia, which expired in December 2007.

The election of Barack Obama as president of the United States renewed prospects for a constructive US-Russia relationship. Obama and Secretary of State Hillary Clinton vowed to reset relations with Moscow, and Obama noted that improved relations should include strengthened human rights and rule of law in Russia. It remains to be seen whether this will result in a strong resolve to confront egregious human rights problems. During his July 2009 trip to Moscow, Obama underscored the importance of a vibrant civil society, civic freedoms, and "a government that's accountable and transparent." Clinton visited Russia in October and emphasized to a group of civil society actors that human rights and democratic values will have an important place in the Russian-American dialogue.

437

In a report published in September, Dick Marty, Parliamentary Assembly of the Council of Europe (PACE) rapporteur on legal remedies for human rights violations in the North Caucasus, noted that the "general climate of impunity at all levels has generated an atmosphere conducive to the spread of violence." Also in September PACE expressed concern about attacks and threats against human rights defenders in the North Caucasus by holding a focused debate on the issue. During the same session PACE adopted another resolution on the August 2008 war over South Ossetia and its fallout, demanding that international monitors and returning Georgian residents be granted unrestricted access to both South Ossetia and Abkhazia.

Russia underwent review by the United Nations Human Rights Council (HRC) Universal Periodic Review mechanism in February, during which it failed to commit to concrete human rights reforms in key areas of concern raised during the review, such as access for UN monitors, reform of the restrictive NGO law, and ending impunity for rampant abuses in the North Caucasus. Russia was reelected to the HRC in May, despite concerns about its human rights record. Following Natalia Estemirova's murder in July, the UN special procedures on torture, enforced disappearances, extrajudicial executions, and human rights defenders requested access to Russia to conduct an investigation, which the Russian government refused. Russia's human rights record came up for close scrutiny again in October during a review by the UN Human Rights Committee, which resulted in strongly-worded conclusions highlighting numerous concerns and urging Russia to take concrete action to address them.

The International Criminal Court continued to keep under analysis crimes committed by all parties to the 2008 conflict over South Ossetia. Russia is not an ICC state party.

The International Olympic Committee (IOC) made several visits to Sochi, the Black Sea resort that will host the 2014 Winter Olympic Games. The IOC did not grant a request to meet with activists or citizens seeking to raise concerns about property rights and environmental violations in connection with preparations for the Games.

SERBIA

Serbia continued on the path toward greater domestic accountability for war crimes, but the government failed to arrest the region's most wanted war crimes suspect Ratko Mladic. Tensions in the Albanian-majority Presevo valley flared into instances of violence in July. The forced eviction of more than 100 Roma from their homes in Belgrade underscored that minority's vulnerable position in Serbia as a whole. The cancellation of the Gay Pride Parade in Belgrade illustrated continuing intolerance toward lesbian, gay, bisexual, and transgender (LGBT) people.

War Crimes Accountability

Serbia failed to bring to justice Ratko Mladic and Goran Hadzic, both indicted by the International Criminal Tribunal for the former Yugoslavia (ICTY) and believed to be in Serbia. The Serbian government has repeatedly undertaken (including in 2009) to arrest Mladic, a precondition for closer ties with the European Union.

In February the ICTY convicted five former top Serbian officials for war crimes and crimes against humanity in Kosovo. Nikola Sainovic, Nebojsa Pavkovic, Sreten Lukic, Vladimir Lazarevic, and Dragoljub Ojdanic were given prison sentences ranging from 15 to 22 years. A sixth defendant, former Serbian president Milan Milutinovic, was acquitted of similar charges.

In July the ICTY sentenced Vojislav Seselj, the former leader of the Serbian Radical Party, to 15 months' imprisonment for breaching witness protection rules. Seselj is currently on trial before the Tribunal for alleged war crimes in Bosnia and Croatia.

The Belgrade War Crimes Chamber continued its efforts to hold alleged perpetrators accountable for wartime abuses, despite limited funding, inadequate political support, and little public awareness of its work. In March the Chamber convicted 13 former Yugoslav army reservists for their participation in the 1991 massacre of around 200 Croats in Ovcara, Croatia, sentencing them to up to 20 years' imprisonment. In June the Chamber sentenced four members of the "Scorpions" paramilitary unit to prison terms of between 15 and 20 years for crimes against Kosovo Albanian civilians committed in 1999.

Significant ongoing trials in the Chamber during 2009 and relating to alleged crimes in Bosnia, Croatia, and Kosovo include the Zvornik trial, the "Tuzla Column" trial, the Lovas trial, the Suva Reka trial, the Banski Kovacevac trial, the Trbojevic trial, the "Bytyqi Brothers" trial (named after the victims), the Podujevo trial, and the Morina trial. Notable new indictments include charges in June against 17 former members of the Kosovo Liberation Army (KLA)'s "Gnjilane group" for alleged war crimes against Serbs, Roma, and Albanians in 1999, and charges in July against Nenad Malic for alleged war crimes against Bosniak (Bosnian Muslim) civilians in 1992.

In September 2009 the Supreme Court delivered the final decision in the "Zvornik I" case, reducing the sentences of two former Bosnian Serb paramilitaries and confirming the sentence and acquittal of two others.

Treatment of Minorities

Forced evictions in Belgrade in April underscored the fact that Roma in Serbia continue to lack full enjoyment of their rights. On April 3, police forcibly evicted 128 Roma people, some of them displaced from Kosovo and including women and children, from their informal homes in a poor neighborhood in New Belgrade. On April 2 the Roma had received official notification from Belgrade municipal authorities that they had 15 days to leave. Less than 24 hours later police arrived with bulldozers to destroy their makeshift homes. The evicted families were left homeless and lost most of their belongings. At this writing they have not been compensated for their lost property.

The evicted Roma are currently living in metal containers in another municipality, near Belgrade. Their move there was initially blocked by local residents, illustrating the widespread discrimination and hostility Roma face in Serbia.

In July the United Nations Committee against Torture found Serbia to have violated the Convention against Torture in the case of Besim Osmani, a Roma man, who had been beaten by police together with his four-year-old son in June 2000 during a forced eviction and demolition operation in an informal settlement in Belgrade. At this writing the Serbian government has yet to respond to the decision.

Longstanding tensions in the Albanian-majority Presevo valley area occasionally flared into violence in 2009. The most serious incidents occurred in July: two Serbian police officers were injured in a grenade attack, and two days later two ethnic Albanians were injured in a bomb explosion in the village of Lucani, prompting the Serbian government to raise the level of alert in the region, which resulted in additional police forces being deployed. Five days later the Presevo municipal assembly requested the withdrawal of the additional police and condemned alleged "general police brutality." In August the regional assembly of Presevo, Medvedja, and Bujanovac passed a declaration demanding the establishment of a separate autonomous region with its own institutions.

In a positive move, the Serbian parliament in March approved an anti-discrimination law, prohibiting discrimination on the basis of race, religion, gender, and sexual orientation, despite opposition to the inclusion of protection for LGBT people from a coalition of churches led by the Serbian Orthodox Church.

In September Prime Minister Mirko Cvetkovic advised the organizers of the Gay Pride Parade in Belgrade to move the event from the streets to a city park, saying the police were otherwise unable to guarantee security to the participants (the only previous parade, in 2001, had ended in violence). The marchers called this "unacceptable" and cancelled the event. Less than a week later, Serbia's public prosecutor called on the government to ban two far right groups linked to the threats that led to the cancellation.

Integration of Refugees and Displaced Persons

According to the United Nations High Commissioner for Refugees (UNHCR), as of August 2009 there were 309,171 internally displaced persons (IDPs) and refugees in Serbia. Many continue to face problems obtaining documentation, accessing housing and other social services, and finding employment. Around 6,000 displaced persons from Bosnia, Croatia, and Kosovo remain in collective centers in Serbia, often in substandard conditions. Roma IDPs from Kosovo face particularly poor economic and social conditions.

Forced returns of Roma from Western Europe continued, absent any program to assist them, placing a particular burden on Roma host communities. According to

UNHCR, between January and May, 163 individuals, including 110 Roma, were involuntarily deported to Serbia from Western European countries. UNHCR did not record any Kosovo Roma being involuntarily returned to Serbia during the first five months of 2009.

Media Freedom

Amendments to the Law on Public Information entered into force in July, prompting widespread criticism by Serbian media and international press freedom organizations because of the excessive size of permissible fines for libel. Critics fear this could discourage investigative journalism and stifle press freedom.

Human Rights Defenders

The LGBT NGO Gay-Straight Alliance came under pressure in 2009. In February the organization was prohibited from holding a news conference in Belgrade's Sava Congress Center by municipal officials. After criticism in the media and by Serbia's human rights minister, the director of the center and Belgrade's mayor both apologized for the decision. In March hooligans threw stones at the door of a conference center in Kragujevac where the organization was holding a press conference to present its annual report. Police arrested and fined three people (including one minor). The Kragujevac city council condemned the attack.

In February a Belgrade municipal court found Natasa Kandic, director of the Humanitarian Law Center, guilty of criminal libel against Tomislav Nikolic, an MP, member of the Serbian Progressive Party and former Radical Party leader, and ordered her to pay Nikolic 200,000 dinars (approximately €2,000) in damages. The suit arose from comments by Kandic that Radical Party members should be investigated for war crimes committed against Croatian civilians in 1992. The Belgrade district court quashed the judgment in June. The government was silent throughout the episode.

Key International Actors

The European Union's Stabilization and Association Agreement (SAA) with Serbia was stalled due to Serbia's failure to apprehend Ratko Mladic. However, in July the European Commission proposed that Serbian citizens should be allowed to travel visa-free to the EU's Schengen area as of early 2010. Approval of the proposal is pending at this writing. The European Commission's annual progress report on Serbia in October 2009 highlighted the need to apprehend Mladic and address the plight of Roma.

During a visit to Serbia in May 2009, US Vice President Joe Biden expressed the Obama administration's desire to "deepen relations with Serbia," stating that Washington supported its plan to join the EU.

During the Universal Periodic Review of Serbia at the UN Human Rights Council in December 2008, key concerns raised included the treatment of Roma, protection of minorities, violence against and trafficking of women, the plight of human rights defenders and independent journalists, and war crimes accountability.

In July 2009 the UN representative on the human rights of IDPs, Walter Kalin, published a report following his visit to Serbia earlier that month, pointing to the ongoing problems with housing and employment faced by Roma and other IDPs from Kosovo.

Political tensions surrounding the status of Kosovo continued. Serbia's claim against Kosovo following its declaration of independence remained pending at the International Court of Justice. A September police cooperation agreement between the Serbian government and the EU police and justice mission in Kosovo (EULEX) stirred political controversy in Belgrade and Pristina. In October, Serbian authorities agreed to collaborate with EULEX on identification of the remains of victims in mass graves from the Kosovo conflict.

Kosovo

The lack of international agreement on Kosovo's status continues to impede efforts to protect the human rights of its inhabitants. Caught between disagreements among its member states, and between Belgrade and Pristina, EULEX struggled in 2009 to fully deploy throughout Kosovo and execute its task of building a functioning justice system. The Kosovo authorities again failed to demonstrate unequivocal commitment to minority rights and the rule of law.

Protection of Minorities

According to data from the UN Mission in Kosovo (UNMIK), 275 inter-ethnic incidents took place during the first eight months of 2009. Roma, Ashkali, and Egyptian (RAE) communities remain the most vulnerable in Kosovo.

There were numerous clashes between Albanian and Serb residents in Mitrovica in July and August, linked to efforts to return Albanians to reconstructed homes in a neighborhood in the town's Serb-controlled north. Renewed clashes on September 4 prompted an intervention by EULEX police and the NATO-led Kosovo Force. In August an elderly Serb couple, Bogdan and Trajanka Petkovic, was found shot dead in their house in Partes near Gnjilane. EULEX and the Kosovo Police Service (KPS) opened an investigation into the killings.

A series of attacks on Roma in the town of Gnjilane in the last week of August raised concern among rights groups about rising hostility in previously peaceful areas. The KPS was slow to respond to these incidents, but eventually opened investigations into all cases reported to the police. On August 25 a group of Roma families from Urosevac petitioned municipal authorities and the KPS, alleging they were being verbally and physically harassed by "unknown perpetrators." While the KPS initiated an investigation into these allegations, neither Kosovo nor international authorities have publicly condemned the incidents.

Return of Refugees and Displaced Persons

Voluntary returns to Kosovo, including from Serbia, continued to decline, with only 508, including 132 Serbs, registered by UNHCR during the first seven months of 2009. The volatile political situation, continuing inter-ethnic incidents in some areas, and poor economic conditions hampered sustainable return.

Forced returns from Western Europe continued, with 3,324 persons returned in the first seven months of 2009. According to UNHCR, Kosovo Serbs, Roma, and Albanians from areas where they are in the minority remain in need of international protection. Despite that, 107 people belonging to UNHCR-protected categories were returned during the first seven months of 2009. In November 2008 Kosovo authorities assumed responsibility for managing forced returns from third countries, a role previously played by UNMIK. At this writing the authorities are

Kosovo

Poisoned by Lead

A Health and Human Rights Crisis in Mitrovica's Roma Camps

HUMAN
RIGHTS
WATCH

negotiating bilateral readmission agreements with Western European countries seeking further forced returns.

Forced returnees experience a host of problems beyond security, many linked to the lack of any assistance or programs to reintegrate them. Roma returnees face particular difficulties accessing housing, education (many children no longer speak Albanian or Serbian), and employment. They depend on help from settled Roma, placing a further burden on Kosovo's poorest group.

Ten years after the destruction of the Roma Mahalla in Mitrovica, its former inhabitants remain in camps in north Mitrovica (Cesmin Lug and Osterode) and in Leposavic. Roma in Cesmin Lug and Osterode are exposed to ongoing and harmful lead contamination, adversely affecting their health, especially children's health. At this writing there is no medical treatment for lead contamination available to current or former camp residents.

A United States Agency for International Development pilot project to relocate 50 families from the Osterode and Cesmin Lug camps to the rebuilt Mahalla or another unspecified place of their choice is in its early stages. The NGO-funded reconstruction of two additional apartment blocks to accommodate 24 families is also underway. Many displaced Roma from the Mahalla are reluctant to return there, with lack of access to Kosovo welfare and problems accessing employment cited as reasons. Many of those who returned there in a 2007 pilot project subsequently returned to northern Kosovo, and some of those who remain are considering doing the same. The reluctance of key donors to engage fully with Serb authorities in the north on resettlement for those unwilling to return to the Mahalla stands in the way of a complete solution.

Impunity and Access to Justice

Despite the new energy and optimism that the deployment of the EULEX rule of law mission brought to Kosovo, the judicial branch remains the weakest of Kosovo's main institutions. At this writing, EULEX has yet to prioritize cases related to the March 2004 anti-Serbian and anti-Roma riots, or to develop a strategy for prioritizing the large number of war crimes files it inherited from UNMIK.

EULEX prosecutors and judges concluded three high-profile cases during 2009. The sole defendant charged with the 2001 bombing of the "Nis Express" bus, which killed 12 Serbs, was acquitted in March. The same month Gani Gashi was convicted and sentenced to 17 years' imprisonment for kidnapping and killing a fellow ethnic Albanian in central Kosovo in 1998. In April Gjelosh Krasniqi was convicted for the 1999 kidnap and murder of a Kosovo Albanian man and sentenced to seven years' imprisonment. In September EULEX arrested four Kosovo Serbs (including one woman) on suspicion of committing war crimes against Kosovo Albanians in 1999 around Novo Brdo.

Shortcomings in witness protection continue to impede justice for the most serious crimes, with witnesses unwilling to testify for fear for their safety. Kosovo still lacks a witness protection law, but the courts regularly fail to employ the array of protective measures that are available to them. EU and other western governments remain reluctant to accept witnesses and their families, despite the widespread recognition that it is the only effective means to protect witnesses in the most serious cases. The lack of EU consensus on Kosovo's status stands in the way of a common EU position on such relocation.

In July the ICTY Appeals Chamber affirmed the conviction and three-month sentence of Bajrush Mornia for intimidating a protected witness in an ICTY trial about alleged wartime abuses in Kosovo. It overturned the conviction of Astrit Haraqija for the same offense. Both men were on provisional release at the time of the verdict, having served the duration of the sentences imposed.

In March EULEX opened what it termed a "preliminary investigation" into the alleged transfers by the KLA in 1999 of around 400 Serbian and other captives to detention facilities in Albania. The Council of Europe investigation into the allegations by Swiss senator Dick Marty continued, but his visit to Kosovo, scheduled for 2009, was postponed for unspecified reasons. The Serbian War Crimes Prosecutor has also initiated an investigation. The Kosovo authorities have dismissed the allegations and refused to investigate them.

In July EULEX and KPS exhumed a mass grave containing remains of 11 individuals, presumed to be missing persons, in the village of Kmetovce, close to Gnjilane. According to the International Committee of the Red Cross (ICRC)

Kosovo, 1,885 persons, the majority Kosovo Albanian, remain missing from the 1999 conflict.

Human Rights Defenders

For most of the year the international Human Rights Advisory Panel (HRAP) continued to process its busy caseload of complaints against UNMIK, despite being understaffed and located in an office to which the public have no access, and a lack of cooperation from UNMIK. In October, however, UNMIK passed an administrative directive with immediate effect that effectively suspended the Panel's operations by requiring, at a time when one panel member post is vacant, that it can only sit with all three members present. The directive also removes jurisdiction over any alleged violations taking place after March 31, 2010.

In November 2008 the Panel ruled that UNMIK had violated the right to life by failing to conduct an adequate investigation into the February 2000 murder of the wife of the complainant Shaip Canhasi; at this writing UNMIK has yet to respond to the ruling. In June 2009 the Panel deemed admissible a claim by a group of Roma current and former residents of the lead-contaminated camps in Mitrovica, including in relation to alleged violations of the right to life, housing, and health, and the prohibition of inhuman and degrading treatment.

In March a public hearing was cancelled in the HRAP case against UNMIK brought by the families of the two Kosovo Albanian men killed by UNMIK police during a February 2007 demonstration. The cancellation followed EULEX and UNMIK statements that they could not guarantee security for such a hearing at any venue. The applicants' families refused to continue the hearing in private, and it was adjourned indefinitely. In September UNMIK offered financial compensation to the families of the two men if they agreed to drop their claims. The families rejected the offer.

In June, after a three-year delay in making an appointment, the Kosovo Assembly elected Sami Kurteshi as Kosovo's ombudsperson, with a five-year mandate. Acting ombudsperson Hilmi Jashari will remain as his deputy.

At this writing, almost 12 months after EULEX's full deployment, the EU Council has yet to approve the creation of an independent review mechanism for EULEX, or to give the mission authorization to initiate formal cooperation with the HRAP or Kosovo Ombudsperson, calling into question the EU's commitment to accountability for potential abuses arising from the exercise of the executive mandate of a flagship European Security and Defence Policy mission.

Key International Actors

Kosovo's international status remains uncertain. At this writing 63 countries have recognized Kosovo's independence, including 22 EU member states. Kosovo joined the World Bank and International Monetary Fund during 2009, but the decision of several EU states to intervene in support of Serbia's claim against Kosovo at the International Court of Justice underscored how divided the EU and United Nations remain on the issue.

The February 2009 visit by US Vice President Joe Biden underscored the Obama administration's continuation of Washington's financial and political support for an independent Kosovo.

In August NATO Secretary General Anders Fogh Rasmussen announced a downsizing of the Kosovo peacekeeping Force (KFOR) from 13,800 to 10,000 by January 2010.

TAJIKISTAN

Human rights violations in Tajikistan remain rampant, affecting disparate spheres of life, from housing to religion, political and media pluralism, and treatment in custody. As the Tajik government implements a broad urban renewal plan in cities around the country, it has forcibly evicted residents from their homes, offering little compensation and often relocating them to remote city outskirts. Due to the lack of an independent and effective judiciary, those who challenge evictions in court rarely have access to an effective remedy.

Torture is routinely used by law enforcement officials, and the Tajik government continues to deny human rights groups access to places of detention. In early 2009 Tajikistan adopted a new religion law that expanded already significant government restrictions on faith groups and worshippers.

The global economic recession has further weakened Tajikistan's shaky economy, which is heavily dependent on remittances from migrant workers working mostly in Russia. Remittances fell by 30 percent in the first quarter of 2009 compared to the same period in 2008, pushing even more Tajiks into poverty.

Institutional Human Rights Reform

In March 2008 President Emomali Rahmon signed a law that called for the creation of a Human Rights Ombudsman's Office. In May 2009 Zarif Alizoda, the president's former legal adviser, was named ombudsman. According to human rights groups in Tajikistan, Alizoda's office is still hiring staff and setting up procedures, and has yet to begin work in earnest. Still, the ombudsman did meet with representatives of Tajik civil society organizations on June 18, when all sides agreed to hold regular meetings on human rights issues, according to the Bureau of Human Rights and the Rule of Law, an NGO.

Property Rights and Forced Evictions

The government's culture of obfuscation on property rights and on broad public initiatives has made people vulnerable to eviction as the country's vast urban redevelopment projects unfold. The public has no information about the planned projects, no input into them, and individuals have no say about whether they can even remain in or return to refurbished areas. They receive no information about the status of their current housing or their future housing options, and residents of an area where building is set to begin only find out about the loss of their property when they receive official notification to vacate their home and move to a new address. Such notification can occur months before an expected move, or days before. Sergei Romanov of the Bureau of Human Rights and the Rule of Law estimates that roughly 650 people have been forced from their homes since the urban renewal process began in 2006.

Residents receive inadequate compensation for their property. Those who lived in the city centers have been relocated to the outskirts, and often to much smaller apartments. When property owners seek legal recourse, they almost always lose. Residents who resist eviction face a range of criminal charges.

A substantial portion of the population in rural areas and in the capital, Dushanbe, lives in so-called "unauthorized" housing. The maze of bureaucracies that homeowners have to navigate to build a house is so daunting—in 2008, building a new home required 49 different government documents—that few people have the legally binding documents for their residences. As a consequence, they have no right at all to compensation when the state forces them to move.

Torture

Torture is practiced by law enforcement officers and within the penitentiary system in a culture of near-impunity. It is often used to extract confessions from defendants, who during initial detention are often denied access to family and legal counsel. To date the Tajik government has refused all requests from human rights groups to visit detention sites, interrogation rooms, and prisons.

In February 2009 Khurshed Islamov was arrested on suspicion of the theft of US$40,000 from a casino in the Dushanbe suburbs. His attorney was only allowed to see him after seven days, and then only in the presence of law enforcement personnel. His mother, Nazokat Islamova, filed a complaint with the prosecutor's office alleging that her son had been tortured during his interrogation: when she saw her son shortly after he had been interrogated, he could not move without help because of his injuries. In July Islamov was sentenced to 23 years in prison.

Tajikistan's definition of torture does not fully comply with recommendations made to the country by the United Nations Committee against Torture in November 2006. In a small sign of progress, local and international human rights groups recently completed a campaign to document instances of torture in Tajikistan, as part of a two-year project funded by the European Union. That project, which was run in Tajikistan by the Bureau on Human Rights and the Rule of Law, determined that over the past two years there had been more than 90 cases of torture.

Freedom of Religion

In March 2009 President Rahmon signed a new religion law that heightens state repression of faith groups. Tajikistan has long curtailed freedom of religion and, under the pretext of battling terrorism, has banned several peaceful Muslim organizations. Under the new law, the state tightened its grip on religious groups: The government now determines where mosques can be built and how many, and where sermons can be given; has censorship authority over religious literature (including material from abroad) and control over children's religious education; and faith groups in Tajikistan must get government permission to contact foreign religious groups. The new law cites the primacy of the Hanafi school of Sunni Islam in Tajik life, which has alienated ethnic minorities such as Uzbeks and Pamiris, who practice Ismaili Shiism.

Certain Christian denominations, such as Jehovah's Witnesses, continue to be banned in Tajikistan. But the Tajik government has focused its restrictions largely on Muslims. A ban on the Salafi school of Sunni Islam came into effect in February 2009; Tajik officials have told rights groups that to be an adherent is not criminalized, but prosecutors have said that they intend to prosecute Salafists who propagate their beliefs. The state bans the wearing of headscarves in schools and universities and has expelled students who violate the prohibition. There continued to be reports of the Tajik authorities prosecuting alleged members of Hizb ut-Tahrir, an international Islamic organization that is banned in several countries in the region, and sentencing them to long prison terms on questionable evidence. In April authorities arrested at least 93 members of the Jamaat Tabligh movement in three cities including Dushanbe. The government has refused to release the names of the detained, their exact number, or the reason for their arrest.

Migrant Workers

Tajikistan's relentless poverty and high unemployment rate have pushed 797,000 Tajiks— one in eight of the population—to leave the country in search of work. Most have gone to Russia hoping to find work, very often in the construction sector. Unlike previous waves of migrants from the former Soviet republics, Tajiks now seeking work abroad are less well-educated, poorer, and have a weaker command of Russian, making them highly susceptible to exploitation.

In February 2009 Human Rights Watch released a report documenting widespread abuse of migrant workers in Russia, including Tajiks. While Human Rights Watch made recommendations in the report to Russian authorities for halting the exploitation, it has also urged the government of Tajikistan to take action against the employment agencies that have sent migrants into forced labor in Russia. To date, Human Rights Watch has not received a response from the government, and the employment agencies continue to operate as before.

Key International Actors

Tajikistan's new religion law drew criticism from the United Nations special rapporteur on freedom of religion or belief and the United States Commission on International Religious Freedom (USCIRF). The special rapporteur told the UN Human Rights Council on March 12 that the law "could lead to undue limitations on the rights of religious communities and could impermissibly restrict religious activities of minority communities." In its 2009 report the USCRIF criticized the law as "highly restrictive," and added Tajikistan to its Watch List because of its "marked decline in respect for and protection of freedom of religion or belief."

In addition to its annual human rights dialogue on September 23, the European Union held a civil society seminar in Dushanbe in July on the right to a fair trial and the independence of the judiciary. Civil society put forth a number of recommendations to bring Tajikistan's law and practice into compliance with international standards. At year's end the EU appeared to be moving ahead with a Partnership and Cooperation Agreement with Tajikistan, which had been frozen for years because of the civil war there.

TURKEY

The government's public announcement in summer 2009, and to the Turkish parliament in November, that it was committed to ensuring the human rights of Kurds in Turkey, was the most hopeful indication that a long-stalled reform process might be restarted. The realization of a plan to uphold minority rights for Turkey's different ethnic and religious groups would represent a fundamental departure from the variously assimilationist or repressive policies of the past, and offers the possibility of advancing the rights of all groups.

The obstacles to change remain clear. Numerous provisions of the current constitution restrict human rights and fundamental freedoms, and a new constitution must be a priority. There were continuing prosecutions and convictions of individuals who expressed nonviolent critical opinion or political views on the Kurdish issue, among other subjects viewed as controversial. Restrictions on press freedom remain a concern. Decisions of Turkey's Court of Cassation continued to flout international human rights law and the case law of the European Court of Human Rights, and demonstrate that the judiciary remains a site of institutionalized resistance to reform. The struggle to assert civilian control over the military in Turkey continues: A June change to the law on military courts ensures that military personnel will be tried in civilian courts for serious offenses, including forming criminal gangs and plotting coups.

The most notable foreign policy achievement of the year came with the signing of an agreement by Turkey and Armenia that opens the way to establishing diplomatic relations and reopening the long-closed border between the two countries. The decision is subject to parliamentary approval.

Freedom of Expression, Assembly, and Association

The criminalization of opinion remains a key obstacle to the protection of human rights in Turkey, although debate is increasingly open and critical. Prosecutions of journalists, writers, publishers, academics, human rights defenders, and officials of Kurdish political parties and associations sometimes resulted in convictions. Journalists and editors were frequently prosecuted for investigative reporting on matters such as the conduct of the military. Temporary closure of newspapers, and long-term restriction of access to websites, including YouTube, continued. The Doğan Media Group received two huge fines (amounting to over US$3 billion) for alleged tax evasion. The Organization for Security and Co-operation in Europe (OSCE) representative on freedom of the media expressed concern that "unprecedented" fines against a media group critical of the government threatened media plurality and hence media freedom in Turkey.

Restrictions on broadcasting in minority languages were progressively lifted in 2009. January saw the opening of a Kurdish-language state television channel, TRT Şeş, and in November there was an easing of restrictions on private channels broadcasting in minority languages.

The Court of Cassation ruled against the closure of the lesbian, gay, bisexual, and transgender (LGBT) Lambda Istanbul Solidarity Association in April. However, the court's ruling included the discriminatory condition that the association not "encourage lesbian, gay, bisexual, transvestite and transsexual behavior with the aim of spreading such sexual orientations."

Demonstrators deemed supporters of the Kurdistan Workers' Party (PKK) are treated similarly to the group's armed militants by courts. Following a March 2008 precedent decision by the General Penal Board of the Court of Cassation, individuals joining demonstrations where the PKK had called for public participation were to be charged with "membership" in the PKK for "committing a crime in the name of the organization." To date, hundreds of demonstrators, a significant proportion of them children, have been convicted or are on trial under these charges for their participation in sometimes violent demonstrations. Most of those on trial spend prolonged periods in pretrial detention.

Since November 2007 the pro-Kurdish Democratic Society Party (DTP), which has 20 members in parliament, has been faced with a closure case pending before the Constitutional Court for alleged separatist activities.

Human Rights Defenders

Three years after the January 19, 2007 murder of Turkish-Armenian journalist and human rights defender Hrant Dink, there was no progress in uncovering state involvement in the conspiracy behind his killing. There have been 10 trial hearings in Istanbul against 20 defendants, including the gunman. Eight gendarmes are on trial in Trabzon for basic negligence in failing to act on intelligence reports pointing to plans to murder Dink. Lawyers for the Dink family have called for their trial to be combined with the Istanbul murder trial; the lawyers have to date applied four times to the European Court of Human Rights complaining of violations of the right to life, fair trial, and the prohibition on discrimination.

In November 2009, 31 mainly Izmir-based members of trade unions affiliated with the public sector workers' trade union confederation KESK stood trial in Izmir on charges of being members of the PKK. The evidence against them mainly referred to their activities in support of such issues as Kurdish-language education. In Ankara in November lawyer Filiz Kalaycı, former head of the Ankara branch of the Human Rights Association and a member of the association's prison commission, stood trial with three other lawyers and the head of a prisoners' solidarity association on charges of PKK membership. The lawyers have been involved in the documentation of prisoners' complaints about prison conditions, ill-treatment, and disciplinary punishments, and there are concerns that they have been targeted for prosecution because of this work. Both proceedings are ongoing at this writing.

Torture, Ill-Treatment, and Killings by Security Forces

Police ill-treatment occurs during arrest, outside places of official detention, and during demonstrations, as well as in places of detention. In October Güney Tuna was allegedly beaten by seven police officers in Istanbul, leaving him with a broken leg and serious head injury that were not recorded in a routine custody medical report. There were far fewer reports than in the past two years of police violence against demonstrators during May 1 demonstrations in Istanbul, although the policing of demonstrations remains a concern, and in April security forces were allegedly responsible for shooting dead two demonstrators during an unauthorized demonstration near Halfeti, Urfa. From July 1 it was obligatory for all police officers in riot gear to wear numbered helmets, for purposes of identification.

The trial of 60 prison guards, gendarmes, and police officers in connection with the October 2008 death of Engin Çeber began in January 2009. Six of the defendants are in custody. Çeber collapsed in Metris Prison and died in hospital, an autopsy recording that he had suffered a brain hemorrhage after being repeatedly beaten.

Impunity

Turkish courts are notoriously lenient toward members of the security forces who are charged with abuse or misconduct, contributing to impunity and the persistence of torture and the resort to lethal force. Long delays and the lack of thorough and independent investigations by prosecutors contribute to impunity.

Of particular concern is the approach of Turkey's top court to the use of lethal force by the security forces. In June the Court of Cassation upheld the acquittal of four police officers for the killing of Ahmet and Uğur Kaymaz in November 2004 in the southeastern town of Kızıltepe. The court ignored substantial forensic evidence demonstrating that the father and 13-year-old son may have been victims of a summary execution. Lawyers for the Kaymaz family will apply to the European Court of Human Rights.

In July 2009 a second "Ergenekon" trial alongside the first began on the basis of second and third indictments probing the alleged plot to overthrow the government by senior retired military and gendarmerie personnel, figures associated with organized crime, journalists, and academics. There are now 192 individuals on trial, in the first such attempt in Turkey's modern history to bring coup plotters to justice.

The most significant attempt at bringing to justice state perpetrators of extrajudicial killings and "disappearances" began in Diyarbakır in September with the trial of a colonel, village guards, and informers for the murder of 20 individuals in the period 1993-95 in Cizre, Şırnak province.

Key International Actors

United States President Barack Obama's April 2009 visit to Turkey marked an important turning point in restoring the credibility of the US with the Turkish public after the US-led invasion of Iraq. The US has been supportive of moves to normalize Turkish-Armenian relations, and is dependent on Turkish support during the withdrawal from Iraq. It now has the potential to play a role in promoting respect for human rights in Turkey domestically for the first time in seven years.

Negotiations with the European Union over Turkey's accession to membership did not progress, with eight negotiation chapters remaining frozen because of stalemate over a divided Cyprus. The EU remains the most important international actor with the potential to foster respect for human rights in Turkey, but the deadlock in negotiations, and the public hostility of some EU member states to eventual EU membership for Turkey, have undermined the EU's leverage. The European Commission's annual report published in October included a more positive political assessment than in the past three years, while raising serious concerns about human rights protection in most areas. The report acknowledged the importance of the Ergenekon trial "as an opportunity for Turkey to strengthen confidence in the proper functioning of its democratic institutions and the rule of law."

Following a visit to Turkey, Council of Europe Commissioner for Human Rights Thomas Hammarberg issued two reports. One was critical of Turkey's continuing failure to recognize religious and ethnic minority groups other than Greeks, Armenians, and Jews—the commissioner urged Turkey to adopt numerous measures to uphold minority rights "with a view to fully aligning law and practice with the Council of Europe human rights standards." The second focused on the situation of migrants and refugees in Turkey.

TURKMENISTAN

The Turkmen government tightened repression in this already extremely repressive and authoritarian country. While retaining excessive restrictions on freedom of expression, association, and religion, it embarked on a new assault on freedom of movement and the right to education by preventing dozens of students studying in private universities abroad from leaving the country.

The authorities released two political prisoners, one of whom had served his full prison term, but they arrested and convicted a well-known environmental activist on trumped-up charges, later releasing him on condition that he renounce his Turkmen citizenship and immediately leave the country. Untold numbers of people continue to languish in Turkmen prisons following unfair trials on what would appear to be politically motivated charges.

The government presents international interest in its hydrocarbon wealth as an expression of international support for President Gurbanguly Berdymukhamedov's policies. A conflict that started in April 2009 between the Turkmen authorities and the Russian gas company Gazprom (over an explosion in a pipeline) served to intensify Western diplomacy aimed at convincing Turkmenistan to commit to supplying its gas via pipelines bypassing Russia.

Elections

The Office for Democratic Institutions and Human Rights of the Organization for Security and Co-operation in Europe (OSCE/ODIHR) did not send a full election observation mission to the December 2008 parliamentary elections in Turkmenistan, stating that "the current political context does not allow for a meaningful competition." About 90 percent of the candidates were members of the Democratic Party, which is led by Berdymukhamedov and is the only political party registered in Turkmenistan. Non-party candidates were nominated by state-controlled groups. Nongovernmental groups in exile reported pressure on individuals not affiliated with the state who attempted to register as independent candidates.

Freedom of Expression and Civil Society Activism

Independent NGOs and media cannot operate openly, if at all, in Turkmenistan. No independent organization has been permitted to carry out research on human rights abuses inside the country, and no international agency—governmental or nongovernmental—has had access to detention facilities.

Independent activists and journalists continue to be subjected to threats and harassment by security services. For example, in spring 2009 customs officials searched two civil society activists for nearly two hours at Ashgabad airport before allowing them to board a flight abroad. Radio Free Europe/Radio Liberty, a US government-funded media outlet, reported that its correspondents' telephone lines were disconnected during the December 2008 parliamentary elections, and one of its correspondents was interrogated and threatened by state security officers the same month.

Andrey Zatoka, an environmental activist who for two years had been banned from traveling abroad, was arrested on October 20 in Dashoguz. Zatoka was attacked by a man without warning while shopping for food at a local market. When Zatoka turned to police officers nearby to report the incident, the policemen proceeded to arrest him. On October 29 Zatoka was convicted and sentenced to five years' imprisonment on false charges of "causing injuries of medium severity." Security services pressured Zatoka to renounce his Turkmen citizenship and leave the country as an unofficial condition for his release. On November 6 the appeals court commuted Zatoka's sentence to a fine equivalent of US$350, and Zatoka and his wife were forced to leave for Russia the next day.

Political Prisoners, Enforced Disappearances, and Deaths in Custody

The harsh repression that prevents civic activism impedes determining the number of political prisoners. Only two individuals believed to be imprisoned for political reasons have been released in the past 12 months—activist Valery Pal in December 2008, and longest-serving political prisoner Mukhametkuli Aymuradov, arrested in 1994 and having served his full prison term, in May 2009. Well-known political prisoners from the era of Berdymukhamedov's predecessor Saparmurad

Niazov, including activists Annakurban Amanklychev and Sapardurdy Khajiev, remain behind bars. Also still imprisoned is the dissident Gulgeldy Annaniazov, who was arrested in June 2008 upon his return from exile and sentenced to 11 years' imprisonment on unknown charges.

There is no information about the fate of Ovezgeldy Ataev (Niazov's constitutionally designated successor) and his wife, who were imprisoned in 2007 just after Berdymukhamedov became president. The fate of about 50 prisoners implicated in the alleged November 2002 attack on Niazov's life likewise remains unknown, including that of former foreign minister Boris Shikhmuradov, his brother Konstantin Shikhmuradov, and the former ambassador to the OSCE, Batyr Berdiev. At least two persons serving prison terms after being purged from government service by Niazov died in prison in 2009 under unknown circumstances: Rejep Saparov, the former head of the presidential administration, and Khabibulla Durdyev, a former provincial governor.

Forum 18, an independent, international religious freedom group, reported that four Jehovah's Witnesses were imprisoned in 2009 for refusing compulsory military service on grounds of religious conscience: Shadurdi Ushotov, sentenced on July 13 to two years; Akmurat Egendurdiev, sentenced on July 29 to one-and-a-half years; and brothers Sakhetmurad and Mukhammedmurad Annamamedov, who were given two-year suspended sentences in November 2008 but transferred to prison in May 2009 following a further court ruling.

Criminal Justice System

Turkmenistan adopted a new criminal procedure code in May. The code has limited progressive clauses related to juvenile justice, appeals, and admissibility of evidence. While declaring that human rights should be respected, the code does not provide any viable mechanisms for their protection: it does not contain habeas corpus guarantees; does not provide for judicial oversight of investigative actions or detention; provides only limited alternatives to pretrial detention; and lacks guarantees for presumption of innocence.

Freedom of Movement

In late July and August Turkmen authorities prevented hundreds of students from boarding planes and crossing land borders to depart for study abroad. Authorities told the students that they did not have appropriate documents to leave the country: The required documents included an invitation from the university, a copy of its license, verification of its state-affiliation status, and a copy of the contract between the student and the university. After weeks of uncertainty, the Turkmen government started to grant permission to leave, but generally to those studying at state-run foreign universities. Dozens of students studying in private universities abroad were not allowed to travel. According to the Vienna-based Turkmen Initiative for Human Rights, at least five students of a private university who tried to leave Turkmenistan in October where informed at the border that they are banned from foreign travel.

Other arbitrary restrictions on foreign travel remain in place and activists and relatives of dissidents are often targeted. Unlike in previous years when some individuals were allowed to travel, there were no reversals of travel bans in 2009. Still banned from foreign travel are Rashid Ruzimatov and Irina Kakabaeva, relatives of an exiled former government official; the daughter of Gulgeldy Annaniazov and her family; Shageldy Atakov, an active Baptist, and his family; Ilmyrat Nurliev, a Turkmen Evangelical Church pastor; and Svetlana Orazova, sister of exiled opposition leader Khudaiberdy Orazov. Her husband Ovez Annaev, who since June 15, 2008, was barred from traveling abroad for medical treatment, died in November 2009.

Key International Actors

Turkmenistan's vast energy wealth and proximity to Afghanistan continue to prompt Turkmenistan's international partners to actively engage with the Turkmen government and to refrain from making human rights improvements an integral part of this engagement.

The European Union in July 2009 formally approved an Interim Trade Agreement (ITA) that gives preferential treatment and promises broader upgraded relations with Turkmenistan. The agreement had been stalled by the European Parliament for more than two years due to human rights concerns. The EU foreign ministerial decision announcing the ITA made no reference to human rights concerns, despite the fact that the European Parliament's April resolution green-lighting the agreement as "a potential lever to strengthen the reform process in Turkmenistan" had highlighted a number of specific steps the Turkmen government should take. These included the need for unconditional release of all political prisoners; removal of all obstacles to free travel; free access for independent monitors; improvements in civil liberties, including for NGOs; and the ability of civil society to develop free from undue government interference; freedom of religion; and open and democratic elections.

In June the EU held its annual human rights dialogue with Turkmenistan, but failed to use it to publicly highlight concern about Turkmenistan's poor human rights record or to urge concrete human rights reforms.

United States officials have generally stated that human rights are an important part of the US government's engagement with Turkmenistan. The US administration issued a statement of concern regarding the arrest of Andrei Zatoka, and raised concern at a high level about students in US-sponsored programs being unable to travel. But there is no evidence that human rights issues were pursued in a manner that fully reflected the serious human rights concerns raised in the State Department Country Reports on Human Rights Practices.

In December 2008 Turkmenistan was reviewed under the United Nations Human Rights Council's Universal Periodic Review (UPR) mechanism. The Turkmen government accepted a number of the recommendations, including acting against any form of harassment and intimidation of journalists, ensuring effective freedom of worship for all religious communities, and taking effective measures to allow NGOs to register and work freely. But it merely undertook to consider several important recommendations such as access to the country for UN special procedures, protecting human rights defenders from persecution, ending the practice of government appointment of editors to all media outlets and removing restrictions on critical media reporting of government policy, and ending torture in places of detention. It also chose to outright reject a number of key recommendations, such as the release of political prisoners, a transparent review of the political cases of past years, holding an independent inquiry into the 2006 death in custody of journalist Ogulsapar Muradova, and the lifting of travel bans on human rights defenders. To date there are no known steps taken by the Turkmen government to implement the UPR recommendations it accepted.

UKRAINE

Another period of instability characterized political life in Ukraine in 2009. Political scuffles between President Viktor Yushchenko and Prime Minister Yulia Timoshenko continued through most of the year. In March Yushchenko proposed a constitutional amendment that would restructure parliament into two chambers—ostensibly the intent is that a bicameral parliament will better withstand political crisis, but critics suggest that the amendment is also designed to limit presidential power after Yushchenko's term ends in 2010. On October 22, parliament voted against the president's proposal.

Relations with Russia continued to deteriorate. As 2008 drew to a close, tensions erupted over a Russian gas pipeline to Europe that crosses Ukraine, prompting the European Union to convene an emergency summit, held in January 2009, dedicated to regional energy security. Although Russia and Ukraine eventually reached a compromise, diplomatic disagreements aggravated political tension between the countries. In August 2009 Russian president Dmitry Medvedev accused the Ukrainian government of "anti-Russian" policies and declared that he refused to work with the Ukrainian government as composed. Ukraine responded by condemning Russia's "empire complex."

Despite some improvements, Ukraine's overall human rights record remains poor, with torture and ill-treatment in detention still commonplace. Hostility to asylum seekers, hate attacks on ethnic minorities, and Ukraine's staggering HIV/AIDS epidemic are problems that the government still fails to address effectively.

Criminal Justice System

The Criminal Justice and Law Enforcement Authorities reform enacted in 2008 achieved some positive changes in 2009, in particular better treatment of mentally ill detainees and improved adherence to due process requirements. However, Ukraine's criminal justice system is still plagued by a high number of arbitrary detentions, ill-treatment in custody, corruption among law enforcement personnel, and a weak judiciary.

Ukraine's human rights groups report high numbers of forced confessions extracted under torture, which are then allowed as evidence during trials. Impunity in the police force is widespread. However, in 2009 mobile monitoring groups composed of Ministry of Internal Affairs personnel and members of the public successfully drew attention to poor conditions in custody. The monitoring groups made 41 visits in the first six months of 2009, uncovering routine violations of detention procedures such as failing to register arrests and to read detainees their rights during arrest, as well as overcrowding and lack of natural light in cells. As a result, by May 2009 more than 50 law enforcement officials had been convicted of crimes related to abuse of power, including ill-treatment.

Treatment of Asylum Seekers and Refugees

With no clear migration policy and a flawed and restrictive refugee law that results in only 3 percent of asylum seekers obtaining refugee status, Ukraine continues to deny asylum seekers protection. However, the Department on Refugees and Asylum-Seekers of the State Committee on Nationalities and Religion has proposed legislation to address these shortcomings.

In 2009 Ukraine continued to refuse to grant refugee status to Chechens, since Ukraine does not recognize war as grounds for granting refugee status. On September 2, six people from the Democratic Republic of Congo, including at least one who sought asylum, were returned two days after arriving in Kyiv. The six were deported despite protests from representatives of the United Nations High Commissioner for Refugees in Ukraine, who were not granted access to them. The Ukrainian authorities cited an August 2009 law requiring persons from Africa, Asia, and several countries of the former Soviet Union entering Ukraine to have at least 12,620 hryvnia (approximately US$1,600), or risk being refused entry. This requirement poses a significant new obstacle for asylum seekers in Ukraine.

In 2009 Ukrainian authorities continued to comply with requests of other governments that violate fundamental refugee rights. In June they provided the Prosecutor General's Office of Kazakhstan with confidential documents from the refugee status applications of four Kazakhstan citizens, in direct violation of article 11 of the Ukrainian refugee law. As a result, Kazakhstan launched criminal cases against people who had provided, in support of the refugee applications, evidence that the four had suffered persecution.

Hate Crimes and Discrimination

Physical assaults and attacks on immigrants, refugees and asylum seekers, foreign students, Roma, and people of non-Slavic appearance persist in Ukraine. On January 18, 2009, a young Nigerian man was stabbed to death, and police promptly ruled out a racial motive without evidence supporting an alternate theory. Ukraine continues to lack legislation on racially motivated crimes, and the current civil and administrative anti-discrimination law does not provide proper protection and access to justice for the victims of racially motivated abuses.

Crimean Tatars continue to endure discrimination, including unequal land allocation, employment opportunities, and access to places of worship, and unavailability of education in their native language. A group of Tatars held a months-long demonstration in front of the government building in Kyiv to protest unequal access to land ownership. On July 30 the protestors were attacked by a group of young people while police looked on.

Health Issues and the HIV/AIDS Epidemic

The Ukrainian National AIDS Center reported 13,039 newly registered cases of HIV infection in the first eight months of 2009, nearly half among injection drug users. On March 19, parliament approved a national HIV/AIDS prevention and treatment program for 2009-13, aiming to provide treatment to 20,000 patients by 2013.

The government expanded provision of antiretroviral therapy (ART) for people living with HIV/AIDS, and increased drug users' access to medication-assisted treatment (MAT) with methadone and buprenorphine (widely recognized as the most effective means to treat opiate dependence and critical to HIV prevention and treatment support for opioid-dependent drug users), though not on a scale sufficient to address the need. As of November 1, 2009, 13,500 people living with HIV/AIDS were receiving ART, and over 4,800 people were receiving MAT in 102 healthcare institutions in 26 regions of Ukraine. There is no MAT in prisons, however, and limited access to ART.

In contrast, Ukraine has made little progress ensuring that patients who face severe pain have adequate access to opioid medications like morphine. Due to excessively restrictive narcotics regulations, tens of thousands of cancer and AIDS patients are likely to suffer from severe pain unnecessarily because they cannot get access to appropriate treatment.

Media Freedom

On June 9, 2009, parliament held the first reading of a draft law imposing criminal liability for violations of public morality, sparking harsh criticism from media and human rights groups concerned that overbroad or subjective definitions of the term "public morality" could make editors and journalists vulnerable to criminal prosecution for publishing otherwise protected speech.

There was welcome progress in the investigation into the murder of journalist Georgy Gongadze. On July 21 Alexei Pukach, a former Ministry of Internal Affairs official suspected of ordering Gongadze's killing in 2000, was arrested after being on the run for four years. He reportedly gave key evidence to investigators, including names of other people involved in the murder.

Key International Actors

On February 9, 2009, the UN Working Group on Arbitrary Detention released a report on its 2008 visit to Ukraine. The report noted positive changes in the detention practices of Ukraine's law enforcement agencies, but expressed concern at the high number of arbitrary detentions, the regular use of torture to extract confessions, and the lack of a separate juvenile justice system.

During an April 2009 visit to Ukraine, Sabine Leutheusser-Schnarrenberger, co-rapporteur of the Parliamentary Assembly of the Council of Europe's Committee on Legal Affairs and Human Rights, cautiously encouraged reform of the parliamentary system in Ukraine. She also expressed regret that those who ordered Georgy Gongadze's murder had still not been brought to justice. The Council of

Europe's European Commission against Racism and Intolerance (ECRI) recommended in May that Ukraine sign and ratify the International Convention on the Protection of the Rights of Migrant Workers and Members of their Families. The ECRI also noted problems in the response by Ukrainian law enforcement to racially motivated crimes.

Procedural obstacles hindered the appointment of a new Ukrainian judge in the European Court of Human Rights in 2009, requiring that judges be appointed ad hoc to hear cases brought against Ukraine. The court has nearly 10,000 pending applications against Ukraine, comprising 8.7 percent of all pending cases for the first eight months of 2009.

United States Vice President Joe Biden visited Ukraine in July 2009 to reassure the Ukrainian government of US support for Ukraine's bid for NATO membership. Biden also encouraged Ukraine to resolve the political crisis in the government, to implement economic reforms to alleviate growing unemployment and inflation, and to become less dependent on Russia for energy.

In 2009 the European Union introduced projects related to migration regulation and equal labor policies in Ukraine. On the initiative of the European Commission, an Eastern Partnership Civil Society Forum was established, including over 60 Ukrainian civil society actors.

Uzbekistan

The Uzbek government's human rights record remains atrocious. In October 2008 the European Union lifted a visa ban against several Uzbek officials, citing progress in human rights. Yet in the wake of that decision the Uzbek authorities intensified their crackdown on civil society activists, members of the opposition, and independent journalists. Torture and ill-treatment remain rampant and occur in a culture of impunity. A January 2008 law on habeas corpus has failed to protect detainees from torture.

Authorities continue to persecute religious believers who worship outside state controls, and freedom of expression remains severely limited. Government-initiated forced child labor during the cotton season continues.

The Uzbek judiciary lacks independence, and parliament is too weak to curtail the reach of executive power. The Uzbek government has ignored repeated calls for an independent inquiry into the May 2005 Andijan massacre, when state security forces killed hundreds of protestors, most of them unarmed.

Human Rights Defenders and Independent Journalists

The Uzbek authorities continue to intimidate, imprison, and torture human rights defenders, independent journalists, and other peaceful civil society activists, and they intensified repression following the EU's easing of sanctions in October 2008. At this writing the Uzbek government holds at least 14 civil society activists in prison because of their legitimate work. They include Gaibullo Jalilov, a member of the Human Rights Society of Uzbekistan whose human rights work focuses on independent Muslims, who was charged in September 2009 with upsetting the constitutional order and disseminating religious extremist materials; at this writing Jalilov is in pretrial detention. Sanjar Umarov, leader of the Sunshine Coalition, was released on amnesty on November 7, 2009, because of his health.

Farkhad Mukhtarov, a member of the Human Rights Alliance of Uzbekistan, was sentenced to five years in prison on October 2, on charges of fraud and bribery. Local defenders believe the charges were fabricated in retaliation for his human rights activities.

The government has moved vigorously to silence activists who oppose official corruption and abuse of power. On July 30 the Tailak district court sentenced Dilmurod Saidov, an independent journalist, to 12½ years in prison on trumped-up charges of extortion and forgery. Local activists believe Saidov was imprisoned because of his investigations into official corruption in Samarkand region and his advocacy for farmers' rights. Also in late July, authorities arrested Oyazimhon Hidirova, chair of the Arnasai branch of the International Human Rights Society of Uzbekistan, on charges of hooliganism, fraud, and tax evasion. In early June Hidirova had written to various officials protesting repeated, unlawful land confiscation and resale by the head of the regional government. Hidirova was released under an amnesty on August 30. In early October Ferghana-based human rights defender Ganihon Mamatkhanov was arrested on trumped-up charges of fraud and bribery. Mamatkhanov works for social and economic rights, including the rights of farmers, a number of whom were the victims of unlawful land confiscation earlier in 2009. Local rights defenders believe that his arrest was in retaliation for his public criticism of the government and his human rights activities.

In several incidents during April and May, five members of the Human Rights Alliance of Uzbekistan were attacked, threatened, and detained. On the morning of April 15, Alliance member Elena Urlaeva was leaving home with her five-year-old son, Mukhammad, when two men assaulted her. Shouting profanities, they told Urlaeva that she "should have left the country long ago." A week later an unknown assailant attacked Mukhammad, beating him repeatedly on the head with a stick and leaving him hospitalized with concussion. On May 27 Urlaeva and fellow Alliance members Salomat Boimatova and Ilnur Abdulov were detained as they travelled to the United Nations office in Tashkent to deliver their recent report on the status of human rights defenders in Uzbekistan. When they objected, Abdulov was severely beaten. Urlaeva was forced to sign a statement that she would cease human rights activities until after June 10, when EU and Uzbek representatives were scheduled to meet in Tashkent for their annual human rights dialogue.

From November 7 to 14, local authorities in six locations detained at least seven activists for attempting to meet with leaders of the Birdamlik opposition movement. Two Jizzakh-based human rights defenders, Mamir Azimov and Bakhtior

Khamroev, were beaten by law enforcement officers for meeting with the opposition leaders.

Criminal Justice, Torture, and Ill-Treatment

Torture and ill-treatment remain endemic to the criminal justice system. The Uzbek authorities have failed to address the culture of impunity for torture or to implement recommendations to combat torture made by the UN special rapporteur in 2003. In January 2008 a much-touted habeas corpus law went into effect in Uzbekistan, but the reform has done little to bolster the rights of defendants or prevent torture and ill-treatment in detention.

Human Rights Watch continued to receive numerous, credible reports of torture and ill-treatment, particularly during pretrial detention. Yet judges routinely ignored allegations of torture and refused to examine such claims. Kushodbek Usmonov, a 67-year-old independent journalist, testified during his trial in March 2009 that he had been beaten with hard objects in the groin and abdomen and had been threatened with rape after being forced to lie face down, naked. The judge reportedly ignored these allegations.

On December 30, 2008, Uzbek prison officials tried to force Alisher Karamatov, an imprisoned human rights activist, to sign a confession regarding a disciplinary violation. After he refused and threatened to complain to the Prosecutor's Office, officials forced Karamatov, who had recently suffered from tuberculosis, to stand outside in sub-freezing weather dressed only in his thin prison uniform. After three hours in the cold, Karamatov signed.

In mid-June 2009 officials at Jaslyk prison put the jailed dissident and poet Yusuf Jumaev in an isolation cell for eight days. His family said that during that time prison guards burned him by holding a hot electric teapot to his shoulders, and for at least two days denied him food and water, as well as use of a toilet.

Freedom of Religion

Although Uzbekistan's constitution ensures freedom of religion, authorities fiercely suppress any religious group that functions outside state control. In particular, authorities have intimidated, beaten, and imprisoned on false charges Muslims who are affiliated with independent organizations and clerics.

In three separate trials in June and July 2009, 32 followers of the late Turkish Muslim theologian Said Nursi were sentenced to prison terms ranging from 5 to 11 years for religious extremism. This brings to 58 the number of Nursi followers who have been imprisoned since late 2008.

Up to 60 pious Muslims in Shakhrihan district, Andijan region, were detained in June 2009 on suspicion of illegal religious activity. In August, 11 pious Muslim men were put on trial on religious extremism charges in Karshi. In November, at least 12 pious Muslim women were detained in Karshi, one of whom is a leader in a local mosque; the charges against them are not known.

Authorities continue to arrest members of minority religions for their peaceful religious activity. Three Jehovah's Witnesses and Pentecostal minister Dmitry Shestakov continue to serve lengthy prison sentences. According to Forum 18, an independent, international religious freedom group, on August 21, 2009, anti-terror police in Tashkent raided the worship service of the registered Donam Protestant church. Seven church members were arrested and four, including the pastor, were sentenced to 15-day prison terms. Christian literature was confiscated during the raid and later destroyed on court order.

The Andijan Massacre and the Situation of Refugees

The government has persisted in its refusal to investigate the 2005 massacre of hundreds of citizens in Andijan, or to prosecute those responsible for it. Instead, authorities have clamped down on any individual they believe to have participated in the events or who may know the truth about what occurred. The government's reliance on surveillance, interrogations, ostracism, and threats against survivors of Andijan and their families continues to trigger further refugees from the area.

On May 26, 2009, hours after a series of violent acts in the Andijan area, including at least one suicide bombing, police visited at least three homes of relatives of individuals imprisoned for alleged involvement in the May 2005 events or who had fled Uzbekistan in their wake.

The Uzbek government continues to work with Kyrgyz authorities to forcibly return Uzbek asylum seekers to Uzbekistan. Since 2005 more than a dozen people have been returned against their will. Haiatjon Juraboev, who was snatched off the streets of Bishkek, Kyrgyzstan, in September 2008, was sentenced in Tashkent to 13 years' imprisonment in February 2009 for religious extremism and illegal border crossing.

Child Labor

Forced child labor in the cotton industry remains a serious concern. Although since mid-2008 Uzbekistan has ratified two conventions prohibiting child labor, the government continues to force hundreds of thousands of schoolchildren into the fields to pick cotton and weed cotton fields.

Children as young as 10 pick cotton for two months a year. They live in filthy conditions, contract illnesses, miss school, and work from early morning until evening daily for little or no money. Hunger, exhaustion, and heat stroke are common. At least five children died during the 2008 harvest, according to the Environmental Justice Foundation.

Key International Actors

The Uzbek government remains uncooperative with international institutions, particularly UN bodies. It has refused to allow access to eight special rapporteurs, including those on torture and human rights defenders.

In December 2008 Uzbekistan's human rights record was reviewed under the Universal Periodic Review mechanism of the UN Human Rights Council. The government denied the existence of a number of well-documented human rights problems and rejected numerous recommendations, including that it release imprisoned human rights defenders and end harassment and intimidation of civil society activists.

The European Union's position on human rights in Uzbekistan remained disappointingly weak. Following a nearly year-long silence in the face of Tashkent's deteriorating rights record, EU foreign ministers on October 27, 2009, lifted the arms embargo against Uzbekistan, removing the last remaining component of the sanctions the EU had imposed after the Andijan massacre in 2005. The June 2009 human rights dialogue between the EU and Uzbekistan yielded no known results.

The United States government also appeared to have weakened its engagement on human rights in Uzbekistan, interpreted by many as a conscious choice to safeguard other interests being pursued by the administration. There were no known policy consequences stemming from new legislation introduced by congress in 2008, which provided for targeted sanctions and spelled out concrete human rights benchmarks the Uzbek government would need to meet in order to normalize relations with the US.

In September 2009 the director of the Organization for Security and Co-operation in Europe's Office for Democratic Institutions and Human Rights (OSCE/ODIHR), Janez Lenarcic, praised the Uzbek government for adhering to commitments it had made as an OSCE member state, including the release of some human rights activists and improvement of detention conditions, despite overwhelming evidence to the contrary.

IRAQ

The Quality of Justice

Failings of Iraq's Central Criminal Court

WORLD REPORT

2010

MIDDLE EAST
AND NORTH AFRICA

ALGERIA

Under a state of emergency imposed in 1992, and with President Abdelaziz Bouteflika easily winning reelection to a third term, Algeria continued to experience widespread human rights violations. These included restrictions on freedom of the media and assembly, police abuse of terrorism suspects under interrogation, impunity afforded to members of the security forces and armed groups for past crimes, and continued failure to account for persons forcibly disappeared by state agents during the civil conflict in the 1990s. On a lesser scale than in previous years, militant groups continued their deadly attacks, mostly targeting the security forces.

Presidential Election

On April 9, 2009, President Bouteflika won reelection with an official tally of 90 percent of the vote, against five challengers. He ran after parliament adopted with no debate a constitutional amendment in November 2008 abolishing a two-term limit for the presidency. Three well-established opposition parties, the Socialist Forces Front, the Rally for Culture and Democracy, and the Islamist Nahdha party boycotted the election, alleging that the conditions for a fair and transparent vote were absent.

Freedom of Expression and Assembly

The broadcast media are state-controlled and air almost no critical coverage of, or dissent on, government policies, but they do provide live telecasts of parliamentary sessions. Privately-owned newspapers enjoy a considerably freer scope, but repressive press laws, dependence on revenues from public sector advertising, and other factors limit their freedom to criticize the government, the military, and the powerful.

The penal code and press law impose prison terms of up to two years along with fines for defaming, insulting, or gravely offending the president, government officials, and state institutions.

In March 2009 Nadjar Hadj Daoud, the managing editor of the news website *al Waha*, began serving a six-month sentence for defamation in connection with a 2005 article accusing a local government official of numerous rape attempts against female coworkers. According to the New York-based Committee to Protect Journalists (CPJ), the court provisionally freed Daoud for medical reasons in consideration of injuries he had sustained in a stabbing a few weeks earlier. Daoud informed CPJ that a "corruption lobby" has lodged 67 complaints for defamation against him since 2003.

In January 2009 Hafnaoui Ghoul, a freelance journalist and member of the Djelfa section of the Algerian League for the Defense of Human Rights (ALDHR), was attacked by an assailant carrying a knife. Hafnaoui claimed to CPJ that local authorities had turned a blind eye to the assault. Ghoul has been frequently prosecuted for defamation over the past years because of his articles accusing officials and powerful individuals of corruption and abuse of power.

Holders of European or North American passports must obtain visas to enter Algeria, which the authorities frequently deny to journalists and human rights workers. Citizens of neighboring Morocco and Tunisia need no visas. However, on April 4 the authorities turned back Sihem Bensedrine, a Tunisian journalist and human rights defender invited by the ALDHR to monitor local media coverage of the presidential election, as she sought to enter Algeria. On April 9 police stopped and interrogated for four hours Moroccan journalists Hicham El Madraoui and Mahfoud Aït Bensaleh, who had come to cover the election for the Moroccan weekly *As-Sahara Al Ousbou'iya*. The two men also reported that they had been followed by plainclothes policemen and that their hotel room was ransacked.

Shortly before the presidential election, authorities confiscated copies of the French weeklies *L'Express, Marianne,* and *Le Journal du Dimanche,* allegedly for violating article 26 of the 1990 Information Code, which forbids the publication of anything that is deemed "contrary to Islamic and national values and human rights, or supportive of racism, fanaticism or treason." Their coverage of Bouteflika and the election campaign was apparently behind the ban.

A 2000 decree banning demonstrations in Algiers remains in effect. Authorities require organizations to obtain authorization from the local governor before holding public meetings.A large contingent of police converged on July 17, 2009, at a downtown Algiers auditorium in order to prevent a conference that organizations representing the victims of civil strife had organized under the title "The Memory of Victims toward the Reconstruction of a Society." The organizers, who said they had received no written notification of the ban, moved the event to the office of the Collective of the Families of the Disappeared in Algeria. In October the ALDHR received a written notification forbidding a meeting on the death penalty it had planned at an Algiers hotel.

Freedom of Religion

Ordinance 06-03, a 2006 law, prescribes prison terms for proselytizing by non-Muslims and forbids them from gathering to worship except in state-approved locations. Authorities refuse applications by protestant Christian groups to use buildings for worship, putting their members at risk of prosecution for worship in unauthorized places.

Impunity for Past Abuses

Over 100,000 Algerians died during the political strife of the 1990s. Thousands more were "disappeared" by security forces or abducted by armed groups fighting the government, and have never been located, dead or alive. Perpetrators of atrocities during this era continue to enjoy impunity. The legal framework for that impunity is the 2006 Law on Peace and National Reconciliation, which provides an amnesty to security force members for the actions they took in the name of combating terrorism, and to armed group members not implicated in the most heinous acts.

The law promises compensation for families of "disappeared" persons but at the same time makes it a crime to denigrate state institutions or security forces for the way they conducted themselves during the period of political strife. Organizations representing the families of the "disappeared" condemned the continued failure of the state to provide a detailed account of the fate of their missing relatives.

Incommunicado Detention, Torture, and the Death Penalty

Reports of long-term "disappearances" have been exceedingly rare in recent years. However, security services in plainclothes often carry out arrests without showing warrants and then sometimes hold terrorism suspects longer than the permitted 12 days before presenting them to a judge, and do not comply with the legal obligation to notify the family. The United Nations Committee against Torture, in its May 2008 examination of Algeria's report to the committee, expressed concern about reports that the legal limit of 12 days in pre-charge detention in terrorism cases "can, in practice, be extended repeatedly" and that "the law does not guarantee the right to counsel during the period of remand in custody, and that the right of a person in custody to have access to a doctor and to communicate with his or her family is not always respected."

For example, according to Algerian human rights organizations, plainclothes men arrested Moussa Rahli of Ouled Aïssa, in Boumerdes governorate, on March 17, 2009. His father's inquiries at nearby police stations and military barracks yielded no information on Rahli's whereabouts. Police returned to search the family's home on March 27 and confiscated Rahli's car, according to his father. It was not until around April 20 that the family learned that authorities were holding Rahli in Blida military prison.

Algeria amended its penal code in 2004 to make torture an explicit crime. The international Committee of the Red Cross regularly visits ordinary prisons in Algeria but not places of detention run by the powerful Department for Information and Security (DRS), an intelligence agency within the military.

Algerian courts pronounced scores of death sentences during 2009, many of them against defendants in terrorism cases and most of them in absentia. Algeria has observed a de facto moratorium on carrying out the death penalty since 1993.

Terrorism and Counterterrorism

Militant attacks were down dramatically compared to the mid-1990s, but Al Qaeda in the Islamic Maghreb (AQIM) continued to launch fatal attacks, directed mostly at military and police targets. Many of the attacks involved roadside ambushes using explosive devices and gunfire, such as a June 17, 2009 attack on a convoy near Bordj Bou Arreridj, 180 kilometers east of Algiers, that killed between 18 and 30 gendarmes, according to reports. AQIM also killed civilians at times. For example, it reportedly claimed responsibility for assassinating a shepherd in Houidjbet, near the eastern city of Tebessa, on March 14 on suspicion of collaborating with authorities.

On January 17, 2009, Hassan Mujamma Rabai Sa'id became the eighth Algerian held by the United States at the Guantanamo Bay detention facility to be returned to Algeria. Upon his arrival, the DRS reportedly placed Sa'id in incommunicado detention for a number of days and questioned him—as the DRS had done to the others who came from Guantanamo before him. Judicial authorities have charged most of the eight with serving a terrorist organization abroad; as of October 2009 they were free awaiting trial. Twelve Algerian detainees remained in Guantanamo as of November 2009.

Key International Actors

Algeria continued during 2009 its non-compliance with longstanding requests for country visits by special procedures of the UN Human Rights Council including the special rapporteurs on torture, on human rights while countering terrorism, and on extrajudicial, summary and arbitrary executions, and the Working Group on Enforced and Involuntary Disappearances.

Algeria "is a major [US] partner in combating extremism and terrorist networks such as Al Qa'ida and is our second-largest trading partner in the Arab world," stated the US government's *Advancing Freedom and Democracy* report of May 2009. The United States provides almost no financial aid to Algeria but is the leading customer of Algeria's exports, primarily gas and oil. The *Advancing Freedom* report stated that the US "continues to urge the government to decriminalize press defamation." Assistant Secretary of State Jeffrey D. Feltman on his visit to Algiers on October 20-21 made no public statements on this or any other human rights issue.

BAHRAIN

Bahrain's government in 2009 continued to subject freedom of expression, assembly, and association to arbitrary restrictions. The year saw increased confrontations between security forces and demonstrators protesting alleged discrimination by the Sunni-dominated government against the country's majority Shia population. Local rights groups accused authorities of using excessive force against protestors and subjecting detained opposition activists to torture and ill-treatment. In March and April clashes led to the deaths of a Pakistani worker (whose car was hit by a Molotov cocktail) and a Pakistani member of the security forces.

On April 11, Shaikh Hamad Bin Isa al-Khalifa, Bahrain's king, pardoned 178 opposition activists charged with and in some cases convicted of security-related offenses. However, the decree never appeared in the official gazette, leaving it unclear whether charges and prison terms might be revived.

On November 10, in line with a pledge it had made to the United Nations Human Rights Council, Bahrain established a National Institution for Human Rights, a government body charged with reviewing and developing legislation to comply with international human rights instruments.

Freedom of Expression and the Media

Authorities continue to use the press law (Law 47/2002) to restrict coverage of controversial matters, including official corruption. In May 2008 the government announced a new draft press law that would remove criminal penalties for most journalistic infractions but appeared to retain the option of criminal penalties for certain types of written or spoken comment, including those found to "harm national unity." The draft still awaits approval by the National Assembly at this writing. Several journalists faced criminal prosecution under the current law for articles alleging favoritism and corruption by government agencies.

Several journalists told Human Rights Watch that Ministry of Interior officials contacted them to complain after they published articles that were even mildly critical of government policies, and in some cases intervened to prevent publication of information. In April 2009 authorities ordered the closure of the daily *Akhbar al-Khaleej*, citing violations of the press law, but lifted the ban after 24 hours.

The country's sole residential internet service provider, Batelco, is government-owned. The independent Bahrain Center for Human Rights (BCHR) reported that in 2009 authorities blocked over 1,000 websites, including sites of political forums, blogs, newspapers, and human rights organizations such as the Arab Network for Human Rights Information.

In June 2009 the University of Bahrain, the country's sole public university, punished business student Noor Abbas by revoking one year of her academic record after she circulated a statement criticizing university policies and facilities. The university later reduced Abbas's punishment to "three warnings," meaning one more infraction would result in her expulsion. Abbas consequently ceased her student activism.

In November 2008, after several Bahraini rights and opposition activists held meetings in Washington, DC, Interior Minister Rashid bin Abdullah al-Khalifa threatened them with prosecution for violating article 134 of the penal code, which states that citizens who fail to obtain government permission to attend meetings abroad to discuss Bahraini domestic affairs may be subject to prison terms and fines.

Freedom of Assembly

Law 32/2006 requires the organizers of any public meeting to notify the head of Public Security at least three days in advance, and authorizes that official to determine whether a meeting warrants police presence on the basis of "its subject ... or any other circumstance." The law stipulates that meeting organizers are responsible for "forbidding any speech or discussion infringing on public order or morals," but leaves "public order or morals" undefined.

The BCHR reported that authorities forced the Al-Attar Center to cancel an August 2009 event at which several opposition leaders were scheduled to speak. Interior Ministry officials informed the center's president that they would deploy security forces to stop the event, and pressured the administrator to sign a statement taking personal responsibility if the event was held. On the day of the event, security forces prevented anyone from approaching the center.

Civil Society and Freedom of Association

The government continues to deny legal status to the BCHR, which it ordered to be dissolved in 2004 after its then-president accused the prime minister of corruption and human rights violations. Several other groups, including the National Committee for the Unemployed and the Bahrain Youth Human Rights Society (BYHRS), attempted in 2005 to register with the Ministry of Social Development, as required by law, but at this writing have received no response to their applications. As of October 2009, Muhammad al-Maskati, president of the BYHRS, was facing up to six months in jail and/or a fine on charges related to working for an unrecognized association.

In 2007 the Ministry of Social Development drafted new legislation on civil society organizations, but at this writing the ministry has not yet submitted the draft to parliament. The draft law contains some improvements over the existing Law 21/1989, but includes numerous provisions incompatible with international standards. A version of the draft law circulated in November 2007 authorizes the Ministry of Social Development to close any organization for up to 60 days without a court order if it deems the organization to have violated any Bahraini law, including the associations law.

Bahrain has ratified some International Labour Organization conventions, but neither of the two core conventions governing freedom of association. Law 33/2002 permits workers to form and join trade unions.Contrary to recommendations of the ILO Committee on Freedom of Association, a November 2006 edict by the prime minister remains in force prohibiting strikes in numerous sectors of the economy on the grounds that they provide essential services.

Migrant Worker Rights

There are an estimated 462,139 migrant workers in Bahrain, primarily from South Asia. In May 2009 Minister of Labor Majeed al-Alawi announced a proposed revision to Bahrain's *kafala* (sponsorship) system designed to reduce the risk of exploitation and abuse of migrant workers. The former system tied migrants' work visas and immigration status to their employers, enabling employer abuses and preventing workers from changing jobs or leaving the country. Under the amended law, which was adopted on August 1, the government officially sponsors each worker, allowing him or her to more easily change employers. At this writing it remains unclear whether the reform has been fully implemented. Bahrain's business community strongly opposed the changes, and workers still need the de facto sponsorship of an individual or company in order to remain in the country legally. Migrant workers complain that some employers illegally withhold passports and fail to pay wages.

The amended law excludes migrant domestic workers, who are at especially high risk of abuse due to their isolation in private homes. In 2009 prominent cases involved physical abuse, forced confinement, and the death of domestic workers.

Women's Rights

In May 2009 Bahrain passed its first written personal status law (Law 19/2009), but it applies only to Sunnis. Shia religious scholars demand a constitutional guarantee that the personal status law cannot be amended, while women's groups are pressing for a unified personal status law for all citizens. The government said that it is working toward social consensus in order to pass a personal status law applicable to Shia as well.

Sharia court judges—generally conservative religious scholars with limited formal legal training—decide marriage, divorce, custody, and inheritance cases according to their individual reading of Islamic jurisprudence and without reference to codified law. They consistently favor men in their rulings and are unapologetically adverse to women's equality. It remains unclear whether codification has alleviated these problems for Sunni women.

In July 2009 the semi-official Supreme Council for Women launched a campaign calling for equal nationality rights. Article 4 of the Citizenship Law of 1963 does not allow Bahraini women married to non-Bahraini men to pass on their nationality to their children, discriminating against more than 2,000 families in Bahrain. The king endorsed Law 35/2009, which mandates that children of Bahraini women married to non-Bahrainis pay the same fees as citizens for government services such as health, education, and accommodation.

Counterterrorism Measures

In August 2006 the king signed into law the "Protecting Society from Terrorist Acts" bill, despite concerns expressed by the UN special rapporteur on human rights while countering terrorism that it contained excessively broad definitions of terrorism and terrorist acts. The law also allows for extended periods of detention without charge or judicial review.

In February 2009 judicial authorities charged several high-profile opposition figures under the counterterrorism law. They were among those freed as a result of the king's April pardon.

Torture and Ill-Treatment

Local rights groups reported numerous allegations of due process violations, including 11 televised confessions that appeared to have been coerced. The government denied that officials had subjected any detainees to torture or inhumane treatment. In its submission to the UN Human Rights Council's Universal Periodic Review mechanism in April 2008, Bahrain stated that "there are no cases of torture in the kingdom."

Decree 56/2002, which confers immunity from investigation or prosecution on government officials alleged to be responsible for torture and other serious human rights abuses committed prior to 2001, remains on the books.

Key International Actors

Bahrain hosts the headquarters of the United States Navy's Fifth Fleet and provides logistical support for military operations in Iraq and Afghanistan.

EGYPT

Egypt continued to suppress political dissent in 2009. The Emergency Law (Law No. 162 of 1958) remained in force, providing a basis for arbitrary detention and unfair trials. The government has never confirmed the number of those detained; Egyptian human rights organizations estimate that between 5,000 and 10,000 people are held without charge.

Authorities harassed rights activists, and detained journalists, bloggers, and members of the Muslim Brotherhood (the banned organization that is the country's largest opposition group). Authorities used lethal force against migrants and refugees attempting to cross into Israel, and forcibly returned asylum seekers and refugees to countries where they could face torture.

Freedom of Assembly and Association

Security forces continued to arbitrarily detain peaceful protestors. In January 2009 security forces arrested journalists covering a protest against Israel's military intervention in Gaza. Muslim Brotherhood representatives said in March that security forces had arrested at least 711 of their members since the start of the Gaza conflict in late December, mostly in connection with the demonstrations they organized. Since then the government has arrested hundreds of Muslim Brothers and charged them with membership in an illegal organization, including senior leaders such as Abdelmenoim Abolfotouh.

Young activists called a nationwide strike over a range of issues for April 6 that was met with heavy security deployment. Police arrested at least 40 people in Cairo, Kafr al-Shaikh, and elsewhere, including journalists covering the protest.

Egypt's law governing associations, Law 84/2002, provides criminal penalties that stifle legitimate NGO activities, including for "engaging in political or union activities." Authorities have not made public proposed amendments to the NGO law, but NGOs have expressed concern at the failure to consult them thus far. The law governing political parties, Law 40/1977, empowers a committee chaired by the ruling National Democratic Party to suspend other parties' activities "in the national interest."

Freedom of Expression

Security officers targeted bloggers and journalists who criticized government policies or exposed human rights violations. State security officers arrested blogger
Diaa Eddin Gad on February 6, after he criticized Egypt's policy toward Gaza, and
detained him without charge under successive emergency law orders before
releasing him on March 27. Kareem Amer (real name `Abd al-Karim Nabil
Suleiman) has been in Borg El Arab prison since November 7, 2006, for writing
about Muslim-Christian tensions in Alexandria and criticizing President Hosni
Mubarak and Al-Azhar religious institution on his blog. On February 22, 2007, a
court sentenced him to four years in prison for "insulting the president," "spreading information disruptive of public order," and "incitement to hate Muslims."
Authorities detained Hany Nazeer, another blogger, on October 3, 2008; at this
writing he remains in Borg El Arab prison under the emergency law and is denied
visits. Nazeer had voiced opinions critical of Christianity and Islam. Musad Abul
Fagr, who criticized rights violations against Sinai Bedouins, remains in prison
despite several court orders for his release. He was first detained in December
2007.

Courts sentenced journalists to prison terms under penal code provisions that
criminalize defamation. Officials frequently press charges of defamation against
individuals who criticize them for corruption. In June 2009 a court sentenced the
editor of the weekly *Al Mugiz* to six months' imprisonment for allegedly slander-
ing parliamentarian Mustafa Bakri.

Airport security officials arrested three bloggers in July and detained them for five
days, and in June detained blogger Wael Abbas for eight hours and confiscated
his laptop after he criticized the government in the presence of National
Democratic Party officials at a conference in Sweden. Authorities detained two
members of the Center for Trade Union and Workers Services at Cairo airport for
several hours in September and again in October while on their way to confer-
ences abroad.

Labor Rights

Egypt witnessed waves of protests and unauthorized strikes throughout 2009, from textile workers in Mahalla and Menoufia demanding better pay, to public transit drivers demanding exemption from high traffic fines. Security officials harassed strike leaders, and employers threatened reprisals. Under Egyptian Labor Law No. 35/1975, the official Egyptian Trade Union Federation (ETUF) or the government must approve all strikes.

Egyptian labor law also prohibits the formation of any union not sanctioned by the government, and requires workers to be members of the ETUF. In December 2008 real estate tax collectors who had successfully conducted several strikes voted to establish an independent trade union. In April 2009 the Ministry of Finance implicitly recognized the union by approving the Real Estate Tax Authority (RETA) application to establish a Social Care Fund, which provides retirement benefits to union members. Members, however, have been subjected to harassment and intimidation, systematic attempts to discredit union leaders, and arrests of members and restrictions on their movement. In August, in response to a complaint by ETUF president Hussein Megawer, the Office of the Public Prosecutor summoned RETA president Kamal Abu Eita for questioning.

Torture and Ill-Treatment

Police and security forces regularly engage in torture and brutality in police stations and detention centers, and at points of arrest. On May 17, 2009, two state security officers pushed Fares Barakat off a fourth-floor balcony when he asked to see an arrest warrant. In hospital intensive care Barakat was handcuffed to his bed.

In August police arrested Rajai Mounir Sultan, who has mental disabilities, as he walked along the beach in Alexandria. They beat him at the police station, fracturing his skull. On November 7 the Alexandria criminal court sentenced Col. Akram Soliman to five years' imprisonment and a fine of 10,000 Egyptian pounds (US$1,838) for using excessive force and causing Sultan permanent disability.

Women's and Girls' Rights

Egypt still lacks a legal environment that protects women from violence, encourages victims to report attacks, or deters perpetrators from committing abuses. A 2009 survey by the National Council for Women, a government-sponsored women's group, found that 62.6 percent of women suffer domestic violence and that four out of five men admit being violent toward their spouse. In July 2009, in a positive step, the government delivered informational booklets on sexual harassment to mosques across the country, but women's groups in Egypt have called for additional measures including legislation.

In August 2009 authorities for the first time arrested and charged a man for circumcising a young girl, under a 2008 law criminalizing the practice.

HIV/AIDS and Privacy Rights

In January 2009 police in Cairo arrested 10 men on suspicion of having consensual sex with other men, forcibly tested them for HIV, beat them, and charged them with the "habitual practice of debauchery"—interpreted in Egyptian law to include criminalizing consensual sex between adult men.

Freedom of Religion

Although Egypt's constitution provides for equal rights without regard to religion, discrimination against Egyptian Christians, and official intolerance of Baha'is, some Muslim sects, and Muslims who convert to Christianity continue. In a positive move, however, on March 9 the Ministry of Interior issued a decree allowing Baha'is and other adherents of "non-recognized" religions to obtain essential identification documents without having to misidentify themselves as Muslims or Christians.

On several days in March, scores of men in the village of al-Shuraniya, in Sohag, attacked the homes of Baha'is, throwing rocks and Molotov cocktails. The police dispersed the crowds but did not make any arrests. Disputes between Muslim and Christian Egyptians flared into violent clashes on several occasions, resulting in deaths and injuries as well as destruction of property. In May a fight between

Muslims and Christians in Bulak al-Dakrour quickly escalated into a shoot-out that injured several people. Authorities used the emergency law to arrest those involved in clashes, but failed to fully investigate many incidents.

Refugees and Migrants

As of November, Egyptian border guards in 2009 had shot dead 16 migrants attempting to cross the Sinai border into Israel. An Egyptian official in September said this policy was to deter migrants from approaching the border.

Egypt continues to detain refugees and migrants and charge them with illegal entry before military courts that do not meet international fair trial standards. Egypt still denies officials of the United Nations High Commissioner for Refugees access to detained refugees and migrants, preventing them from making asylum claims. Authorities also continued to deport refugees and migrants without assessing their protection needs. In December 2008 and January 2009, Egypt violated the international prohibition against refoulement by forcibly repatriating at least 45 Eritreans.

Key International Actors

The United States remains Egypt's largest donor, but significantly reduced its funding for democracy and human rights in 2009. The United States also agreed to Egyptian demands not to directly fund unregistered organizations. On August 18 President Mubarak visited Washington, DC for the first time in four years.

On June 4 President Barack Obama chose the occasion of a speech at Cairo University to declare US intent to rebuild a relationship of trust with the Muslim world.

IRAN

Following the disputed June 12 presidential election and the massive protests it provoked, the government unleashed the most widespread crackdown in a decade. Security forces were responsible for at least 30 deaths, according to official sources. On August 13, Judiciary spokesman Ali Reza Jamshidi said that authorities had detained 4,000 people following the election, mostly in street protests that were largely peaceful. Security forces also arrested dozens of leading government critics, including human rights lawyers, whom the government held without charge, many of them in solitary confinement. The Judiciary, the Revolutionary Guard, the Basij militia, and the Ministry of Intelligence—all of which report to Supreme Leader Ali Khamenei—were responsible for many serious human rights violations. Meanwhile, long-standing human rights issues, including restrictions on freedom of expression and association, religious and gender-based discrimination, and the frequent use of the death penalty, including on juvenile offenders, continued unabated.

Torture and Ill-Treatment of Political Prisoners

Following the disputed election, both ordinary protestors and prominent opposition figures faced detention without trial, harsh treatment including sexual violence and denial of due process including lack of access to lawyers of their choosing. Human Rights Watch documented at least 26 cases in which detainees were subjected to torture and/or coerced to make false confessions, though local activists believe that there were many more such cases. Some released detainees told Human Rights Watch that they were held in solitary confinement, and deprived of food and proper healthcare. Security forces used beatings, threats against family members, sleep deprivation, and fake executions to intimidate detainees and to force them to confess that they instigated post-election riots and were plotting a "velvet coup." The government held a series of show trials in which prominent political figures such as former Vice President Mohammad Ali Abtahi, Mohamed Atrian Far, Saeed Hajarian, Saeed Shariati, Abdullah Momeni, Hedayat Aghaie, and journalists and analysts such as Maziar Bahari, Amir Hussein Mahdavi, and Hussein Rassam publicly "confessed" to these charges.

Freedom of Expression

Iranian authorities continued to imprison journalists and editors for publishing critical views, and strictly controlled publishing and academic activities.

In the aftermath of the election authorities arrested more than 30 journalists and bloggers. Some imprisoned journalists and their families claimed that security forces subjected them to mistreatment and abuse during detention.

Throughout 2009 Iran's National Security Council gave newspapers formal and informal warnings against covering issues such as human rights violations and social protests. The Ministry of Culture and Islamic Guidance continues to monitor and censor independent newspapers before publication.

On June 15 the authorities suspended the publication of Kalameh Sabz (The Green Word), a newspaper owned by opposition presidential candidate Mir Hossein Mousavi. On August 17, *Etemad Melli*, a newspaper aligned with another candidate, Mehdi Karrubi, was shut down for publishing a letter by Karrubi alleging that some post-election detainees in Iran were sexually harassed and raped in detention.

State universities prohibited some politically active students from registering for graduate programs despite undergraduate test scores which ordinarily would have guaranteed them access.

Following the election, the government sharply increased restrictions on domestic and foreign media, detaining at least two journalists working with foreign outlets and prohibiting at least a dozen journalists from covering the post-election developments, forcing them to leave the country. In early October security forces confiscated the passports of three prominent Iranian journalists—Badrolsadat Mofidi, Farzaneh Roostai and Zahra Ebrahimi—at Tehran airport, preventing them from leaving Iran.

The government systematically blocks Iranian and foreign websites that carry political news and analysis and disrupted SMS services prior to gatherings by opposition groups.

Freedom of Association

The government increased restrictions on civil society organizations that advocate human rights and freedom of speech. Security forces on December 23, 2008 shut down the Center for Defenders of Human Rights, led by 2003 Noble Peace Prize Laureate Shirin Ebadi. The authorities later threatened human rights lawyers associated with the center and demanded that they stop cooperating with Ebadi.

On August 17, on the basis of a warrant issued by Saeed Mortazavi, Tehran's prosecutor general, officials shut down the Association of Iranian Journalists on the day of the association's annual meeting, putting an end to operations of the only independent and the largest journalists' association in Iran, with more than 3,700 members.

On January 21, Minister of Science, Research and Technology Mohammad Mehdi Zahedi declared Daftar-e-Tahkim Vahdat (Office for Consolidating Unity), a national independent student association an illegal organization, and prohibited it from continuing to operate on the premises of any university. On October 2, authorities arrested 14 of the association's leaders when they met informally at a park in northern Tehran. The government also continues to ban the activities of civil society organizations such as Volunteer Actors (a resource center for civil society organizations), the NGO Training Center, and the Rahi Institute, all led by prominent civil society activists and all of which the government had arbitrarily shut down in 2007 and 2008.

Since 2006, authorities have responded harshly to workers, teachers, and women's rights groups who advocate for better working conditions, better wages, benefits, and demands for changes in discriminatory laws. In 2009 the authorities arrested union leaders, women activists, and suppressed gatherings of teachers and workers.

Death Penalty

Iran carries out more executions annually than any other nation except China. These executions frequently occur after unfair or political crimes with inadequate access to legal counsel. In 2009 authorities hanged 20 persons in the city of Karaj on charges of drug trafficking, and 13 members of Jondollah, an armed opposition group operating in Sistan and Baluchistan province.

Iran leads the world in the execution of juvenile offenders. As of October Iran had executed three juvenile offenders in 2009. Iranian law allows death sentences for persons who have reached puberty, defined by Iranian law as age 9 for girls and 15 for boys. At least 130 other juvenile offenders are currently on death row. In many cases these sentences followed unfair trials.

On January 21 Iran executed a 21-year-old Afghan citizen Molla Gol Hassanm, for a crime allegedly committed when he was 17 years old. On May 1 Iran secretly hanged Delara Darabi, 22, accused of a murder committed when she was 17, despite a flawed trial and a two-month stay of execution issued on April 19 by Ayatollah Shahroudi, Head of the Judiciary. On October 12 despite an initial pardon by the victim's family, authorities executed Behnoud Shojaie for a killing that he committed in 2005, when he was 17.

Human Rights Defenders

The government escalated its crackdown on human rights lawyers in 2009, subjecting some to arbitrary detention, travel bans, and harassment. Since the contested June 12 election, authorities arrested at least four human rights lawyers, including Abdolfattah Soltani, Shadi Sadr, Mohammad Mostafayee and Mohammad Ali Dadkhah. The government's crackdown on such prominent lawyers was an attempt to intimidate not only them but also younger, less prominent lawyers who are considering representing political detainees.

Judiciary officials did not allow families of detainees to choose prominent independent human rights lawyers to represent their detained family members. Family members of detainees said that officials told them that if they picked from those lawyers, their loved ones would "stay in prison for a long time." Several released detainees told Human Rights Watch that they were forbidden to name Shirin Ebadi or other prominent human rights lawyers when they applied for an attorney.

Treatment of Minorities

The government continues to deny members of the Baha'i faith, Iran's largest non-Muslim religious minority, freedom of religion. In May 2008 authorities arrested seven leaders of the national organization of Baha'i based on fabricated security related accusations. The government accused them of espionage without providing evidence and has denied their lawyers request to release them on bail and promptly conduct a free and fair trial. As of November 2009 the seven remain in detention.

In the northwest provinces of Azerbaijan and Kurdistan, the government restricts cultural and political activities, including the organizations that focus on social issues. The government also restricts these minorities from promoting their cultures and languages.

Key International Actors

The government accused foreign media and governments of instigating demonstrations after the contested presidential election in mid-June, expelled most foreign correspondents, and arrested Iranian nationals employed in the British embassy in Tehran.

Following the elections, the Obama administration condemned violence against protestors and urged respect for human rights in Iran, while steering clear of language that would imply support for the opposition movement.

On October 26, Sweden, which then held the European Union presidency, issued a strong statement condemning the human rights situation in the aftermath of the election, and in particular the rise in death sentences, the mass trials of around 150 prisoners accused of crimes against national security, and the arbitrary detention of journalists, human rights defenders and political activists.

Since 2005 the government has prevented independent experts of the United Nations Human Rights Council from visiting to investigate alleged human rights violations. On November 20, the UN General Assembly's Third Committee, which comprises all the member states of the General Assembly itself, approved a resolution criticizing Iran for "harassment, intimidation and persecution, including by arbitrary arrest, detention or disappearance, of opposition members" as well as "violence and intimidation by government-directed militias."

IRAQ

Human rights conditions in Iraq remain extremely poor, especially for displaced persons, religious and ethnic minorities, and vulnerable groups such as women and girls, and men suspected of homosexual conduct. Iraq marked the June 30, 2009 withdrawal of United States combat forces from its towns and cities with parades and a national holiday. In the subsequent weeks, violence shook the country as extremists launched multiple attacks in several locations.

Serious tensions between the Kurdistan Regional Government (KRG) and the Iraqi central and provincial governments continued over control of territories lying between the mainly Kurdish- and Arab-inhabited areas in northern Iraq. Escalating conflict there worsened the human rights situation of non-Kurdish and non-Arab minority groups living in these contested areas.

Political Developments

In January 2009, 14 of Iraq's 18 governorates held provincial elections (the three governorates comprising the Kurdistan region had their elections in July; no elections were held in the disputed Kirkuk governorate). The participation of more political parties, in particular Sunni Arab parties, resulted in a dramatic change of power in areas where Sunni Arabs had boycotted the 2005 elections, notably in Nineveh governorate. Overall, the election results reflected sectarian divisions.

On June 24, 2009, the Kurdistan National Assembly (the regional parliament) passed a draft regional constitution that laid claim to disputed areas, provoking outrage from central government leaders. The KRG insists, in the face of central and provincial government recalcitrance, that the referendum mandated by article 140 of Iraq's 2005 constitution finally be held (the constitutional deadline was December 31, 2007), confident that the referendum would endorse the incorporation of the disputed areas into the semi-autonomous Kurdish region.

Iraqi security forces in July 2009 raided Camp Ashraf, an area controlled for over two decades by several thousand members of an Iranian opposition group, the Mojahedin-e Khalq Organization. The raid, in which the government tried to assert its authority by establishing a police station inside the camp, resulted in the deaths of 11 Camp Ashraf residents, some by gunfire, and dozens injured. The government said it would conduct an investigation into the incident, but as of mid-November it had provided no information about the progress of any investigation or its results.

In November Iraq signed the Convention on Cluster Munitions, an international treaty that prohibits the use, production, and transfer of cluster bombs.

Attacks on Civilians and Displacement

Civilians remained the targets of attacks across the country. In the first six weeks following the June 30 withdrawal of US forces from cities to their bases, coordinated bombings and other violence killed more than 700 Iraqis, mainly Shia. On August 19, coordinated truck bombs outside the foreign and finance ministries in Baghdad killed nearly 100 people and wounded more than 600. On October 25, two vehicle bombs, driven by suicide bombers, destroyed three major government buildings, including the Ministry of Justice. That attack, the country's deadliest in more than two years, killed more than 155 people and wounded over 500.

Sunni Arab insurgents appeared to have been responsible for these and other attacks, such as the January and April 2009 bombings of Baghdad's Kadhimiyya mosque, a major Shia place of worship, killing more than 100 people. The perpetrators also targeted groups of Shia refugees waiting for food rations, children gathering for handouts of candy, religious pilgrimages, weddings, funerals, mosques, and hospitals in Shia areas. Sunni leaders forcefully condemned such attacks, and Shia militias refrained from engaging in widespread reprisal attacks.

Displacement caused by sectarian violence continued, but economic pressures and difficulties maintaining legal status in Syria, Jordan, and Egypt induced some refugees to return. The government remained without a workable plan for the return of Iraqis displaced internally or who had fled to neighboring countries, according to the office of the United Nations High Commissioner for Refugees. In Baghdad returnees were seldom able to reclaim their former homes. In rural communities many returnees found their houses destroyed or in complete disrepair, and they lacked access to income and basic services including, water, electricity, and healthcare. With the resurgence of attacks in the latter half of 2009, some returnees reportedly found themselves forcibly displaced again. People mostly returned to neighborhoods or districts under the control of members of their sect; very few families returned to former home areas where they would be in a minority.

Detention Conditions and Torture

Reports continued of widespread torture and other abuse of detainees in detention facilities run by Iraq's defense and interior ministries and police. Government-run detention facilities struggled to accommodate almost 30,000 detainees, and serious delays in the judicial review of detention exacerbated overcrowding: Some detainees have spent years in custody without charge or trial. The situation worsened in 2009 as the US military transferred detainees to Iraqi custody (more than 1,200 in the first nine months) under the 2008 US-Iraqi security agreement. The US military's remaining detainee population stood at under 9,000 as of September 2009, from a peak of approximately 26,000 in late 2007.

In June 2009 Prime Minister Nuri al-Maliki set up an eight-member special committee, composed of representatives from the government's security ministries as well as human rights and judicial agencies, to investigate allegations of widespread abuse and torture in Iraq's prisons. As of mid-November the government had provided no information about the progress of any investigation or its results.

Accountability for Past Crimes

In August the Iraqi High Tribunal (IHT) sentenced former deputy prime minister Tariq Aziz and Ali Hassan al-Majid (known as "Chemical Ali") each to seven years in jail for their roles in planning the forced displacement of Kurds from northern Iraq in the late 1980s. The conviction followed a separate 15-year jail sentence that both received in March for the former government's execution of merchants accused of profiteering under sanctions in 1992. Also in March 2009 the IHT sentenced al-Majid to death for the murder of Shia Muslims in 1999 (he was previously sentenced to death for his role in the 1988 Anfal campaign against the Kurds, and suppression of a Shia uprising after the 1991 Gulf War).

In July 2009 a public inquiry was launched in the United Kingdom into the death of Iraqi civilian Baha Mousa while in British custody in Basra in 2003. A postmortem examination showed that Mousa had at least 93 injuries to his body, including a broken nose and fractured ribs. The inquiry is examining the British military's treatment of Iraqi detainees, including interrogation techniques.

Gender-Based Violence

Violence against women and girls continues to be a serious problem, with members of insurgent groups and militias, soldiers, and police among the perpetrators. Even in high-profile cases involving police or security forces, prosecutions are rare. Insurgent groups have targeted women who are politicians, civil servants, journalists, and women's rights activists. They have also attacked women on the street for what they consider "immoral" or "un-Islamic" behavior or dress. "Honor" killings by family members remain a threat to women and girls in Kurdish areas, as well as elsewhere in Iraq.

Female genital mutilation is practiced mainly in Kurdish areas of Iraq; reportedly 60 percent of Kurdish women have undergone this procedure, although the KRG claimed that the figures are exaggerated. Girls and women receive conflicting and inaccurate messages from public officials on its consequences. The Kurdistan parliament in 2008 passed a draft law outlawing FGM, but the ministerial decree necessary to implement it, expected in February 2009, was inexplicably cancelled.

Violence against Men Suspected of Homosexual Conduct

In early 2009 a killing campaign against men suspected of being gay, or of not being sufficiently "masculine," erupted. Armed gangs kidnapped men and dumped their mutilated bodies in the garbage or in front of morgues. Men interviewed by Human Rights Watch in April recounted death threats, blackmail, midnight raids by masked men on private homes, and abductions from the streets. The campaign was most intense in Baghdad, but extended to other cities including Kirkuk, Najaf, and Basra.

IRAQ

"They Want Us Exterminated"

Murder, Torture, Sexual Orientation and Gender in Iraq

HUMAN RIGHTS WATCH

Graffiti in a neighborhood in Najaf: "Death to the People of Lot."
"People of Lot" is a derogatory term in Arabic for men who engage in
homosexual conduct, derived from the story of Sodom and Gomorrah.
© 2009 Private

Most survivors and witnesses pointed to Moqtada al-Sadr's Mahdi army, the largest Shia militia, as the driving force behind the killings. Sadrist mosques and leaders have warned loudly that homosexuality threatens Iraqi life and culture. Some Sunni militias may have joined the violence, competing to show their moral credentials. While there was no accurate tally of the victims, the number may have well been in the hundreds. Iraqi police and security forces did little to investigate or halt the killings. Authorities announced no arrests or prosecutions; it is unlikely that any occurred.

Violence against Minorities

Armed groups continued to persecute ethnic and religious minorities with impunity. After US forces withdrew from Iraqi cities, assailants launched horrific attacks against minority groups: in Nineveh province alone, bombings in four towns and cities killed more than 137 and injured almost 500 from the Yazidi, Shabak, and Turkmen communities.

As the conflict intensified between the Arab-dominated central government and the KRG over control of the disputed territories running across northern Iraq from the Iranian to the Syrian borders, minorities found themselves in an increasingly precarious position. Leaders of minority communities complained that Kurdish security forces engaged in arbitrary arrests and detentions, intimidation, and in some cases low-level violence, against minorities who challenged Kurdish control of the disputed territories.

Key International Actors

An agreement signed between the United States and Iraq in 2008 requires a complete US withdrawal—including of non-combat military forces—from Iraq by the end of 2011. Having withdrawn to bases since the end of June 2009, US forces must now seek Iraqi permission to launch operations in the cities. As of October the United States had approximately 120,000 troops in Iraq (down from 160,000-170,000 at the height of the 2007 "surge"). The United Kingdom, the only other country with a significant number of military personnel in Iraq, held a ceremony in April in the city of Basra to mark the official end of the six-year British military mission in Iraq.

IRAQ

On Vulnerable Ground

Violence Against Minority Communities
in Nineveh Province's Disputed Territories

HUMAN
RIGHTS
WATCH

In August the United Nations Security Council voted to extend the mandate of the UN Assistance Mission for Iraq (UNAMI) for one year. The UNAMI Human Rights Office monitors human rights violations as part of a plan aimed at developing Iraqi mechanisms for addressing past and current abuses.

ISRAEL / OCCUPIED PALESTINIAN TERRITORIES (OPT)

The human rights crisis in the Israeli-occupied Palestinian territories worsened in 2009, particularly in Gaza, where Israeli forces killed hundreds of Palestinian civilians and destroyed civilian homes and infrastructure during Operation Cast Lead, a major military offensive that began on December 27, 2008 and ended on January 18, 2009. Israel's continued blockade of Gaza denied basic goods to Gaza's 1.5 million residents and prevented post-war reconstruction.

Hamas, Islamic Jihad and other Palestinian armed groups in Gaza fired rockets indiscriminately at Israeli cities and towns. At their peak during Operation Cast Lead, more than 100 rockets per day hit Israel, killing three Israeli civilians. Longer-range rockets placed 800,000 Israelis at risk of attack.

During and after the war, Hamas forces in Gaza killed alleged collaborators with Israel and shot and maimed scores of political rivals.

In the West Bank, Israel maintained many restrictions on freedom of movement for Palestinians, demolished hundreds of homes under discriminatory regulations, continued unlawful settlement construction, and continued to arbitrarily detain children and adults.

Gaza Strip

Palestinian Armed Groups

From November 2008 through March 2009 the military wings of Hamas, Islamic Jihad, the People's Front for the Liberation of Palestine (PFLP) and other groups fired hundreds of largely locally made rockets at population centers in Israel, killing three civilians and severely wounding four. Up to 800,000 people were within range of the attacks. In several cases, the rockets fell short of their intended targets in Israel and harmed Palestinians in Gaza, including two young girls killed by a rocket in the northern Gaza Strip. Rocket attacks greatly diminished since March 2009.

ISRAEL/OCCUPIED PALESTINIAN TERRITORIES

Rockets from Gaza

Harm to Civilians from Palestinian Armed Groups'
Rocket Attacks

HUMAN
RIGHTS
WATCH

The repeated attacks on population centers by rockets that cannot be targeted and statements from Palestinian armed groups indicate that the attackers intended to harm civilians. Hamas and other groups stated the attacks were intended as reprisals for unlawful Israeli attacks or as a means of resistance to occupation. Deliberate or indiscriminate attacks on civilians are a serious violation of international humanitarian law regardless of their rationale.

Palestinian armed groups unnecessarily placed Palestinian civilians at risk from retaliatory attacks by firing rockets from densely populated areas. Additionally, reports by news media and a nongovernmental organization indicate that in some cases, Palestinian armed groups intentionally hid behind civilians to unlawfully use them as shields to deter Israeli counter-attacks.

From late December 2008 to at least March 2009, masked gunmen apparently affiliated with Hamas, killed at least 32 alleged collaborators with Israel—including men in custody or who posed no threat at the time—and shot or severely beat scores of other Palestinians, primarily members of the rival Fatah party. In response, the Fatah-run authorities in the West Bank increased repressive measures against Hamas members and supporters there.

Hamas and other Palestinian factions have conducted no known investigations into unlawful rockets attacks against Israeli civilians, actions by Palestinian armed groups that put Palestinian civilians at unnecessary risk, or the killings or mistreatment of alleged collaborators or political rivals. Hamas pledged in October to investigate alleged war crimes including rocket attacks.

Palestinian armed groups in Gaza continued to detain incommunicado the Israeli soldier Gilad Shalit, captured in June 2006, refusing to allow the International Committee of the Red Cross to visit him or to carry messages to and from his family. In October Israel released 20 female prisoners in return for a video of Shalit, proving he was alive.

Israel Defense Forces

Civilians suffered tremendously during the conflict in Gaza. At least 773 Palestinian civilians were killed during Operation Cast Lead, according to the Israeli human rights group B'Tselem; the group listed 330 combatants killed, and

248 policemen. (Human Rights Watch has not been able to assess whether and to what extent Gaza's police were civilians immune from attack or were directly participating in the hostilities and thus lawful targets.) The Israel Defense Forces (IDF) damaged hospitals and United Nations facilities where displaced persons were sheltering. Israel and Egypt refused to open their borders, preventing civilians from fleeing the conflict, a step criticized by the UN High Commissioner for Refugees.

Israeli forces shelled densely populated areas with heavy artillery, including 155mm high explosive, and white phosphorous obscurant munitions, which are inherently indiscriminate when used in densely-populated areas. In one case, on January 15, IDF high explosive and white phosphorus artillery shells struck the main compound of the UN Relief and Works Agency for Palestine Refugees in the Near East (UNRWA) in Gaza City, wounding three people and starting fires that destroyed four buildings, food aid, and medical supplies. The IDF had previously suspended the use of heavy artillery in residential areas of Gaza in November 2006, after an artillery attack that killed 23 civilians. Israel had never previously used white phosphorus in Gaza and initially denied using it in Operation Cast Lead.

Israeli soldiers unlawfully shot and killed at least 11 Palestinian civilians, including five women and four children, who were in groups waving white flags to convey their civilian status.

Israeli aerial drones launched missiles that killed 87 civilians (not including police) in Gaza, according to human rights NGOs. Victims included children playing on rooftops and students waiting for a bus in areas where there was no evidence of military activity. Drone operators have the time and capacity to clearly see their targets on the ground.

In several areas of Gaza, the IDF destroyed or damaged civilian structures—including a flour mill, food factories, cement factories, and greenhouses—without military necessity as required by international law. In total, Israeli forces damaged or destroyed 14,000 homes, around 60 health facilities, 68 government buildings, and 31 offices of nongovernmental organizations, according to the UN.

Rain of Fire

Israel's Unlawful Use of White Phosphorus in Gaza

HUMAN
RIGHTS
WATCH

Throughout the war Israeli authorities banned journalists and human rights monitors from entering Gaza, and placed restrictions on peaceful protests against the
war. Israeli government authorities sought to cut off funding to Breaking the
Silence, a group of IDF veterans that published the testimonies of 26 Israeli soldiers who participated in and were critical of abuses committed during Operation
Cast Lead.

In April the IDF released the results of five internal investigations into its actions
in Gaza, concluding that it "operated in accordance with international law" and
that "a very small number" of incidents occurred due to "intelligence or operational errors." In July the Israeli Ministry of Foreign Affairs released a report that
repeated these claims and blamed Hamas for using civilians as shields. In
November the ministry reported that the IDF had opened investigations into 128
incidents. These included operational debriefings by military units of personnel
within the chain of command, whose findings cannot be used as evidence of
criminal wrongdoing, and 27 criminal investigations by military police. As of
November Israeli authorities had prosecuted only one soldier involved in the
Gaza war, for stealing a credit card.

The board of inquiry appointed by the UN Secretary-General to examine incidents
where UN property and personnel were harmed during the war concluded, in May,
that "the government of Israel was responsible for the deaths and injuries ... and
the physical damage" in seven of nine cases examined; in another case, a
Palestinian rocket damaged a warehouse. (Responsibility for the ninth case could
not be determined.) The UN Fact Finding Mission on the Gaza Conflict, established by the UN Human Rights Council, headed by Justice Richard Goldstone,
found that both parties to the conflict committed war crimes and possibly crimes
against humanity in a report published in September. Israel refused to cooperate
with the mission.

Blockade

Israel's comprehensive blockade of the Gaza Strip, imposed since June 2007, continued to have severe humanitarian and economic consequences for the civilian
population, particularly during the war. Hundreds of thousands of people lacked
electricity, running water, cooking gas, gasoline and other goods for weeks on

ISRAEL/OCCUPIED PALESTINIAN TERRITORIES

White Flag Deaths

Killings of Palestinian Civilians during Operation Cast Lead

HUMAN
RIGHTS
WATCH

end; raw sewage flooded some city streets; hospitals were overcrowded, lacked essential medicines, and were often inaccessible to the wounded.

As of September roughly 20,000 people remained homeless and 10,000 remained without water. Items Israel prohibited from entry included reconstruction materials, chickpeas, dates, macaroni, a water purification system, and 120 truckloads of school supplies. The only exports that Israel allowed consisted of several shipments of carnations.

Israeli officials stated that the blockade would remain in place until Hamas releases Gilad Shalit. The blockade, supported by Egypt at Rafah's Gaza border, amounts to a form of collective punishment of Gaza's 1.5 million civilians in violation of international law. Israel is Gaza's major source of electricity and sole source of fuel, which Israel does not permit from other sources, so its restrictions on their supply cripple transportation as well as water-pumping, sewage, and sanitation facilities.

In September, the office of the Coordinator of Government Activities in the Territories (COGAT), a unit of the Israeli defense ministry, severed contacts with Israeli human rights organizations handling individual applications for exit permits from Gaza, even in emergency humanitarian cases. Gaza residents have no direct access to the Israeli military authorities.

West Bank

Palestinian Authority

Four men, all reportedly Hamas supporters, died in the custody of Palestinian Authority (PA) security services in the West Bank. In only one case were suspects brought to trial: the death of Haitham Amr, whose body showed signs of torture after he was arrested by the General Intelligence agency in Hebron in June. (A military trial of officials allegedly involved was ongoing in November.) The Independent Commission for Human Rights, a Palestinian rights body, received 150 complaints of torture in PA custody in the West Bank as of October.

OCCUPIED PALESTINIAN TERRITORIES

Under Cover of War

Hamas Political Violence in Gaza

HUMAN
RIGHTS
WATCH

Home Demolitions and Evacuations

As of late October Israeli authorities had demolished 103 residential structures in the West Bank (including East Jerusalem), displacing 581 people, justifying the demolitions on the grounds that the structures were built without permits; in practice such permits are almost impossible for Palestinians to obtain. In one case in June Israeli authorities demolished the homes and animal pens of 18 shepherd families in the northern Jordan Valley, displacing approximately 130 people, five days after ordering them to evacuate because they were living in a "closed military zone." Some of the displaced families had been living there since at least the 1950s.

In August, following a court ruling, Israeli police forcibly removed 53 Palestinians, including 20 children, from their homes in the Sheikh Jarrah neighborhood of East Jerusalem. Israeli settlers immediately moved into their homes.

Israel continued its policy of demolishing the homes of families of convicted Palestinian militants, after the High Court of Justice upheld the policy as a deterrent against future attacks, even though the family members had not been implicated in militant activity.

During the first half of 2009, Israel completed 881 housing units and began construction of 666 new units in illegal settlements in the West Bank. At least 96 new structures were built in unauthorized settlement "outposts" as of July, and Israeli authorities approved construction of 455 new housing units in September, according to Peace Now.

Freedom of Movement

Israel maintained onerous restrictions on the movement of Palestinians in the West Bank. In September Israeli authorities announced the imminent removal of 100 closure obstacles (ranging from checkpoints to earth mounds and concrete blocks), which if carried out, would leave 519 closure obstacles.

Israel continued construction of the wall or separation barrier. Its ostensible purpose was to protect against suicide-bombing attacks, but rather than build it along the Green Line separating Israel from the West Bank, some 87 percent of it has been built on territory within the West Bank. The confiscation of private land meant, among other things, that farmers and pastoralists were separated from their lands. Between May and August 2009 the UN reported that Israeli security had injured 94 Palestinians during anti-barrier demonstrations.

The High Court of Justice in March upheld a travel ban on Shawan Jabarin, the director of Al Haq, a human rights organization in the West Bank, which prevented him from traveling to the Netherlands to collect a human rights award. Israeli authorities presented secret evidence, which Jabarin and his lawyer were not allowed to see, that allegedly showed him to be an active member of the PFLP, but did not charge him with any crime.

In August Israeli authorities began restricting certain foreign nationals who have family, work, business or academic ties in the West Bank and who entered the West Bank via Jordan to areas controlled by the Palestinian Authority, thereby barring them from Israel, East Jerusalem, and "Area C" of the West Bank.

Arbitrary Detention

While Israeli civil courts define Israelis under 18 years of age as children, Israeli military courts continue to treat Palestinians over the age of 16 as "adults," and sentence them on the basis of their age at sentencing rather than when they committed the offense. The nongovernmental organization Defense for Children International reported multiple cases where Israeli authorities allegedly mistreated Palestinian children in custody to coerce them to sign confessions in Hebrew, which they did not understand.

In July the IDF established a separate military court for the prosecution of Palestinian West Bank children. Previously the IDF had prosecuted Palestinian children and adults in the same court system.

As of November Israel held 335 Palestinians in administrative detention under Military Order Number 1229 of 1988, which authorizes detention without charge for indefinitely renewable periods of up to six months.

Expulsion of Asylum Seekers

Israel continued its policy of "hot returns," a procedure in place since 2007 in which IDF troops forcibly return migrants who irregularly enter the country from Egypt back across the border within 72 hours of detention, without adequately allowing them to present asylum claims. As of September 12 Israel forcibly returned 217 migrants to Egypt this year. Egyptian border guards killed at least 16 migrants near the Sinai border with Israel as of November.

Key International Actors

Israel is the largest recipient of aid from the United States, receiving US$2.7 billion in military aid in 2009, without any human rights conditions. The Obama administration urged Israel to halt all new settlement construction but later endorsed as "progress" a temporary freeze on new construction that did not include existing plans or East Jerusalem. The US continued to train and equip Palestinian security forces.

The current European Union-Israel Action Plan only vaguely mentions human rights concerns, in contrast to similar plans between the EU and other countries in the region. The EU unofficially froze an upgrade in relations with Israel following Operation Cast Lead.

After the Gaza war, international donors pledged US $4.4 billion in reconstruction aid; despite this, due to Israeli import restrictions, UNRWA stated in August that "not one penny of aid has reached Gaza."

Both the UN Human Rights Council and the General Assembly passed resolutions endorsing the report of the UN Fact-Finding Mission on the Gaza Conflict and calling for a mechanism to monitor steps that Israel and Hamas take to investigate serious laws-of-war violations, including war crimes, committed by their respective forces.

JORDAN

No significant change in Jordan's human rights policies or practices occurred in 2009. Jordan twice revised its NGO law, in 2008 and again in 2009, further restricting freedom of civic organizations. After becoming, in 2008, the first country in the region to extend its labor law to cover domestic workers, the specific protections provided to them in a 2009 regulation fell short. Jordan maintains the death penalty but since 2006 has observed a moratorium on its practice.

Torture, Arbitrary Detention, and Administrative Detention

Torture, which independent prison inspections conducted by the United Nations and Human Rights Watch in 2006, 2007, and 2008 found to be routine and widespread, continues. Positive initiatives, such as training programs run by the National Center for Human Rights and other groups to raise awareness about torture among law enforcement officials, are far from sufficient considering Jordan's lack of both political will and effective mechanisms to bring perpetrators to justice.

Jordan has a prison reform program that seeks to rehabilitate prisoners through incentives and activities while reducing overcrowding and improving prison services. It does not address accountability for abuses against inmates by prison staff and members of the security forces. Among new instances of prisoner abuse, Islamist prisoners transferred from Swaqa to Juwaida prison in February 2009 said guards and gendarmes subjected them to repeated beatings upon arrival, and in September officials at Juwaida turned off drinking water for Islamist prisoners on hunger strike, relatives said. Torture also occurs at police stations to extract information. Despite reporting severe beatings, and in one 2008 case use of electricity on sensitive parts of the body, torture victims received no redress. Near-total impunity for torture is assured by a police-run system of accountability in places of detention, composed of a deficient complaint mechanism, lackluster investigations and prosecutions, and police court judges who impose lenient sentences.

Under the Crime Prevention Law provincial governors can administratively detain persons. The law requires governors to have evidence of criminal conduct, but in practice this is not always the case. Administrative detention is frequently used to circumvent the obligation to present suspects to the prosecutor within 24 hours, or to overrule judges who have released suspects on bail. The Foreign Ministry in May 2009 reported 14,000 administrative detainees being held in 2008 (including 800 women), comprising one in five prison inmates, down from 20,000 in 2006.

Freedom of Expression and Association

Criticism of the king, defamation of government officials and institutions, and comments deemed offensive to Islam carry heavy penalties under the penal code. Other penal code provisions criminalize speech deemed to diminish the prestige of the state or to harm international relations. A draft revision of the penal code, expected before parliament in November 2009, would maintain them intact. Article 5 of the 2007 Press and Publications Law requires publications to adhere to "Islamic values."

On June 21, 2009, Amman's court of first instance sentenced Islam Samhan to one year in prison for insulting Islam in a published poem. In March an Amman appeals court struck down a guilty verdict against Radio Balad for breaching the visual and audio media law by airing listener comments that allegedly insulted parliament, and in April Amman's criminal conciliation court cleared newspaper columnist Khalid Mahadin of libeling parliament in an article criticizing parliamentarians' privileges, the case having been brought following a complaint by Fayiz Shawabka, secretary-general of parliament's lower house. In June Jordan's major daily newspapers boycotted reporting on parliament after parliamentary administrators restricted media access to its deliberations and members, and after the body voted for a 5 percent special tax on media institutions.

In August, defying three years of lobbying by NGOs for a more permissive law, parliament passed an amended Law of Societies that maintained the authority of the government to intrude in the internal activities of NGOs. The new law gives authorities discretionary power to reject applications for new NGOs and wide powers to close existing ones. It obliges NGOs to inform the authorities in advance of planned activities and certain meetings, which they must allow offi-

JORDAN

Guests of the Governor

Administrative Detention Undermines Rule of Law in Jordan

HUMAN
RIGHTS
WATCH

cials to attend. The government may scrutinize NGO bank accounts and must approve foreign funding, which it can deny at its discretion.

Women's and Girls' Rights

Jordanian governors detain in protective custody women whose families threaten them with violence. In 2008 Jordan moved these women from Juwaida prison either to a government-run or to an NGO-run shelter where they enjoy increased freedoms but still require a family member to agree to their release.

Jordanian courts continue to issue lenient verdicts for "honor" crimes perpetrated by family members against women and girls suspected of "immoral" behavior; by August there had been 14 such killings in 2009, comprising the majority of female murders in Jordan. In January a court halved the sentence of a man who had attempted to murder his sister twice for reasons of family honor, after she had dropped personal claims against him. The Ministry of Justice in August announced a special tribunal for "honor" killings but made no progress in amending penal code articles that allow lenient sentences for killing spouses caught during illicit sex and for committing crimes in a state of "rage," or provide discretionary sentence reductions when victims drop personal claims.

Against opposition from the Islamic Action Front, the biggest opposition political party, Jordan in August 2009 lifted reservations on article 15 (4) of the UN Convention on the Elimination of All Forms of Discrimination against Women, giving women the same rights as men to travel freely and to decide their place of domicile.

Labor Rights

In July police and gendarmerie forces violently broke up a sit-in by Aqaba port workers striking to protest plans to end subsidized housing. Authorities arrested more than 80 workers and injured three, after protesters "verbally attacked" security forces, according to Minister of Interior Nayif al-Qadi, who accused "Israel and those who work for its interests within" Jordan of spreading false rumors of police brutality.

The National Labor Committee, a US advocacy group, reported abuses against Asian migrants working in Jordan's Qualified Industrial Zones, including late payment of wages, withholding of passports, unsanitary lodging conditions, and police breaking up impromptu strikes. Unionized Jordanians may only strike with government permission; non-Jordanians, although allowed to join unions since 2008, are not allowed to strike.

New regulations on domestic workers, issued in September 2009 following the inclusion of domestic workers under the labor law in July 2008, restricted essential rights, such as freedom of movement, and failed to adequately protect workers from working long hours and from remaining trapped in abusive households. The regulations impose "all financial obligations" on a worker who leaves her employment unless she can meet the difficult criterion of proving the fault is the employer's. The regulations contain positive clauses requiring the employer to ensure regular payment of salary, adequate living quarters, and medical coverage. The Ministry of Labor in 2009 closed four recruitment agencies and warned eight others over violations of the labor law.

Prosecutors filed charges against suspects under Jordan's Anti-Human-Trafficking Law, passed in January 2009, but the courts had not yet adjudicated them as of November 2009.

Key International Actors

The United States concluded a five-year agreement, starting in 2010, to provide Jordan with US$360 million in economic assistance annually, and US$300 million in foreign military financing. This represents an increase over previous US administration annual requests for aid to Jordan, but in the past those were often supplemented with ad hoc aid, which raised actual US aid to over US$1 billion in 2008 (compared to the European Union's €265 million for 2007-2010).

The EU engaged Jordan in a joint project aimed at improving "respect for human rights as regards the treatment of detainees." In April the EU's progress report cited "some progress," in eliminating torture, but lamented the lack of judicial independence and the existence of "special courts," and criticized "increase[d] state control," over NGOs. In an April statement, Benita Ferrero-Waldner, external relations and neighbourhood policy commissioner, "encourage[d] Jordan to make ... progress in good governance and create the conditions that will enable the civil society to support the government in its efforts."

During consideration at the UN Human Rights Council under the Universal Periodic Review mechanism, Jordan accepted recommendations for independent investigations of torture allegations, but rejected acceding to the Optional Protocol of the Convention against Torture, which provides for such independent investigations.

Kuwait

Kuwait has improved its record in some aspects of women's human rights, and its parliament has debated ways to improve migrant workers' rights. However, broad discrimination continues against women in nationality, residency, and family law, and in their economic rights, despite women in 2005 gaining the right to vote and run for office. Kuwait continues to exclude the stateless Bidun from full citizenship, despite their long-term roots in Kuwaiti territory. In 2009 there was deterioration in respect for freedom of expression and the rights of lesbians, gays, and transgender persons.

Kuwait retains the death penalty, and voted in December 2008 against a United Nations General Assembly resolution calling for a worldwide moratorium on executions. The last reported execution took place in May 2007.

Women's and Girls' Rights

Kuwait's nationality law denies Kuwaiti women married to non-Kuwaiti men the right to pass their nationality on to their children and spouses, a right enjoyed by Kuwaiti men married to foreign spouses. The law also discriminates against women in residency rights, allowing the spouses of Kuwaiti men but not of Kuwaiti women to be in Kuwait without employment and to qualify for citizenship after 10 years of marriage.

The government grants low-interest housing loans only to Kuwaiti men; Kuwaiti women, whether single or married, are ineligible. Upon divorce, married women lose their claim to homes purchased through this program, even if they made payments on the loan. A single mother can claim rent subsidy only if she intends not to remarry.

There exists no data on the prevalence of violence against women in Kuwait. Victims are often reluctant to file complaints with the police because redress for domestic abuse through the criminal justice system remains elusive. Perpetrators are rarely arrested even when women file with the police complaints that are supported by medico-legal evidence.

In 2005 Kuwaiti women won the right to vote and to run in elections. In May 2009 voters elected four women to Parliament. In November Kuwait's Constitutional Court rejected an appeal by a Kuwaiti citizen that two of the women parliamentarians be required to step down because they do not wear the Islamic headscarf. In August a court struck down article 15 of the Passport Law 11/1962 as unconstitutional and allowed married women henceforth to obtain a passport without their husband's permission.

Bidun

Kuwait hosts approximately 120,000 stateless persons, known as the Bidun. The state does not recognize the right of these long-time residents to Kuwaiti nationality or permanent residency. Children of the Bidun are also stateless.

As a consequence of their statelessness, the Bidun cannot freely leave and return to Kuwait; the government issues them one-time travel documents at its discretion. As non-Kuwaitis, they face restrictions in employment, healthcare, education, marriage, and founding a family. Kuwait issues Bidun with identity cards, but issue and renewal can be accompanied by pressure to sign affidavits renouncing any claim to Kuwaiti nationality. Prosecution and deportation to Iraq and other countries as illegal aliens are possible consequences of failing to sign such waivers.

A 2007 draft law would grant the Bidun civil rights, but not nationality. At this writing it has not been passed.

Freedom of Expression and the Media

In separate cases in October 2009, courts fined two Kuwaiti members of parliament 3,000 dinars (US$10,500) each for "slandering the government." The first was fined for criticizing the Interior Ministry's treatment of the Bidun, and the second for making allegations of corruption in the Ministry of Health.

Kuwaiti authorities in August 2009 banned the TV show *Your Voice is Heard* after it criticized officials. A 2006 reform of the press law replaced imprisonment as punishment for infractions of the law with high fines.

Sexual Orientation and Gender Identity

Kuwait continues to criminalize consensual homosexual conduct, in contravention of international best practices. Article 193 of Kuwait's penal code punishes consensual sexual intercourse between men over age 21 with up to seven years' imprisonment; if the conduct involves persons under 21, then imprisonment is increased to 10 years.

Kuwait's National Assembly in December 2007 introduced restrictions on privacy and on a person's free choice of dress. The new article 198 of the penal code criminalized "imitating the appearance of a member of the opposite sex," punishable with a sentence of up to one year in prison or a fine of up to 1,000 dinars (US$3,500). Immediately after the new law passed, police began arresting "crossdressers," jailing at least 14 people in the first month and subjecting them to abuse and violence while in detention. In mid-March 2008 another wave of arrests took place, and arrests and harassment of individuals who defy state-imposed rules on gender presentation have continued sporadically.

Migrant Worker Rights

More than one million foreign nationals reside in Kuwait, constituting an estimated 80 percent of the country's workforce. Many of them experience exploitative labor conditions including private employers who confiscate their passports or who do not pay their wages, claiming they need to recoup their fees for hiring the worker. Migrant workers themselves often pay exorbitant recruitment fees to labor agents in their home countries, and must then work off their debt in Kuwait. Kuwaiti law limits wage deductions for debt, but these limits are not enforced in practice.

Parliament in May 2009 debated a draft revision of the Labor Law that would incorporate more protective provisions on wages, working hours, and safety. However, it does not establish monitoring mechanisms for workers' rights, and continues to exclude domestic workers from its protections.

Approximately 700,000 migrant women—chiefly from Indonesia, Sri Lanka, and the Philippines—are employed in Kuwait as full-time live-in domestic workers. Their exclusion under the current labor law deprives them of protections afforded other workers, such as a weekly rest day and limits on working hours. Many domestic workers complain of confinement in the house, long working hours without rest, months or years of unpaid wages, and sometimes verbal, physical, and sexual abuse. Domestic workers who fled abusive situations at their workplace have often become stranded at their embassies, at deportation centers, or at recruitment agencies. In October 2009 Indonesia banned further migration of domestic workers to Kuwait in response to having 600 workers trapped in its embassy.

A major barrier to the redress of labor abuses is the sponsorship (*kafala*) system by which a migrant worker's legal residence in Kuwait is tied to his or her employer, who serves as a "sponsor." Migrant workers can only transfer employment with their sponsor's consent, although a reform in August 2009 frees them of this requirement if they have worked more than three years (migrant domestic workers do not benefit from this provision). Sponsorship traps workers in abusive situations, including in situations of forced labor, and blocks their access to means of redress. If an employer withdraws sponsorship, workers who flee abusive workplaces can be arrested and deported for being out of status in the country. Kuwaiti law enforcement officials rarely bring to justice Kuwaitis who abuse their powers as sponsors.

Key International Actors

The United States in the 2009 State Department Trafficking in Persons report classified Kuwait as Tier 3—that is, among the most problematic countries—but chose not to impose sanctions for Kuwait's failure to combat human trafficking. The US considers Kuwait a strategic partner in combating terrorism, and in February had US$8.4 billion in open foreign military sales contracts with Kuwait's Defense Ministry.

The International Labour Organization in October 2009 urged Kuwait to end the sponsorship system.

LEBANON

2009 was a year of lost opportunities for Lebanon. Parliamentary elections held on June 7 were praised as free and fair. However, it took five months for a government to be formed, reflecting the country's deep-seated divisions, and needed reforms were stalled amidst the political paralysis. Proposed laws that would abolish the death penalty, reduce pretrial detention, and grant women the right to pass nationality to their husband and children await governmental debate.

Torture, Ill-Treatment, and Prison Conditions

Lebanese law prohibits torture, but accountability for torture and ill-treatment in detention remains elusive. A number of detainees, especially suspected Islamists, told Human Rights Watch and other groups that their interrogators beat and tortured them in a number of detention facilities, including the Military Intelligence unit of the Ministry of Defense, the Information Branch of the Internal Security Forces, and certain police stations. The Ministry of Interior did not make public the results of an investigation it commissioned in August 2008 into allegations of abuse occurring inside Lebanese prisons.

On December 22, 2008, Lebanon ratified the Optional Protocol to the Convention against Torture (OPCAT), which calls for the creation, within one year of ratification, of a national preventive mechanism to visit and monitor places of detention.

Conditions in prisons and detention facilities remain poor, with overcrowding and lack of proper medical care a perennial problem. According to a report prepared by the Internal Security Forces, as of August 24, 2009, there were 5,324 detainees in Lebanon, while detention facilities can accommodate a maximum of 3,653. According to the same report, pretrial detainees represent around 65 percent of the total number of detainees, while foreigners with completed sentences but awaiting deportation represent another 13 percent.

Lebanon maintained its de facto moratorium on executions, but a number of death sentences were passed in 2009. The minister of justice presented a draft law on abolition of the death penalty to the Lebanese government in October 2008, but its adoption is still pending.

Palestinian Refugees

The estimated 300,000 Palestinian refugees in Lebanon live in appalling social and economic conditions, and remain subject to wide-ranging restrictions on housing and work. Palestinians from the Nahr al-Bared refugee camp—destroyed in the 2007 battle between the Lebanese army and the armed Fatah al-Islam group—continue to live in dire conditions. Reconstruction efforts officially began in March 2009, but in August the State Shura Council, the highest administrative court, declared a two-month suspension after a leading politician submitted a petition noting that reconstruction may damage archeological finds uncovered under the rubble. Palestinian former residents of the camp held protests against the continued delays. Reconstruction finally resumed at the end of October following expiry of the court's injunction.

In March the Ministry of Interior stopped issuing temporary identification papers to Palestinians in Lebanon who are without legal documentation. The issuing of ID cards had begun in August 2008 as part of a plan to improve the legal status of at least 3,000 non-ID Palestinians who had previously lived in constant fear of arrest. However, the ministry issued only 750 cards before it stopped the process, citing fraudulent applications. In October 2009 the minister of interior announced that the process would soon resume, but at this writing no new cards have been issued.

Iraqi Refugees

An estimated 50,000 Iraqi refugees live in Lebanon. The United Nations High Commissioner for Refugees (UNHCR) recognizes all Iraqis from central and southern Iraq seeking asylum in Lebanon as refugees on a prima facie basis. However, since Lebanon has not ratified the 1951 Refugee Convention, it does not give legal effect to UNHCR's recognition of Iraqi refugees and generally treats the vast majority of them as illegal immigrants subject to arrest. In September 2009, 80 recognized refugees remained in detention on grounds that they did not hold proper residency papers.

Women's and Girls' Rights

Despite women's active participation in most aspects of Lebanese society, dis-criminatory provisions continue to exist in personal status laws, nationality laws, and penal laws relating to violence in the family. Current Lebanese law does not allow Lebanese women to confer nationality on their spouses or children. As a result, thousands of children born to Lebanese mothers and foreign fathers are denied full access to education (public schools will only take non-Lebanese if there is space), healthcare, and residency. Following a multi-year campaign by local civil society groups, in August the minister of interior submitted to the Cabinet a draft law that would allow Lebanese women to pass their nationality to their husbands and children, but the Cabinet has not yet approved the proposal. Women's political representation remains very low, with only four women elected to Lebanon's 128-member parliament in 2009.

A new bill that aims to criminalize domestic violence is currently under review by the Cabinet. The Family Violence Bill aims to reduce domestic violence by trans-ferring such cases to specialized courts. The bill requires anyone who witnesses domestic violence to report it, and obliges perpetrators to provide the plaintiff with alternative living arrangements and an allowance, and to pay medical expenses.

Migrant domestic workers face exploitation and abuse by employers, including excessive work hours, non-payment of wages, and restrictions on their liberty. Many suffer physical and sexual abuse at the employer's hands, in a climate of impunity for the employer. In January 2009 the Ministry of Labor introduced a standard employment contract that clarifies certain terms and conditions of employment for domestic workers (such as the maximum number of daily working hours), and a new regulation for employment agencies. However, enforcement mechanisms to apply the rules are still lacking. Migrant domestic workers contin-ue to die in high numbers (there were eight deaths in October alone), a majority being classified as suicides or deaths while "trying to escape from the employer."

Legacy of Past Conflicts and Wars

More than a year after the end of the fighting that broke out in May 2008 between the Hezbollah-led opposition and pro-government groups, killing at least 71 people in two weeks, Lebanese judicial authorities have failed to hold accountable fighters responsible for attacks against civilians.

More than three years after the end of the war between Israel and Hezbollah, neither the Israeli nor the Lebanese government has investigated the violations of the laws of war committed by the warring parties. The submunition "duds" left behind by Israel's bombing campaign continue to harm civilians: according to the official Lebanon Mine Action Center, such duds killed two civilians and wounded 18 in 2009, raising the post-war casualty toll from clusters to 44 killed and 305 wounded. In May Israel handed to the United Nations data and maps on the cluster munitions it fired over southern Lebanon in the 2006 conflict. Lebanon signed the Convention on Cluster Munitions in December 2008.

Despite a pledge in the government's ministerial declaration of August 2008 to take steps to uncover the fate of the Lebanese and other nationals who "disappeared" during and after the 1975-1990 Lebanese civil war, and to ratify the International Convention for the Protection of all Persons from Enforced Disappearances, the government took no practical steps to uncover mass graves or collect information on the "disappeared."

The fate of Lebanese and other residents of Lebanon who "disappeared" at the hands of Syrian security forces remains unknown. An official joint Syrian-Lebanese committee established in May 2005 to investigate such cases has not published any findings at this writing.

Hariri Tribunal

In March 2009 the international tribunal to try those responsible for killing former prime minister Rafik Hariri in 2005 and other politically motivated assassinations officially began its operations. In April the tribunal ordered the release of four former heads of Lebanese intelligence and security services—Gen. `Ali al-Hajj, Gen. Raymond Azar, Brig. Gen. Jamil al-Sayyed, and Gen. Mustafa Hamdan—who had been held for almost four years in detention without charge following their arrest in 2005 on suspicion of their involvement in Hariri's assassination. The tribunal has not issued any indictments to date, and the UN-appointed international commission continues its investigations.

Key International Actors

Multiple international and regional actors compete for influence in Lebanon.

France, the United States, and the European Union are key supporters of the Lebanese government and provide assistance for a wide range of programs, including armed forces training, torture prevention seminars, and civil society activities. However, these countries have not used their leverage to push Lebanon to adopt concrete measures to improve its human rights record, such as investigating specific allegations of torture or adopting laws that respect the rights of refugees or migrant workers.

Regionally, Syria, Iran, and Saudi Arabia maintain a strong influence on Lebanese politics through their local allies.

UN peacekeepers are still present in large numbers at Lebanon's southern border.

LIBYA

Libya's international reintegration continued to move ahead despite the government's ongoing human rights violations. Driven by business interests and Libya's cooperation in combating terrorism and irregular migration, European governments and the United States strengthened ties with Libya during 2009.

On the domestic front, government control and repression of civil society remain the norm, despite some movement toward reform. The authorities continue to imprison individuals for criticizing the country's political system or its leader, Mu`ammar al-Gaddafi, and Libya maintains harsh restrictions on freedom of assembly and expression, including penal code provisions that criminalize "insulting public officials" or "opposing the ideology of the Revolution." Nevertheless, 2009 saw some space for criticism in the press, proposed reform of the penal code, and greater tolerance for public protest by victims' families seeking disclosure and redress for a 1996 prison massacre.

Political Prisoners

Libya continues to detain scores of individuals for engaging in peaceful political activity. Hundreds more have been "disappeared," some for decades. In 2009 the authorities freed a number of political prisoners, including, in March, Jamal al-Haji and Farag Hmeid, the last of a group of 14 prisoners arrested in 2007 for planning a peaceful demonstration to commemorate the anniversary of a violent crackdown on demonstrators in Benghazi (another of the 14, Abderrahman al-Qotaiwi, initially reported as "disappeared," was released apparently in 2008, but his release not initially disclosed). Many others remain detained, however, such as Abdelnasser Al-Rabbasi, serving a 15-year sentence imposed in 2003 for writing a novel about corruption and human rights.

Fathi al-Jahmi, Libya's most prominent political prisoner, died in a Jordanian hospital on May 20, 2009, age 69, after six-and-a-half years' imprisonment in Libya. In March 2004 Internal Security agents imprisoned al-Jahmi after he called for democratization and criticized al-Gaddafi, and in July 2007, suffering from diabetes, hypertension, and heart disease, he was transferred to the state-run Tripoli Medical Center, where he remained under Internal Security control and was not free to leave the hospital. Al-Jahmi was flown to Jordan 15 days before he died, having lapsed into a coma two days earlier.

Arbitrary Detention

By the General People's Committee (Ministry) for Justice's own reckoning, about 500 prisoners who have served their sentences or been acquitted by Libyan courts remain imprisoned under orders of the Internal Security Agency. The agency, under the jurisdiction of the General People's Committee for Public Security, controls two prisons, Ain Zara and Abu Salim, where it holds "security" detainees. It has refused to carry out judicial orders to free these prisoners, despite calls from the secretary of justice for their release.

The 1996 Abu Salim Prison Massacre

In December 2008, Libyan authorities started informing the families of the 1,200 prisoners killed on June 29, 1996, in Tripoli's Abu Salim prison of the death of their relatives, by issuing death certificates (without specifying the cause of death, in many cases). This followed the June and September 2008 decisions by the North Benghazi Court ordering the government to reveal the fate of those who had died. The Libyan authorities have offered compensation of 200,000 dinars (US$162,000) to families who agree to relinquish all legal claims, but most of the victims' families in Benghazi have refused to accept compensation on those terms and continue to call for disclosure of what occurred on the day of the killings and criminal accountability for those responsible. The authorities have not made public any account of the events or held anyone responsible. On September 6, 2009, the acting secretary of defense established a seven-judge investigation panel, headed by a former military tribunal judge, to conduct an investigation.

Freedom of Expression, Association, and Assembly

While there has been an opening for greater debate and discussion in the press, freedom of expression remains severely curtailed. Article 178 of the penal code carries penalties of up to life imprisonment for disseminating information considered to "tarnish [the country's] reputation or undermine confidence in it abroad." Negative comments about al-Gaddafi are frequently punished, and self-censorship is rife. Two private newspapers, *Oea* and *Quryna*, publish limited criticism of the Libyan authorities, but journalists say they face harassment for expressing any criticism. Lawsuits for defamation, which carries criminal sanctions in Libya, are common.

Libya has no independent NGOs, and Libyan laws severely restrict freedom of association. Law 71 bans any group activity opposing the ideology of the 1969 revolution, and the penal code imposes the death penalty on those who join such groups. The government has refused to allow independent journalists' and lawyers' organizations. The only organization able to criticize human rights violations publicly is the Human Rights Society of the Gaddafi Foundation, which is chaired by Saif al-Islam al-Gaddafi, the Libyan leader's son.

In a tightening of restrictions, on June 29, 2009, the General People's Committee issued a decision requiring anyone wishing to hold a meeting or seminar to obtain 30-day advance approval from a newly established government committee, and requiring the meeting organizers to provide a list of all participants and the issues to be discussed.

Demonstrations are also illegal in the country, but during 2009 a number of demonstrations by the families of victims of the Abu Salim prison killings took place in Benghazi, the biggest of which, involving over 100 demonstrators, was on June 29. The government, for the most part, has allowed the families to demonstrate, and the Libyan press at times has covered their activities and demands, but some of the organizers have faced harassment, intimidation, and in March, arrest from security officials. The families have also formed a committee to present their demands.

Violence against Women and Girls

On October 21, 2009, at least 10 women ages 18 to 27 who live in a state-run care residence for women and girls who were orphaned as children, organized a rare demonstration calling for an end to sexual harassment they said they had experienced in the residence. A journalist who covered the demonstration for *Al Manara* was immediately afterwards called in for questioning by local police, and a few days later by the General Prosecutor's Office. Libyan news website *Libya al Youm* reported that officials had threatened to expel those who demonstrated from the residence, and pressured them to retract their statements and to sue the journalist for defamation. On October 29, however, the General Prosecutor's Office opened an investigation into the claims and on October 31 charged the head of the residence with sexual harassment.

Treatment of Foreigners

Libya continues to abuse and mistreat non-Libyan migrants caught trying to leave the country by boat. In May 2009 Human Rights Watch interviewed migrants in Malta and Italy who had been detained at some point in Libya. All reported that Libyan authorities had mistreated them and subjected them to indefinite detention, often in inhuman and degrading conditions. Interviewees described how Libyan guards beat them with wood and metal sticks, and detained them in severely overcrowded and unsanitary conditions. They also spoke about police corruption and brutality and of migrants being dumped in the desert near Libya's land borders. When Human Rights Watch visited Libya in April 2009, officials refused access to any of its many migrant detention centers.

Libya has no asylum law, has not signed the 1951 Refugee Convention, and has no formal working agreement with the United Nations High Commissioner for Refugees.

Fate of Returned Detainees

Libya continues to share intelligence on militant Islamists with Western governments, and the United States and United Kingdom continue to consider it a strategic partner in counterterrorism efforts. A number of those the US has returned or rendered to Libya over the past five years remain in detention after unfair trials, and Libyan authorities continue to detain Mohamed al-Rimi and Sofian Hamoodah, Libyan citizens whom the US government returned in 2006 and 2007 from detention in Guantanamo Bay. In April 2009 Human Rights Watch was able to confirm the detention of five former CIA secret detainees in Abu Salim prison.

In May, Ali Mohamed al-Fakheri (also known as Ibn al-Sheikh al-Libi) was found dead in his cell in Abu Salim prison. The State Security Court had sentenced al-Libi to life imprisonment following his transfer to Libya in 2006 after the US had rendered him to Jordan, Morocco, and Egypt (where he was tortured). Human Rights Watch spoke with him briefly in prison on April 27, though he refused to be interviewed. Libyan newspaper *Oea* first reported al-Libi's death on May 10, saying he had committed suicide.

Key International Actors

On November 20, 2008, the US Senate confirmed Gene Cretz as the first US ambassador to Libya since 1972. In September 2009 al-Gaddafi visited the US for the first time, and gave a 96-minute speech before the United Nations General Assembly.

On August 20, Scottish Justice Minister Kenny MacAskill ordered the release of Abdelbaset al-Megrahi, the only man convicted for the 1988 Lockerbie bombing. Saif al-Islam al-Gaddafi accompanied al-Megrahi back to Tripoli where he was greeted at the airport by crowds waving Scottish flags. The UK and US severely condemned this welcome, and the media accused the UK of releasing al-Megrahi in a bid to improve business dealings. The UK later acknowledged that for strategic and commercial reasons, UK government policy had favored al-Megrahi's release.

Italian-Libyan cooperation over migration intensified, based on the Treaty of Friendship, ratified in March 2009, which provides compensation for Italian colonialism, and joint measures to control migration. Al-Gaddafi paid a state visit to Italy in June 2009 and returned in July for the G8 meetings. In May Italy began interdicting and forcibly returning boat migrants directly to Libya in coordination with Libyan authorities (see also European Union chapter).

In February the African Union elected al-Gaddafi as chairman, and in June 2009 held its summit in Sirte, Libya. There, al-Gaddafi pushed for the creation of a Union of African States, and continued efforts to undermine the International Criminal Court , which helped lead to the adoption of a decision calling for AU members not to cooperate with the ICC in the arrest and surrender of Sudan's President Omar al-Bashir, subject of an ICC arrest warrant for war crimes and crimes against humanity.

Morocco / Western Sahara

Human rights conditions deteriorated overall in 2009 in Morocco, although the country continued to have a lively civil society and independent press. The government, aided by complaisant courts, used repressive legislation to punish and imprison peaceful opponents, especially those who violate taboos against criticizing the king or the monarchy, questioning the "Moroccanness" of Western Sahara, or "denigrating" Islam.

Restrictions on rights are particularly tight in the restive Western Sahara region, which Morocco claims sovereignty over and administers as if it were part of its national territory. A pro-independence movement known as the Polisario Front (Popular Front for the Liberation of the Saguía al-Hamra and Río de Oro) demands a referendum on self-determination for the Sahrawi people. The Polisario rejected an April 2007 Moroccan proposal for enhanced autonomy for the region, mainly because it nowhere mentions a referendum in which independence would be an option. Numerous Sahrawis were charged or imprisoned because of their peaceful advocacy of self-determination for the contested Western Sahara. Politically motivated restrictions on the right to travel increased.

Terrorism and Counterterrorism

Hundreds of suspected Islamist extremists arrested in the aftermath of the Casablanca bombings of May 2003 continue to serve prison terms. Many were convicted in unfair trials after being held that year in secret detention for days or weeks, and subjected to mistreatment and sometimes torture while under interrogation. Some were sentenced to death, a punishment that Morocco has not abolished even though it has not carried it out since 1993. Since August 2006 police have arrested hundreds more suspected Islamist militants, many of whom were convicted and imprisoned for belonging to "a criminal gang" or preparing to join "the jihad" in Iraq.

Intelligence agencies continued to interrogate terrorism suspects at an unacknowledged detention center at Temara, near Rabat, according to numerous reports from detainees. Many suspects alleged that police tortured them under interrogation, while holding them in pre-charge custody for longer than the 12-day maximum the law provides for terrorism cases. For example, several of the defendants in the so-called Belliraj mass trial (see below) contended that the police abducted them and held them incommunicado for between two and four weeks before presenting them to a judge. Some of these contended at trial that police at Temara tortured them in order to extract false confessions.

Confronting Past Abuses

Following the pioneering work completed in 2005 by Morocco's Equity and Reconciliation Commission (ERC), the state acknowledged responsibility for "disappearances" and other grave abuses in the past, and compensated some 16,000 victims or their survivors. However, no Moroccan officials or security force members are known to have been prosecuted for violations committed during the period from 1956 to 1999 that the ERC investigated, and the government has yet to implement most of the institutional reforms recommended by the ERC to safeguard against future abuses. In addition, as of October, the families of the "disappeared" persons whose cases were handled by the ERC and, afterwards by the Advisory Council on Human Rights, had not received a full account of the ERC's findings concerning the "disappearance" of their relatives.

Police Conduct and the Criminal Justice System

Police are rarely held accountable for violating human rights. In cases with political overtones, courts seldom provide fair trials; judges routinely ignore requests for medical examinations lodged by defendants who claim to have been tortured, refuse to summon exculpatory witnesses, and convict defendants on the basis of apparently coerced confessions. On July 28 the Rabat Court of Appeals convicted all 35 defendants in the "Belliraj" case of forming a terrorist network, sentencing them to terms of up to life in prison. The defendants included the heads of two parties and four other well-known political figures. The court based the guilty verdicts almost entirely on the statements attributed to the defendants by the police, even though most defendants had repudiated those statements before the investigating judge and all repudiated the statements at trial. The court refused to investigate allegations of torture, falsified statements, and statements written in Arabic for defendants unable to read that language. The appeals hearing was due to begin in December 2009.

Police arrested seven non-violent Sahrawi activists on October 8 upon their return from openly visiting the Polisario-run refugee camps near Tindouf, Algeria. A Casablanca judge referred their case to a military court on the grounds that the alleged offenses included harming "external state security," by "causing harm to Morocco's territorial integrity." The referral of civilians to a military court, where the procedural rights of defendants are abridged, was a rare and ominous development.

Freedom of Association, Assembly, and Movement

Morocco boasts thousands of independent associations. However, government officials arbitrarily impede the legalization of some organizations, undermining their freedom to operate. Groups affected include those defending the rights of Sahrawis, Amazighs (Berbers), sub-Saharan immigrants, and unemployed university graduates, as well as charitable, and cultural and education associations whose leadership includes members of Justice and Spirituality, one of the country's largest Islamist movements.

The government generally tolerates the work of the many human rights organizations active in Rabat and Casablanca. In northern Morocco, authorities on February 17, 2009 arrested Chekib el-Khayari, president of the Association for Human Rights in the Rif, after he accused certain Moroccan officials of complicity in narcotics trafficking. On June 24 a Casablanca court convicted el-Khayari of "gravely insulting state institutions" and minor currency violations, and sentenced him to three years in prison and a heavy fine. He was still in jail awaiting his appeal as of November.

Authorities generally do not hamper foreign human rights groups visiting Morocco, although the security forces sometimes question Moroccans who have had contact with them. Beginning in October the police enforced new restrictions on groups visiting the homes of Sahrawi activists, breaking up at least seven such visits on the grounds that visitors would henceforth require clearance for such meetings. Most types of outdoor gatherings require authorization from the

Interior Ministry, which can refuse permission if it deems them liable to "disturb the public order." Although many of the frequent public protests run their course undisturbed, baton-wielding police have brutally broken up others.

The government prevented Sahrawi activists from traveling abroad more often than in recent years. On August 5, authorities prevented six Sahrawi students from departing from Agadir airport to travel to the United Kingdom to participate in a program of cross-cultural dialogue. On October 6, Moroccan authorities detained and turned back five well-known Sahrawi activists who were on their way to Mauritania via the land border crossing. They confiscated the men's passports and had not returned them as of early November. Authorities declined to issue a passport to Brahim Sabbar, secretary-general of a Sahrawi human rights organization.

Media Freedom

Press freedom declined in 2009.The press law provides prison terms for "maliciously" spreading "false information" likely to disturb the public order or for speech that is defamatory, offensive to members of the royal family, or that undermines "Islam, the institution of the monarchy, or [Morocco's] territorial integrity." After the Arabic daily *Akhbar al-Youm* published on September 26 a cartoon about a cousin of King Mohammed VI, authorities froze its bank account and sent police to shut down its editorial offices – actions that have no basis in Moroccan law. A court on October 30 ordered the closure of *Akhbar al-Youm*'s offices and sentenced the cartoonist and director of publication to fines and suspended prison terms. Driss Chahtane, editor of *al-Mish'al* weekly, went to prison on October 15, the day a court of first instance sentenced him to a one-year term for maliciously publishing "false news" about the king's health. On August 1 the minister of the interior ordered the seizure of the new issues of *TelQuel* and *Nichan* because the two weeklies had published the result of a public opinion poll on King Mohammed VI, even though the results were favorable. Disregarding the applicable law, the authorities then destroyed copies of the issues before the publisher could appeal the seizure in court.

MOROCCO

Freedom to Create Associations

A Declarative Regime in Name Only

HUMAN
RIGHTS
WATCH

Key International Actors

Morocco is the biggest beneficiary of the European Neighbourhood and Partnership Instrument, with €654 million in aid earmarked for 2007-2010, including grants to many independent Moroccan human rights organizations. In 2008 the European Union voted to give the kingdom "advanced status," placing it a notch above other members of the EU's "neighbourhood policy."

A European parliamentary delegation conducted a fact-finding mission to Morocco and Western Sahara in January 2009 that Morocco had blocked for three years. The delegation said it was able to conduct its visit without obstacles. Among its recommendations was that Morocco "ensure that the clauses relating to territorial integrity do not apply to the mere expression of opinions, including those in support of independence, provided that they respect the principle of non-violence."

While supporting autonomy for Western Sahara under Moroccan sovereignty, US diplomats traveled to Western Sahara, where they met with Sahrawi human rights activists.

In the first visit to North Africa by a senior official of the Obama administration, Secretary of State Hillary Clinton met in Morocco with King Mohammed VI on November 2. In her public rermarks the next day, Clinton saluted the reforms that have enabled Moroccan women to "bring their considerable talents to strengthening democratic institutions, accelerating economic growth and broadening the work of civil society."

France is Morocco's leading trade partner and the leading source of public development aid and private investment. France gave Morocco €460 million in Overseas Development Assistance in 2007-2009, making it the leading recipient of such assistance. France rarely criticized publicly Morocco's human rights practices.

The United Nations Security Council in April 2009 renewed for one year the MINURSO peacekeeping force in Western Sahara but once again declined to extend its mandate to include human rights observation and protection. Morocco opposes giving MINURSO such a mandate, whereas the Polisario says it supports it.

Morocco ratified the International Convention on the Protection and Promotion of the Rights and Dignity of Persons with Disabilities on April 9. King Mohammed VI announced on December 10, 2008 that Morocco would lift its reservations to the Convention for the Elimination of All Forms of Discrimination against Women but that had yet to happen as of November 2009. Morocco hosted a visit in June by the Working Group on Enforced and Involuntary Disappearances, the first by the group in an Arab or African country. The group praised the ERC but expressed concern that its mandate, which excluded the prosecution of perpetrators, could promote impunity.

SAUDI ARABIA

Human rights conditions remain poor in Saudi Arabia. In February 2009 King Abdullah replaced conservatives in the religious establishment, judiciary, and education system with more progressive-minded officials, but domestic and international pressure to improve human rights practices is feeble.

Authorities continue to systematically suppress, or fail to protect, the rights of fourteen million Saudi women and girls, eight million foreign workers, and some two million Shia. Thousands of people have received unfair trials or were subject to arbitrary detention. Curbs on freedom of association, expression, and movement, as well as a pervasive lack of official accountability, remain serious concerns. In May the government cancelled scheduled municipal elections.

Women's and Girls' Rights

The government told the United Nations Human Rights Council in June that it would dismantle the system of male legal guardianship over women, but it continues to treat women as legal minors by allowing male guardians to determine a woman's right to work, study, marry, travel, and even receive a national identification card. Officials refused to let Heba Neguib, a 27-year-old Egyptian living with her family in Saudi Arabia, travel back to Egypt without permission from her father, who initially refused. Women who are victims of domestic violence face societal and governmental obstacles in obtaining redress.

In February, Norah al-Fayez was appointed deputy minister of education, the highest post attained by a woman in Saudi Arabia. In September the first coeducational facility, King Abdullah University of Science and Technology, was inaugurated. Yet sex segregation is strictly enforced throughout the kingdom and impedes women's full participation in public life. Women are prohibited from working in offices or entering government buildings without female sections, or pursuing degrees in disciplines not taught in women's colleges. Women cannot work as judges, prosecutors, or court-accredited lawyers. In March a court in Ha'il convicted a 75-year-old woman for "illegal mingling" with her nephew and his friend who had delivered food to her.

The government has not yet set a minimum age for marriage, against a recommendation by the governmental Human Rights Commission. In April a court in 'Unaiza reaffirmed its earlier verdict, overturned on appeal, refusing to annul the marriage of a girl age 8 to a middle-age man. In March a 70-year-old man demanded US$130,000 to divorce his new 13-year-old bride, who had run away from him. In May a girl age 10 in the Eastern Province was betrothed to a man 15 years her senior.

Migrant Worker Rights

An estimated eight million largely Asian and Arab foreign workers fill manual, clerical, and service jobs. Many suffer multiple abuses and labor exploitation, sometimes rising to slavery-like conditions. A new anti-trafficking law passed in July set prison sentences of up to 15 years for forced labor. However, Saudi Arabia made little progress reforming the restrictive *kafala* (sponsorship) system that ties migrant workers' residency permits to their employers, fueling abuses such as employers confiscating passports, withholding wages, and forcing migrants to work against their will.

In July 2009 the advisory Shura Council extended some labor protections to the 1.5 million migrant domestic workers, but excluded the right of workers to leave the house or keep their passports, and obliges them to obey the employers. Asian embassies report thousands of complaints each year from domestic workers forced to work 15-20 hours a day, seven days a week, and denied their salaries. Domestic workers frequently endure forced confinement, food deprivation, and severe psychological, physical, and sexual abuse.

Migrants sometimes face severe delays in the immigration and justice systems, and obstacles such as lack of access to interpreters, legal aid, or their consulates. Few migrants successfully pursue criminal cases against abusive employers. Following a dispute with his sponsor, officials on October 26 detained pending deportation Usama Hijazi, an Egyptian legal adviser living in Saudi Arabia for 16 years. Hijazi had just won a court ruling in his favor against his sponsor, granting him 155,000 riyal (US$41,000) and allowing him to transfer his sponsorship. Authorities repatriated Keni binti Carda, an Indonesian domestic worker, in late 2008 before she could formally complain about her employers causing her severe burns and prying out her teeth. She returned to Riyadh to press charges, but as of November 2009 criminal proceedings had yet to begin. In August Saudi morality police raided a shelter run by a Filipino support group, though prosecutors later dropped charges against 18 persons present.

Criminal Justice, Arbitrary Detention, Torture, and Ill-Treatment

Detainees, including children, are commonly the victims of systematic and multiple violations of due process and fair trial rights, including arbitrary arrest and torture and ill-treatment in detention. Saudi judges routinely sentence defendants to thousands of lashes. The kingdom carried out some 53 executions as of September 2009, including of one woman, slightly fewer than in 2008.

Judges can order arrest and detention of children at their discretion. Children can be tried and sentenced as adults at any age if the defendant is determined to have attained majority, a concept based on puberty. Shaikh Salman al-'Awda, a prominent cleric, in September criticized death sentences for children; no executions of children were reported in 2009.

Authorities rarely inform suspects of the crime with which they are charged, or of the supporting evidence. Saudi Arabia has no penal code, and prosecutors and judges largely define criminal offenses at their discretion. During interrogation detainees are not assisted by lawyers, and they face excessive pretrial delays, and difficulty examining witnesses or presenting evidence at trial. Secret police (*mabahith*) in 2009 detained or continued to detain without trial or access to lawyers, in many cases for years, around 2,000 persons suspected of sympathies with or involvement in terrorism or for their peaceful political views. Muhammad al-'Utaibi, and Khalid al-'Umair, two human rights activists arrested in January for trying to organize a peaceful Gaza solidarity demonstration, continue to be held in al-Ha'ir prison without trial beyond the six-month limit allowed under Saudi law.

In July Saudi Arabia announced that a specialized criminal court had found 330 persons guilty of terrorism-related offenses, but did not provide further details. Trials were closed and defendants did not have access to lawyers of their choosing. A total of 991 terrorism suspects were referred to court in October 2008.

SAUDI ARABIA

Human Rights and Saudi Arabia's Counterterrorism Response

Religious Counseling, Indefinite Detention, and Flawed Trials

HUMAN
RIGHTS
WATCH

On August 28, 2009, guards in al-Ha'ir prison severely beat a Yemeni prisoner. In another case, prosecutors began probing whether an al-Ha'ir guard beat prisoner Abd al-Karim al-Dahamshi in July. Detainees reported beatings in Buraiman and Malaz prisons and inhumane conditions in Jeddah's deportation center.

Freedom of Expression

Saudi authorities brooked little public criticism of officials or government policies in 2009. Print and broadcast media remained heavily censored and internet critics faced arrest. The government tolerated hate speech, including by officials, while courts criminalized free speech.

Interior Minister Prince Nayef in June criticized a reporter for *Al-Watan* newspaper for asking why there are more religious than ordinary police stations in Riyadh. Jamal Khashoggi, *Al-Watan*'s chief editor, published a contrite article praising Nayef and promising reflection on its reporting. In September MBC1 television canceled two episodes of the popular Ramadan series *Tash Ma Tash*, which regularly pokes fun at conservative and liberal Saudi attitudes: one dealt with excessively amplified calls to prayer, and the other imagined Barack Obama growing up in the kingdom. Authorities in August closed local LBC television offices after a Saudi man spoke about his sexual conquests on one show in July; he received a five-year prison sentence with 1,000 lashes for advocating vice. A judge in May filed a libel case that can carry a prison sentence against Hayat al-Ghamdi of *Arab News* for reporting that at a conference on domestic violence the judge had spoken approvingly of a husband slapping his wife for lavish spending. An Abha court accepted the case, although only the Ministry of Information has jurisdiction over the content of publications.

Saudi domestic intelligence on July 29 arrested Syrian blogger Ra'fat al-Ghanim, who had signed a petition calling for the release of al-'Utaibi and al-'Umair, the two human rights activists arrested in January.

In early 2009 Saudi authorities lifted bans on foreign travel on Muhammad Sa'id Tayyib, Abd al-Rahman al-Lahim, and Najib al-Khunaizi, imposed in 2003 after they advocated constitutional reform, but maintained bans on Ali al-Dumaini, Matrook al-Faleh, Abdullah al-Hamid and Muhammad Bajadi, fellow advocates.

Denied Dignity

Systematic Discrimination and Hostility toward
Saudi Shia Citizens

**HUMAN
RIGHTS
WATCH**

Freedom of Religion

Saudi Arabia systematically discriminates against its religious minorities—in particular, Shia in the Eastern Province and around Medina, and Ismailis (a distinct branch of Shiism) in Najran. Official discrimination against Shia encompasses religious practices, education, and the justice system. Government officials exclude Shia from employment and decision making, and publicly disparage their faith.

Clashes between Shia pilgrims and security guards in Medina in February 2009 led to the worst sectarian tensions in years. Authorities arrested scores of pilgrims and protestors demonstrating in solidarity with them, releasing most without charge by July. That month, authorities in Khobar arrested Shia who hosted communal prayers in their homes, and on September 4 sealed shut the city's only Ismaili mosque. In al-Ahsa', authorities by September had arrested at least 42 Shia religious and community leaders in 2009.

In Najran, new governor Prince Mish'al, the king's son, in June announced land distribution to local residents, and, in August, pardons for the remaining 17 prisoners sentenced after sectarian clashes in April 2000. In September King Abdullah released Ismaili leader Shaikh Ahmad bin Turki Al Sa'b, detained without charge since May 2008 for complaining about discrimination against his community. However, a court in August 2009 sentenced Hadi Al Mutif, an Ismaili on death row since 1994 for allegedly insulting the Prophet Muhammad, to an additional five years in prison for criticizing his imprisonment in a videotaped message broadcast on Al-Hurra television in January 2007.

Key International Actors

Saudi Arabia is a key ally of the United States and the United Kingdom. US pressure for human rights improvements was imperceptible. UK efforts through the Two Kingdoms Dialogue to protect human rights had no tangible effect, if such efforts were made at all.

SYRIA

Syria's poor human rights situation deteriorated further in 2009, as the authorities arrested political and human rights activists, censored websites, detained bloggers, and imposed travel bans. No political parties are licensed. Emergency rule, imposed in 1963, remains in effect and Syria's multiple security agencies continue to detain people without arrest warrants. The Supreme State Security Court (SSSC), an exceptional court with almost no procedural guarantees, resumed trials in March 2009, following an eight-month suspension.

Syria's repressive policies toward its Kurdish minority continue. Security agencies prevented political and cultural gatherings, and regularly detain and try Kurdish activists demanding increased political rights and recognition of Kurdish culture.

Arrest and Trial of Political Activists

The SSSC sentenced over 45 people in 2009 on various grounds, including membership in the banned Muslim Brotherhood, Kurdish activism, membership in unauthorized political groups, and independent criticism of the government. On February 4, political security detained two members of the Communist Party for collecting signatures opposing a government decree that imposes new restrictions on real estate transactions in border areas. Three months later, on May 21, political security detained five members of the Communist Work Party during a gathering at a member's house. At this writing, all remain in detention.

On March 15 a Damascus criminal court sentenced writer and political analyst Habib Saleh to three years in jail for "spreading false information" and "weakening national sentiment" for writing articles criticizing the government and defending opposition figure Riad al-Turk.

Twelve leaders of the Damascus Declaration, a prominent gathering of opposition groups, continue to serve 30-month prison terms imposed in October 2008 after attending a political meeting. Among those detained is Riad Seif, 62, a former member of parliament who is in poor health. A Damascus criminal court tried Walid al-Bunni, another of the 12, for voicing criticism of the government while in prison, but acquitted him of the new charge on June 17.

In March 2009 the United Nations Working Group on Arbitrary Detention deemed arbitrary the imprisonment of Kamal al-Labwani, a physician and founder of the Democratic Liberal Gathering, who is serving a 15-year sentence for advocating peaceful reform.

Authorities released prominent writer Michel Kilo and political activist Mahmud `Issa, in May and June respectively, after the two finished serving three-year sentences for signing a petition calling for Syrian-Lebanese relations to be based on mutual respect for sovereignty.

Freedom of Expression and Civil Society Activism

Syria has no independent press. The government has extended to online outlets restrictions it imposes on other media. Internet censorship of political websites is pervasive and extends to popular websites such as Blogger (Google's blogging engine), Facebook, and YouTube.

On September 13 the SSSC sentenced blogger Karim `Arbaji to three years in prison on the charge of "spreading false information that can weaken national sentiment" for moderating a popular online youth forum, akhawia.net, that contained criticisms of the government.

Also on September 13, security forces shut down the office of Mazen Darwish, president of the Syrian Center for Media and Freedom of Expression (SCM), without providing any explanation or legal order.

In April a military prosecutor charged human rights lawyer Khalil Ma`touk with "insulting the president and public administrations" and "inciting sectarian conflict" after Ma`touk called for prosecuting security officials suspected of killing his nephew in October 2008 while reportedly pursuing smugglers. Ma`touk's trial is ongoing at this writing.

On July 28, 2009, State Security detained Muhannad al-Hasani, president of the Syrian Human Rights Organization (Swasiah), and two days later an investigating judge charged him with "weakening national sentiment" and "spreading false or exaggerated information" in connection with his monitoring of the SSSC. His trial is ongoing. On November 10 the Syrian Bar Association issued a decision to permanently disbar him.

On October 14, State Security detained Haytham al-Maleh, 78, a prominent human rights lawyer, following his appearance on an opposition television station in which he criticized the ongoing repression of freedom of expression in Syria. On November 3 a military judge charged him with "spreading false or exaggerated information that can weaken national sentiment." His trial is ongoing.

The government continues to prevent activists from traveling abroad, and in some cases, their families. Among the human rights activists whom security services prevented from traveling in 2009 are Musa Shanani, a lawyer, Abdel Karim Rehaoui, president of the Syrian Human Rights League, Abdel Rahim Ghamaza, a lawyer with the National Organization for Human Rights, and Najib Dadam, board member of the Human Rights Association of Syria. The SCM issued a report in February listing 417 political and human rights activists banned from traveling.

All Syrian human rights groups remain unlicensed, as officials consistently deny their requests for registration. The National Organization for Human Rights has challenged before an administrative court the decision of the Ministry of Social Affairs and Labor to deny its registration request. The ministry responded by calling for the organization's members to be prosecuted.

Arbitrary Detention, Enforced Disappearances, and Torture

Syria's multiple security services continue to detain people without arrest warrants and frequently refuse to disclose their whereabouts for weeks and sometimes months—in effect forcibly disappearing them. The fate of at least 10 men detained in August 2008 from the region of Deir al-Zawr because of suspected ties to Islamists remains unknown. The authorities have also kept silent about the fate of at least eight Kurds detained since September 2008 on suspicion of ties to a separatist Kurdish movement.

As in previous years, the government failed to acknowledge security force involvement in the "disappearance" of an estimated 17,000 persons, mostly Muslim Brotherhood members and other Syrian activists detained by the government in the late 1970s and early 1980s, as well as hundreds of Lebanese and Palestinians detained in Syria or abducted from Lebanon. The vast majority remains unaccounted for and many are believed to have been killed.

More than one year after security forces opened fire on rioting inmates in Sednaya prison, killing at least nine, the government has not disclosed any information about the casualties. The authorities have not released Nizar Rastanawi, a prominent human rights activist who was scheduled to complete a four-year sentence in Sednaya on April 18, 2009, and there is no information about his well-being or whereabouts.

Human Rights Watch received numerous reports of ill-treatment and torture by security agencies. On January 10, 2009, the security services returned the body of Muhammad Amin al-Shawa, 43, who had been detained in August 2008, to his family. According to Syrian human rights groups, he died under torture. Ten Kurdish activists told Human Rights Watch that agents of security agencies tortured them in 2009.

Discrimination and Repression against Kurds

Kurds, Syria's largest non-Arab ethnic minority, remain subject to systematic discrimination, including the arbitrary denial of citizenship to an estimated 300,000 Syria-born Kurds. Authorities suppress expressions of Kurdish identity, and prohibit the teaching of Kurdish in schools. On February 28, 2009, security forces violently dispersed Kurds who had gathered to protest the decree restricting real estate transactions in border areas, and subsequently detained 21 demonstrators. In March police stopped a musical event organized by a Kurdish political party in Qamishli, and security forces broke up gatherings celebrating the Kurdish New Year in Qamishli and Derbassiyeh.

Security forces detained at least nine prominent Kurdish political leaders in 2009, including, on January 10, Mustapha Jum`a, acting general secretary of the Azadi Party. On April 14 a military court sentenced two Yekiti party leaders, Fuad `Aliko and Hasan Saleh, to 8 and 13 months in prison respectively for membership in an unlicensed political organization. On May 11 a criminal court sentenced Mesh`al Tammo, spokesperson for the Kurdish Future Movement in Syria, to three-and-a-half years in prison for "weakening national sentiments" and "broadcasting false information." On October 20 a criminal court sentenced Ibrahim Berro, a Yekiti party leader, to eight months in prison for membership in an unlicensed political organization.

Women's and Girls' Rights

Syria's constitution guarantees gender equality, and many women are active in public life, but personal status laws as well as the penal code contain provisions that discriminate against women and girls. On June 5 the Syrian media revealed that the Ministry of Justice had submitted a new draft personal status law that still kept discriminatory clauses against women intact, such as denying women married to non-Syrians the right to pass on their nationality to their husbands and children, and requiring women to receive male permission to travel abroad and to work outside the home. After numerous protests from Syrian women's rights groups, President Bashar al-Asad cancelled the draft law in July.

On July 1 President al-Asad amended the Penal Code to require a minimum two-year sentence for so-called "honor" crimes. While the number of honor crimes is unknown, the Syrian Women's Observatory, an unlicensed group, documented at least 12 in 2009, including the killing in August of an 18-year-old by her father because a neighbor had tried to rape her.

Situation of Refugees Fleeing Iraq

Syria hosts more Iraqi refugees than any other country. Resurgent violence in Iraq caused Iraqis to continue to arrive in Syria: During the first six months of 2009 the United Nations High Commissioner for Refugees officially registered 19,000 new Iraqi refugees, bringing the total number of registered Iraqi refugees to 210,000. This represents only a portion of the Iraqis in Syria, the actual number being an estimated 1–1.5 million. Syria gives Iraqi refugees, registered or not, access to public hospitals and schools, but prohibits them from working. While Syria has generally maintained its doors open to Iraqi refugees, it has implemented since 2007 more restrictive entry requirements. Syria has forcibly returned to Iraq some Iraqi refugees whom Syria accused of committing criminal acts or working illegally.

Syria continues to refuse entry to Palestinians fleeing Iraq. At this writing, at least 2,700 remain at makeshift camps in the no-man's-land between Iraqi and Syrian border checkpoints. Chile and Sweden have accepted to resettle some of these refugees.

Key International Actors

Syria's diplomatic isolation eroded further in 2009, with at least nine high-level foreign officials visiting Damascus, including German foreign minister Frank-Walter Steinmeier and United States envoy George Mitchell. The renewed ties have had little impact on Syria's human rights record, however. During 2009 the European Parliament issued public statements expressing concern over the human rights situation in Syria, but this did not impede progress toward signing an Association Agreement, a process that had been frozen following the assassination of Lebanese Prime Minister Rafik Hariri in February 2005.

TUNISIA

President Zine al-Abidine Ben Ali and the ruling party, the Democratic Constitutional Rally (RCD), dominate political life in Tunisia. The government uses the threat of terrorism and religious extremism as a pretext to crack down on peaceful dissent.

Ben Ali was elected to a fifth term on October 25, 2009, with an official tally of 89.6 percent of the vote, against three challengers. Laws designed to exclude outspoken opponents, and acts of intimidation and censorship against those authorized to challenge the incumbent, prevented the campaign from being a period of serious debate and prevented the vote from being free and fair. In the legislative elections held the same day the RCD won the popular vote and thus was awarded 75 percent of the seats, the other 25 percent being set aside for candidates of the other parties.

Pre-Election Violations

Despite President Ben Ali's proclamation that the October presidential and legislative elections would be conducted in a democratic and transparent manner, laws adopted by the RCD-dominated parliament disqualified two key potential presidential candidates. The only outspoken one among the three authorized contenders was Ahmed Brahim of the formerly communist et-Tajdid movement. Brahim's party saw authorities annul the nominations of 13 of 26 members running for parliamentary seats, and block distribution of the issue of its newspaper containing its electoral platform. The Ministry of Interior also demanded that Brahim retract five points from his campaign manifesto, including those that criticized the way the elections were being conducted and references to a prevailing "mentality of one-party rule."

Human rights lawyer Radhia Nasraoui and her husband Hamma Hammami, head of the banned Communist Party of Tunisian Workers, were assaulted on September 29 by plainclothes policemen at Carthage airport in Tunis. Hammami had just returned from Paris, where he had given an interview to Al Jazeera television in which he accused the Tunisian government of human rights violations and urged a boycott of the elections.

Human Rights Defenders

Authorities have refused to grant legal recognition to every truly independent human rights organization that has applied over the past decade. They then invoke the organization's "illegal" status to hamper its activities.

Human rights defenders and dissidents are subject to heavy surveillance, arbitrary travel bans, dismissal from work, interruptions in phone service, physical assaults, harassment of relatives, suspicious acts of vandalism and theft, and slander campaigns in the press. Members of the unrecognized International Association in Support of Political Prisoners (AISPP) are regular targets for harassment by the security forces. In April 2009 Human Rights Watch spoke with former political prisoners in meetings arranged by AISPP. Plainclothes police officers closely monitored both Human Rights Watch researchers and the people they interviewed, stopping some of the latter to check their IDs and question them about the meetings.

On September 15, plainclothes police detained for nine hours human rights defender and former political prisoner Abdallah Zouari in Hassi Djerbi. They interrogated him about his media and human rights work in the past seven years, threatening him if he did not stop criticizing the government, Zouari said. Just weeks earlier, Zouari had completed seven years of post-prison town arrest in a remote village far from his home in greater Tunis, including two years that the authorities imposed by an oral order (without ever providing a legal basis) at the conclusion of his original five-year sentence of "administrative control."

Criminal Justice and Rule of Law

Although Tunisia's constitution provides for an independent judiciary, the executive branch strongly influences judicial decisions and controls the appointment, tenure, and transfer of judges. In cases that have a political character, courts fail to guarantee defendants a fair trial. Prosecutors and judges usually turn a blind eye to torture allegations, even when defense lawyers formally demand an investigation. Trial judges convict defendants solely or predominantly on the basis of coerced confessions, or on the testimony of witnesses whom the defendant does not have the opportunity to confront in court.

The International Committee of the Red Cross continued its program of visiting Tunisian prisons. However, authorities have not allowed access by independent human rights organizations. They continue to refuse to honor an explicit commit-ment made in April 2005 to allow visits by Human Rights Watch, first by delaying approval, then imposing conditions on the visits that would undermine the credi-bility of the data obtained, and then by ignoring revised proposals for the visits submitted by Human Rights Watch.

Tunisian law allows judges to sentence defendants both to prison terms and to post-prison terms of "administrative control." However, the authorities subject ex-prisoners convicted for their suspected affiliation with Islamist movements to a variety of restrictions that exceed what the law permits, such as giving them oral instructions to present themselves regularly at police stations, denying them passports without written justification, and pressuring employers to refrain from hiring them.

Tunisian citizens often find no redress for government violations against them. For example, the Ministry of Interior still refuses ex-prisoner Hocine Jelassi a passport even though the administrative court ruled in his favor on the matter in 2007.

Media Freedom

None of the domestic print and broadcast media offers critical coverage of gov-ernment policies, apart from a few low-circulation magazines such as *al-Mawkif*, an opposition party outlet, that are subject to occasional confiscation. Tunisia has privately-owned radio and television stations, but private ownership is not syn-onymous with editorial independence. The government blocks access to certain domestic and international political or human rights websites featuring critical coverage of Tunisia.

On August 15, 2009, pro-government journalists ousted the board of the National Syndicate of Tunisian Journalists (NSTJ) and replaced it with a new one controlled by pro-government members. This action followed a smear campaign against the previous board and its democratically elected president, after the NSTJ in May had released a report critical of the government's suppression of the media.

Authorities barred Florence Beaugé, the North Africa correspondent for *Le Monde*, from entering the country on October 20, accusing her of having "always shown blatant malevolence and a systematically hostile bias toward Tunisia."

Counterterrorism Measures and Human Rights

Since 1991 there has been one deadly terrorist attack in Tunisia: an April 2002 truck bomb that targeted a synagogue on the island of Djerba, for which al Qaeda claimed responsibility. In addition, security forces have clashed once with armed militants, in December 2006 and January 2007, outside the capital.

The 2003 Law in Support of "International Efforts to Fight Terrorism and the Repression of Money Laundering" contains a broad definition of terrorism that the United Nations Human Rights Committee criticized on March 28, 2008, for its "lack of precision." Authorities have charged many hundreds of men, and some minors, under the law. Nearly all of the hundreds who were convicted and imprisoned stood accused of planning to join jihadist groups abroad or inciting others to join, rather than of having planned or committed specific acts of violence. In July 2009 the Tunisian parliament adopted an amendment narrowing the law's definition of a terrorist act by restricting the extent to which "incitement to hatred" would meet the definition.

Suspects arrested in the context of the counterterrorism law commonly face a range of procedural abuses that includes the failure by authorities to notify their kin promptly, in violation of Tunisian law, extension of pre-arraignment detention beyond the legal six-day limit, and the refusal of judges and prosecutors to act on requests for a medical examination.

Socioeconomic Unrest

At least 200 people were prosecuted in connection with socioeconomic protests in 2008 in the depressed mining region surrounding the southern town of Redhayef. Charges included "forming a criminal group with the aim of destroying public and private property" and "armed rebellion and assault on officials during the exercise of their duties." In February 2009 an appeals court upheld the convictions of Adnan Hajji, secretary general of the local branch of the General Union of Tunisian Workers, and 37 other trade unionists and protestors. On May 11 a peaceful demonstration by relatives of the detainees calling for their release led to the arrest of some 30 individuals, eight of whom were charged with minor offenses and sentenced to up to one year in prison, according to Amnesty International.

On November 4 some 68 prisoners held in connection with the 2008 protests were conditionally released in a presidential pardon issued by Ben Ali to mark the 22nd anniversary of his coming to power. Approximately 50 people who were tried in absentia continue to face charges related to the protests.

Key International Actors

France is Tunisia's leading trade partner and its fourth largest foreign investor. In April 2009 France concluded a nuclear energy cooperation deal and an €80 million aid package for Tunisia. On March 22 French foreign minister Bernard Kouchner acknowledged, "It's true that there are human rights abuses in Tunisia, journalists who are harassed, sometimes imprisoned, and a general policy of firmness." He then went on to praise Tunisia's economic and social achievements, notably regarding the status of women and the values of secularism. In response to a spate of post-election arrests, Bernard Valero, spokesperson for the French foreign ministry, declared on November 6, "We are concerned by the difficulties faced by journalists and human rights defenders in Tunisia ... We have conveyed our concerns to the Tunisian ambassador and raised them with our European partners."

The European Union-Tunisia Association Agreement continues to be in force, despite the government's human rights record and its blocking of EU grants to some NGOs. More than 80 percent of Tunisia's trade is conducted with Europe. EU officials occasionally criticize their partner's rights record, while praising its economic performance and the state of bilateral relations overall. On July 3, 2009, EU External Relations Commissioner Benita Ferrero-Waldner criticized Tunisia for shutting down Radio Kalima, a web-based radio station critical of the government, which earlier in the year authorities had refused to license, seizing its equipment and harassing its journalists.

United States Department of State spokesperson Ian Kelly on October 26 said the US was "concerned" about the Tunisian elections, adding,"We are not aware that permission was granted to any credible independent observers.... We'll continue to pursue bilateral cooperation in areas of mutual interest, and we'll continue to press for political reform and respect for human rights."

At this writing Tunisia is negotiating a visit by the UN special rapporteur on human rights while countering terrorism. It has not agreed to a long-standing request for a visit by the special rapporteur on torture.

UNITED ARAB EMIRATES (UAE)

The UAE's economy stumbled in 2009 and the human rights situation worsened, particularly for migrant workers. Construction and related industries sent thousands of migrant workers home after projects were scrapped or suspended. Authorities jailed a number of UAE citizens and foreigners for debt and corruption, with some languishing in jail for months without charge or after completing their sentences.

Migrant Worker Rights

During six years of spectacular growth in the construction sector, mainly in Dubai, the UAE brought in hundreds of thousands of South Asian migrant workers. But the financial crisis that began in late 2008 slowed construction, and by July 2009 tens of thousands of workers had returned home from the UAE, judging from Indian government statements describing a situation likely to be typical of labor-sending countries. Some companies sent migrant workers home on unpaid "vacations" as a way to avoid compensating workers whose contracts they had broken.

Despite the economic downturn, foreigners still officially account for 83.5 percent of UAE residents and nearly 99 percent of the private-sector workforce. Immigration sponsorship laws grant employers extraordinary power over the lives of migrant workers. Other laws in force fail to protect workers' rights to organize and to bargain collectively, provide punishments for workers going on strike, and exclude from coverage domestic workers employed in private households. Although the Labor Law of 1980 calls for a minimum wage, the Ministry of Labor has yet to adopt such a measure.

Many female domestic workers are subjected to unpaid wages, food deprivation, forced confinement, and physical or sexual abuse. In August 2009 the Philippines government paid to fly home 44 Filipinas who had been living for months at a shelter. The women were among 127 Filipinas, mostly housemaids, who fled their workplace after complaining of mistreatment, long working hours, insufficient food, and nonpayment of salaries. The standard contract for domestic workers introduced in April 2007 provides some protections and calls for "adequate

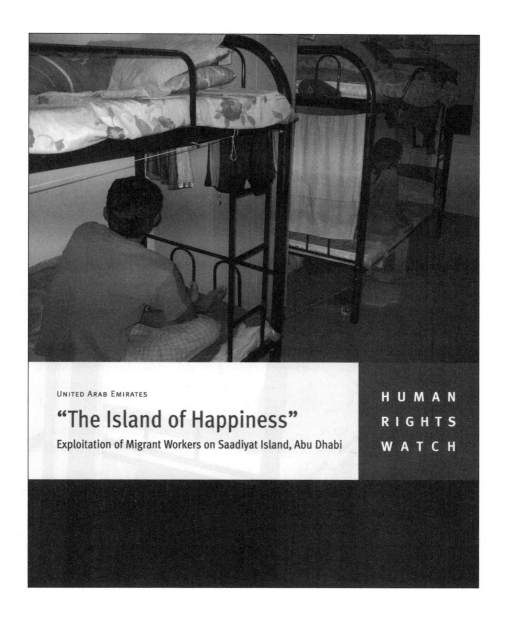

UNITED ARAB EMIRATES

"The Island of Happiness"

Exploitation of Migrant Workers on Saadiyat Island, Abu Dhabi

HUMAN
RIGHTS
WATCH

breaks," but does not limit working hours or provide for a weekly rest day, over-time pay, or workers' compensation.

Exploitation of migrant workers by construction companies across the country is also severe: abuses include maintaining unsafe working environments that con-tribute to avoidable illness or deaths, and withholding workers' travel documents. On August 31, 2009, police and labor officials quickly dispersed a demonstration over low wages by as many as 2,000 striking migrant workers employed by con-struction and engineering company Al Habtoor in Dubai. A Ministry of Labor investigation into the strike cleared the company of any wrongdoing after deter-mining it had not broken any rules regarding pay.

Workers from South Asia have been building the infrastructure of Saadiyat Island since 2005. The UAE government hopes to turn a US$27 billion development on the island into a global tourist destination, with international institutions plan-ning to open branches there, including the Guggenheim, New York University, and the Louvre Abu Dhabi (under the responsibility of Agence France-Muséums). Migrant workers working on the island interviewed by Human Rights Watch said they were caught in a cycle of abuse that left them deeply indebted and unable to stand up for their rights or even quit their jobs. The UAE government and the authorities responsible for developing Saadiyat Island have failed to tackle the root causes of worker abuse: unlawful recruiting fees charged to migrant workers, wages below what was promised, and a sponsorship system that gives employers virtually complete power over their workers.

In June 2009 the UAE cabinet approved compulsory housing standards to improve living conditions for migrant workers. Employers still have five years to comply with the rules, which took effect in September.

In its 2009 annual report on human trafficking the United States Department of State put the UAE back at Tier 2 of its list of countries cited for their records on trafficking, after having removed the country from the 2008 list. The US consid-ered that the UAE has yet to take crucial measures to fight trafficking and forced labor, such as stronger monitoring of recruitment agencies and prosecuting those who traffic in forced labor.

Torture

In May 2009 UAE authorities detained a royal family member in connection with the torture of an Afghan grain dealer, after international coverage of a video showing the torture. The video showed Sheikh Issa bin Zayed al Nahyan, with the assistance of what appear to be police agents, torturing Mohammed Shah Poor using whips, electric cattle prods, and wooden planks with protruding nails. Near the end of the video, Al Nahyan positioned Poor on the desert sand and then drove over him repeatedly. The UAE had announced in April that the Abu Dhabi Judicial Department would conduct an expeditious and "comprehensive review" of the torture incident, and in July the government issued a public statement that the investigation was ongoing. Previously, the Ministry of Interior had character-ized the abuse as an assault that the parties subsequently settled "privately." At this writing UAE officials still have not released details about the investigation.

In October the Federal Supreme Court convicted Naji Hamdan of terrorism-related charges, and sentenced him to 18 months in prison. The chief justice, Khalifa al-Muhairi, did not give a written or oral decision explaining the ruling or whether Hamdan was convicted of all three charges. Hamdan, an American of Lebanese origin, has denied the allegations and his lawyer told the court that Hamdan suf-fered torture and threats in detention and was coerced into signing a confession "to whatever they wanted to hear." Hamdan was released in November on the basis of time served, and deported to Lebanon.

Criminal Justice System

Under criminal procedure laws, public prosecutors can order detainees to be held for 21 days without charge. Courts may then grant 30-day renewable extensions for an indefinite period and without requiring prosecutors to file charges. A sus-pect is entitled to an attorney only after the police have completed their investi-gation. As a result, accused persons often go for days or weeks without access to legal counsel. In March 2008 authorities detained American businessman Zack Shahin, the former chief executive officer of Dubai-based property developer Deyaar Development PJSC, and he was eventually charged with corruption-related offenses after being held for 13 months without formal charges; at this writing Shahin is still behind bars awaiting trial. He says that initially his jailers denied him food for three days, held him in solitary confinement, subjected him to harsh interrogation methods, and threatened him with torture.

With the UAE impacted by the global economic downturn, many people were imprisoned in 2009 for failing to pay off their debts. More than 1,200 people in Dubai's central jail, about 40 percent of that prisoner population, have been convicted for defaulting on bank loans. Even after completing their sentence, debt prisoners are likely to remain in jail until their debt is paid off, usually by a relative.

Freedom of Association and Expression

Human rights defenders and government critics face harassment, including trumped-up charges. In 2009 the Jurist Association, an NGO established in 1980 to promote the rule of law and to raise professional standards among jurists, was subjected to mounting restrictions from the government. The government did not permit association representatives to attend meetings abroad. Members also complained of pressure to quit the association, including questioning by the Judiciary Supreme Council and threats of dismissal for those with public sector jobs. Former association president Muhammad al-Mansoori, who has been harassed by UAE authorities for years, was arrested on June 7 without explanation but released the same day. Authorities have refused to renew his passport since March 2008.

The UAE is the media hub of the Gulf, with a dozen daily newspapers, each with circulations in the tens of thousands. The government monitors press content, and journalists routinely exercise self-censorship. Although Prime Minister Sheikh Muhammad stated in 2007 that journalists should not face prison "for reasons related to their work," a 1980 law still in force provides for the imprisonment of journalists and suspension of publications for publishing "materials that cause confusion among the public."

On January 20, 2009, the legislature (the Federal National Council) passed a new draft media law drawn up by the National Media Council. As of November the law had still not been signed into effect by President Sheikh Khalifa Bin Zayed Al Nahyan. While containing some improvements over the 1980 media law, the pending law would continue to punish journalists under civil law for infractions such as "disparaging" the royal family or publishing "misleading" news that "harms the country's economy." The law would impose administrative penalties that could bankrupt media outlets and silence dissenting voices with fines as high as 5,000,000 dirhams (US$1,350,000) for "disparaging" senior government officials. The pending law also would grant the government more control in deciding who is allowed to work as a journalist and which media organizations are allowed to operate in the country.

The government has on numerous occasions used the country's laws to penalize, fine, and close media establishments. In July 2009 the Abu Dhabi Federal Court of Appeal upheld the conviction of the local newspaper *Emarat Alyoum*. The court suspended its publication for 20 days, and fined its editor 20,000 dirhams (US$5,445), because of a 2006 article alleging that a UAE-based company gave steroids to local race horses owned by the Abu Dhabi royal family.

Key International Actors

The United Nations special rapporteur on racism and xenophobia visited the UAE in October 2009 and raised concerns about the working and living conditions of construction and domestic workers, the situation of the Bidun (stateless persons), and the victims of human trafficking. The UN special rapporteur on the sale of children, child prostitution and child pornography also visited the UAE in October and urged the government, despite the progress already made, to make stronger efforts to protect vulnerable children, including Bidun and migrants.

YEMEN

The human rights situation in Yemen deteriorated significantly in 2009. Yemen's previous advances in the rule of law have been eroded by hundreds of arbitrary arrests and use of lethal force against peaceful demonstrators as the central government responded to increasing political unrest in the south. A resurgence of conflict with Huthi rebels in the north saw both sides reportedly commit laws of war violations, and use child soldiers, and the government continued to deny humanitarian access to the displaced. Al Qaeda in the Arabian Peninsula launched attacks from Yemen inside the country and in Saudi Arabia.

Conflict in the North

On August 12, sporadic clashes between Huthi rebels and government forces in the northern Sa'da governorate erupted into the sixth round of heavy fighting since June 2004. The conflict has displaced more than 150,000 people, many of whom remain out of the reach of humanitarian agencies. Saudi Arabia in September blocked refugees' access to the kingdom, denied humanitarian access to Yemen through its territory, and forcibly returned refugees who had crossed its border. In November Saudi forces became a party to the armed conflict.

Yemeni authorities continued to restrict access by international aid agencies to persons in need in Sa'da governorate, shutting down telephone lines as well. The United Nations in August called for humanitarian corridors and localized cease-fires, to allow aid to reach civilians, and for civilians to be able to flee to safety.

Government forces and Huthi fighters both recruited children for combat. Huthi fighters carried out summary executions and put civilians in harm's way by firing from populated areas. Government forces reportedly conducted indiscriminate aerial bombardment in civilian-populated areas, including a crowded market in al-Talh on September 14 and a gathering of displaced persons in al-'Adi on September 16.

Suppression of Southern Separatism

Security forces carried out mass arbitrary arrests surrounding protests of the peaceful Southern Movement, a loose grouping with broad backing demanding secession. Security forces erected checkpoints on days of announced protests and arrested suspected participants, but also uninvolved bystanders. The number of arrests at a July 7 Aden protest led authorities to move detainees into industrial hangars and even to the sports stadium.

Other arrests targeted perceived leaders of the Southern Movement. In early June police stopped Walid Shu'aibi, the head of the Union of Southern Youth in al-Dhali', and dragged him into their car as he was walking from his student housing in Aden. Lawyer Muhammad Hasani on May 7 tried to represent detainees, but was arrested and detained at the Criminal Investigation Division for six days instead. Ahead of the planned July 7 protest, authorities on July 2 arrested two leaders of the Southern Movement, Qasim al-Da'iri and Ali al-Sa'di, who remain in detention at this writing.

Security forces also "disappeared" people. In April they arrested Ahmad Ba-Mu'allim in Hadhramawt; his whereabouts remained unknown until lawyers for HOOD, a rights organization, got access to him in San'a's War Prison in July.

During an April 15 protest in Habilain, riot police without warning or provocation fired automatic weapons directly at protestors, wounding one man in the foot. During a May 21 protest in Aden security forces on several different occasions opened fire without warning or provocation, wounding 23 protestors including Nasr Hamuzaiba, a former army officer and Southern Movement activist. Protestors responded by throwing rocks at the security forces, who again responded with deadly force. Rock-throwing by the protestors, while possibly criminal, does not warrant lethal responses in such circumstances. On May 30, protestors marched peacefully in Shahr, demanding the release of some 75 persons detained during a protest two days earlier. When they came to within meters of riot police blocking the road, police fired first into the air, but then at the protestors, killing 'Awwad Baram. The government held no inquiry into the fatal shooting. In al-Dhali', security forces shot and killed Tawfiq al-Ja'di during a May 31 demonstration without warning or provocation.

Media Freedom

On May 11 the judiciary created a new court to try journalists. On July 11 this Specialized Press Court held its first criminal hearing, relating to earlier (December 2006) charges against Sami Ghalib, editor of *Al-Nida* newspaper, over an article about corruption at the Ministry of Endowments' Hajj and 'Umra department. A special prosecutor for press and publication matters can take journalists and media personnel to court over violations of the penal code and the Press and Publications Law.

Information Minister Hasan al-Luzi on May 4 announced a ban on the distribution of eight of Yemen's leading independent daily and weekly newspapers, *Al-Ayyam, Al-Masdar, Al-Watani, Al-Diyar, Al-Mustaqilla, Al-Nida, Al-Shari'*, and *Al-Ahali,* for publishing articles "against national unity and the country's highest interests" and "incit[ing] violations of law and order, spreading hatred and enmity among the united people of Yemen." The government also imposed informal censorship, imposing "red lines" that included publishing interviews with Southern Movement leaders and gory pictures of injured or killed southern protestors, and mentioning the names of the organizations behind the protests. Pressure by authorities on media outlets extended to physical attacks on *Al-Ayyam*, Yemen's oldest and largest independent newspaper. On May 1, armed individuals stopped *Al-Ayyam*'s delivery van in the Milah area of Lahj governorate and burned 16,500 copies. On the night of May 2, soldiers at two military checkpoints outside Aden confiscated more than 50,000 copies of *Al-Ayyam*, providing employees with a receipt signed by the police, the intelligence service, and the Ministry of Information. On May 4, *Al-Ayyam* suspended publication due to a siege of their offices. On May 12, security forces exchanged fire with guards at the *Al-Ayyam* compound in Aden, leaving one bystander dead and another gravely wounded.

Terrorism and Counterterrorism

Al Qaeda in the Arabian Peninsula, a new merger of al Qaeda's Yemeni and Saudi branches, carried out attacks on both countries from Yemen, where about two dozen wanted Saudi militants, including nine former detainees of the United States at Guantanamo Bay, are said to be hiding. In March a suicide bomber killed four South Korean tourists in Hadhramawt, and in August a suicide bomber who crossed into Saudi Arabia nearly assassinated the Saudi counterterrorism chief, Prince Muhammad bin Nayef. Islamist militants are among the possible suspects in the June abduction of nine foreigners in north Yemen, three of whom—two German nurses and a South Korean teacher—were killed.

Security forces arbitrarily detained more than 135 terrorism suspects without charge, including one former Guantanamo detainee held for five months, and two children held as hostages to induce relatives to surrender.

US concerns about Yemen's counterterrorism measures stalled repatriation of more than 90 Yemenis at Guantanamo—nearly half the remaining detainees. Only two Yemenis have been returned since 2007: Salim Hamdan in November 2008 and Ala' Ali Ahmad in September 2009.

Death Penalty

In 2009 Yemen executed more than 30 persons as of October, including Aisha al-Hamza for murdering her husband, whom she alleged had abused their daughter. Courts sentenced to death members of al Qaeda, Huthi rebels, and alleged spies for Israel and Iran.

Women's and Girls' Rights

In a positive step, parliament in February gave women the right to pass their nationality on to their children, and set the minimum legal age for marriage at 17. However, early marriage remains widespread, exposing young girls to domestic violence and maternal mortality, and cutting short their education. In September a 12-year-old married girl died in childbirth. Yemen has one of the world's highest maternal mortality rates, with an estimated eight women dying each day from childbirth complications. Seventy-five percent of Yemenis live in rural areas with no hospitals.

Women who marry against parental wishes are sometimes charged with adultery and imprisoned. Marital rape is not criminalized, trapping forcibly married girls and women in relationships with abusive husbands. Women fleeing domestic violence are sometimes incarcerated, and may face prolonged detention when male relatives refuse to collect them. A new policy allows female relatives to collect female detainees as well, but to date it is not consistently observed.

Key International Actors

Saudi Arabia, Qatar, and other Persian Gulf states provide substantial amounts of assistance to Yemen, including to tribal leaders and religious institutions.

Nine European Union states also provide aid to Yemen. The largest donor, the United Kingdom, plans to give the equivalent of US$189 million between 2007 and 2011. For fiscal year 2010 the Obama administration requested from Congress US$55.5 million, an increase of US$20 million compared to 2009, bringing US aid levels back to 2007 levels. The biggest increases went to programs of "governing justly and democratically," and to human rights and the rule of law within that category. Washington publicly supported Yemen's unity but criticized attacks on *Al-Ayyam* newspaper.

The UN and donor states played a greater role in 2009 pressing the government to grant humanitarian access to civilians affected by the Sa'da conflict.

UNITED STATES

Testing Justice

The Rape Kit Backlog in Los Angeles City and County

H U M A N
RIGHTS
WATCH

WORLD REPORT

2010

UNITED STATES

UNITED STATES

US citizens enjoy a broad range of civil liberties and have recourse to a strong system of independent federal and state courts, but serious human rights concerns remain, particularly in criminal justice, immigration, and counterterrorism law and policy. The Obama administration has said it will address many of these concerns but, at this writing nearly one year into Barack Obama's presidency; it had taken few concrete steps.

Domestically, 2009 saw an increase in executions and continued growth in the US incarcerated population, already the world's largest. Black men and members of other racial and ethnic minorities make up a disproportionate share of that population.

Other longstanding problems include the sentencing of individuals to life imprisonment without parole for crimes committed as children (the US is the only country in the world to do so), the use of corporal punishment in schools, inadequate protections for child laborers and pregnant women, inadequate responses to rape and domestic violence, and violations of the rights of non-citizens.

In a positive development, President Obama signaled his intention to break with the Bush administration's abusive counterterrorism policies. On his second full day in office, Obama issued executive orders to close the CIA's secret prisons, ban torture and other mistreatment, and set a one-year deadline for closing the military prison at Guantanamo Bay. After that promising start, his administration backtracked on counterterrorism, taking a number of disturbing decisions relating to detention policy, trials, and government secrecy.

Death Penalty

As of November 2009 there had been 45 executions in the United States in 2009, up from 37 in all of 2008. In March 2009 New Mexico abolished capital punishment, bringing to 15 the number of US states that do not impose the death penalty.

Between January and November 2009, nine prisoners were exonerated and released from death row, bringing to 139 the number of death-sentenced prisoners released since 1973 due to evidence of their innocence.

Ohio's September 2009 attempt to execute Romell Broom by lethal injection failed after executioners tried unsuccessfully for more than two hours to locate a suitable vein, with Broom reportedly grimacing and crying as executioners stuck him with the execution needle at least 18 times. The botched execution attempt led Ohio's governor to impose a moratorium on executions pending review of the state's lethal injection protocol.

Juvenile Life without Parole

In May 2009 Human Rights Watch revised upward to 2,574 its estimate of the number of US prisoners serving sentences of life without the possibility of parole for crimes committed when they were under age 18. There are no persons known to be serving life without parole sentences for crimes committed as children anywhere else in the world.

At year's end, legislation was pending to end juvenile life without parole in the US Congress and in the legislatures of Alabama, California, Florida, Iowa, Michigan, Missouri, Nebraska, and Pennsylvania. In November the US Supreme Court heard two cases challenging the constitutionality of sentencing juveniles to life without parole for non-homicide crimes.

Incarceration

A March 2009 report by the US Justice Department's Bureau of Justice Statistics found that the incarcerated population had reached an all-time high of nearly 2.4 million. The United States continues to have both the largest incarcerated population and the highest incarceration rate in the world.

In many states prison crowding has led to serious threats to prisoner health and safety. The California prison system, with nearly 160,000 prisoners, is operating at almost double its intended capacity; some facilities have populations approaching 300 percent of their intended capacity. In August 2009 after finding

UNITED STATES

Decades of Disparity

Drug Arrests and Race in the United States

HUMAN
RIGHTS
WATCH

that this crowding results in unconstitutionally deficient medical and mental health care for prisoners, a panel of federal judges ordered the state to devise a plan to reduce its prison population by approximately 40,000 within two years.

The burden of incarceration continues to fall disproportionately on members of racial and ethnic minorities. Black men are incarcerated at 6.6 times the rate of white men, and more than 10 percent of all black men ages 25 to 39 are behind bars on any given day. Human Rights Watch's March 2009 report *Decades of Disparity: Drug Arrests and Race in the United States* found that in every year from 1980 to 2007, blacks were arrested on drug charges at rates that were 2.8 to 5.5 times higher than white arrest rates, despite the fact that blacks and whites engaged in illegal drug behavior at similar rates.

Incarcerated pregnant women saw increasing, but still insufficient, recognition of their rights. The number of states restricting the shackling of pregnant prisoners grew from three to six, and a federal appeals court ruled that shackling women during labor and childbirth violates the US Constitution. The Federal Bureau of Prisons and the US Marshals Service limited this practice in 2008; US Immigration and Customs Enforcement (ICE) still lacks sufficient restrictions.

Tens of thousands of prisoners in the United States are sexually abused by staff or other prisoners each year because officials have not instituted basic measures to protect them. In 2003 Congress passed the Prison Rape Elimination Act (PREA), which created the National Prison Rape Elimination Commission, charged with studying the causes and consequences of prison rape. In June 2009 the Commission presented its findings and recommended standards for all federal, state, and local confinement facilities, including public and privately run prisons, jails, lockups, juvenile facilities, immigration detention facilities, and community corrections settings. Under PREA, the US attorney general has until June 2010 to adopt national prison rape standards that will immediately be binding on federal facilities; states will have a year to comply with the standards or forfeit a portion of the federal corrections funding they receive.

Despite the large number of prisoners with histories of substance use and addiction, US prisons and jails remain resistant, even hostile, to evidence-based treatment. Human Rights Watch's March 2009 report *Barred from Treatment:*

Punishment of Drug Users in New York State Prisons found that evidence-based treatment is available only on a limited basis to the substantial population of New York prisoners whom prison officials have identified as needing treatment. Medication-assisted therapy with methadone or buprenorphine, proven to be the most effective treatment for opioid dependence, is unavailable in most prisons. Prisoners who use drugs—including those who relapse, a common symptom of drug dependence—are penalized with disproportionate severity, facing months, even years, locked down in harsh conditions which often amount to cruel and inhuman punishment.

A number of states impose mandatory HIV testing upon prisoners at entry or upon release, a practice that violates their right to informed consent and can result in discrimination in prison employment, programming, and work release opportunities. In Alabama, South Carolina, and Mississippi, HIV-positive prisoners continue to be segregated from the general population, forcing involuntary disclosure of their HIV status and promoting discrimination.

The Prison Litigation Reform Act (PLRA), enacted by Congress in 1996, creates a variety of obstacles for prisoners seeking to vindicate their rights in court. In its June 2009 report *No Equal Justice: The Prison Litigation Reform Act in the United States*, Human Rights Watch found that the PLRA's restrictions have resulted in dismissal of lawsuits alleging sexual abuse and other significant injuries, and constitute a significant barrier to the protection of prisoners' health and safety.

Drug Policy

While the Obama administration has made efforts to address the health and human rights of people who use drugs and to reduce barriers to treatment, much remains to be done. The administration sent an important signal by announcing that it accepts the scientific evidence behind needle exchanges, but its failure to support the elimination of funding bans on domestic and international needle exchanges, or to support other evidence-based interventions, has impeded progress.

UNITED STATES

No Equal Justice

The Prison Litigation Reform Act in the United States

HUMAN
RIGHTS
WATCH

Rights of Non-Citizens

There are some 38 million non-citizens living in the United States, of whom approximately 12 million are undocumented. In 2009 the US government took some preliminary positive steps but largely failed to resolve the myriad human rights problems faced by this population.

In 2009, nearly 100,000 non-citizens, including many lawfully present immigrants, were deported from the United States after serving prison sentences, often for minor nonviolent crimes such as marijuana possession. Under restrictive laws passed in 1996, judges in many such cases are given no discretion to allow the immigrants to remain, regardless of their lawful presence in the country, status as a spouse or parent of a US citizen, economic contributions, service in the US military, or likelihood of persecution after deportation.

Human Right Watch's April 2009 report *Forced Apart (By the Numbers)* analyzed government data and disproved the popular belief that US deportation policy focuses almost exclusively on undocumented (or illegally present) non-citizens with violent criminal histories. In reality, three-quarters of non-citizens deported from the United States over the last decade had criminal histories limited to nonviolent offenses and one in five had been in the country legally, sometimes for decades. At least one million spouses and children, many of whom are US citizens, were separated from their family members by these deportations.

The United States detains approximately 300,000 non-citizens each year in a network of some 300 facilities. Immigrants are often initially detained close to their attorneys and witnesses, in locations such as New York or Los Angeles, only to be transferred later to detention centers in rural Texas or Louisiana. Between 1999 and 2008, 1.4 million detainee transfers occurred. The transfers interfere with detainees' rights to be represented by counsel, to defend against deportation, to present witnesses and other evidence, and to be free from arbitrary and prolonged detention.

Human Rights Watch's March 2009 report, *Detained and Dismissed: Women's Struggles to Obtain Health Care in United States Immigration Detention*, documented inadequate provision of routine gynecological care, cervical and breast cancer screenings and diagnosis, family planning services, pre- and post-natal

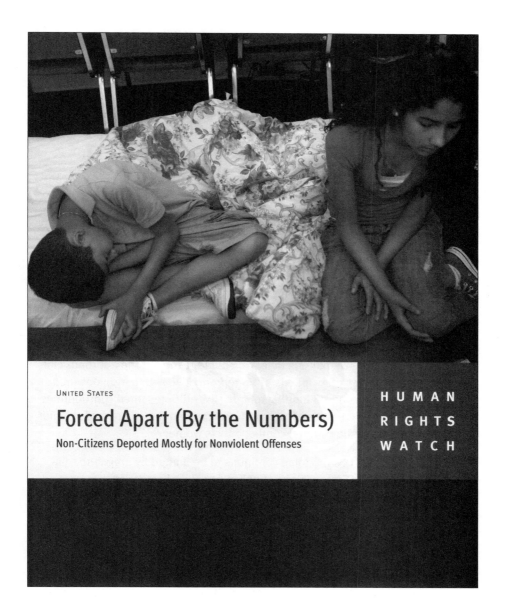

UNITED STATES

Forced Apart (By the Numbers)

Non-Citizens Deported Mostly for Nonviolent Offenses

HUMAN
RIGHTS
WATCH

care, and services for survivors of sexual and gender-based violence. Many of these problems are traceable to official ICE policy that focuses on emergency care and discourages staff from providing certain core women's health services.

In late 2008 ICE revised its detention standards and included some improvements to the medical care provided to detainees but the revisions fell short of reforms that had been sought. In July 2009 ICE officials refused to make the detention standards enforceable regulations, stating that its revised policies were adequate.

In 2008 Congress repealed legislation barring HIV-positive noncitizens from entry, stay, or residence in the United States. In November 2009 the Department of Health and Human Services announced that the ban would be fully lifted effective January 1, 2010.

Women's and Girls' Rights

In his first year in office President Obama signaled his intent to emphasize women's rights in domestic and foreign policy. He created the White House Council on Women and Girls, a coordinating body composed of cabinet members, and established an ambassadorship-at-large on global women's issues. The president also repealed the Global Gag Rule, which had restricted the abortion-related speech and activities of recipients of US reproductive health aid, loosened problematic restrictions on US funding to fight HIV/AIDS, resumed contributions to the United Nations Population Fund, and championed the creation of a senior UN position to address how armed conflict affects women.

Women's status in the US workforce continues to be limited by pregnancy discrimination. The United States is one of only a handful of countries that have no guarantee of paid family leave, and pregnancy discrimination claims have risen sharply in recent years. A 2009 Supreme Court decision limited remedies for past discrimination but enactment of the Lilly Ledbetter Fair Pay Act removed some barriers to pay discrimination suits.

Thousands of domestic violence survivors' requests for shelter and critical services go unmet every day in the United States, a situation exacerbated by the economic crisis. Shelters reported an increased need for services in 2009 even as

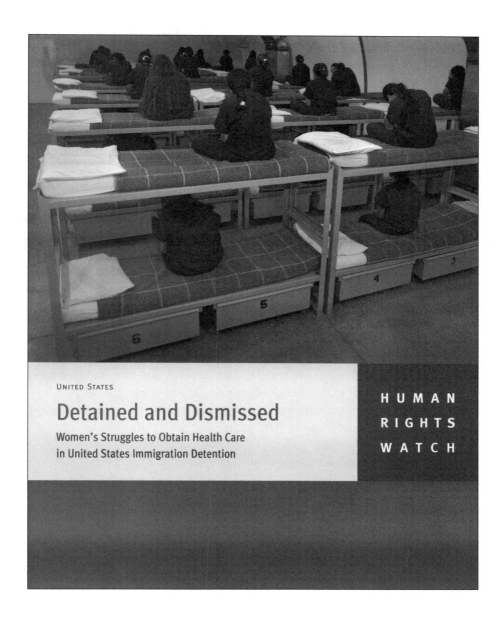

Detained and Dismissed

Women's Struggles to Obtain Health Care
in United States Immigration Detention

HUMAN
RIGHTS
WATCH

key programs remained underfunded, private donations declined, and state and local budget crises jeopardized existing funding, with some shelters forced to close.

In women's health, African-American women face grossly disproportionate rates of HIV/AIDS infection and death, with the disease the leading cause of death among African-American women ages 25 to 34. The reproductive rights of all women remain under attack, with abortion providers burdened by unnecessary regulations, harassment, and physical violence. Dr. George Tiller, one of few late-term abortion providers in the United States, was murdered in May 2009.

Sexual Violence

In the United States the crime of rape has one of the lowest arrest, prosecution, and conviction rates among serious violent crimes. When reporting a sexual assault a victim is asked to submit to a four- to six-hour physical examination to collect DNA evidence that, if tested, may aid in the criminal investigation. Human Rights Watch's March 2009 report *Testing Justice: The Rape Kit Backlog in Los Angeles City and County* found more than 12,500 untested rape kits in law enforcement storage facilities in Los Angeles County alone. Following release of the report the Los Angeles Police and Sheriffs' Departments instituted a policy of testing every booked rape kit, and found the resources to hire new crime lab personnel. News reports of 10,000 untested rape kits in Detroit and 4,000 in Houston underscore the national scope of the problem, but comprehensive rape kit data remain elusive because no state or federal agency tracks this information.

Children's Rights

Hundreds of thousands of children work on US farms yet are exempt from the legal protections granted to all other working children in the United States. The 1938 Fair Labor Standards Act specifically exempts farmworker youth from minimum age and maximum hour requirements, exposing them to work at younger ages, for longer hours, and under more hazardous conditions than children in other jobs. Federal protections that do exist are often not enforced and state child labor laws vary in strength and enforcement. As a result, child farmworkers, most of whom are Latino, often work 12-and-14-hour days, and risk pesticide poisoning, heat illness, injuries, and life-long disabilities. Many drop out of school; girls are sometimes subject to sexual harassment.

According to the US Department of Education more than 200,000 public school students received corporal punishment at least once during the 2006-2007 school year. Corporal punishment—which typically takes the form of one or more blows to the buttocks with a wooden paddle—is legal in public schools in 20 states; Ohio banned corporal punishment in its public schools in July 2009. An August 2009 Human Rights Watch report, *Impairing Education: Corporal Punishment of Students with Disabilities in US Public Schools,* found that students with mental and physical disabilities are subjected to corporal punishment at disproportionately high rates.

Guantanamo, Indefinite Detention, and Military Commissions

When President Obama took office, there were 242 prisoners at Guantanamo, approximately 50 of whom had been cleared to leave but could not be sent to their home countries due to credible fears of abuse. Although a number of European countries have agreed to accept a small number of detainees for resettlement, the US government's refusal to do so itself has hindered resettlement efforts. At this writing only 20 Guantanamo detainees have been transferred or released since President Obama's inauguration, and the administration now concedes that it is unlikely to meet the January 2010 closure deadline.

Even more worrying than delays in closing Guantanamo is the possibility that the administration will continue to hold prisoners indefinitely without trial. Although the administration appears to have scrapped plans to ask Congress to enact preventive detention legislation, it has continued to rely on the Bush-era wartime rationale as a justification for holding suspected terrorists indefinitely without trial.

The Obama administration sent a positive signal that it would provide fair trials to suspected terrorists when it announced federal indictments against two men formerly held without charge as "enemy combatants." In May, however, President Obama announced that he planned to revive the system of military commissions to try Guantanamo detainees. Working with Congress, the administration signed legislation providing greater protections for suspects tried in such commissions, including banning evidence obtained through coercion and tightening hearsay rules. The commissions, however, remain a substandard system of justice that lacks legitimacy; their continued use will result in needless litigation, delays, and flawed trials.

Accounting for Past Abuses

Although there is overwhelming evidence that senior Bush administration officials approved brutal and illegal interrogation methods, the Obama administration showed little enthusiasm for initiating a thorough investigation of these abuses. In an important step, Attorney General Eric Holder appointed a federal prosecutor to review post-9/11 interrogation practices. By all indications, however, the investigation was narrowly circumscribed and unlikely to examine the responsibility of senior officials who set the policies and authorized abuses.

Secrecy

The Obama administration has invoked an overly broad understanding of the "state secrets" privilege, arguing that litigation related to the US secret detention and rendition program, as well as lawsuits filed by victims of torture and illegal surveillance, should be dismissed because they might divulge classified information. While it released several important Bush-era interrogation-related memoranda, the administration backtracked on a commitment to release photographs depicting detainee abuse, claiming that doing so could jeopardize US troops abroad.

Renditions

The Obama administration has said that it will continue to rely on "diplomatic assurances"—non-binding promises from the receiving country that detainees will be treated humanely—in carrying out prisoner transfers. Human Rights Watch research has found that such assurances against torture are unreliable and has urged the administration to reconsider this position.

Key International Actors

In his May 2009 report the UN special rapporteur on extrajudicial, summary, or arbitrary executions called on the United States to improve due process protections in its application of the death penalty, finding that the current system's flaws increase the likelihood that innocent persons will be executed. The UN special rapporteur on contemporary forms of racism, racial discrimination, xenophobia, and related intolerance called in his April 2009 report for the establishment of a commission to evaluate progress and failures, and recommend action, in the fight against racism and what he called "the ongoing process of resegregation" in housing and education.

In November, a Milan court found 23 Americans, including 22 alleged CIA operatives, guilty of kidnapping an Egyptian cleric in 2003. A landmark judgment, it was the first time that a court had assessed the legality of the CIA's rendition program. In Spain, a criminal case was filed in March against six lawyers believed responsible for formulating the legal justifications for Bush-era abuses.

Selling Justice Short

Why Accountability Matters for Peace

**HUMAN
RIGHTS
WATCH**

WORLD REPORT
2010

2009
HUMAN RIGHTS WATCH
PUBLICATIONS

By Country

Afghanistan

"We have the Promises of the World": Women's Rights in Afghanistan, December 2009, 93pp.

Angola

"They Put Me in the Hole": Military Detention, Torture, and Lack of Due Process in Cabinda, June 2009, 29pp.

Democracy or Monopoly? Angola's Reluctant Return to Elections, February 2009, 47pp.

Armenia

Democracy on Rocky Ground: Armenia's Disputed 2008 Presidential Election, Post-Election Violence, and the One-Sided Pursuit of Accountability, February 2009, 66pp.

Bangladesh

Ignoring Executions and Torture: Impunity for Bangladesh's Security Forces, May 2009, 78pp.

Brazil

Lethal Force: Police Violence and Public Security in Rio de Janeiro and São Paulo, December 2009, 122pp.

Burma

The Resistance of the Monks: Buddhism and Activism in Burma, September 2009, 117pp.

Burma's Forgotten Prisoners, September 2009, 36pp.

Perilous Plight: Burma's Rohingya Take to the Seas, May 2009, 17pp.

"We Are Like Forgotten People" – The Chin People of Burma: Unsafe in Burma, Unprotected in India, January 2009, 95pp.

Burundi

Forbidden: Institutionalizing Discrimination against Gays and Lesbians in Burundi, July 2009, 28pp.

Pursuit of Power: Political Violence and Repression in Burundi, May 2009, 88pp.

Central Africa Republic

Improving Civilian Protection in Northwest Central African Republic, December 2008, 23pp.

Chad

The Risk of Return: Repatriating the Displaced in the Context of Conflict in Eastern Chad, June 2009, 46pp.

China

"An Alleyway in Hell": China's Abusive "Black Jails", November 2009, 53pp.

"We Are Afraid to Even Look for Them": Enforced Disappearances in the Wake of Xinjiang's Protests, October 2009, 46pp.

An Unbreakable Cycle: Drug Dependency Treatment, Mandatory Confinement, and HIV/AIDS in China's Guangxi Province, December 2008, 44pp.

Cuba

New Castro, Same Cuba: Political Prisoners in the Post-Fidel Era, November 2009, 125pp.

Democratic Republic of Congo

A "mixed chamber" for Congo? September 2009, 11pp.

Soldiers Who Rape, Commanders Who Condone: Sexual Violence and Military Reform in the Democratic Republic of Congo, July 2009, 58pp.

The Christmas Massacres: LRA attacks on Civilians in Northern Congo, February 2009, 68pp.

Killings in Kiwanja: The UN's Inability to Protect Civilians, December 2008, 30pp.

Equatorial Guinea

Well Oiled: Oil and Human Rights in Equatorial Guinea, July 2009, 104pp.

Eritrea

Service for Life: State Repression and Indefinite Conscription in Eritrea, April 2009, 97pp.

France

Lost in Transit: Insufficient Protection for Unaccompanied Migrant Children at Roissy Charles de Gaulle Airport, October 2009, 62pp.

Georgia

A Dying Practice: Use of Cluster Munitions by Russia and Georgia in August 2008, April 2009, 84pp.

Up In Flames: Humanitarian Law Violations and Civilian Victims in the Conflict over South Ossetia, January 2009, 209pp.

Germany
Discrimination in the Name of Neutrality: Headscarf Bans for Teachers and Civil Servants in Germany, February 2009, 69pp.

Greece
No Refuge: Migrants in Greece, November 2009, 13pp.

Unsafe and Unwelcoming Shores, October 2009, 10pp.

Left to Survive: Systematic Failure to Protect Unaccompanied Migrant Children in Greece, December 2008, 111pp.

Honduras
"Not Worth a Penny": Human Rights Abuses against Transgender People in Honduras, May 2009, 47pp.

India
Sabotaged Schooling: Naxalite Attacks and Police Occupation of Schools in India's Bihar and Jharkhand States, December 2009, 103pp.

Unbearable Pain: India's Obligation to Ensure Palliative Care, October 2009, 93pp.

No Tally of the Anguish: Accountability in Maternal Health Care in India, October 2009, 152pp.

Broken System: Dysfunction, Abuse, and Impunity in the Indian Police, August 2009, 120pp.

Indonesia
"Wild Money": The Human Rights Consequences of Illegal Logging and Corruption in Indonesia's Forestry Sector, December 2009, 75pp.

"What Did I Do Wrong?" Papuans in Merauke Face Abuses by Indonesian Special Forces, June 2009, 17pp.

Workers in the Shadows: Abuse and Exploitation of Child Domestic Workers in Indonesia, February 2009, 75pp.

Iran
Iran: Freedom of Expression and Association in the Kurdish Regions, January 2009, 43pp.

Iraq
On Vulnerable Ground: Violence against Minority Communities in Nineveh Province's Disputed Territories, November 2009, 47pp.

"They Want Us Exterminated": Murder, Torture, Sexual Orientation and Gender in Iraq, August 2009, 69pp.

The Quality of Justice: Failings of Iraq's Central Criminal Court, December 2008, 42pp.

Israel

White Flag Deaths: Killings of Palestinian Civilians during Operation Cast Lead, August 2009, 63pp.

Rockets from Gaza: Harm to Civilians from Palestinian Armed Groups' Rocket Attacks, August 2009, 30pp.

Precisely Wrong: Gaza Civilians Killed by Israeli Drone-Launched Missiles, June 2009, 39pp.

Rain of Fire: Israel's Unlawful Use of White Phosphorus in Gaza, March 2009, 73pp.

Italy

Pushed Back, Pushed Around: Italy's Forced Return of Boat Migrants and Asylum Seekers, Libya's Mistreatment of Migrants and Asylum Seekers, September 2009, 88pp.

Jordan

Guests of the Governor: Administrative Detention Undermines the Rule of Law in Jordan, May 2009, 58pp.

Kazakhstan

An Atmosphere of Quiet Repression: Freedom of Religion, Assembly and Expression in Kazakhstan, December 2008, 55pp.

Kenya

"Bring the Gun or You'll Die": Torture, Rape, and Other Serious Human Rights Violations by Kenyan Security Forces in the Mandera Triangle, June 2009, 53pp.

From Horror to Hopelessness: Kenya's Forgotten Somali Refugee Crisis, March 2009, 56pp.

A Question of Life or Death: Treatment Access for Children Living With HIV in Kenya, December 2008, 100pp.

Libya

Truth and Justice Can't Wait, December 2009, 78pp.

Pushed Back, Pushed Around: Italy's Forced Return of Boat Migrants and Asylum Seekers, Libya's Mistreatment of Migrants and Asylum Seekers, September 2009, 88pp.

Mexico
Uniform Impunity: Mexico's Misuse of Military Justice to Prosecute Abuses in Counternarcotics and Public Security Operations, April 2009, 78pp.

Morocco
Freedom to Create Associations: A Declarative Regime in Name Only, October 2009, 47pp.

Human Rights in Western Sahara and in the Tindouf Refugee Camps, December 2008, 216pp.

Nepal
Still Waiting for Justice: No End to Impunity in Nepal, October 2009, 49pp.

Nigeria
Arbitrary Killings by Security Forces: Submission to the Investigative Bodies on the November 28-29, 2008 Violence in Jos, Plateau State, Nigeria, July 2009, 28pp.

Palestinian Territories
White Flag Deaths: Killings of Palestinian Civilians during Operation Cast Lead, August 2009, 63pp.

Rockets from Gaza: Harm to Civilians from Palestinian Armed Groups' Rocket Attacks, August 2009, 30pp.

Precisely Wrong: Gaza Civilians Killed by Israeli Drone-Launched Missiles, June 2009, 39pp.

Under Cover of War: Hamas Political Violence in Gaza, April 2009, 28pp.

Rain of Fire: Israel's Unlawful Use of White Phosphorus in Gaza, March 2009, 73pp.

Pakistan
Cruel Britannia: British Complicity in the Torture and Ill-Treatment of Terror Suspects in Pakistan, November 2009, 45pp.

Philippines
"You Can Die Any Time": Death Squad Killings in Mindanao, April 2009, 105pp.

Russia
"Who Will Tell Me What Happened to My Son?" Russia's Implementation of European Court of Human Rights Judgments on Chechnya, September 2009, 40pp.

"What Your Children Do Will Touch Upon You": Punitive House-Burning in Chechnya, July 2009, 59pp.

An Uncivil Approach to Civil Society: Continuing State Curbs on Independent NGOs and Activists in Russia, June 2009, 71pp.

A Dying Practice: Use of Cluster Munitions by Russia and Georgia in August 2008, April 2009, 84pp.

"Are You Happy to Cheat Us?" Exploitation of Migrant Construction Workers in Russia, February 2009, 113pp.

Up In Flames: Humanitarian Law Violations and Civilian Victims in the Conflict over South Ossetia, January 2009, 209pp.

Saudi Arabia

Denied Dignity: Systematic Discrimination and Hostility toward Saudi Shia Citizens, September 2009, 29pp.

Human Rights and Saudi Arabia's Counterterrorism Response: Religious Counseling, Indefinite Detention, and Flawed Trials, August 2009, 26pp.

Serbia

Kosovo: Poisoned by Lead: A Health and Human Rights Crisis in Mitrovica's Roma Camps, June 2009, 70pp.

Somalia

"Hostages to Peace": Threats to Human Rights and Democracy in Somaliland, July 2009, 59pp.

"So Much to Fear": War Crimes and the Devastation of Somalia, December 2008, 104pp.

South Africa

No Healing Here: Violence, Discrimination and Barriers to Health for Migrants in South Africa, December 2009, 87pp.

Sri Lanka

War on the Displaced: Sri Lankan Army and LTTE Abuses against Civilians in the Vanni, February 2009, 46pp.

Besieged, Displaced, and Detained: The Plight of Civilians in Sri Lanka's Vanni Region, December 2008, 49pp.

Trapped and Mistreated: LTTE Abuses against Civilians in the Vanni, December 2008, 17pp.

Sudan

The Way Forward: Ending Human Rights Abuses and Repression across Sudan, October 2009, 27pp.

No One to Intervene: Gaps in Civilian Protection in Southern Sudan, June 2009, 16pp.

"It's an Everyday Battle": Censorship and Harassment of Journalists and Human Rights Defenders in Sudan, February 2009, 25pp.

"There is No Protection": Insecurity and Human Rights in Southern Sudan, February 2009, 46pp.

Syria

Group Denial: Repression of Kurdish Political and Cultural Rights in Syria, November 2009, 66pp.

Far From Justice: Syria's Supreme State Security Court, February 2009, 75pp.

Turkey

Closing Ranks against Accountability: Barriers to Tackling Police Violence in Turkey, December 2008, 80pp.

Uganda

Preparing for the Polls: Improving Accountability for Electoral Violence in Uganda, December 2009, 28pp.

Open Secret: Illegal Detention and Torture by the Joint Anti-terrorism Task Force in Uganda, April 2009, 88pp.

United Arab Emirates

"The Island of Happiness": Exploitation of Migrant Workers on Saadiyat Island, Abu Dhabi, May 2009, 82pp.

United Kingdom

Cruel Britannia: British Complicity in the Torture and Ill-Treatment of Terror Suspects in Pakistan, November 2009, 45pp.

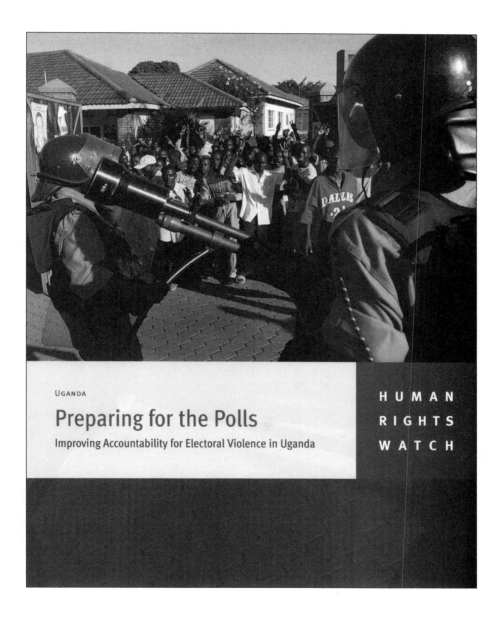

UGANDA

Preparing for the Polls

Improving Accountability for Electoral Violence in Uganda

HUMAN
RIGHTS
WATCH

United States

Locked Up Far Away: The Transfer of Immigrants to Remote Detention Centers in the United States, December 2009, 101pp.

Impairing Education: Corporal Punishment of Students with Disabilities in US Public Schools, August 2009, 71pp.

No Equal Justice: The Prison Litigation Reform Act in the United States, June 2009, 48pp.

Forced Apart (By the Numbers): Non-Citizens Deported Mostly for Nonviolent Offenses, April 2009, 66pp.

Testing Justice: The Rape Kit Backlog in Los Angeles City and County, March 2009, 63pp.

No Direction Home: Returns from Guantanamo to Yemen, March 2009, 51pp.

Barred from Treatment: Punishment of Drug Users in New York State Prisons, March 2009, 55pp.

Detained and Dismissed: Women's Struggles to Obtain Health Care in United States Immigration Detention, March 2009, 80pp.

Decades of Disparity: Drug Arrests and Race in the United States, March 2009, 19pp.

The Employee Free Choice Act: A Human Rights Imperative, January 2009, 12pp.

Vietnam

Not Yet a Workers' Paradise: Vietnam's Suppression of the Independent Workers' Movement, May 2009, 33pp.

On the Margins: Rights Abuses of Ethnic Khmer in Vietnam's Mekong Delta, January 2009, 111pp.

Yemen

No Direction Home: Returns from Guantanamo to Yemen, March 2009, 51pp.

Zimbabwe

False Dawn: The Zimbabwe Power-Sharing Government's Failure to Deliver Human Rights Improvements, August 2009, 21pp.

Diamonds in the Rough: Human Rights Abuses in the Marange Diamond Fields of Zimbabwe, June 2009, 59pp.

Crisis without Limits: Human Rights and Humanitarian Consequences of Political Repression in Zimbabwe, January 2009, 34pp.

UNITED STATES

Impairing Education
Corporal Punishment of Students with Disabilities
in US Public Schools

HUMAN
RIGHTS
WATCH

ACLU
AMERICAN CIVIL LIBERTIES UNION

BY THEME

Arms Issues

A Dying Practice: Use of Cluster Munitions by Russia and Georgia in August 2008, April 2009, 84pp.

Business and Human Rights Issues

"Wild Money": The Human Rights Consequences of Illegal Logging and Corruption in Indonesia's Forestry Sector, December 2009, 75pp.

Well Oiled: Oil and Human Rights in Equatorial Guinea, July 2009, 104pp.

Diamonds in the Rough: Human Rights Abuses in the Marange Diamond Fields of Zimbabwe, June 2009, 59pp.

"The Island of Happiness": Exploitation of Migrant Workers on Saadiyat Island, Abu Dhabi, May 2009, 82pp.

"Are You Happy to Cheat Us?" Exploitation of Migrant Construction Workers in Russia, February 2009, 113pp.

United States – The Employee Free Choice Act: A Human Rights Imperative, January 2009, 12pp.

Children's Rights Issues

Sabotaged Schooling: Naxalite Attacks and Police Occupation of Schools in India's Bihar and Jharkhand States, December 2009, 103pp.

No Refuge: Migrants in Greece, November 2009, 13pp.

France – Lost in Transit: Insufficient Protection for Unaccompanied Migrant Children at Roissy Charles de Gaulle Airport, October 2009, 62pp.

Impairing Education: Corporal Punishment of Students with Disabilities in US Public Schools, August 2009, 71pp.

Soldiers Who Rape, Commanders Who Condone: Sexual Violence and Military Reform in the Democratic Republic of Congo, July 2009, 58pp.

Workers in the Shadows: Abuse and Exploitation of Child Domestic Workers in Indonesia, February 2009, 75pp.

A Question of Life or Death: Treatment Access for Children Living With HIV in Kenya, December 2008, 100pp.

Left to Survive: Systematic Failure to Protect Unaccompanied Migrant Children in Greece, December 2008, 111pp.

Health and Human Rights Issues

No Healing Here: Violence, Discrimination and Barriers to Health for Migrants in South Africa, December 2009, 87pp.

Unbearable Pain: India's Obligation to Ensure Palliative Care, October 2009, 93pp.

No Tally of the Anguish: Accountability in Maternal Health Care in India, October 2009, 152pp.

Returned to Risk: Deportation of HIV-Positive Migrants, September 2009, 29pp.

Serbia – Kosovo: Poisoned by Lead: A Health and Human Rights Crisis in Mitrovica's Roma Camps, June 2009, 70pp.

Discrimination, Denial, and Deportation: Human Rights Abuses Affecting Migrants Living with HIV, June 2009, 26pp.

United States – Barred from Treatment: Punishment of Drug Users in New York State Prisons, March 2009, 55pp.

"Please, do not make us suffer any more...": Access to Pain Treatment as a Human Right, March 2009, 47pp.

An Unbreakable Cycle: Drug Dependency Treatment, Mandatory Confinement, and HIV/AIDS in China's Guangxi Province, December 2008, 44pp.

A Question of Life or Death: Treatment Access for Children Living With HIV in Kenya, December 2008, 100pp.

International Justice Issues

Memorandum for the Eighth Session of the International Criminal Court Assembly of States Parties, November 2009, 33pp.

A "mixed chamber" for Congo? September 2009, 11pp.

Selling Justice Short: Why Accountability Matters for Peace, July 2009, 130pp.

Lesbian, Gay, Bisexual, and Transgender Issues

"They Want Us Exterminated": Murder, Torture, Sexual Orientation and Gender in Iraq, August 2009, 69pp.

Forbidden: Institutionalizing Discrimination against Gays and Lesbians in Burundi, July 2009, 28pp.

"Not Worth a Penny": Human Rights Abuses against Transgender People in Honduras, May 2009, 47pp.

Together, Apart: Organizing around Sexual Orientation and Gender Identity Worldwide, May 2009, 46pp.

This Alien Legacy: The Origins of "Sodomy" Laws in British Colonialism, December 2008, 66pp.

Refugees/Displaced Persons Issues

Locked Up Far Away: The Transfer of Immigrants to Remote Detention Centers in the United States, December 2009, 101pp.

No Healing Here: Violence, Discrimination and Barriers to Health for Migrants in South Africa, December 2009, 87pp.

No Refuge: Migrants in Greece, November 2009, 13pp.

Greece – Unsafe and Unwelcoming Shores, October 2009, 10pp.

France – Lost in Transit: Insufficient Protection for Unaccompanied Migrant Children at Roissy Charles de Gaulle Airport, October 2009, 62pp.

Pushed Back, Pushed Around: Italy's Forced Return of Boat Migrants and Asylum Seekers, Libya's Mistreatment of Migrants and Asylum Seekers, September 2009, 88pp.

The Risk of Return: Repatriating the Displaced in the Context of Conflict in Eastern Chad, June 2009, 46pp.

Perilous Plight: Burma's Rohingya Take to the Seas, May 2009, 17pp.

From Horror to Hopelessness: Kenya's Forgotten Somali Refugee Crisis, March 2009, 56pp.

"We Are Like Forgotten People": The Chin People of Burma: Unsafe in Burma, Unprotected in India, January 2009, 95pp.

Left to Survive: Systematic Failure to Protect Unaccompanied Migrant Children in Greece, December 2008, 111pp.

Morocco/Western Sahara/Algeria – Human Rights in Western Sahara and in the Tindouf Refugee Camps, December 2008, 216pp.

Terrorism and Counterterrorism Issues

Cruel Britannia: British Complicity in the Torture and Ill-Treatment of Terror Suspects in Pakistan, November 2009, 45pp.

Human Rights and Saudi Arabia's Counterterrorism Response: Religious Counseling, Indefinite Detention, and Flawed Trials, August 2009, 26pp.

Open Secret: Illegal Detention and Torture by the Joint Anti-terrorism Task Force in Uganda, April 2009, 88pp.

No Direction Home: Returns from Guantanamo to Yemen, March 2009, 51pp.

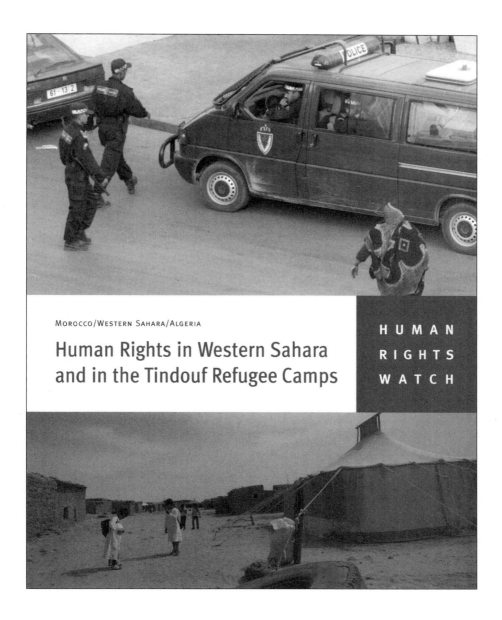

MOROCCO/WESTERN SAHARA/ALGERIA

Human Rights in Western Sahara and in the Tindouf Refugee Camps

HUMAN RIGHTS WATCH

Women's Rights Issues

"We have the Promises of the World": Women's Rights in Afghanistan, December 2009, 93pp.

Soldiers Who Rape, Commanders Who Condone: Sexual Violence and Military Reform in the Democratic Republic of Congo, July 2009, 58pp.

Detained and Dismissed: Women's Struggles to Obtain Health Care in United States Immigration Detention, March 2009, 80pp.

United States – Testing Justice: The Rape Kit Backlog in Los Angeles City and County, March 2009, 63pp.

Discrimination in the Name of Neutrality: Headscarf Bans for Teachers and Civil Servants in Germany, February 2009, 69pp.

All reports can be accessed online and ordered at www.hrw.org/en/publications.